This book
belongs to

Jackie Ziegler

NEW AGE
POLITICS

Other Delta Books of Interest

TOWARD A SCIENCE OF CONSCIOUSNESS
by Kenneth R. Pelletier

MIND AS HEALER, MIND AS SLAYER
by Kenneth R. Pelletier

BEYOND BIOFEEDBACK
by Elmer and Alyce Green

LISTENING TO THE BODY
by Robert Masters and Jean Houston

ROLLING THUNDER
by Doug Boyd

GOLF IN THE KINGDOM
by Michael Murphy

ENERGY PRIMER
by Richard Merrill and Thomas Gage (Eds.)

NEW AGE POLITICS

Healing Self and Society

Mark Satin

A Delta Book

A DELTA BOOK
Published by
Dell Publishing Co., Inc.
1 Dag Hammarskjold Plaza
New York, New York 10017

This book is a revised edition of NEW AGE POLITICS
published in Canada by Whitecap Books.

Delta ® TM 755118, Dell Publishing Co., Inc.

ISBN: 0-440-55700-3

Printed in the United States of America

First printing—November 1979

Library of Congress Cataloging in Publication Data

Satin, Mark Ivor, 1946–
New age politics: healing self and society.

(A Delta book)
Bibliography: p.
1. Civilization, Modern—1950–   2. Social values.
3. Radicalism—North America. I. Title.
CB428.S26   1979   909.82   79–16317
ISBN 0-440-55700-3

VB

*I would like to dedicate
this edition of my book
to the memory of my mother,
Selma Satin (1925–1978).
With abiding love.*

Contents

A Personal Word

Until last spring, I'd been a draft resister in Canada for nearly twelve years. I'd come to Canada convinced that I hated the United States and everything in and about it, but after many adventures, petty and grand, I began to realize that I was engaged in a lover's quarrel with my country. It was so fine on paper, and so awful in practice. (For many years before coming to Canada I'd wanted to be a city planner. I'd wanted to build a city that would express what's really unique and really fine about this country.)

I spent my last eight years in Canada trying not to wish I was back in the United States—in other words, wishing I was back in the States. And in the meantime, like every other draft resister I knew, I paid close attention to political developments; not only those in the national spotlight, but also those on the fringes of society where the real beginnings, the real rediscoveries often take place. One fierce winter's day in Montréal, over a cup of steaming cocoa and the *New York Times*, it dawned on me that the ideas and energies from the various "fringe" movements—feminist, ecological, spiritual, human potential, and the rest—were beginning to come together in a new way . . . in a way that was beginning to generate a coherent new politics. But I looked in vain for the people or groups that were expressing that new politics (instead of merely bits and pieces of it).

I realized then that living in Canada had been good for me in a way. It had given me exactly the perspective I needed in order to see the new politics whole. Beyond that, it had given me perspective on my "hatred" of America. It had given me exactly the perspective I needed in order to grow.

I no longer wanted to bring socialism to our shores. Or any "ism," for that matter. Instead, I wanted us to create a new and *healing* politics out of the indigenous social movements of our time.

So I resolved to describe this emerging new politics, as simply and as clearly as I could, and to publish the results myself if need be. If I ever got amnesty, I told myself, I would offer my writings to my country as a kind of gift, and go anywhere anyone asked me to go to speak about the emerging new ideas. (And I still mean that—see the last page of this book.)

I could never build my city, or so it seemed. But I could certainly write my book.

I *did* need to publish the first edition myself. And I did all the typing and typesetting and layout myself (because I believe in doing my own dirty work). I wrote the last draft of it in a house trailer on one of the islands off the Vancouver coast, where on clear days you could see all the way to Mt. Baker in Washington state.

The first edition came out in 1976 as an 84-page pamphlet. I did no advertising, I just started mailing them out from my house, and after a year I was selling a couple hundred copies a month. The second edition—240 pages long—was published by a Canadian friend of mine in 1978. It sold 10,000 copies in less than a year with no paid advertising and no American distributor—except me. (I have a sash with dozens of exhibitor's badges from all the fairs I've been to.)

I came down to this country after my amnesty with one speaking invitation and no notion that I would be invited to dozens of fairs. I was up all night before that talk (too much excitement, too much *fear*, too much waiting for that chance) and could never have made it to the speaker's stand the next day had someone not befriended me and walked me through the woods for hours. My speech got a standing ovation, and I cried—I couldn't believe that so many people were so receptive to what I had to say. And I felt that I'd come *home*.

When Delta offered to publish this book, I was in a quandary. Did I really want to give my book up to a big corporation that would do it all for me—to a "monolithic institution," to use my own terminology?

Three things convinced me to go with Delta.

First, there were some important changes that I wanted to make in the manuscript, and I couldn't face doing the whole typesetting job a third time (I type with one finger). Especially, I had come to realize that what I was calling "New Age politics" wasn't new at all in this country. It had always been with us, though it had always been expressed in bits and pieces before. It represents an entire "third force" in American politics—and it represents what this country at its best has really been about: personal responsibility, self-reliance, freedom of choice, belief in ethical values and ideals, and an all-encompassing love for what some of us choose to call God.

Another important change: I wanted to make this edition as practical and concrete as possible. And so I've added a model New Age "political platform" of 200 concrete political proposals that each of us can work for *now*. And while we're on concrete: I've expanded the resources section to include fifty New Age magazines and one hundred New Age groups. There should be at least one magazine, at least one group that's right for each of us.

A second reason I went with Delta is that after six months on the road I was sure that New Age politics could speak to a majority of Americans, to the Proposition 13 constituency, to any constituency that values self-reliance and cooperation more than top-down government and corporate control. After all, the only alternative to government or corporate control *is* a self-reliant and cooperative people. And that means New Age politics.

But I wasn't able to reach many Americans on my own. For the most part, I was only able to reach "the converted."

The third reason I went with Delta is that I very much needed the sense of accomplishment that people are able to feel once their work has been accepted and approved by a "monolithic institution." I am not strong enough inside myself to be able to do without the recognition, the status, the prestige, the "success" that is bestowed on people whose books are published by multimillion-dollar corporations in New York.

I am telling you this partly because I want to make it very clear that this is a book of self-criticism and not just social criticism. I am not writing this book from "on high," and I need to make real a lot of what's in here just like anybody else.

Don't trust anybody who tells you that they have all the answers . . . for self *or* society. You're liable to end up in Canada too.

I would like to acknowledge some of the people who fed me, housed me, and/or otherwise nurtured and supported me during the years that I traveled around writing this book. Without their help, this book might not have been possible: Cathy Aaron, Mike Abbott, John Amadeo, Averill, Pam Belyea, Joan Bostwick, Michael Burch, Robert Buxbaum, David Charlsen, Michael Chechik, Bob Cole, David Cutler, Joao da Motta, Mark Drew, Mac Elrod, Gary Faigin, Alanna Hartzok, Jim Hickman, Sue Hildreth, Linda James, Marilyn Kalman, Nancy Kellum-Rose, Donald Keys, Martha Keys, Bonnie Kreps, Jodean Marks, Jacqueline Ménard, John Mogey, Wendy Mogey, Carl Monk, Ross Nelson, Barb Newton, Andrea Piraino, Melanie Ray, Lou Riverso, Mark Roseland, Sári Ruskin, Val Scott, Elizabeth Shefrin, Sallie Shelley, Judith Skutch, Patty Summers, Eric Swan, David Thaler, Fred Wylie, the San Pablo House, and the Tuesday Night Men's Consciousness-Changing Group. I would also like to acknowledge the staffs of three bookstores who let me use their books and did me many other favors: Ariel Women's Books (Vancouver, B.C.), Banyen Books (Vancouver), and Sphinx and Sword of Life (Cambridge, Mass.).

Montréal—Toronto—Vancouver, B.C.—Cambridge, Mass.—San Francisco

October 1975–February 7, 1979

Part I
THE PRISON
WITHIN US

CHAPTER 1

What Is New Age Politics?

This book is based on a simple premise. It's that we don't have a usable politics any more—and that the politics we need, in America today, will not and cannot come from our old political "ism's." Not from capitalism, not from socialism, and *certainly* not from just "muddling through." Muddling along, we won't get through.

The situation we're in is so new, so unprecedented, that we need a whole new way of looking at the world. A whole new way of *seeing* things and thinking about things—especially political things. One that comes out of our own experience for a change, as distinct from the experience of Europe in the nineteenth century (which is where "modern" capitalism comes from, and Marxism and anarchism).

The point of this book is that a new way of seeing and a new politics is arising *already* in bits and pieces, here and there, across the country; but that we (and especially our intellectuals) have been so desperately set on pretending that nothing is *fundamentally* wrong—or that socialism is *fundamentally* the answer—that we've missed the coming together of these pieces, *right before our eyes.*

The new politics is arising out of the work and ideas of the people in many of the social movements of our time: the feminist, environmental, spiritual, and human potential movements; the appropriate technology, simple living, decentralist, and "world order" movements; the business-for-learning-and-pleasure movement and the humanistic-transformational education movement.

The new politics is also arising out of the work and ideas of a couple of hundred sympathetic economists and spiritual philosophers, business-people and workers' self-management people, systems analysts and psychoanalysts, physicists and poets. . . .

Each of these movements and each of these writers has something to add to the new politics. Their contributions come together like the pieces of an intricate jigsaw puzzle.

More and more of us have, over the last ten years or so, become deeply involved in one or more of the movements mentioned above. At the same time, though, the radical political movements of the 1960s seem to have collapsed.

Could there be a connection?

I believe that the radical political movements declined as soon as they began to promote a doctrine of us-against-them, of "we have all the answers," of separation rather than healing; as soon as they began to promote a dogmatic Marxism that overstressed our need for *things* and tried to make us feel guilty about our deeper needs, which are emotional, psychological, and spiritual (and which are what got us into the radical political movements in the first place). And I believe that the spiritual, feminist, environmental, etc., movements rose partly, at least, because they did contain a politics that did speak to our deeper needs. To *all* our needs.

But it was only an implicit politics, hard to see at first. And it was doubly hard to see just because it was so new and different from the politics that had gone before.

The purpose of this book is to make this politics explicit. To draw out, in some detail, its analysis of society (Paris I-III), its worldview (IV), its goals (V), its economics (VI), and its strategy (VII-XIX).

This book does not attempt to speak for the social movements of our time in the same way that, say, *The Greening of America* attempted to speak for the counterculture. The basic approach to politics that this book takes has always been with us here in America, in bits and pieces at any rate. The beauty of the social movements of our time is that each of them represents one of those pieces—and if you put them together, you are able to see clearly and coherently, maybe for the first time, what I like to call the perpetual "third force" in American politics. It is a force that can be traced all the way back, not to Roger Williams *or* John Cotton, but to Thomas Hooker; not to Thomas Jefferson *or* Alexander Hamilton, but to John and John Quincy Adams; and so on (see Chapter 25). It will certainly survive the social movements of our time.

Third force politics is a radical politics, not so much in the sense of radical *versus* liberal as in the sense of going to the roots of things. Specifically, third force politics goes to the psychocultural roots of our problems. It does not concentrate exclusively on the institutional and economic symptoms of our problems.

It is a radicalism that is neither of the left nor right—a radicalism that is modest enough to borrow what it needs from each of the old political "ism's" but bold enough to transcend them. (It is not a wimpy "mean" between the so-called "extremes" of American power politics.)

It is a radicalism that is more interested in healing society than in championing the exclusive claims to rightness of any one faction or segment of society; a radicalism that is more interested in reconciling people to each other's needs and priorities than in winning people over to its side (and in doing so, producing a losing side, poised for revenge).

It is a radicalism that is less interested in blaming groups and governments for our problems than in attempting to work out new and viable solutions to our problems (see Mark Markley). (All books, authors, periodicals, and groups cited in parentheses are listed in Chapter 27 below.)

It is a radicalism that is less interested in standing up for *alternative* ways of doing things than in standing up for *appropriate* ways of doing things. Jim DeKorne, a New Age builder, puts it well when he says (in *New Age*, April 1978), "The emphasis must shift from 'difference for difference's sake' to the concept of appropriateness—the idea that time, place, and circumstances are all factors pointing to specific, useful solutions."

It is a radicalism that traces our problems not to economic poverty (as was done between 1960–1966) or even to political powerlessness (1966–1972), so much as to a more general kind of *purposelessness*—to our lack of sustaining and believable ethics and values; to our lack of community; to our lack of inner strength (see, e.g., Jerry Fletcher, *O D Practitioner* Spring 1978, and Garry Wills, listed under Ghelardi).

It is a radicalism that acknowledges and accepts complexity, irony, paradox, and ambiguity—a radicalism that acknowledges the richness of life even when aspects of that richness are not particularly politically "correct."

It is a radicalism that opposes large concentrations of property and wealth, not because it believes that money is "bad" but because of a desire to protect *everyone's* right to a *sufficient* amount of property (see Richard Gregg).

It is a radicalism that recognizes the existence of a force in all things that is God or Truth or Love, and that derives its guiding ethics and values from that recognition or worldview or sensibility; or from a passionate commitment to life in all its forms, which amounts to the same thing.

Above all, perhaps, it is a radicalism that understands that the real problem is not how to get people, groups, and governments to agree on the "one best way" to do things, but how to get all the different ways, all the old political "ism's," to agree to live and work synergically together ("synergically" means: so that people, groups, and governments can get more by cooperating together than they can by competing against one another). It is a radicalism that asks: what are the specific ethics and political values that must be shared by everyone in order for everyone to survive, flourish, grow?

It is a radicalism that says, with social philosopher James Ogilvy, "Let the Birchers have their enclaves, let the Marxists have their communes, let the moderates have their modest communities and the utopians have their experiments in living. . . . [And let each group come] to recognize the others not only as Other but also as a projection of what has been repressed in our selves."

Dozens of people have tried to give a name to this third force politics, now that it has begun to emerge as a coherent and recognizable whole. Here are some of the names that are being used:

> "Anarchic Capitalism"—William Irwin Thompson, cultural historian
> "Cooperative Capitalism"—Joe Falk, community organizer

"Enlightened Humanism"—John Maher, organizer of ex-felons
"Global Humanism"—Richard Falk, professor of international law
"The New Localism"—David Morris and Karl Hess, political economists
"Participatory Divinity"—David Spangler, spiritual philosopher
"Personalism"—Nikolai Berdyaev, religious philosopher
"The Politics of the Person"—Theodore Roszak, cultural historian
"Radical Humanism"—Erich Fromm, psychologist
"Synergic Politics"—Jim Craig, management consultant, and Marge Craig, group facilitator

I have begun to call this politics "New Age politics." Partly because so many members of the movements mentioned above have begun using the term "New Age" themselves in their work. Partly because the term "New Age" is broad enough to encompass all these other definitions—and flexible enough to be constantly open to redefinition. And partly because it suggests that the years since World War II represent the beginnings of a radical break with the past, or at least, with many aspects of that past. It implies that the world is being not just changed but transformed, and it implies that we had better see to it that it's transformed in a life-giving manner.

Aspects of the transformations can be grouped under six headings:

New technologies. New means of transportation and communication have shrunk the Earth to such a degree that we're all united now, for better or worse, in a kind of "planetary village." For example, in sixty years we've gone from Kitty Hawk, North Carolina, to the moon. Consider that since 1945 the atomic bomb, the neutron bomb, the 'electronic battlefield' and God knows how many military horrors have all been developed. Consider that since 1945, eighty-six nations have appeared on the scene (more than half the total), world population has doubled, and the Gross World Product has gone up from $700 billion to $3.2 trillion (in constant dollars)—more than a 450 percent increase.

New problems. The new weapons. Overpopulation. Our suicidal consumption levels (resources, energy), and the failure of other countries to learn from our mistakes. The new techniques of political repression and control. Our severance from the spirit, loss of the sense that we're of any ultimate value. Futurologist Edward Cornish puts it well when he says, "The current transformation is not just a transformation; it is also a global crisis, perhaps the greatest that [we have] ever experienced."

New possibilities. Never before have we had the capacity to eliminate all hunger, disease, hard-core poverty, etc.—all physical manifestations of human suffering. In the affluent countries, meanwhile, as psychologist Abraham Maslow liked to point out, for the first time we can consciously decide *what we are to become* as human beings.

New awareness. "A peculiar feature of the current transformation," says Cornish, "is that people are aware that it is occurring. . . . Even the eighteenth-century English never knew they were experiencing the Industrial Revolution."

New consciousness. Donald Keys, registrar of Planetary Citizens, thinks we can begin to speak about a "new evolutionary step" for people in terms of their consciousness. People are becoming less egocentric, less dependent on science as the *one* way to truth, etc. At the same time, says William Irwin Thompson, founder of the Lindisfarne community, we are beginning to see the emergence of a new *collective* consciousness. Previously, "collective consciousness" meant that the individual was wiped out; but today, more and more, "the individual is aware of the presence of [a] group-mind, but [his or her] own integrity is not crushed by it."

New energies. Sensitive and spiritually oriented persons the world over have recently become aware of a subtle change in energies that the earth appears to be undergoing. The reason for this may be astrological—but at this point no one can really be sure.

Another thing I mean by New Age politics is a politics that recognizes that the concept of the person is expanding. In this view, New Age politics is the politics that seeks to speak to the needs of that "new person."

I like to say that our concept of the person has been expanding both horizontally and vertically. Vertically, our concept has expanded to take in our higher or "spiritual" natures and needs (see, e.g., Roberto Assagioli, 1965, or Maslow, 1971). In the other direction, our definition has expanded to take in our emotional or "subconscious" natures and needs (see, e.g., Erich Fromm, 1973, or Rollo May). In the new definition of the person, our "higher" and "lower" selves are as real as our visible selves, with needs that are equally vital, equally real (in fact, Fromm thinks that our need for love is even more pressing than our need for food).

Horizontally, we're "people" now, not "men." And if we want to think of our selves historically or sociologically or anthropologically, we can no longer think of our selves as isolated individuals. The *smallest* unit of inquiry is, or should be, the person *plus the environment*. (For family therapist Dennis Jaffe, the environment is the rest of the family. For poet Gary Snyder, it's the natural world. For anthropologist Gregory Bateson, it's the entire immediate natural and social surround.)

In this way, the spiritual, human potential, feminist, and environmental movements have created the social and perceptual *context* for a New Age politics.

Another defining aspect of the new politics is that it would link us here in America with the Fourth World rather than the First World. The First World consists of the overdeveloped capitalist countries, the Second World of the overdeveloped communist countries, and the Third World of the insufficiently developed countries. The Fourth World consists of all those native and natural peoples who *like* being who they are and where they are, and it consists of all those countries (and communities and regions) whose people prefer the pleasures and responsibilities of "voluntary simplicity," to the spiritual *sacrifices* and ecological *irresponsibilities* of trying to keep their seats on the poverty-prosperity merry-go-round. They are people who have *enough* for their needs—which are primarily to lead lives of rich personal experience and to be of service to others.

And here are some more definitions, for those of you who like definitions.

By the term "New Age" I mean to convey a dual sense of *possibility* and *responsibility*. The sense of possibility is captured nicely by Dionne Marx, a brilliant young instructor at the California Institute for Asian Studies, when she says that many traditions are reflecting growth into a "new age of wholeness, synthesis, and unity." The sense of responsibility is suggested by political scientist William Ophuls when he speaks of our "new age of scarcity," and by world order theorist Ervin Laszlo when he mentions the fact that the "new age of global community" is upon us whether we like it or not.

By "politics" I definitely mean to include the struggle for power. To create a haven for the "expanded person" without state power is to create a subculture, one that is admittedly nice and warm, but it is not to create a culture that can heal this country.

But the struggle for power is only part of what I mean by politics. For me, politics is all the ways we treat one another, as individuals, as groups, and as governments; and all the ways we treat our environment; and all the ways we treat our *selves*. And so New Age politics is a politics in which we learn to assume *personal and collective responsibility* for the ways we treat one another, and nature, and our selves. A politics in which we assume this responsibility not out of a sense of grim duty, but out of a sense of real, virtually untapped *possibility*.

This may be the first time that a politics along these lines has become coherent and whole. But it is not the first time that such a politics has *begun* to take shape in the world.

United States, 1840s–1870s: The Spiritualist movement is easily the largest movement of a politically, ecologically, and socially radical nature in nineteenth-century America. Millions of Americans join in the search for a new moral belief system and a new ethically/spiritually based politics. But the incipient Marxist movement decides that the Spiritualists' stress on ethics and consciousness is a distraction from "the struggle" (for Marxism), and so it helps to discredit the Spiritualists' political ideas as "antiscientific" and pro-free love (see Marian Leighton, "Victoria Woodhull Meets Karl Marx," *Liberation*, Fall 1977).

Prerevolutionary Russia: A collection of articles called *Landmarks*, published in 1909 and circulated widely, lashes out at the materialist worldview, at scientific single vision, and at all the old political "ism's," and calls for a return to spiritual values as a precondition for social, cultural, and political change. After the Revolution the book is banned, and its contributors, including the ex-Marxist philosopher Nikolai Berdyaev, flee the country.

Harlem and other black communities, U.S.A., 1920s: Black people are beginning to work out a political alternative that puts special emphasis on culture and on ethnic group identity. But the black intellectuals are, according to black writer Harold Cruse, "so overwhelmed at being 'discovered' and courted" by white Marxists that they allow their insights to degenerate into a pampered cultural vogue (the Harlem Renaissance), meanwhile accepting political leadership from these same white Marxists.

India, 1920s–40s: Mahatma Gandhi articulates a coherent new political philosophy under the slogan "self-rule and self-restraint." People are to lead simple lives, free of want and luxury; villages are to practice political and economic self-sufficiency as much as possible, and are to prefer human-scale technology to huge modern factories.

The "self-rule" movement is successful but Gandhi is killed, and most of the rest of the independence leaders, good Marxists and liberals who are embarrassed by the rest of Gandhi's political program, proceed to try to "modernize" India in the best traditions of the industrial West.

France, 1930s–1950s: A popular political movement called "Personalism" arises that aspires to be genuinely different from Marxism and liberalism. Its leading journal, Emmanuel Mounier's *Esprit*, holds that the person is sacred; redefines "bourgeois" to mean, he who has banished all mystery from life; speaks out against "over-industrialism" and calls for a decentralized economy; and condemns the nation-state. The movement comes out of World War II stronger than ever, with branches in many other European countries, but within five years of the Cold War it is effectively dead.

Roger Garaudy, dissident French communist, claims that Personalism died because it had failed to construct a genuinely different worldview for its politics—and so it had simply crumbled under the for-us-or-against-us kinds of pressures of the Cold War.

North America and to some extent Western Europe, 1960s: The new activism is proud, at first, of its refusal to rely on any known ideology, and of its first efforts to work out an "independent" political program based largely on its own actual experience of the world. The "Triple Revolution" manifesto argues that the cybernetics, weapons, and human rights revolutions are precipitating a "historic break" with the past. Students for a Democratic Society, the leading radical student group, puts out a literature list that includes pamphlets by McLuhan, education reformers, neopacifists, and therapists, as well as by Marxists and liberals. SDS activists attempt to identify a new, "revolutionary" social class that would include some students and professionals. Nonviolence is "discovered" (through Camus); the dangers of totalitarianism are stressed (Orwell). Books of spiritual concern are popular, especially those by J. Krishnamurti and Aldous Huxley, and are found to contain an underlying, and often enough a congenial, political dimension.

Liberals and Marxists alike are aghast at the unorthodox ideas and reading matter of the new activists, and regularly criticize their "lifestyles" (a code word for their ideas) and their motives. Generally the activists respond on the same level as the criticisms. They laugh.

But then comes Vietnam, and most of them—most of us, me included—begin to want to come up with an analysis fast, an analysis that can tell us exactly what is happening and why and exactly "what is to be done" about it. There is only one such analysis in town— Marxism—and so many of us become Marxists. But it is a decision that many of us are later to regret. For example: Julius Lester, who used to write the token black man's column for the Marxist weekly, the *Guardian*, has recently said that he'd always felt that "real change was spiritual," but that his experiences in "The Movement" had caused him to become self-righteous and hateful and ultimately to lose touch with himself. By 1969, he tells us, he felt himself to be "a dummy for a revolutionary ventriloquist, an actor in a bad play." Jerry Rubin, in his recent book, *Growing (Up) at 37*, says much the same thing—"We activists in the 1960s eventually lost touch with ourselves"—and he adds: "People out of touch with their bodies and souls cannot make positive change."

By the early 1970s, most of us had begun to associate "politics" with rhetoric and guilt, and had wisely left "politics" behind.

If the experiences of the past can teach us anything, it is surely that we have to look at the world with fresh eyes and from our own point of view.

In the United States, New Age political thinking is most advanced and may soon be in a position to capture the imagination of the general public . . . partly because we are the first people to learn-by-doing that the pursuit of affluence does *not* lead to happiness. But, significantly, New Age political ideas are surfacing today in many other places as well. For example:

In **Britain,** the environmental movement has published *A Blueprint for Survival* (1972) which argues that a decentralized society is not only *preferable* to what we have now, but may soon be *necessary* because of environmental and resource constraints. The *Blueprint* serves as an intellectual basis for the Ecology Party and the increasingly influential Green Alliance; and it has had a profound impact on the up-and-coming Values Party of New Zealand (see Chapter 27). At the same time, the magazine *New Humanity* is advertising itself as "the world's first politico-spiritual journal," and an increasingly large number of independent scholars and activists are speaking out against make-work projects, questioning the usefulness of economic class analysis, calling for political decentralization, calling for "social transformation" rather than revolution *or* reform, and so on (see *Peace News*, July 9, 1976).

In **France,** many "graduates of the streets" of May 1968 have recently been turning *away* from Marxism and anarchism and *toward* a point of view, if not yet a politics, that looks very much like that of New Age politics. In at least fourteen books, all published since 1975, these "new philosophers" accuse the French left of "intellectual betrayal" (for consistently lying about the events in the socialist countries); trace the Soviet labor camps back to Marx, rather than Lenin or Stalin; and attack the intellectual foundations of Marxism *and* liberalism, which they trace back to "scientific rationalism" and the Western European enlightenment.

At the same time, a new, ecologically oriented political party, "The Greens," recently stunned the traditional political parties (liberal and Marxist) by receiving 12 percent of the popular vote in the French municipal elections. Many of the Greens have been influenced deeply by the new philosophers' critique of socialism, and by a number of the authors listed in Chapter 27 below. Their rallying cry is "auto-gestion" —decentralized self-government. As one of them explains it, autogestion is the political version of the "auto-regulation" (self-regulation) of the ecosystems which owe their stability to their diversity.

Green activists include regional separatists, workers' self-management people, antinuclear activists, consumer activists, anarchists, nonviolent activists, and various women's groups—a heterogeneous lot that's fighting a decisive battle right now over whether or not to break with the rhetoric of the traditional antiauthoritarian left (see Sylvia Crossman, "The Greens," *CoEvolution Quarterly*, Winter 1977).

With regard to **Russia,** Alexander Solzhenitsyn and half a dozen other Soviet dissidents have put together a book, *From Under the Rubble* (1975), that is consciously modeled on the old *Landmarks* of Berdyaev and company. In it, the spiritual wing of the dissident movement reveals istelf as being totally committed to nonviolence—as an ethic as well as a tactic; speaks in the strongest terms about the material limits to growth; calls for political and economic decentralization; and urges us to practice "repentance and self-limitation" as individuals and as nations. "Once understood and adopted, this principle diverts us—as individuals, in all forms of human association, societies and nations—from *outward* to *inward* development. . . ."

You can't say that New Age politics is "left wing" or "right wing." It is perfectly compatible with public or private ownership of the means of production, and it speaks equally to rich and poor, young and old, white collar and blue. Still, New Age politics does stand in a definite relation to the other political ideologies. From the perspective of New Age thinkers, there are two defining political choices that every society must make . . . and neither of them is covered by the old political categories "left" and "right."

The first choice has to do with this. Do we want our society to encourage us to seek rich individual experience and to be of service to others—or do we want our society to encourage us to seek material riches in the form of possessions and status? Another way of putting this is: do we want our society to be based on the Prison, or do we want our society to be based on a complex of more life-giving ethics and values? (For more on the Prison, see Chapters 3 and 13.)

The second choice has to do with this. Do we want our society to extend state and institutional control over our lives (for whatever reason)—or do we want our society to encourage us to be self-reliant and self-determining? Another way of putting this is: do we want our society to extend our "monolithic" institutions, or do we want it to replace them with "biolithic" institutions? (For more on our institutions, see Chapters 7 and 14.)

In order to develop an accurate and telling substitute for the old left-right continuum and so better indicate the real political energies that are at work in the world and the choices that we really must make, I created two new continua based on the above, experience-versus-possessions and autonomy-versus-obedience, and crossed them at right angles, making the quadrant below:

**individual autonomy;
community and/or regional
self-determination
(biolithic institutions)**

emphasis on individual experience and social service (Prison-free)			emphasis on individual possessions and social status (Prison-bound)
	New Age politics	**United States (in theory)**	
	China	**Soviet Union**	

**individual conformity;
state and/or institutional
domination
(monolithic institutions)**

It seems to me that New Age politics might most comfortably fit into the upper left hand quadrant; the United States, in the upper right in theory and the lower right in practice; the Soviet Union, in the lower right; and China, in the lower left (though whether the Chinese emphasis on being is meant to last, or is only an expedient while it builds up a material base, is probably impossible now to say).

CHAPTER 2

Why We Need a New Age Politics

This chapter will attempt to show why only a minority of New Agers still call themselves capitalists or socialists, and why even these tend to be deeply opposed to *liberal* capitalism, *Marxist* socialism.

Beyond Liberalism

If our politics are liberal, we might say that people are having a hard time making ends meet financially. And that would be true enough. But it is also true that our average per person incomes are over $7,500 a year now, children included—and our average household incomes are over $18,000 a year. To a New Ager this is no small sum—many of us are living satisfying lives on a fraction of that income. It tends to suggest that our problems have a lot to do with the kinds of foods we eat (all that meat—all that packaged stuff); with the kinds of clothes we wear (chosen for fashion rather than comfort); with the kinds of living arrangements we make for our selves (which tend to encourage isolation and discourage sharing); with the kinds of cars we drive (their size) and the fact that we would *rather* drive cars than walk or even use the public transit (more families have two cars now than none); with the ways we entertain ourselves ("nights on the town" rather than true intimacy); and so on. Many New Age writers have suggested that we tend to get our sense of worth from buying and owning things, rather than from, say, friendship and service. Many others have pointed out that, with 5 percent of the Earth's people we account for nearly 30 percent of the Earth's yearly resource use—about six times our fair share.

Or consider this: our incomes can buy over 60 percent more now than they could in the late 1940s, even after allowing for taxes and inflation (cited in Easterlin). To me this suggests that our material wants—including our desire to have others do *for* us what we once did for our selves—have also gone up by 60 percent since the late 1940s, or even faster. And are we really as satisfied now, even on the material plane, as we were in the late 1940s? (Easterlin cites a number of studies that show that we are no happier now.) Consider that personal debt rises as we go on up the income scale.

To a New Ager, all these facts suggest that our problems are only superficially economic, and that they have much more to do with culture: with who we are and what we want from life. Of course, it's not part of the accepted political wisdom to tell people that their values

and priorities are doing them in: they won't vote for you if you do. But
by encouraging people to feel that they need only more of the same—
and, worse, that they can make use of top-down bureaucratic government to "give it to them"—the liberals may only be adding to the
problems that they say they hope to solve.

If our politics are liberal, we might also say that we are just not
putting the "right men" in office. (If we're liberal historians we'd say
we've never really put our best men in office. If we're liberal lawyers
we might try putting our selves in office. And if we're militant liberals
we might try putting black people in office, or women, or even black
women!) But all these liberals are assuming that other people, "men in
office," can solve our problems *for* us. And anyway, they're begging
the question. Why *can't* we put the "right" people in office?

Some liberals understand that our problems go deeper than "more
money" or "bad politicians." But they're at a loss to know how to define
our deeper problems, let alone what to do about them.

Some of these liberals are willing to speak of a "crisis in values." But
as Ruben Nelson, management consultant and theologian, points out—
putting the problem in this way is implying that the crisis is happening
"out there," *to* us. And that it can therefore be patched up by top-
down government technicians ("the best and the brightest") through a
kind of mass merchandising of newer and better values.

Others of these liberals have argued that our problems are too com-
plicated to grasp—for now. Meanwhile, they think that pumping a lot
of money into the problems might do some good. Unfortunately, however, as Nelson and many other New Agers point out, we not only
need to *try* to do the right things, but we must actually do them.
Otherwise our projects may end up doing a lot more harm than good.
Partly by reinforcing, inadvertently, some of the problems that we
most need to solve, such as our overdependence on the top-down state
and on our other monolithic institutions. And partly by reinforcing and
perpetuating the *consciousness that causes* these problems in the first
place—what I like to call the Prison.

So the lessons of liberalism are: (1) we can't do good until we
understand what our problems really are; and (2) we can't do good
until we understand and then redefine who *we* are, and what we want
from life.

(For a thorough critique of liberalism, see Robert Ghelardi, *Economics, Society and Culture*.)

Beyond Marxism

If our politics are Marxist, we would probably say that the problem
is capitalism: a handful of bosses are "ripping off" the workers. But
most corporations have been averaging only 5-10 percent profit per
year—and most of that is reinvested. (A socialist bureaucracy has to
spend at least as much on extra administrative costs.) Economist William Nordhaus has recently shown that there's been an "absence of

'net' profitability in the corporate sector" since the late 1940s; "that is, price was just sufficient to cover all costs including the cost of capital" (*New York Review of Books*, Feb. 17, 1977). And Seymour Melman, a political scientist, and Harvey Leibenstein, an economist, have recently proposed different (but complementary) theories to show that corporations do not, generally speaking, minimize costs or maximize profits.

H. B. Wilson, who is a chartered accountant as well as an advocate of workers' self-management, has had what should be everybody's last word on the subject: "[Profit] is a word used by everyone but understood by very few because it is an abstract accounting concept having, at most, an incidental connection with cash. . . . What financial statements describe as 'net income' (profit) is not really net income in the sense in which anyone but an accountant would understand the term. . . . It is neither a measure of success nor a measure of the extent of the exploitation of labor. . . . We may refer to the profit or loss figures to support our positions, but this is just a debating trick, or a rationalization, and is not what determines our opinions."

If we are "forward-looking" Marxists we might then say: "It's not just the profits, it's that the goods are useless and the work degrading." But people are still clamoring for all those "useless" goods. And consider the fate of those politicians who have dared to call for "meaningful" work or guaranteed incomes or reducing the work week.

"But that's because of all the propaganda in the media, and because of all the advertising."

But why do people believe the propaganda that they read? Why do they respond to ads for goods that will knowingly harm them? Are we to conclude that we are brainwashed by the media—are suffering from "false consciousness," as a Marxist might put it?

No. Social psychologist Daryl Bem has convincingly shown that the media have only a very slight capacity to persuade us one way or the other. And he cites a number of recent studies that show that personal contacts, especially with friends, have a much greater capacity to affect our opinions and decisions. His conclusion: the media can help to persuade us (but not much)—and ultimately, we and our friends decide.

Moreover, if we are said to be suffering from "false consciousness," then we must also conclude that we *can't be held responsible* for the things we think and do. And then what can we say when a political party comes along to force us to act "in our own best interests," as in the Soviet Union or the People's Republic of China?

(For a more thorough critique of the Marxist analysis, see Chapter 26.)

Beyond the Anarchist Alternative

The New Age position may seem closer to anarchism than to Marxism or liberalism, but it differs from anarchism too in many ways. For example:

Most strains of anarchism are rooted in the socialist tradition. New Age politics is rooted in an amalgam of traditions of which feminism, ecology theory, Eastern philosophy, and Western psychology are probably the most important.

For anarchism our main enemies are capitalism and the state. For New Age politics the main obstacles to our development are monolithic institutions—which are *common* to capitalism and socialism but not, strictly speaking, *necessary* to either—and the Prison, a cultural complex of values and attitudes that make us *want to give up* our autonomy to our monolithic institutions . . . including the top-down state.

Michael Albert, "libertarian-Marxist" writer, notes (in *What Is To Be Undone*, 1974) that anarchism "still lacks a 'psychological model' that can be a basis for common collective tactical analyses." New Age politics seeks to remedy this lack with its seven stages of self-development, its theory of the "stroke economy," and its psychocultural class analysis.

Nikolai Berdyaev and many others have pointed out that anarchism still shares the nineteenth century, materialist worldview. New Age politics seeks to avoid falling into the opposite trap of the non-material worldview and is busily helping to articulate a new, trans-material worldview.

Anarchist philosophy believes in the natural goodness of human beings. New Age politics is, I think, more realistic. It believes that "defensive" aggression (aggression that aims at the removal of a threat) is an instinct in us, and that "malignant" aggression (destructiveness and cruelty) is a *potential* in us—less than an instinct, but "more than a learned pattern of behavior that readily disappears when new patterns are introduced" (see esp. Erich Fromm, *The Anatomy of Human Destructiveness*). It is a potential that apparently "actualizes" itself whenever our important psychic needs—for love, friendship, esteem, etc.—are not met. Whenever we fail to nourish our selves materially or emotionally or psychologically or spiritually.

Anarchist philosophy believes that it is important to avoid structures and leaders as much as possible and that the ideal society could do without them altogether. New Age politics believes that—as Joreen expresses it in the anthology, *Radical Feminism*—there can be no such thing as a structureless group. Any group of people that comes together for any length of time will inevitably structure itself in *some* fashion. Therefore, while the idea of structurelessness may help to prevent the formation of formal or "directive" structures, it cannot help to prevent the formation of informal or "anarchic" ones that will be dominated by the strong or the charismatic or the manipulative. New Age politics has come up with the concept of "synergic power" which can provide a genuine alternative to both directive and anarchic kinds of power; see Chapter 15.

Most strains of anarchism tend to believe in the ultimate necessity of revolution and violence. New Age politics is uncompromisingly evolutionary and nonviolent, though it does believe that evolution can be speeded up and that nonviolence is potentially the most *effective* tactic as well as an ethical imperative.

The Emerging New Alternative

So. Politically we seem to be in a next to impossible situation right now in America. The anarchist alternative isn't thorough or realistic enough to speak for more than a temperamental minority. The liberal analysis leads to impotence and despair, and to a longing for a messiah (consider Jimmy Carter's 1976 campaign imagery: it made masterful use of our longing for a messiah). And the Marxist analysis leads to bitterness and despair—to an anger that can, ultimately, only be directed back against "the people" (who know not what they do) through a revolutionary "vanguard" that claims to represent the people's "true" consciousness, as opposed to their false, or actual consciousness.

There are at least half a dozen *competing* revolutionary vanguards now in every major city.

And yet and yet. Any political theory should be able to tell us what's wrong with our society, and what we can do to heal it. If neither liberalism, nor Marxism, nor anarchism can do the trick, the point is not to give up in despair, and even less is it to return to other industrial-era political philosophies such as libertarianism or Henry George-ism (though New Age politics has borrowed quite a bit, from both of these). It is, rather, to work out a new political theory that can help us get our bearings in the new age we are entering. Or, since new political theories always seem to come along just when they're most needed, the point is to look around and see if a new political theory isn't arising already among the supposedly "apolitical" or "semipolitical" movements that many of us are involved in now.

As I suggested in Chapter 1, I believe that a new political theory— New Age politics—*is* emerging out of the work of these movements.

It differs from liberalism and Marxism in many ways. With regard to the discussion above: it does not feel that the personnel of the system is the problem; in free elections, people do tend to get the politicians they deserve. As California State Assemblyperson John Vasconcellos puts it, "We choose those people who most approximate our consciousness."

Nor does New Age politics feel that the economic system is the problem. As economic systems, capitalism and socialism each have their strong points (freedom and security, respectively); a human-scale capitalism and a democratic socialism would appear to make the most of these strong points; but infected by the Prison and its institutions, socialism's security tends to become regimentation, and capitalism's freedom tends to become dog-eat-dog.

The New Age position suggests that the basic problem has partly to do with the scale of our society: the human scale *is* beautiful and nearly everything we have now is much too big (and powerful and speedy). And that has little to do with capitalism per se: Russia's SST is even bigger than ours would have been. Accordingly, the New Age solution does not call for top-down bureaucratic government, but for much more local autonomy than we have at present, and much more planetary cooperation. Similarly, the New Age solution does not call for socialism or capitalism (that kind of question would be decided on by the individual communities), but for an economy of life-oriented, mostly human-scale enterprises.

But the New Age solution does *not* call for an extreme version of a small-scale, labor-intensive, appropriate technology (A.T. for short) society for everyone. Even some of the line drawings in *CoEvolution Quarterly* and *New Age* suggest that an extreme A.T. society would be as monolithic, in its way, as the kind of society we try to live in now. This is why I emphasize, again and again, that the central problem is not how to get everyone to agree on the "one best way" to do things. It is, rather, how to get everyone to cooperate around a series of basic political values that would allow all the different New Age communities, economies, technologies, polities, etc., to get *more* by cooperating than they could by competing. The New Age model is to try to reach a point where nations and, within nations, regions and communities, can say things like: "All right—we've agreed on 'maximization of environmental quality' as an overriding political value and we've worked out specifically what that means. Therefore, X, if you really want to automate, you know you're going to have to pay the rest of us some taxes. Why don't you pay us with some of the goods you produce? We could use some computer typesetters. . . ."

Beyond size and scale, beyond technology, the New Age analysis suggests that the problem is with "the people" themselves: with *us*, with what we have become. And it holds that "what we have become" goes back to a cultural complex—the Prison—whose six main elements predate capitalism by hundreds or thousands of years.

CHAPTER 3

The Six-Sided Prison

Many New Age writers and activists have pointed out that our social problems—war, exploitation, racism, environmental degradation—have their roots not so much in our institutions as in our mentality or consciousness. Gregory Bateson, the anthropologist, believes that "this massive aggregation of threats to [people and their] ecological systems arises out of errors in our habits of thought at deep and partly unconscious levels"; Wendell Berry, a writer on agriculture (and a farmer and poet), points out that it is the "mentality of greed and exploitation" that is ultimately responsible for war, racism, and environmental degradation; Grace Stuart, a psychoanalyst, traces the fact of exploitation back to our "hating and self-hate" which has, she reminds us, been with us for thousands of years; E. F. Schumacher, author of the book *Small Is Beautiful*, says it is the "violence of greed, envy, hate and lust" in each of us that ultimately causes our problems; and so on.

Our institutional arrangements are, in this view, ultimately a reflection of our mentality or consciousness: we get back what we give out. Krishnamurti puts it well when he says, "What you are within has been projected without, on to the world; what you are, what you think and what you feel, what you do in your everyday existence, is projected outwardly, and that constitutes the world." Our institutions may *help* to determine the world—including our consciousness! (see Part II)—but our consciousness is ultimately, or as Marx might say, "in the final analysis," the determining factor. (For more on this subject, see Chapter 26.)

What is there, then, that is most central to our mentality or consciousness? What is there that defines it? What are the beliefs, attitudes, values, myths, that are so important to us that they make up the taken-for-granted context of our lives?

Dozens of New Age writers and activists have been trying to define our most basic beliefs, and if you put their writings together, you'll come up with this. Our basic beliefs make up a cultural complex whose six main elements are: patriarchal attitudes, egocentricity, scientific single vision, the bureaucratic mentality, nationalism, and the big city outlook.

I like to think of these six elements as making up a "Six-Sided Prison," partly because at least fifteen authors in Chapter 27 have used the Prison metaphor in their own work, and partly because it is so apt. Calling the cultural elements a Prison implies that we're trapped not so much by the institutions of the society as by the culture of things and of death that we carry around in our *minds*. Michael Novak, political scientist, goes so far as to state, "Institutions are what their perceivers wish them to be. Their life in the psyches of the community is their main source of power [and] stability. . . . When sufficient numbers of the community begin to think differently, those institutions lose their power [and] stability. . . ."

Basically the Prison is a way of *seeing* the world, a mental construct (as sociologists would put it) or an illusion (as Eastern philosophers would) that we create every day anew. And because we create it in our minds, we can undo it in our minds. We can change our consciousness individually and collectively so that we're not Prison-bound. (Carlos Castaneda's books, Ram Dass's books, Chogyam Trungpa's books, are about *seeing* the world differently, which is why they're more transformative, for our time and place, than the *Communist Manifesto*.)

And if enough of us do this—if enough of us can transcend and transform the Prison—then *and only then* would the institutions, goods, and services that are set up to meet the needs of Prison-bound people lose the Prison-bound aspects of their appeal. We might still watch television, but not twenty-eight hours a week (the national per adult average) and not because we weren't living as intensely as the people on the screen. We might still drive cars, but not to the corner store, and not because we needed to feel powerful and in charge. We might still get married, but not because we felt we had to, and not because we wanted to control our partner's growth.

Once we were free of the Prison, all the propaganda and all the advertising in the world wouldn't be enough to make us want to lose our selves in our things; to make us want to give up our power and responsibility to our institutions.

Then we could begin to really heal self and society.

Some New Age writers have attempted to prove that *one* of the first three sides of the Prison has been the really determining one. For example, June Singer derives egocentricity from patriarchal attitudes— and Alan Watts derives patriarchal attitudes from egocentricity. The important point, to my mind, is that the origins of at least the first three sides of the Prison are lost in the mists of time . . . and are crucially and independently determining today.

The second three sides appear to be more clearly connected to certain institutional forms—to bureaucracies, to the nation-state, and to big cities. Therefore, it's tempting to conclude that the second three sides can be done away with by "breaking up" the bureaucracies and by reducing the size of our nations and cities. But the second three sides are reinforced and perpetuated by the first three sides—to such an extent that they would probably survive the physical break-up of the bureaucracies, nations, and cities, and seek to stifle us in other ways (and seek to recreate the bureaucracies, etc.). They are also

reinforced and perpetuated by many of our monolithic institutions—
see Part II.

Patriarchal Attitudes

The patriarchy is a system of power in which men "determine what
part women shall or shall not play, and in which the female is everywhere subsumed under the male" (Adrienne Rich). It is the means by
which men are able to get women to be their secretaries, make their
beds, prop up their egos, and enjoy doing it. Aspects of the patriarchy
may be enforced by law or through such venerable institutions as wife-
beating; but mostly it's enforced by a series of patriarchal attitudes that
we don't even notice.

Patriarchal attitudes are the attitudes, values, and beliefs that are
supportive of the patriarchy. The patriarchy wouldn't exist for a moment without these attitudes, which are "socialized" into us literally
from the day we're born in the form of sex-role stereotypes. Hogie
Wyckoff, a therapist, puts it this way (see Steiner): "As women and
men we are socialized to develop certain parts of our personalities
while suppressing the development of other parts. This programming
promotes a predetermined, stilted, and repetitive way of acting in life."

For example, men are taught to be aggressive, independent, rational,
objective, intelligent, competent, ambitious, unemotional, and detached. And women are taught to be pretty much the opposite: passive, dependent, irrational. . . . Is it any wonder that men want to rule,
or that most women obey?

It is important to understand that our sex-role stereotypes are just
that—stereotypes. In their book *The Psychology of Sex Differences,*
Eleanor Maccoby and Carol Jacklin take a look at virtually all of the
studies of sex differences that have been carried out in recent years.
They are able to show conclusively that women are *not* "naturally"
passive, dependent, irrational, etc. (though they may be less malig-
nantly aggressive than men). Their last lines: "Social institutions and
social practices are not biologically inevitable. . . . It is up to human
beings to select those that foster the life styles they most value."

We get our sex-role stereotypes mostly and most importantly from
our parents. Our parents teach us their own sex-role stereotypes that
have nothing to do with our own unique temperaments and interests
but that lend themselves perfectly to the taken-for-granted patterns of
submission and dominance. (They don't do most of this consciously,
of course. They do it more by the raised eyebrow and the exasperated
voice, and by the example they set as "mommies" and "daddies.")

But where do our parents get these stereotypes from? Just how far
back do they go? Only one thing is certain: they go back thousands of
years before capitalism, and have survived all sorts of social and economic and political "revolutions." Anne Koedt, a founder of the radical feminist movement, makes the essential political point: "The pur-

pose of male chauvinism is primarily to obtain psychological ego satisfaction, and . . . only secondarily does this manifest itself in economic relationships." For thousands of years the male identity has been sustained "through its ability to have power over the female ego." For thousands of years man has acquired his self-esteem "in direct proportion to his ability to have his ego override woman's."

Some anthropologists believe that societies have always been patriarchal in their power relationships. But many years ago Margaret Mead was able to prove that that is itself a patriarchal assumption. She went to New Guinea and reported on tribes that were patriarchal and matriarchal and even androgynous (*Sex and Temperament in Three Primitive Societies,* 1935). Nevertheless, the overwhelming majority of societies over the centuries—over the millennia!—do appear to have been patriarchal.

There is some evidence that thousands of years ago the world was dotted with matriarchies. And these may have been more than just patriarchies spelled with an "m". According to Elizabeth Gould Davis, a feminist theorist, there is archaeological evidence that suggests that in some of them there had been no sacrifices of any living beings, no violent deaths, and—hard to believe!—no wars for a thousand years. According to Merlin Stone, a feminist historian, there is cultural evidence that suggests that some of them were societies of genuine political equality—e.g., "the earliest Sumerian myths included both female and male deities in the decision-making assemblies of heaven."

Nobody seems to know why the matriarchies ended. Predictably, Marx and Engels say that it happened because women lost control of the means of production. Not so, says cultural historian Helen Diner: we now know of matriarchies that existed in spite of that fact. Davis says that the matriarchies were conquered by power-hungry males. Kate Millett, writer and sculptor, thinks that it might have had something to do with men figuring out how babies are started.

But even if the matriarchies never did exist, even if, as Adrienne Rich puts it, it is simply that "we all carry in our earliest imprintings the memory of, or the longing for, an individual past relationship to . . . female warmth, nurture, and tenderness," it is impossible to deny these writers' main point: that fairly early on, women had lost whatever power they might have had in society.

Andrea Dworkin reminds us that, at different times and in different places, men have indulged in, for example, the practice of footbinding in China, an exceedingly painful practice that only began to end with Sun Yat-sen's revolution of 1911; or, for example, the persecution of "witches" in Europe and the United States, especially from the fifteenth to the eighteenth centuries when possibly millions of women were slaughtered—and along with the women, their entire, separate culture.

Obviously, in the United States today, patriarchal attitudes don't produce such horrors. But all things considered, women may not be "better off today than ever before." Davis, for one, contends that women have been rendered more and more useless over the centuries, with an ensuing loss in power and in self-esteem. And even if women are better off today in a material sense, and are "allowed to do more," that doesn't mean that the patriarchy runs any less deep or that it does us less harm.

For in *any* society characterized by patriarchal attitudes, those of us who are women are made to feel powerless, inferior, incompetent, and unattractive. Or, if we don't feel these things, then we've had to go through quite a struggle to free our selves from them. Partly just because—as Jean Baker Miller, a psychologist, points out—women's psychological strengths are not *recognized* as such by men, nor by those women who want to "make it" in "the man's world." Miller encourages women to recognize their strengths *as* strengths, and to add to them, not change them: women are better able to admit to feelings of weakness and vulnerability than men; women have a greater sense of the emotional dimensions of all human activity; women have a greater sense of the pleasures of close connection with physical, emotional, and mental growth; women have a greater recognition of the cooperative nature of human existence; and women have a greater ability to create for themselves a new concept of personhood.

Many New Age writers have pointed out that patriarchal attitudes are harmful to those of us who are men. Patriarchal attitudes make it almost impossible for us to love or be emotional; turn us into success objects (as opposed to sex objects—though we can be that, too); keep us out of touch with our bodies; teach us to see women as inferior, and to hate women; and keep us from getting to know our children. Marc Feigen Fasteau puts it well when he says, "The male machine is a special kind of being, different from women, children, and men who don't measure up. He is functional, designed mainly for work. He is programmed to tackle jobs, override obstacles, attack problems, overcome difficulties, and always seize the offensive. . . . His circuits are never scrambled or overrun by irrelevant personal signals. His relationship with other male machines is one of respect but not intimacy; it is difficult for him to connect his internal circuits to those of others. In fact, his internal circuitry is somewhat of a mystery to him, and is maintained primarily by humans of the opposite sex."

If we try hard enough and know where to look, we can begin to change our patriarchal attitudes: men's and women's consciousness-changing groups are helping some of us do that right now (see Chapter 21). But we can't change our patriarchal attitudes completely until we go on to change—not capitalism, necessarily—but the Prison as a whole. For each of the other sides of the Prison *reinforces and perpetuates* our patriarchal attitudes.

Egocentricity

In the tradition of Western psychology, egocentricity refers to selfishness and false pride, and to the notion that the world exists for our own, personal benefit. In the tradition of Eastern philosophy, and in this book, egocentricity also refers to the notion that we are solid and isolated beings, sealed up in our skins like so many tin cans on a shelf.

In this view, egocentricity includes the notion that we are our bodies, period, or our social roles, period—the notion that we only exist in the material state of consciousness (see Chapter 11). It includes the notion that we are different from other people, period (as opposed to the idea that we can also and sometimes more usefully be seen as One, though we play the game of life in different ways). And it includes our fear of losing our egos, a fear that we try to avoid by constantly trying to extend our selves in the world—all those tall buildings, all those highways. (If we are adepts at Eastern philosophy, we tend to have the opposite fear, the fear of losing our egolessness!)

The notion that we are separate from trees, animals, stars, wind, rocks, minerals—from the life that is in all these things (which native Americans have traditionally called the Great Spirit)—is a half-truth; and when we take it as the whole truth, it is reasonable to call it an illusion. It is an illusion that nearly all of us share: not only our separation from these things, but our domination of them, has been celebrated in our folklore for thousands of years, and is celebrated in Marxist economics (E. F. Schumacher: "Even the great Dr. Marx fell into this devastating error [of treating] as valueless everything that we have not made ourselves").

But if our egocentricity doesn't come from capitalism—where does it come from?

Grace Stuart traces it back to the fact that we are not constantly held and stroked and loved when we are young. This lack of happy and close physical intimacy with people makes it very difficult for us to love other people later on, and leaves us with a generalized fear of loving others and of expressing our love for them; and that makes it almost impossible for us to get out of our selves.

To Oscar Ichazo, founder of the Arica Institute, egocentricity is the limited mode of awareness, the distorted consciousness, that develops as a result of the socializing process (as we know it today). Between four and six years old "the child begins to imitate [his or her] parents, tell lies, and pretend. . . . Personality forms a defensive layer over the essence [of the self], and so there is a split between the self and the world."

To Joel Kramer, a meditation teacher, egocentricity is born of the fact that we seek pleasure—the pleasure of judging things, the pleasure of prolonging things. When we experience a landscape, an event, or whatever, at first there is no gap between the experiencer and the experience—it is one thing. But what always seems to happen is that we say to our selves, This is beautiful! or, How can I keep on with this? We separate our selves out from the experience in order to *retain* it—and as soon as we do this we have constructed a *barrier* between our selves and the experience.

Whatever their differences, Stuart, Ichazo, and Kramer would agree that egocentricity is a very deep quality in us. But we shouldn't conclude that it's always been with us.

Until quite recently most Asiatics would have been baffled by the "civilized" idea of self. So would many of those Europeans who, until modern times, stood outside of the Judeo-Christian tradition. Traditional American native peoples are still baffled by it. Probably most people in the world have done without it.

Theodore Roszak, Alan Watts, and many other New Age writers, have said that it goes back to the beginnings of the Judeo-Christian tradition, when God was first seen as being something apart from us. As Watts puts it: in most forms of Judeo-Christianity, "the creature is as distinct from the Creator as the table from the carpenter." Worse, the Creator is also the Boss, and "the Boss notices: he loves and judges every creature separately, and his demands are stern." Philip Slater, a psychotherapist, says that it began with the first kings. Acute self-consciousness engendered in kings an acute fear of death which led to their (and now our) desire to extend our selves into the environment, a desire that, according to Slater, "constitutes the single greatest threat to our species."

That is my real point: whichever theories about egocentricity turn out to be most accurate or useful, the fact is that for thousands of years our egocentricity has been doing us all great harm.

- It cuts us off from each other;
- It keeps us from realizing our obligation to love and respect our environment;
- It makes us keep wanting to go places, do things, have more. It makes us live in and for the future—or the past. As Ram Dass says, we can never really *be* where we are now;
- It causes us constantly to emphasize our separateness from others through craving, hate, anger, fear, jealousy;
- It keeps us from being able to reach any kind of common agreement about the world—what it's all about, what life is *for*;
- It makes us terribly afraid of death.

We can try to get out of our egocentricity. Through Yoga, through Zen, and through many other Eastern traditions and disciplines, and through encounter and growth groups, many of us are beginning to lose at least the most destructive aspects of our egocentricity. But we'll never be able to really strip our selves of our egocentricity unless and until we change the Prison as a whole. For each of the other sides of the Prison reinforces and perpetuates our egocentricity.

Patriarchal attitudes encourage men to be arrogant and women, defensive. Scientific single vision encourages us to see our selves as the center of the universe. The bureaucratic mentality encourages us not only to "get ahead" but to trample on others in the process. Nationalism encourages us to get ahead as a *nation* and to trample on other *nations*. And our big city outlooks encourage us to loathe and fear other people and to separate our selves from them as much as we can.

Scientific Single Vision

"May God us keep, From Single vision and Newton's sleep"—William Blake. Scientific single vision (or the "scientific outlook") is one way, our way, of seeing the world. It's the way that most of us think about things, including our selves, life in general, and the material in this book.

Scientific single vision is intellectual rather than sensuous, active rather than receptive, analytic rather than intuitive, verbal rather than spatial. It tends to be more interested in argument than in experience, more interested in understanding things sequentially (in terms of cause and effect) than as patterned wholes, more concerned with time than with eternity.

According to George Lodge, a New Age business theorist, scientific single vision is characterized by: specialization (and overspecialization); "reductionism" (the way to understand whole things is to break them apart and examine the parts); "objectivity" (knowledge must be quantifiable—if you can't count it, it doesn't really count); "rationalism" (reason is all); and "materialism" (what's real is what I can feel, touch, see—especially if I own it!).

In the United States, scientific single vision is the outlook *par excellence* not only of scientists but of doctors and lawyers, politicians and revolutionaries, businessmen and scholars—of nearly everyone who's managed to "make it big" outside of the arts. Which is, maybe, why most of us are convinced that it's the *only* way of seeing the world, of getting at "the truth." People who come up with other ways of seeing are usually called "crazy" or worse. But are they?

Over the last ten years or so, many of us have begun to discover whole cultures that share in an alternate way of seeing the world. Zen, Vedanta, Sufism, American Indian culture—whatever their differences, each of them seems, in its way of seeing, to be the polar opposite of the scientific outlook: sensuous rather than intellectual, receptive rather than active, intuitive rather than analytic.

At the same time, many recent investigators have begun to gather evidence that the two sides of the brain are specialized for different modes of consciousness. The left side of the brain is, apparently, specialized for analysis, verbal facility, linear time-orientation, and the like; the right side of the brain for pattern recognition, spatial orientation, holistic thinking, and the like (see Ornstein or Singer).

So the reality would appear to be that, not only do different ways of seeing exist, not only do some of them go back thousands of years, but that these alternate ways of seeing are rooted in the workings of the right half of the brain just as much as scientific single vision is rooted in those of the left. Even in science's *own* terms, the alternate outlooks are as real and as valid as the scientific outlook.

The real question is, why is our culture so "crazy" as to promote—to be partially based on!—an outlook that requires us to ignore the signals that are coming to us from the right side of our brains?

Theodore Roszak traces the scientific outlook back to the ancient Jewish belief that people who worshiped objects were being abusive of God (who was supposed to be invisible). According to Roszak, the Jews were simply suffering from a cultural misunderstanding; they didn't realize that for the peasants, God was manifest equally in all things. But the damage was done; from that point on, *things* began to lose their transcendent qualities and became merely objects to be manipulated.

And that was only the beginning. Later we would come to *actively dislike* the natural world. According to Joel Kovel, a psychohistorian, this dislike began when we learned to dislike our feces (for as we became more "civilized" we learned to practice some pretty wicked versions of toilet-training); but it quickly and inevitably spread outward to all natural things.

Soon it was only a matter of time before we devised a system for subduing and punishing nature (as opposed to simply working with her), and cutting our selves off from her as much as possible. According to Roszak, the most important step here was taken by Galileo, for he did more than any other person to define the "real" world as only what could be precisely defined in physical terms: if it couldn't be counted, it didn't really count. According to George Leonard, psychologist and philosopher, the most important step was Isaac Newton's "grand synthesis" of the ideas of Galileo, Copernicus, Descartes, etc.; a synthesis that caused or at least encouraged us to see the world as a machine.

Either way, the point is that the scientific outlook arose well before capitalism, and that, because it was so narrow, it's done us all great harm.

• It has encouraged us to lose touch with our selves and our bodies;

• It has cut us off from other dimensions of reality besides the material;

• It has led to our worship of machines and of technique;

• It has led to a situation where the human scale is lost, and "progress" means mostly destruction;

• It has helped us forget that after all the "objective" facts are in, we still have to make moral choices and value judgments;

• It has led to a separation of means and ends in almost every human endeavor;

• It has fostered a society made up of mostly unrelated specialties and specialists;

• It hasn't even delivered on what it promised in its *own* terms. We haven't understood the material world "with absolute certainty" by ignoring our subjective experience of that world. We haven't understood human nature by describing it statistically. We haven't understood history by reading it "scientifically."

Many of us are trying to expand our scientific outlooks now by immersing our selves in Eastern disciplines or in encounter and growth groups or by working on our bodies—by getting back in touch with the sensuous, intuitive, holistic side of our selves. We are not going to be able to change our selves deeply, however, unless and until we also change the other sides of the Prison. For each of the other sides reinforces and perpetuates the scientific outlook. Patriarchal attitudes, for example, teach us that the traits that are associated with the scientific outlook are *male* traits, and therefore the ones we'll need if we want to "make it" in society. And the bureaucratic mentality has helped to give that teaching the irresistible force of truth.

The Bureaucratic Mentality

The bureaucratic mentality—or, more accurately, the "functional" or "rationalized" mentality—is an extremely important aspect of the Prison. According to sociologists Peter Berger and William Howton, some of its key elements are:

- Status-consciousness. Every person has his or her place—"above" or "below" you.
- Depersonalization. Every person comes to see him or herself as a thing, an object, a number.
- Predictability. Everything is supposed to fit neatly into some category. If it doesn't fit neatly then it doesn't really exist for us, we put it out of our minds.
- Efficiency. This is not only the highest social value, it is the greatest metaphysical virtue.
- Arbitrariness. Rules and rituals are followed because they are supposed to be followed—because they are there.
- Discipline. Every person is supposed to abide by the rules, or else.

The bureaucratic mentality is far from being a product of capitalism —it goes back thousands of years. It isn't even a product of mechanization, at least not originally. According to Lewis Mumford, "the meticulous order that characterizes bureaucracy" probably derives from the ritual observances of the Temple; and even in the first organized wars "we find remarkably early records, in definite figures, of prisoners captured, animals rounded up, loot taken." Behind every later process of organization and mechanization Mumford is able to find "primordial aptitudes . . . for ritualizing behaviour" and for finding satisfaction in repetitive order.

The bureaucratic mentality is, then, in the final analysis, responsible for bureaucracies, and not the other way around; but in the rich interplay of consciousness and society, bureaucracies have had a significant effect on the bureaucratic mentality, reinforcing and extending it at every turn.

Bureaucracies are organizations that are run from the top down and that see people, us, as *means* to the bureaucracies' own ends (above all that of self-preservation). According to Mumford they go back 5,000 years, to Egypt and Mesopotamia. According to Howton they go back "only" 2,000 years, to Rome, because the Roman bureaucrats were the first to know that they owed their power to their offices, rather than to God. According to Simon Leys, a Sinologist, the Chinese bureaucracy had ten distinct hierarchical classes in the sixth century B.C.

But bureaucracies have by no means managed to dominate society everywhere or at all times. Why, then, does bureaucracy become so determining in Prison society in our time?

According to Kenneth Boulding, the economist, it has little to do with our *need* for large, hierarchical organizations. It has a lot more to do with the improvement in the skills of organizations and—even more important—in the ability of the organizations to grow, unchecked (after the sixteenth century or so) by any widely held ethics or values that were not Prison-bound. Possibly the change in our *demand* for large, hierarchical organizations came as a result of the growth in strength of the other sides of the Prison: patriarchal attitudes caused us to become more domineering; egocentricity, more ambitious; and scientific single vision, more arrogant. And "important," centralized, and hierarchical organizations are nothing if not a means for allowing us to be domineering and ambitious and arrogant (in our different ways).

At any rate, the important point is that the bureaucracies—and the bureaucratic mentality—are "here now," and that they are doing us all a great deal of harm.

• To begin with, take another look at those seven key elements of the bureaucratic mentality. Every single one of them encourages us to lose sight of our humanity in the interests of a "higher" logic. Every single one of them encourages us to think of other people as a means —or, worse, as "sand in the gears"—rather than as vulnerable, valuable, and unique;

• The bureaucratic mentality causes us to fear and oppose all substantial change;

• The bureaucratic mentality makes it seem more interesting to manipulate the environment than to live in it, more rewarding to (try to) manage the world than to (try to) understand it;

• The fact that the bureaucratic mentality is depersonalized makes it seem objective—a cardinal value to Prisoners, as we saw in the section on scientific single vision—and so the public interest naturally comes to be redefined as part of the private interest of bureaucracies (look at our "defense" policies!);

• Bureaucracies have become so big that they can't even deliver on some of their own values (efficiency, predictability, orderliness). Liberals and Marxists may rail against bureaucracy and call for increased and improved organization of services, but as Jacques Ellul points out, increased and improved organization would serve "only to fortify the [bureaucratic] system and to improve its operation," making it more versatile, discriminating, intelligent—ultimately, more all-encompassing;

• To work well, says Boulding, bureaucracies seem to require what

I later call Prison-bound personalities (see Chapter 9)—people who aren't able to have warm and open personal relationships, and who are therefore apt to translate their frustrations into personal ambition or into "serving the people";

 • But it isn't even a question of bad, or rather frustrated, individuals. No matter how life-loving we are, our consciences will be diminished at the point where we enter a bureaucratic structure. What happens is this: when we enter an authority system—or when we're living in one!—we no longer see our selves as autonomous, as acting on our own. We come to see our selves as *agents* for carrying out the wishes of others. Psychologist Stanley Milgram calls this the "agentic state of mind" (he could just as well have called it the "bureaucratic mentality supreme"), and he argues that when we're in this state we no longer see our selves as responsible for our actions but as instruments for carrying out the wishes of others. "An element of free choice determines whether the person defines [him- or herself] in this way or not," says Milgram (the bureaucratic mentality is *not* part of human nature), "but . . . the propensity to do so is exceedingly strong, and the shift [back to an autonomous state of mind] is not freely reversible." This goes a long way toward explaining why so many of us are psychologically able to sell cars that are built to break down in five years (or is it three?), work strip mines, and murder each other.

Nationalism

The "sense of identity with a small, earthbound 'in-group' is extremely ancient," writes Mumford; "the sentiment of nationality long antedates any conscious belief in nationalism." Similarly, Vadim Borisov, a Russian historian—born in 1945, deprived of all employment—tells us (in Solzhenitsyn, ed.) that nationalism is "above all an *ideology*, which directs the existing elemental national instincts into a particular channel."

The "sentiment of nationality" that predates nationalism—those "elemental national instincts"—have nothing to do with the large nation-state, but are regional, even local in scope. Carlton Hayes, a well-known historian, has written several scholarly books whose message is that it's natural for us to love our own immediate surroundings —town, neighborhood, countryside—but that it takes an artificial effort to make us love a whole nation (or at least, a geographically immense and socially-culturally diverse nation). It is natural for us to feel loyal to family and friends and to the people in our immediate communities, but it takes special civic training to make us feel loyal to all the people who are supposed to constitute our nation. It is natural for us to feel loyal to some ideas or ideals that are shared by our friends, but it takes systematic efforts to make us feel loyal to an entire national ideology.

So—localism is natural to us, regionalism is natural, but nationalism only *seems* natural because we're living in giant nation-states (and because of the Prison). In tribal society, our highest loyalties were to our friends and to our immediate communities. And even after tribal society was replaced by the great military empires, nationalism wasn't forced on us. All (all?) the Egyptians or Persians or Romans wanted from us was money and soldiers. They didn't want to weld us together into "one people."

Well into the sixteenth century, most of Europe was localistic or "universalistic"—not nationalistic. The peasants, by virtue of the work they did and the community they enjoyed with each other, were loyal to lord and village. Many religious people and scholars, by virtue of the Christian religion and the Latin language, were "universalists," the kind of people that dedicated nationalists have always mistrusted—and mistreated.

In the sixteenth century, the triumph of Prison values plus new developments in military technology led to the "emergence"—as they say in the polite history books—of the monarchical nation-state. And the nation-state was nationalist from the very beginning. It had to be and has to be, because it has to convince people to feel loyal to *it* rather than to their immediate or self-chosen surroundings. (This task was made easier because the Black Death and the schisms in the Christian church had caused us to lose our faith and become afraid, and so we needed something to cling to and believe in.)

Even so, among all but the intelligentsia, the new nationalism spread slowly; it was given its first big boost by the French revolution. The revolutionary "patriotes," nationalists, singers of the "Marseillaise," shortsightedly identified the ideals of liberty and equality with the idea of nationalism. And so they crushed the peasants who tried to fight against the nationalization of the historic provinces of France and the elimination of provincial rights. Then they tried to export their revolution.

Nationalism continued to grow in the nineteenth century, but mostly in the cities, and mostly even there among those who were rootless (good soldiers but bad workers). It was partly in order to foster our nationalism that our national governments introduced the system of universal, compulsory schooling. According to Hayes, universal schooling was intended "to unify a people by belittling their economic, social, [cultural], occupational and religious differences and by emphasizing their national language and the inculcation of a common national patriotism." This strategy was fully justified during World Wars I and II, when there seemed to be a direct connection, in nearly every country on Earth, between the number of "schooled" people and the degree of unquestioning national loyalty.

So nationalism has nothing to do with human nature—and nothing to do with political ideologies, either (by 1900 even communism had become a nationalistic force). But just because it's been forced on us—has it really done us that much harm? Can we really speak of it as part of the Prison?

From the beginning, nationalism has served as a kind of *vulgarized religion* with its "sacred" rituals and texts and its missionary zeal. And so we've come to believe that we are a chosen people; that our nation is eternal; that the deaths of its sons add to its glory; that we need to guard our selves against foreign "devils"; and so on.

Nationalism has made us insufferably chauvinistic. If we are from big nation-states, we tend to feel that the world revolves around us and that other places, other ideas, other *peoples*, are of lesser importance. If we are from smaller nation-states, we tend to feel so defensive that often we shut our selves off from outside influences even more completely.

Nationalism compensates for feelings of inferiority or worthlessness in an extremely unproductive (and often downright dangerous) way. Krishnamurti says, "Living in a little village or a big town or whatever it might be, I am nobody; but if I identify myself with the larger, with the country . . . it flatters my vanity." Erich Fromm says that the degree of nationalism is "commensurate with the lack of real satisfaction in life," is a function of material and cultural scarcity, of boredom. He says it's much more dangerous than personal narcissism, because "an individual, unless [he or she] is mentally very sick, may have at least some doubts about [his or her] personal narcissistic image. The member of the [nation] has none, since [his or her] narcissism is shared by the majority."

In other words, nationalism has encouraged us to live vicariously, through an abstraction called the nation-state. Even our self-esteem becomes dependent on what strangers think of our nation and its culture. As Richard Barnet points out—when foreign governments reject Coca-Cola, General Motors, Alcan, etc., we tend to feel *personally* rejected, personally attacked.

Many New Age writers have pointed out that the nation-state system leads almost inevitably to war. Margaret Mead points out that it is literally impossible for each and every nation to have a favorable balance of trade. Kenneth Boulding points out that the nation-state has *never* been a "trading" organization so much as a "fighting" one—that "it is only a mild exaggeration to say that all states are the creations of their enemies" (the U.S. owes its existence to George III, Canada to the U.S., etc.). Gerald and Patricia Mische point out that individual nation-states *must* engage in "balance-of-weapons competition, balance-of-payments competition, and competition over scarce resources"—and that all of these are zero-sum games (there will always be "winners" and "losers," poised for revenge).

Over the last few years, many of us have tried to change our loyalties—at least in our hearts and minds. Some of us have become "planetary citizens" through constant travel or through exposure to other ways of seeing the world. Some of us have returned to a form of localism by doing intensive political work in our local communities or by starting community enterprises of one sort or another. Some of us have done both.

But we won't be able to lose our nationalism, really, until we leave the rest of the Prison behind. Because the rest of the Prison reinforces and perpetuates our nationalism. Egocentricity, for example, feeds Americans' sense that they are superior human beings, and Canadians' sense that they are morally superior to the Americans.

The Big City Outlook

By a "big city" I mean any place that has more than half a million inhabitants or so; and, yes, I mean "big city" as a negative term. Because above that size, as E. F. Schumacher and many other New Age writers have told us, nothing is added to the value of a city, to its street life, its cultural offerings, its virtue.

It's a little-known fact, but 124 million North Americans—54 percent of us—now live in urban areas of half a million or more. Seventy-one million of us—31 percent—live in urban areas of *two million* or more!

(Incidentally: according to Schumacher's teacher, Leopold Kohr, population size is only part of what determines the "social" or "effective" size of a community. The other factors are: density of a population; degree of its administrative integration; and velocity of its movements. So we should take "half a million" with a grain of salt. Still, it's a good rule of thumb.)

The big city outlook is what happens inevitably to our outlook on life when we end up living in big cities no matter how "nice" or "cosmopolitan" they are. (It might not happen right away. Urban economist Elizabeth Bardwell speaks of an "incubation period" of three generations for the effects of urban living to really begin taking their toll on people.) What happens is this: the very existence of the extra hundreds of thousands (or millions) of people, all crowded together, creates enormous problems that we can't get away from—and our big city outlooks are shaped by these problems.

Air pollution. Big city air is four times as dirty as rural air, and particulates and other pollutants in the air are expected to increase from now on as population increases (Bardwell). Researchers have established significant connections between polluted air and bronchitis, asthma, pneumonia, lung cancer, eye allergies, and mental depression.

Noise pollution. Background noise has increased dramatically since World War II—in fact, some experts estimate that background noise is now more responsible for impaired hearing than industrial noise (Bardwell). Constant noise is known to produce annoyance, fright, irritability, tension, and headaches in us.

Isolation. "There is a decrease of all-round trusted friends and neighbors who share the total process of living, and a resulting loss of emotional ties of affection and regard, and of a sense of social responsibility. Out of this lack comes a tendency to breakdown of ethical standards . . ." (Arthur Morgan).

Lack of privacy. The other side of the coin from isolation—made even worse because it often goes together with isolation.

Rootlessness. The average American moves every four years—the big city dweller more often than that. And can *anyone* feel rooted in a high-rise?

Anonymity. In a big city, most of our transactions are carried on with strangers. "Urban anonymity increases fear and suspicion, which in turn make people less mutually supporting members of the community" (Bardwell).

Overcrowding. A considerable amount of research has demonstrated that density of living "has definite negative effects on the behavior and the body chemistry" of people (Bardwell). Not to mention on rats: when rats are allowed to multiply freely in a fixed space, catastrophe soon ensues. Mothers abandon their young; many rats withdraw from interaction, others wander about in a disoriented daze; still others become extremely aggressive. Of course, rats and people have nothing in common. . . .

Crime. The crime rate is five and a half times as high in our big cities as it is in our rural areas. Or, more specifically: the crime rate per 100,000 people in rural areas was 985 in 1970; in cities pop. 50–100,000, 2,960; in cities pop. 500,000–1,000,000, 5,530. Significantly, the crime rate failed to rise (much) once the size of the city topped 500,000.

Danger. Because of the crime rate, we become fearful and afraid. We expect trouble all the time—and that helps bring it about.

Hustle. The only way to keep your head above water in these conditions!

Stress. "Diseases associated with stress, particularly ulcers, coronary disease, and high blood pressure, are . . . prevalent" in big cities (Ehrlich and Ehrlich).

Mental illness. Anne and Paul Ehrlich, population experts and environmentalists, have suggested that "the high numbers of contacts with individuals not part of one's circle of regular social acquaintances may lead to mental disturbance"—and they offer quite a bit of evidence to prove their point. In one study conducted in Manhattan on the effects of density on people, it was found that all but 18 percent of the people interviewed were suffering from some degree of neurotic or psychotic disturbance (this survey did not include the poorest neighborhoods).

Higher death rates. In New York State the death rates for both sexes are higher in metropolitan areas. The U.S. Public Health Service reports that coronary heart disease is 42 percent higher for people in metro areas. In Iowa, cancer is 40 percent more prevalent among urban dwellers (Ehrlich and Ehrlich).

Look out kid you better stay hid. Even a generation or two ago big city children "spent much of their time exploring and participating in the activities of the city, while today children are confined to dreary school rooms, their homes, and the local park" (Ehrlich and Ehrlich). And even if they *are* allowed to roam, says Alison Stallibrass (in Holt, 1976), the environment is rapidly becoming one "which they cannot become familiar with through the senses, cannot understand, and in which they cannot, therefore, use their own judgement." Some children, finding that their "tentative efforts towards independence or adventure and experiment" are (reasonably enough!) discouraged, may eventually conclude that "passivity is the best policy."

Materialism. Urban anonymity has contributed to our materialism —so say many sociologists. "External appearance becomes important because so little is known about a person's character or ethical principles. The type of clothes, the cut of the hair, or the cost of an automobile or a home are often all one has to go on in sizing up people. In addition, the great variation in standards of living in [big] cities tends to heighten people's dissatisfaction with the quantity and quality of their own possessions" (Bardwell)—no matter what that quantity or quality might be!

Communications overload. The big city dweller can't escape a constant bombardment of information and impressions. "Excessive stimulation creates confusion and fatigue, sometimes to the point where the mind has to turn off" (Bardwell).

The tie that blinds. "The larger a city the more likely it is for people to get caught up in it," says Mike Nickerson, New Age author and activist. In other words: the more likely it is for us to get caught up in thinking that only urban technology, urban life-styles, urban values, are natural to us, or at least, suitably "modern."

Skyrocketing costs. Urban economist Richard Bradley, in a study done for a Colorado Springs, Colo., citizens group (*The Costs of Urban Growth*, 1973), concludes that "all things considered, county areas having a population of about 25,000 people cost their residents the least amount of money per capita. Above this population size, per capita costs of all local governments tend to increase." Bardwell finds that total expenditures increase gradually with size in the 50–250,000 range but go up much more quickly after that—"the law of diminishing returns sets in and produces significant diseconomies of scale." In fact, a city of one million population costs *three times* as much to run, per capita, as a city of 100,000. I believe that the big city taxpayer learns a "lesson" (usually subconscious) from these skyrocketing costs: other people cost us too much money—other people are burdensome. Therefore, other people are expendable.

Loss of the connection with life-as-a-whole-process. In a big city, says Nickerson, "where goods and food come from store shelves and end up in garbage cans or the sewage system, it is hard for people to be aware of the impact their lives have on the world around them."

Loss of the connection with nature and with the spiritual and religious states of consciousness. Walking Buffalo, a Stoney Indian from Alberta, says (in *The Mother Earth News*, May–June 1977), "Living in a city is an artificial existence. Lots of people hardly ever feel real soil under their feet, see plants grow except in flowerpots, or get far enough beyond the street lights to catch the enchantment of a night sky studded with stars." And he adds: "When people live far from scenes of the Great Spirit's making, it's easy for them to forget [the Great Spirit's] laws."

Because our big cities are so "modern," so technologically advanced, it is tempting to conclude that the problems they pose for us are new and therefore traceable to capitalism or technology. But according to Lewis Mumford, nothing could be further from the truth. Huge, over-sized cities ("megalopolises," the city planners call them) go all the way back to Egypt and Mesopotamia, where the first kings, eager to consolidate their new power, managed to replace the decentralized village economy with a highly centralized and therefore primarily urban one—"centralized," that is, around the king's needs.

But big cities haven't always been dominant since then. According to Mumford, they tend to become really big only toward the end of a civilization—which tends to suggest that their overexpansion has less to do with economic forces than with cultural ones (the Prison). Certainly that is the case today: all over North America, the whole cultural structure of rural life has been collapsing, and people have been pouring into the biggest cities even with no prospects of finding decent work there. The *biggest* cities—because these provide us (or appear to provide us) with what rural life never seemed to be able to: "excitement," vicarious pleasures, "real life"—in a phrase, the consolations of the Prison.

A similar situation prevails in France: according to Schumacher, "the French planners fight against France becoming 'Paris surrounded by a desert'." Similarly in the Soviet countries: Barbara Ward tells us that Moscow and Leningrad "have continued to double in size after all policies likely to lead to further growth had been strictly banned," and she concludes, "There must be evidence of some innate, forceful, and all but uncontrollable influences at work." Mumford says much the same thing: "The persistence of these overgrown containers [every-where] would indicate that they are concrete manifestations of the dominant forces in our present civilization."

I believe that they are manifestations of the Prison. And I also believe that they help to reinforce and perpetuate the Prison in us. For living in a place where endless streams of anonymous people pass us by every day, helps to convince us that human life is cheap (a *jailer's* mentality). And living in a place where pollution, overspecialization, rootlessness, etc., appear to be unavoidable facts of life, helps to convince us that Prison values are necessary for our survival—that they are, in fact, natural and good.

CHAPTER 4

Racism:
A Product of Capitalism—
or of the Six-Sided Prison?

Several times now I've said that the Prison, as distinct from capitalism or human nature, is ultimately responsible for racism, war, imperialism, ecological destruction. In this chapter I wanted to show *how* the Prison is responsible for one of these horrors. I drew straws—I really did—and picked racism. To simplify things I'll focus on white racism in the United States.

What is racism exactly? Most of us seem to think that it's a prejudice against people on biological grounds (as in "they have low IQ's" or "they smell funny") and that it can therefore be done away with by showing people that their prejudices have no basis in fact, or that "the facts" are misleading. But if you actually sit down and talk with people who are racists I think you'll find that their biological prejudices are really just rationales, excuses, that give a kind of scientific validity to a much deeper form of prejudice.

In this view, racism is not just a question of biologically mistaken beliefs or economically convenient beliefs (though both these play a part). It is also, and more profoundly, a kind of cultural prejudice writ large, and with a scientific twist. And cultural prejudice goes back at least as far as the ancient Greeks. In fact, Roderic Gorney tells us that in the vast majority of cultures for which there are written records we can find some degree of connection between whiteness and truth, beauty, divinity, etc., and blackness and falsehood, ugliness, evil, etc.

So the question becomes, what is there about our *culture* that makes us prejudiced against blacks (and other dark-skinned peoples)? Why are we so prejudiced that improvements in the economic and educational status of nonwhites may cause us to feel even more prejudiced against them? Why were we prejudiced against nonwhites from the very beginnings of the settlement of the United States?

The answer, I believe, lies in the workings of the Six-Sided Prison.

Patriarchal attitudes gave us a precedent for oppression, the oppression of women throughout history and in the family. As Shulamith Firestone points out, black and native and Chicano oppression is modeled on the oppression of women—the parallels are exact and startling.

In addition, the patriarchy gives us an image of masculinity that leads inevitably to racism. For example, most white males are brought up to believe that the repression of emotion is normal, and so they come to look down on people like blacks and Chicanos who are (supposedly) able to express their emotions more freely.

Egocentricity encourages us to build walls around our selves, and therefore contributes mightily to our tendency to see nonwhites as "the other" . . . if not as "the enemy."

Scientific single vision causes us to think of the traits associated with the left side of our brains as "light," and those with the right side of our brains as "dark" (see Ornstein). And it causes us to be prejudiced against the traits that are associated with the right side of our brains. And so we think of dark-skinned people as sensuous ("lazy"), receptive ("passive"), intuitive ("stupid"), etc.

In addition, scientific single vision led to our mistrust and eventual domination of natural things in the name of a "higher rationality"; and this led in turn to our alienation from our bodies and to our culture's distortion of natural functions—in plainer words, to our love-hate relationship with feces. And in our culture, as any first-year psychology student can tell you, most of us subconsciously identify blackness with feces, and darkness with "impurities" (see Joel Kovel, *White Racism*, for a thorough explanation of this point).

The bureaucratic mentality encourages us to feel that the world is *naturally* made up of powerful and powerless, winners and losers, jailers and jailed—whites and nonwhites.

Nationalism requires us to conform to the characteristics of the dominant cultural group. In the United States, the dominant group is white, Anglo-Saxon and Protestant (the "WASP's"). Minorities that are obviously, even physically unlike this cultural group are automatically suspect.

In addition, the nation-state encourages us to think of other nation-states as "weaker," "poorer," "menacing," etc. And these qualities naturally rub off—in our minds—on the people who are living in these other nation-states.

The big city outlook encourages us to see our selves as separate and isolated, and so it contributes to our tendency to see human differences as alien and threatening. (The big city itself, overlarge and overbearing, gives us an arena in which all our racial prejudices can be acted out in an appropriately vicious and satisfying manner.)

I could go on—but by now I hope my point is made. Racism is a product of the Prison. It is not a part of human nature, and it is not confined to capitalism, either. (Does anyone doubt that Stalin could have carried out the extermination of the Jews, which he'd planned, had he lived? Or that the Communist Party could convince the Chinese in a very short time to fear—and believe in—the "white peril"?)

The conditions for cultural prejudice are deep-seated in all of us, for they were put there by the Prison. And if we don't change the Prison, changing our economic system or changing our schools won't do much to change our racist attitudes. It might even make us more subtly and deeply racist. For if we pass and enforce "good laws" our racism might simply be driven underground, to live on in the fantasies and symbols that nourish the Prison. Moreover, if we pass "good laws" and ignore the Prison we may only succeed in driving a wedge between our selves and our society. Barbara Amiel, a well-known Canadian journalist, tells us (in *Maclean's*, April 4, 1977) that Britain's liberal immigration laws have made a definite contribution to "the growing alienation Britons feel from their society," that the presence of large numbers of black and brown immigrants in the big British cities "may be one of the reasons for [Britain's] indifference to its future."

CHAPTER 5

Tri-Level Analysis:
How to See Through
to the Prison

Because it's so pervasive and runs so deep, the Prison isn't immediately obvious to everyone. In order to see through to it, it helps to keep in mind a method that I call "tri-level analysis."

I call it that because it looks at the world on three levels at once. The first is concerned with the passing events of daily life; the second, with economic and political power; and the third, with the Prison itself (and with the worldview that the Prison spawns—see Chapter 11).

I didn't invent this method of analysis. It's been used under other names, or simply intuitively, by many New Age-oriented people over the years. In the field of psychology, for example, Daryl Bem has done a tri-level analysis of the levels of belief—he calls them "primitive," "higher-order," and "nonconscious." In economics, Robert Theobald distinguishes among first-, second-, and third-order "connections" that we make between phenomena. In sociology, Peter Berger distinguishes among ideas, ideologies, and worldviews.

In political theory, New Age authors and activists distinguish among "reform," "revolution," and "transformation" (See Chapter 20). And Willis Harman says that there are three levels on which we can "view society's problems": (1) the level of symptoms—e.g., poverty, crime, racism, pollution, inflation; (2) the level of basic institutions—built-in distributions of economic and political power; and (3) the level of cultural premises, dominant values, and our *image* of our selves (i.e., our basic worldview).

To my mind, the greatest practitioner of tri-level analysis (he doesn't call it that, of course) is a French historian, Fernand Braudel. In his magnum opus, *The Mediterranean*, history moves on three levels at once.

On the first level, the most superficial, are the *events* that fill our daily newspaper—elections, murders, wage demands; "surface disturbances," says Braudel, "crests of foam that the tides of history carry on their strong backs." This is the level that the liberals concentrate on, because it lends itself to irony and can be written about without challenging "the system," any system.

On the second level is the history of *groups and groupings*, of changes in governmental and economic forms (monarchy to democracy, feudalism to capitalism, and so on). This is the level that the Marxists concentrate on, in order to "prove" that communism is inevitable.

On the third level, invisible to liberals and Marxists alike, is the history of *structures*. In *The Mediterranean* Braudel focuses mainly on changes in geography and climate, on what Ernest Callenbach might call "ecohistorical" changes, but many historians have pointed out that this level could—and should—also refer to *inner* structures; to deep-seated changes in states of mind, points of view, custom and routine, personality and consciousness (see, e.g., Hexter, listed under Braudel). Therefore, this is the level where the Six-Sided Prison can be found.

This third level of history isn't impossible to change; but it is the hardest to change. It's the level William Irwin Thompson is operating on, in *Passages About Earth*, when he sets out to describe a "transformation of culture so large that it isn't an event any more." No wonder most political activists have chosen to ignore it!

And yet—and yet—if it's true that governments and economic systems determine the nature of events, as the Marxists say, then it's also true that the third level of history determines the nature of governments and economic systems, and the context, the atmosphere, the quality of events. If we simply ignore the third level of analysis until "later" we'll end up with no social evolution at all, in any deep sense. And we may end up with a stronger Prison.

CHAPTER 6

History as if People Mattered: the Stages of Human Development

Tri-level analysis tells us that the minds and hearts of people were the determining factors in history, and that governments, economics, and so on, were not so determining. Does this make our history read any differently? Does our history make more sense when it's read in this way? And does it hold out hope for the future?

This chapter is an attempt to answer these questions. (It answers "yes" to each of them.)

Before I begin, though, Id like to say something about what I think are the two main barriers to history-as-if-people-mattered: the idea that there are "laws" in history, and the idea that we are primarily tool-making and tool-using beings (i.e., the idea that *who we are* must conform to material constraints).

The idea that history is governed by a series of unchangeable laws that are taking us from "lower to higher," in Engels's phrase, or "onward and upward," in Stalin's, obviously diminishes people's role in history—and provides a convenient excuse for authoritarian governments who would override the will of the people, or pay no heed to the views of dissenting minorities. For a critique of the currently most influential series of historical laws—Marxist dialectics—see Chapter 26.

The other barrier is the idea that we are primarily tool users and tool makers ("man the maker"). A number of New Age-oriented people have recently pointed out that tool-making and tool-using are not our most characteristic activities.

Marshall Sahlins, an economic anthropologist, says that we're basically meaning-seeking beings and that we turn even the things we *need* to do into a vehicle for the expression of our search for meaning. In this view, culture is the sum total of our efforts to find out about our selves and to realize our selves—even when we're engaging in directly economic activities, our search for meaning remains primary. What is distinctive about human culture is not "that it must conform to material constraints but that it does so according to a definite symbolic scheme which is never the only one possible" (see *Manas*, Dec. 21, 1977).

Roderic Gorney, psychiatrist and social philosopher, says that "the functional capacity that truly separates man from ape and all other animals is that of using *complex symbols*. . . . Tool-using and especially tool-making are manifestations of the symbolic process."

Lewis Mumford says that we're not primarily tool-making, we're primarily "mind-making, self-mastering, and self-designing," and so we've always been. For until we developed a culture (he says), our inner life must have been a madhouse—we wouldn't have been able to recognize a tool, let alone use one. Our first and greatest need wasn't to change the world but to change our *selves*, and the only instruments we had for doing this were our own gestures and sounds. The most important thing tools did for us is that they helped us carry food, and freed our mouths for speech.

Speech, language, allowed us to create a symbolic culture, and (here Mumford's argument dovetails with the others) it's this that got us out of the animal world: not our tools. Many birds and mammals were more proficient with their tools. The unique human achievement was the *shaping of a self* by means of this symbolic culture; and from that point on, our main business was our own self-development.

The point is this, that in the last analysis we ourselves determine our consciousness. The material world helps, but *we're responsible*. Lawrence LeShan, an experimental psychologist, puts it nicely when he says, "A human being is an organizer of reality with a wide variety of options. The more [he or she] exercises those options, the more human and the less animal he or she is."

The Stages of Human Development

If I had to choose one grand, global explanation as to why the Prison arose—one explanation as to how it achieved its "leading role" —I would point to the finally uncontrollable desire for power over things (as distinct from the power to cooperate "synergically" with people and with nature—see Chapter 15).

Many New Age authors have imagined (or simply assumed) a history in which our growing fascination with coercive power and control is the dominant theme. In other words, in which our mentality or consciousness is the dominant theme, in which the Prison is the dominant theme. If you put their writings together I believe you'll come up with two main *stages of human development*—along with the notion that we're on the brink of a third stage, or on the brink of destruction.

The first great stage in our history was Prison-free, but it was monolithic in the sense that it allowed us no choice in how we wanted to do things: custom and tradition constrained us in exactly the same way that our monolithic institutions do today (see Chapter 7). The second great stage was, is, characterized by the rise of the Prison and its monolithic institutions. The third stage—if it happens—will be Prison-free, or at least headed in that direction, and will be characterized by biolithic institutions—institutions that allow us a great deal of choice in how we want to do things (see Chapter 14).

The first great stage was characterized by decentralized or tradition-bound or anarchic power relations. The second great stage is characterized by coercive power relations. And the third great stage will be characterized by synergic power relations (see Chapter 15).

The first great stage was concerned with meeting our needs in all four "states of consciousness" and at all seven "stages of self-development" (see Chapters 8 and 11)—and all too often our material needs got lost in the shuffle. The second stage is concerned with meeting our material needs. The third stage will certainly be concerned with meeting our material needs, but it will not stop there. It will also allow and encourage us to meet our "higher" needs—for love, for self-esteem, for meaning, and for transcendence (see Chapters 8 and 11). The pursuit of these needs will *characterize* this society, just as today the pursuit of material gratifications characterizes at least the dominant part of our society.

Now let's run through the stages a little more concretely.

The first stage is that of *traditional society* and it may be characterized by the fact that it was Prison-free. By "traditional" I don't mean Europe before 1492, I mean the world as it existed until some time after we had begun to practice agriculture. For until that time our fascination with power—though definitely not absent—expressed itself only weakly and sporadically, and more often than not for the common good.

There is a difference between romanticizing the past and accepting that there are important things that we need to recover from the past. New Age people have been studying traditional society not so much for models as for lessons, clues; what is it that we lack, what is it that we need to learn before we can break the Prison's grip on our society?

And they've come up with some suggestive "finds." Marshall Sahlins says that traditional people formed the original affluent society. "An affluent society is one in which all the people's material wants are easily satisfied," and in traditional society our material wants were easily satisfied not because we could produce much but because we wanted little—because our material wants were "finite and few." Traditional people were able to temper their material wants largely because their worldview included a spiritual-religious and also a mythic-aesthetic dimension (largely because there was so much more *to* life, for them, than material things).

Certainly we worked hard in those days, says Mumford, but not any harder than we needed to. We didn't think of the world as a project, and we didn't feel a need to pour into our working lives the energy that could and did go into sex and play and rituals. (According to Sahlins, we may have worked as little as fifteen hours a week!)

Sahlins finds it significant that the vast majority of our experience—and certainly our formative experience as a people—was not in complex civilization (let alone huge cities) but rather in small-ish bands. Gary Snyder, the poet, reports (in *East West*, June 1977) that these bands may have enjoyed "the existence of a tremendous interest, exchange and sympathy between people and animals."

Again: no one is suggesting that traditional people lived in a "golden age" or that we should imitate them in any way today. But it is impossible to confront the anthropology of the New Age and not begin to suspect that the following (at least) may represent deep-seated social needs that we can only ignore at our peril: the need for a concept of "enough"; the need for a more sophisticated, many-sided worldview than the materialist one; the need for a compelling series of ethics and values; the need for a much closer tie to nature and the natural world; and the need for a much smaller *scale*, for many small societies rather than a few large ones. (These points will all be taken up in Parts IV–V).

The second stage of human development is that of so-called *modern society*, and it has lasted from the beginnings of the agricultural era up to our own day. It is characterized by our growing fascination with coercive power; by the decline of all ethics and values that might have tempered this fascination; and by the birth and growth of the Prison.

Our quest for power over things (and eventually also over one another—whom we treat more and more like things) probably began as no more than a pragmatic and "innocent" response to immediate dangers (e.g., traps for marauding animals). Unfortunately, however, the quest for power, once begun, seems to have no natural bounds. Our culture can restrain the power drive—primarily by subordinating it to a series of ethics and values—but if and when those ethics and values begin to disintegrate, the power drive becomes dominant . . . gets out of control.

New Age authors have isolated three historical events that seem to have been turning points with regard to the strength of our power drive—with regard to its significance as a force in history.

The first turning point came with the accumulation of our first agricultural surpluses, for these gave us our first real opportunity to exercise our coercive power—at least, on a grand and costly scale— and many of our first civilizations chose to do just that (war-chariots, pyramids, bureaucracies, empires, megalopolises . . .).

The second turning point came in the third century B.C. when Alexander the Great invented the concept of "humanity"—the idea of the one-naturedness of people everywhere. What this idea did, says Ivan Illich (in *East West*, April 1976), was to substitute the concept "human nature," an abstraction, for the idea of a multiplicity of distinct, flesh-and-blood peoples, each with their own particular needs, wants, priorities. It implied that everybody had, or should have, the same priorities, and it gave most of us the notion that we knew—that we *could* know—what was best for everyone.

The third turning point was the Black Death and the schisms in the Christian church—for these things made us feel fearful, and betrayed by our old ethics and values; and in response, we grasped at the sides of the Prison as if we were drowning.

Our new nations, our new cities, our new products and technologies did manage to offset our loss of certainty; but they also took us farther away from the natural world and from the world of natural behavior.

They took us so far away that we began to love life less and love things more. In time we began to crave the Prison's products mainly because we could think of nothing better to do. And we tore up half the planet just to give our selves these false gifts. And we worked longer hours in the twentieth century than we did in the thirteenth, and we enjoyed our selves less, both on and off the job (see, e.g., deGrazia). (How *could* Prison-bound people have enjoyed themselves more?)

The third stage of human development is that of *New Age society,* and it's the alternative to the final triumph of the Prison—in other words, to spiritual suicide. A description of New Age people and New Age society is attempted in Part V; here I just want to examine the historical evidence for signs that we may be moving in that direction. (Signs, not laws as in a Marxist reading of history. Giving up that "certainty" is the price we have to pay for disbelieving in scientific single vision.)

First, following Braudel's lead (Chapter 5), some evidence from geography—from astronomy even. David Spangler puts it accurately enough: "Earth moves through 12 ages during the course of 26,000 years as the equinoctial points revolve around the ecliptic through each of the 12 zodiacal signs or arcs. We are now leaving one age and entering another . . . [and it] is not farfetched to assume that [this] may bring about the exposure of Earth and the life-strains upon it to differing energies from the cosmos." If we can develop our selves enough to be open to these energies, we should be able to break out of the Prison—and go on to create something better.

My next two arguments are rooted more firmly in the history we've just been reviewing. They suggest that the Prison is *producing its own gravediggers* by going against deep-seated, third-level tendencies in our hearts and minds.

The first "gravedigger" is the fact that the Prison has become a threat to our physical survival on Earth (because of its "ecocidal" tendencies and because of its system of military defense). Most psychologists believe that we have an innate, biological need to survive. Therefore, our need to survive may help to carry us out of the Prison and into a New Age where our desire to *have* more can be replaced by a desire to *be* more: by a desire to develop our selves and to relate to each other in a life-loving manner; and by a desire to serve others (but as a means of developing self rather than as a means of fighting self).

Well—we've always managed to make the right biological adaptations before.

The second "gravedigger" is the fact that the Prison has taken away our rationale for the inevitable pain and sadness of life. (I don't mean the pain that comes from starving, I mean the pain that comes when, for instance, someone we love dies.) Peter Berger calls this rationale a "theodicy," and he claims that having a theodicy is an inherent human need.

To provide us with a theodicy—to explain, without explaining away, our suffering—is what religion used to do, before we lost our faith and tried to replace it with the Prison's values. However, neither the scientific outlook nor any other side of the Prison has been able to generate an alternate theodicy. There are, of course, secular theodicies, such as nationalism and Marxism. But while these may be comforting to those of us who face death on the barricades, they are not going to be very comforting to those of us who have heart attacks in the penny arcade—to those of us whose lives lack the (phony) grandeur of armed struggle. The Six-Sided Prison can't answer our need for a theodicy, and it's our search for a theodicy—for "something to live for," in the watered-down popular phrase—that's carrying many of us out of the confines of the Prison, and beyond the materialist worldview.

Part II
MONOLITHIC INSTITUTIONS

CHAPTER 7

The Monolithic Mode of Production: How the Prison Is Institutionalized

The Prison doesn't exist only in our hearts and minds. It is institutionalized by means of what I call the "monolithic mode of production."

I am sorry to have to introduce another cumbersome new term, but I couldn't see any way around it since it refers to something cumbersome and all too real. Marx used to speak of the "capitalist mode of production," but the monolithic mode is common to both capitalism and socialism—it's a third-level concept if anything is. More recently, Kenneth Boulding has spoken of "monolithic" and "polylithic" organizations; Ivan Illich of the "industrial mode of production"; Jacques Ellul of "technique"; E.F. Schumacher of "modern" versus "appropriate" technologies; Lewis Mumford of "poly-, mono-, and biotechnics" —in fact, at least twenty-six authors cited in Chapter 27 have spoken out against what I am calling monolithic institutions and technologies —and the "monolithic mode of production" is a synthesis of their views.

Description

The monolithic mode of production makes it almost impossible for alternatives to exist to the products it creates. In the United States some of its leading products are: institutionalized medical care, mass-produced housing, compulsory schooling, organized religion, nuclear-family child care, and nuclear power. These products are produced by monolithic institutions: the medical profession, the housing industry, the compulsory school, the church, the nuclear family, the nuclear power-plant.

I call these institutions "monolithic" because they establish a kind of monopoly over the production of "goods" and services. When we hear about monopolies it's usually Exxon's or Alcan's—some corporation's monopoly. Applying tri-level analysis that would be a second-level monopoly, a *brand-name* monopoly. Monolithic institutions are third-level monopolies, more seep-seated, more profound, much harder to root out. Their monopolies are those of the *products* they create. Not the University of California but the university system of learning, not the American Medical Association but professional medicine, not the Catholic Church but church-centered religion, not the Atomic Energy Board of Canada but, if there are no serious accidents (fat chance), nuclear power—these are the kinds of monopolies that have been and are being produced by monolithic institutions.

It is, of course, theoretically possible for alternatives to many of these products to exist. And many of them do exist, at the edges and in the corners of society. But that is just my point: chances are good that if you've given birth at home, or built your own home, or taken your kids out of school, or put a solar heater up on your roof, then you're not really part of the mainstream of society. And even if you are part of the mainstream, you have probably spent an incredible amount of time and money and energy on creating your alternative. Not everybody can do it the way you did. Not everybody should have to.

Two sections down I have listed and briefly described sixteen *examples* of monolithic institutions, patterns, technologies. This is not meant to be a complete list, but it is meant to give some idea of the range of monolithic institutions—they are everywhere. But first, a little background. . . .

Origins

The monolithic mode of production creates a monopoly not only of products but of products that—when they are dominant in a society— reinforce and perpetuate Prison values (standardization, efficiency, hierarchy, order, etc.). In fact, to a great extent, the monolithic mode owes its origins to the Prison: it is the natural and possibly inevitable institutional underpinning of a society whose members are Prison-bound.

Patriarchal attitudes have certainly contributed to our desire to have our institutions service us (and/or to devote our selves to serving our institutions). Philip Slater doubts that our monolithic institutions could exist without egocentric impulses having provided fuel for them in the first place. Theodore Roszak traces the roots of many of our monolithic institutions back to scientific single vision. And Lewis Mumford shows that the monolithic nature of our institutions would be impossible without the bureaucratic mentality.

A dependence on monolithic institutions is transmitted to us in earliest childhood by our parents. Joseph Chilton Pearce has given us a fine description of this process: "In the case of the injured child, for instance, the average parent [has] little capacity for responding to the needs of the situation. . . . Conditioned to surrender personal power and ability to the professional, the parent would have to rush the child to a hospital or doctor. . . . The child whose parent panics and rushes him/her to the professional (the person who stands between self and personal power) undergoes a deep and abiding learning. S/he learns that the parents do not have the personal power s/he believed them to have. S/he learns that the parents cannot act on his/her behalf, . . . that [power and possibility] must be bought from the professionals. . . . The parent who panics and shifts responsibility thus dispels the child's own sense of personal power and ability. The child learns that s/he is as impotent as the parents. The stage is then set for the child's own surrender of responsibility to the professional."

According to Mumford (and to Jacques Ellul), the monolithic mode of production was dominant at least twice before in our history—at the time of the Pharaohs, and in ancient Rome. In its current form, the monolithic mode can be traced all the way back to the beginnings of modern culture. As we saw in Chapter 6, by the fifteenth century most people were in no mood to see that the old values (reverence, leisure, play, ritual) needed to be added to, not destroyed. After the Black Death and the splits in the Christian church, they cast their old values aside and seized on Prison values with a vengeance. Spurred on, then, not by a desire to live more joyously, but by patriarchal fantasies of conquest, egocentric visions and desires, scientific arrogance, and bureaucratic-hierarchical notions of order, they managed not only to develop *but to abuse* standardization, prefabrication, and mechanization centuries before the Industrial Revolution (appropriately enough, these monolithic standbys were all first developed in the *state-organized* military arsenals in an early megalopolis, Venice).

It wasn't until the early twentieth century that the monolithic mode actually triumphed. Alongside monolithic tendencies there had always been what Mumford calls the "polylithic mode of production," which drew on a pool of tools, machines, materials, and processes that went back hundreds or even thousands of years. This "technological pool" was, in an important sense, our material heritage, and it had been passed on from generation to generation by skilled craftspeople and work teams. But when the jobs of these people were finally eliminated (by standardization, prefabrication, and mechanization), the technological pool, and the polylithic mode of production that had depended on it, was of course eliminated too.

The triumph of the monolithic mode has taken place in three main stages, well described by Ivan Illich:

Each institution appears to earn the right to achieve a monopoly in its field. In medicine, for example, around World War I medical school graduates became almost as good as herbalists at curing diseases. That was enough to convince us to identify healing with patriarchal, scientific, bureaucratic, professionalized health care. Professional medical associations were given the right to set standards and limit entry—and all other kinds of healers were prosecuted. Even self-care became more difficult.

Each institution comes to frustrate the end it was originally designed to serve. In transportation, for example, the creation of faster and faster vehicles led to the creation of greater and greater distances within cities. Soon it was taking us longer to get to work than it ever had before. Or, for example, we spent an average of 1,600 hours on our cars last year (driving them, earning money to pay for them, parking them, etc.) and we drove them less than 7,500 miles: less than five miles an hour!

Each institution becomes a threat to society. Again in transportation,

60,000 Americans were killed on the roads last year, and over four million were injured. Fewer of us were killed or injured in the war on Vietnam. But that was an easier threat to deal with, because it didn't involve changing our selves (or at least that's what we thought).

Examples

The transportation industry is an excellent example of a monolithic institution. Its product is the private automobile (and other speedy vehicles: planes, trucks, busses). Of course, auto manufacturers don't advertise their product as "the automobile." They tell us to "buy GM instead of Chrysler" and so on. And there are always reformers who are telling us to "break up GM" and so on. But on the third level of analysis, all of the manufacturers, and most of the reformers too, are telling us the same thing: without the private automobile we are diminished as human beings. And our cities are designed and our society is run on the basis of, you might even say for the convenience of, the private automobile. (More than half of the ground space in our cities is taken up now by roadways, parking lots, and gas stations; more than half of our urban air pollution comes from the automobile; more than three-quarters of our noise pollution. . . .)

But—and this is my other crucial point—if the monolithic mode were changed to one that gave priority to bicyclists and walkers tomorrow, most of us would be very unhappy. For the Prison has made us feel that it's *important* to get where we're going as fast as possible and with as little exertion as possible and in as "distinguished" or flashy a manner as possible. "Dominant social values become embedded in the technology that they produce," says David Dickson, author of the book *The Politics of Alternative Technology*. Just so, the Prison is embedded in our monolithic institutions. (Barbara Ward tells us that Russia had attempted to delay motorization but was forced to relent in the 1960s "under consumer pressure." You can't blame advertising for that.)

In this view, providing a "good" system of rapid public transit (solution of the traditional "ism's") would only be compouding the problem. For the problem is not the domination of the private automobile so much as it is the Prison-bound notion that we've got to get to wherever it is we're going as quickly, smoothly, etc., as possible. It isn't even speed per se that's the problem but the fact that we can't escape from it, or from its effects, if we want to be a part of our society.

Professional, institutional medicine depends on restricting our access to medical information and restricting the numbers of people who are allowed to practice "medicine," formerly known as "healing." Like any other monopoly, its claims are inflated and its ill effects understated.

As for its claims, Ivan Illich tells us that the great strides that we have, indeed, made over the last one-hundred years or so have come primarily from better nutrition, better housing, and the like, rather than from doctors.

As for its ill effects, Illich mentions three: first, modern medical practice often *causes* illness by prescribing the wrong drugs, too many drugs, etc., or by allowing something to go wrong in the hospital (there are more reported accidents in hospitals than in all industries but mines and high-rise construction!). Second, modern medical practice encourages us to become dependent on . . . modern medical practice . . . rather than to take any responsibility for our own healing (in Britain, one quarter of all visits to the doctor for free service are for the untreatable common cold!). Third, modern medical practice saps our will to master the arts of suffering and dying, and encourages instead merely an obsessive desire to "kill" any kind of discomfort or pain. "This progressive flattening out of personal, virtuous performance," writes Illich, "constitutes a new goal which has never before been a guideline for social life."

Universal, compulsory schooling makes it nearly impossible for us to educate our selves outside of the school system. And partly for that very reason, universal compulsory schooling teaches us what educators John Holt and Ivan Illich call "the hidden curriculum."

The hidden curriculum, says Holt, consists of the things schools teach "simply by the fact of being schools, of having the power to compel children to attend, to tell them what to learn, and to grade, rank, and label them." The hidden curriculum consists of the things schools teach whether the curriculum is designed to make us good Americans or good communists or whether the teacher is strict or kind. . . .

The hidden curriculum consists of several interrelated messages. Illich identifies them as follows: only through schooling can we prepare our selves for adulthood; what is not taught in school is of little value (and what is learned outside of school is not worth knowing); the degree of success we will enjoy in society depends on the amount of schooling we consume; learning *about* the world is more valuable than learning *from* the world.

Holt identifies many more messages, including: "if we didn't make you come here you wouldn't learn anything, you'd . . . grow up to be a bum"; "even if you could be trusted to find out about the world, you are too stupid to do it"; "learning is separate from the rest of life"; "your own questions are hardly ever worth asking or answering"; "what is not rewarded is no good"; "everything important about us can be measured"; "there must be experts somewhere who know better than we do what is best for us"; and "real life is a struggle, a zero-sum game, where no one can win without someone else, or everyone else, losing."

All these messages can be seen as parts of a single message—"learning is a commodity, it is not something that we do."

But the New Age critique of schooling does not begin and end with the idea that universal, compulsory schooling is self-defeating. It also includes a critique of the *kinds* of teaching that schools do. Especially, schools are said to focus too exclusively on developing our intellectual selves; whereas New Age education, as articulated by people like Jack

Canfield and Paula Klimek (of the Institute for Wholistic Education) and Jerry Fletcher (still at the Department of Health, Education and Welfare) would *also* focus on developing our bodies, our emotions, our imaginations, our intuitions, our wills, and our higher or "transpersonal" selves.

The housing industry has two purposes. The first is to build our housing *for* us. The second is to keep us from housing our selves simply and cheaply, and to keep us from building our own.

In 1945, Ivan Illich tells us, 32 percent of our homes were still self-built. By 1970 the proportion had gone down to 11 percent. We had actually grown more capable of producing tools and materials that fostered self-building, but unions, building codes, and mortgage rules —all of them reflecting the values and priorities of the Prison—had turned against self-building. And not only against self-building, but against *all* housing that was inexpensive and simple and easy to understand.

To take but one example: Buckminister Fuller's dymaxion domes, three-bedroom homes with natural air conditioning that would have cost $1,250 to put up in 1940, plumbing, wiring, and furniture included, never got off the ground. Fuller's opposition came equally from three sources: from the building codes, from greedy investors, and from the plumbers' and electricians' unions. After five years or so, Fuller gave up in despair.

Church-centered religion tells us—more or less bluntly—that we can only "really" get to the spiritual and religious states of consciousness by means of the church. Church-centered religion tends to cordon the spirit off from the rest of life, and God becomes just another commodity to be purchased, along with the soap and the Wheaties. (Ironically, church-centered religion plays right into the hands of the materalists.)

The job economy makes it hard for us to exist if we don't want to work at a regular, 40-hour-a-week job. Illich puts it well when he says, "The loss of one liberty after another to be useful when out of a job or outside professional control is the unnamed but also the most resented experience" of our time. And Tom Bender has recently said (in de Moll and Coe, eds.), "[Jobs] lock us into a cash economy, specialization and not taking care of our own needs. They split us into opposing and self-serving roles—producer and consumer, employer and employee, management and labor. Jobs, like store-bought bread, rarely come in different sized slices—it's full- or no-time. Thought of providing jobs to counter unemployment easily falls into who can 'provide' jobs—large institutions—rather than the less centralized and less manipulable alternative of people creating work for themselves. . . ."

Advocates of the full-employment economy would guarantee 40-hour-a-week employment to all, thereby *strengthening* both the job economy and the Prison-bound rationale behind it ("if they don't wanna work let them starve"). For an alternative to this proposal, see Chapter 24.

Monogamy, heterosexuality, marriage, all become monolithic when they're seen as moral or cultural imperatives—as choices that we *must* make if we want to escape the feeling that we're unnatural, selfish, sick, immoral (not to mention the pain of our parents and the prejudice of our neighbors). In the United States, most of us haven't even bothered to ask our selves whether or not we *want* to be monogamous, heterosexual, married—we simply are, or assume that we do. And if we do question these things, it is usually only an intellectual questioning.

Compulsive heterosexuality cuts us off from half the world as love partners and may diminish our overall enjoyment of people of our own sex. It also perpetuates sex-role stereotypes (partly by keeping us out of touch with the opposite-sex person within us, what Jung has called our "anima" or "animus"), and it perpetuates patriarchal attitudes—as Lucia Valeska puts it (in *Quest*, Fall 1975), it is "a mandate that all women be forever divided against each other through a compelling allegiance to one man at home and all men outside the home."

Compulsive monogamy may have served some essential purpose two or three million years ago. But today, as Robert Thamm points out, compulsive monogamy tends to lead "more to a dependent attachment than to a loving commitment." And compulsive marriage tends to lead to "mutual overdependence and restricted gratification"; tends to imply "a more or less monotonous day-to-day living together"; and tends to change "romantic love to dependent, possessive, and jealous love." No wonder studies have found that the stability of marriage is a function of the couple's isolation from other important relationships, and that unhappiness tends to increase with the length of marriage—one recent study of middle-aged married couples (cited in LeMaster) found that the *typical* marriage "represented a facade with no substantial marital relationship behind it."

The nuclear family can be devastating to parents and children alike —if it isn't consciously chosen, and if its inherent dangers are not then consciously dealt with.

For one thing, it tends to embody some—and usually all—of the monolithic institutions of monogamy, heterosexuality, and marriage. For another thing, it tends to embody the first four sides of the Prison in almost pure form—making it into a kind of transmission belt for the Prison. The patriarchy is embodied in the dominant male—husband or father; egocentricity is embodied in the isolated family's notion that it's "us" against "them"; the scientific outlook is embodied in the dualism this notion implies; and the bureaucratic mentality is embodied in the functional hierarchy, pets-kids-Mommy-Daddy.

John Holt says that the relationships in the nuclear family are "too intense," partly at least just because of its size; that "too much is always at stake." And the family "is so dependent on these high-powered feelings, so shut in on itself, . . . so devoid of purposes outside of itself, that it is fragile, easily threatened by a quarrel." Which is, perhaps, one reason why there's so much suppression of feelings in the nuclear family.

Finally, it's worth mentioning some of Thamm's objections to the

nuclear family (he lists forty-four objections in all!)—"fails to provide
an ongoing stability and security for members over generations";
"friends take second place to relatives in the obligation hierarchy";
"cannot function as a democracy when only two adults share the
power."

Some of the nuclear family's worst effects have to do with child-
rearing. It gives the child a terrible model of adult and social life
(typically—and this has been borne out by many studies—the father
flops down on the easy chair after a hard day at work, and watches TV
that night and for much of the weekend; the mother cooks food and
cleans house). Then there's the fact that—starved for strokes, for
friendship and esteem—we turn our children into objects for our own
gratification, with ill effects for all concerned. We turn them into love
objects, which we desperately need (Holt: "It is very painful to have
more love to give away than people to whom we can give it"). We turn
them into help objects ("We value their dependency and helpless-
ness"). And we turn them into hate objects, to work off the rage that
we feel toward a world in which we can never get enough (*every year*
in the United States, 50,000 children die and 300, are permanently
injured by maltreatment).

Monolithic technology—generally known as "modern" or "industrial-era" or "Western" technology—has come to dominate our society
to such an extent that many of us are hardly aware that there *are* other
technologies, other ways of doing things; or we think that the choice is
between more of the same and "going back to the Middle Ages." All
mass production technologies are by definition modern and good, or at
least, "functional"; all smaller-scale technologies are by definition
backward and bad, or at least a little silly.

There is, however, nothing particularly modern about the *nature* of
our large-scale technologies. Lewis Mumford has shown us that, "Almost from the beginning of civilization, two disparate technologies
have existed side by side: one 'democratic' and dispersed, the other
totalitarian and centralized. . . . The large-scale organization of the
proletariat in specialized workshops and factories, using what now
seem like 'modern' methods, is reasonably well developed for the
Hellenic and Roman world but must have begun much earlier. . . ."

Moreover, there is nothing rhetorical about Mumford's use of the
term "totalitarian"—if we continue on our present course, our technology will make a totally planned, totally administered society all but
inevitable. Consider these key characteristics of monolithic technology:
grand in scale; costly; prodigious use of nonrenewable resources; considerable environmental damage; difficult to maintain; difficult if not
impossible for most people to understand; indifferent to its surroundings (could be anywhere). Clearly, some powerful central authority is
going to have to be (is already) necessary to construct and pay for the
technological apparatus; to make sure that other governments or corporations don't muscle in on the needed resources; to train the "keep-
ers" of the system; and so on.

Monolithic technology is, then, neither particularly modern in nature nor particularly democratic in essence; but—and this "but" is inevitable—doesn't it deliver the goods?

Well, up to now it has (for one-sixth of the globe perhaps)—but no New Ager would deny that, as Tom Bender puts it, "The assumptions upon which present production processes have been built are no longer supportable." Three of the most important assumptions are (a) continuously increasing the size of production facilities is the best way to maximize production and minimize costs; (b) we will continue to be able to buy more and more goods and services; (c) the economic effect of how we do things is more important than the political, environmental, or psychocultural effects.

Assumption (a) has been disproved by economists whose accounting practices figured in the "secondary" and "external" costs of goods (e.g., time lost in strikes; declining quality of goods) and who looked more closely at the so-called "economies of scale"; see, e.g., Barry Stein, *Size, Efficiency and Community Enterprise* (1974). Assumption (b) is obviously untrue—if the whole world "enjoyed" the American standard of living we would run out of many crucial and irreplaceable raw materials by the end of the century. And assumption (c) is true only if people are held to be primarily economic beings, an assumption that's challenged—I think successfully—in Parts III and IV.

One of the advantages in seeing our technology as monolithic is seeing that, as David Dickson puts it, our problems result "as much from the nature of technology as from the way it is used." In other words, technology is not neutral—it has a kind of life of its own. New Age writers like Theodore Roszak and William Irwin Thompson have gone so far as to claim that we've made our technology (and the science on which it is based) "a culture in its own right—the *one* culture to be uniformly imitated or imposed everywhere." And Langdon Winner gets to the heart of the matter when he says that our technology "reflects our own life, crippled, incomplete, and not fully in our control."

Peter Berger has recently shown us that our monolithic technology serves to *reinforce and perpetuate* the Prison in us. How does it do this? When we operate our machines, follow our bureaucratic regulations, etc., we learn the following lessons, among others: reality consists of static self-contained units, it is not an ongoing flux; reality consists of identical components, not unique entities; there is no necessary connection between means and ends; every action, however concrete, needs to be understood in an abstract frame of reference—abstractions are what count; work is separate from private life; it is functional to define other people as functionaries; the self can only be expressed in a partial and segmented way.

Nuclear power is, beyond some point that we may soon reach, an irreversible energy strategy. So it is important that we become aware of some of the dangers of nuclear power plants:

● "A single large nuclear reactor," says Dr. Patrick Moore, head of the Greenpeace Foundation (in *Greenpeace Report: 1976*), "produces as much nuclear waste in one year as would result from the explosion of 100 Hiroshima-sized atomic bombs. . . . Due to the slow rate of decay of many of these poisonous nuclear wastes it is necessary that they be kept isolated from the environment for many thousands of years. . . . Thus we are confronted with the problem of trying to construct gigantic storage tanks that must not leak for thousands of years."

• An even more serious result of nuclear fission, according to Moore, is the production of a substance known as plutonium—"aptly named after the Greek god of Hell. . . . Plutonium is [one of] the most toxic [chemicals] known to [people]. A piece of this element the size of a grapefruit is enough to poison every person on earth. . . . Plutonium is highly radioactive and the ingestion of even the most minute particle can cause cancer. . . . Plans for future nuclear power plants call for the production of many hundreds of tons of plutonium. . . . It is inevitable that some of this material will find its way into the environment."

• The *Clamshell Alliance News* (Oct.-Nov. 1977) reports that Dr. Ernest Sternglass, of the University of Pittsburgh, has discovered evidence of "exceptionally high cancer rates, infant mortality rates, and birth defects among people living near existing nuclear power plants." ("Honicker vs. Hendrie" is a meticulously documented medical indictment of nuclear power, and is available for $5 from The Book Publishing Co., 156 Drakes Lane, Summertown, Tenn. 38983.)

• "Accidents can happen," says a Clamshell Alliance pamphlet, "causing release of radiation and possible contamination of land and water for years, with thousands of deaths and injuries. There have been close calls already: at the Fermi plant in Michigan in 1966 and at Brown's Ferry, Alabama, where a fire in 1975 almost led to a 'meltdown' and subsequent release of radiation."

• "An accident in the transportation of radioactive materials is even more likely [than an accident in a nuclear power plant]," write environmental experts Dennis Pirages and Paul Ehrlich. "If the great number of reactors needed to fill projected electricity demand in the year 2000 are built, trains and trucks loaded with deadly radioactive materials will constantly be crisscrossing the United States. . . . [And] it should be kept in mind that our experience with such dangerous cargoes has not been very satisfactory."

• It is difficult to build a nuclear bomb from uranium—the construction of a plutonium bomb is, however, relatively simple. "It is not difficult," says Dr. Moore, "to separate the plutonium from the rest of the elements present in nuclear waste. Once their separation is made it is then possible, for a few thousand dollars, to construct a workable nuclear bomb." Dr. Edward Teller—father of the H-bomb—has estimated that there are over 100,000 people who have enough knowledge to build a nuclear bomb.

• Even if all these things could be kept "under control"—and they are already out of control—nuclear power would, as Gil Bailie puts it (in *Planet/Drum* no. 4), "limit the range of possible choices for future generations" more completely than anything else on the planet (this is what makes it a monolithic institution, as well as a particularly dangerous one). "Politically, centralization will be important for the required social control"—to oversee the transportation and storage of radioactive wastes, guard the storage tanks, regulate the producers, etc.

Amory Lovins, a well-known physicist, adds, "Discouraging nuclear violence and coercion requires some abrogation of civil liberties; guarding long-lived wastes against geological or social contingencies implies some form of hierarchical social rigidity or homogeneity to insulate the [technocrats] from social turbulence; and making political decisions about nuclear hazards which are compulsory, . . . disputed, unknown, or unknowable, may tempt governments to bypass democratic decision in favor of elitist technocracy."

• Finally: if we *had* access to unlimited energy, all signs point to the fact that we would *use* it and create an almost inhumanly high-technology society (even compared to our present-day society which many people feel has already lost all sense of the human scale). As Bailie says, "Maturity is the wisdom not to use all the power you have," and we have yet to demonstrate that we have that wisdom.

Our defense system is totally dependent on monolithic institutions. Our tanks, our planes, our bombs, our military officers and so on, could only be produced by monolithic institutions and technologies. If we want to transform our monolithic institutions, we're going to have to transform both the *scale* and the *nature* of our system of defense.

Marxists like to say that capitalism is responsible for the military economy; and it's a well-known fact that one out of every ten jobs in the U.S. depends directly or indirectly on the Pentagon. But it is also true that, as Seymour Melman puts it, there is no "economic necessity inherent in capitalism which gives war economy such competence. That is a political choice." Canada, Great Britain, Japan, and many other capitalist countries have done without an undue amount of military spending. Nor is the military economy exclusive to capitalism— the Soviet Union is outspending even the U.S. Nor is the military economy particularly *good* for capitalism—on the contrary, as Melman has convincingly shown, what's good for the defense industries is eroding the productivity of the rest of the U.S. economy.

The monolithic state is a product of our wanting—and needing— the government to do things *for* us. By now it is, as Jacques Ellul puts it, "the most important reality in our day. . . . We cannot conceive of society except as directed by a central omnipresent and omnipotent state." And as we become more dependent on the state, the state continues to grow. "The means through which the state can act are constantly growing. Its personnel and functions are constantly growing. Its responsibilities are growing. All this goes hand in hand with inevitable centralization and with the total organization of the society in the hands of the state." In the U.S., expenditures directed by all levels of government increased from 15 percent of all expenditures in

1930 to 40 percent in 1973. The costs of government rose from 3 billion dollars in 1913 to 400 billion in the mid-1970s. Sixteen percent of the labor force now works for one or another governmental agency. In proportion to our population, says George Lodge, government in the United States is probably bigger than in those countries we call socialist.

"The nation-state is much more fundamental in our world than economic reality," says Ellul. "Nowadays the state directs the economy." This important point has been carefully documented by a number of New Age writers. Richard Barnet, for instance, has accumulated much evidence to show that World War II "brought the federal bureaucracy to a new position of command over American society. . . . The corporations continue to exercise the dominant *influence* in the society, but the *power* keeps passing to the state." Similarly, Seymour Melman holds that "the traditional role of government in capitalism as the servant of business has been in transition. During the Cold War this relationship shifted toward collaboration, a partnership between government and big business. More recently, following the great institutional changes of the Kennedy-McNamara regime, a newer pattern emerged of business as the well-rewarded servant of government." Melman points out that corporate taxes have risen about twice as fast as corporate profits since 1950—proof positive that corporate decision-making power has declined vis-à-vis that of the state. "I made a point of inquiring of officers of a few major firms, Why was such a reduction in decision power accepted. The typical reply was that the senior officers have been essentially 'bought off' with handsome salaries and fringe benefits, not to mention occasional access to the highest places of power in the federal government."

Ellul draws the essential political point: "Marxist analysis was valid only in the nineteenth century, when the emergence of uncontrolled, explosive economic power relegated a weak, liberal, and unclearly delineated state to the shadows and subjugated it. But today the major social phenomenon is the state, becoming ever more extended, ever more assured. . . ."

The governing elite monopolizes the key decisions—the policy decisions—and should therefore be classified as a monolithic institution no matter how open to new members it is.

However—it is also true that, in the United States today, policy is no longer "imposed from the top" by sixty wealthy families (or whomever). Franz Schurmann, a well-known political scientist, has recently shown that policy emerges from an ongoing struggle between the "realm of ideology" and the "realm of interests."

The realm of ideology consists primarily of the executive branch of the government—the President and his or her advisors. The realm of interests consists of all the different legislative, executive, and military bureaucracies, as well as the pressure groups that feed them (this is where the corporations come in). The realm of ideology and the realm of interests are constantly at loggerheads, but the realm of ideology is also, generally, the stronger of the two (a point Schurmann makes with great skill in his long-drawn-out discussion of U.S. foreign policy).

The concept of the realm of ideology suggests that by our choice of President we may have much more power to affect the policy-making process than we think. But why, then, if we have this power, is the governing elite still so obviously selfish, so obviously unjust? Primarily because we are our selves selfish and unjust; bound by the Prison. *We are not essentially different* from the President and his or her advisors, from the people we choose to govern us (if anything, we're *less* tolerant and *less* humanitarian; see Monsma). According to Ferdinand Lundberg, we are not even different from the denizens of the realm of interests—and Lundberg has spent at least one lifetime studying them. Our ethics are the same, our values the same, our attitudes the same, our motives the same; and what "they" do in South Africa, in Chile, and elsewhere is what most of us would do too, if we were in their place. Condemning the governing class for its deeds is not unlike looking into a mirror—and then blaming the mirror.

As Lundberg puts it at the end of his book *The Rich and the Super-Rich*: "The causes of [our] insufficiency . . . are political, not economic, or at least political before they are economic. Better put, they are cultural. Serious problems cannot be solved on the basis of a consensus of value-disoriented dolts."

The large corporation may or may not be monolithic by nature (New Agers disagree over whether the corporation needs to be "broken up" or simply better controlled . . . by the communities themselves)—but there can be no doubt that our large corporations are monolithic today. We have permitted them to drive smaller enterprises systematically out of business (worse, we have encouraged them to do so: tax advantages for large corporations often make it impossible for small businesses to compete). We have permitted them to set prices. We have permitted them to impose a Prison-gratifying (and therefore profitable) culture of monolithic plastic sameness on our places and regions. At the moment, the 500 largest industrial corporations control nearly one *trillion* dollars in corporate assets (in the United States); and the 600 largest multinational corporations will, us willing, control over 40 percent of *planetary* production by the end of the 1980s (and that's not counting the centrally planned nations where monolithic "state enterprises" are even more powerful).

Taking their lead from George Lodge, a number of New Age people have argued that the motive force behind the large corporation has changed (or is changing). Corporation managers and technical personnel are no longer primarily concerned with how much money they can make for their bosses; nor are they primarily concerned with how they can best extend their own power and privileges (though they're certainly not indifferent to these things!). Rather, a new breed of managers and technicians is emerging whose primary concern is, How can I further the interest of the *industry of which I am a part*? Exxon and Texaco people are asking, How can I further the oil industry through my work; CBS and *New York Times* people, the power-and-authority-of-the-media; and so on.

This makes a lot of psychological sense when you consider that the corporate managers and technical personnel are people who believe in "the system" and in the basic goodness of their work. It might even be said to be a kind of idealism. Trouble is, it's a particularly monolithic kind of idealism.

Monolithic social roles require us to say things, do things, and (inevitably) think and feel things, that we might not necessarily feel like doing or saying or thinking and feeling, but that are nevertheless deemed appropriate—by "society"—to the occasion at hand. All social roles will, of course, require us to suppress certain parts of our personalities at certain times—there's nothing particularly harmful in that—but in the United States many social roles require us to suppress our selves as a general rule, if we want to retain the role at all. Moreover, most of us are *more than willing* to repress our spontaneous selves on behalf of an easy social harmony and peace—what we like to call "smooth personal relations." Most of us are actually more interested in avoiding possible public embarrassment than in achieving any kind of genuine self-expression. (That's because we're trapped by the Prison—trapped and afraid to walk out.)

Nearly every possible role in the United States today is, for most of us, a monolithic one: mother, son, wife, secretary, boss, factory worker, patient, friend. . . .

To some extent roles are useful and necessary—they give us a shape, an outer identity, and also a sense of inner continuity. The problem comes when the roles become monolithic—when there is no distance between our selves and our roles and when we fail to make a significant personal contribution to the way we see and live our roles.

• We lose touch with our selves—the different parts of our selves do not mesh;

• We tend to *become* our roles—we subordinate our personality to what we suppose to be the role's demands and "a new creature replaces autonomous [humanity], unhindered by the limitations of individual morality, . . . mindful only of the sanctions of authority" (Stanley Milgram);

• Roles represent institutions and, to a great extent, *are* institutions —"roles make it possible for institutions to exist" (Peter Berger). Therefore, rigidly defined, coercive roles are what keep all the monolithic institutions, above, going strong;

• "The life process itself renders [the] continuance [of roles] impossible; e.g., the aging of beautiful women; the loss of athletic strength; the disruption of the mother role through the maturity or death of her children. All these may produce very serious crises . . ." (Roberto Assagioli).

The monolithic mind races on and on endlessly, never giving us a chance to simply be, never giving us a chance to experience the world with openness and vulnerability. As Luke Rhinehart puts it in his book about *est*: "Since the being inevitably identifies [his or her] being with [his or her] mind, the purpose of the mind becomes the survival of the mind: the survival of the tapes, the points of view, the decisions, the beliefs, the rightness of the mind. The mind thus seeks always for agreement and to avoid disagreement, always to be right and avoid being wrong, to dominate and avoid domination, to justify itself and avoid invalidation."

The monolithic mind is more intent on being right than on seeing clearly; more intent on proving others wrong than on healing society.

Effects

Summing up, New Age people have leveled four important criticisms at our monolithic institutions and technologies: they are counterproductive; they encourage us to become overly dependent on them; they are wasteful; and they are not natural to us, they do not suit.

Their counterproductivity. Our monolithic institutions are making it harder for us to get around, harder for us to care for our selves, harder for us to learn. Our jobs are less productive, our relationships less satisfying, our technologies less efficient. Every day the nation-state becomes more coercive; our roles more stereotyped. And every day our transportation systems, technologies, governments, etc., are costing us proportionately more: in money, in energy, in resources, in time; in wear and tear on the nerves.

The overdependence that they foster in us. "Our industrial categories," says Ivan Illich, "tend to define results as products of specialized institutions and instruments," rather than as products that *we* create using institutions and instruments as our tools. Doctors produce healing, schools produce learning, churches produce salvation, agribusiness produces food, armies produce defense, marriage produces intimacy, and so on. Meanwhile, we are encouraged to become consumers of these "products," giving up in the process much of our capacity for personal responsibility and active choice. River, a rural self-builder, puts it this way: "It all boils down to the desire of our security-centered culture for the illusion of painless, worry-free, and totally comfortable living. Conditioned to believe that Big Daddy will somehow make us safe, we have mistakenly looked to business and government to provide this impossibility."

Their wastefulness. Energy is not infinite. Resources are not infinite. Therefore, every car that we put on the road denies *many* people good transportation by bus. Every dollar spent on supersophisticated medical equipment denies *many* people adequate paraprofessional medical care. And so on, ad infinitum. (This is especially true in the Third World; and it would be more visibly true in the United States if the percentage of our material wealth were at all proportionate to our population.)

Their unnaturalness—the fact that they do not suit. Because of our monolithic institutions, says Jacques Ellul, we must adapt our selves, "as though the world were new, to a universe for which [we were] not created." We were made to go ten miles an hour and we go a thousand; we were made to follow the natural rhythms of the body and our psyches and of nature, and we go by the clock; we were made to share the earth with living things and we live in a world of plastic.

Biolithic institutions—the New Age alternative to monolithic institutions—are described in Chapter 14.

Part III
ON THE PRISONERS THEMSELVES (ON OUR SELVES)

CHAPTER 8

Are We Economic People— or Self-Developing Persons?

Capitalists tend to believe that our need for material things is endless— a belief that obviously helps to justify the monolithic mode of production. Socialists tend to believe that our need for things will eventually be satiated, but they can't say when. The Marxist psychologist, Wilhelm Reich, still seems terribly avant-garde to Marxists because of his suggestion that love should be thought of as a basic need.

What gives us the authority, what gives us the right, to ask people to live differently? What gives us the *gall* to ask people to live lives in which work and consumption would matter much less to them than love and play, spirituality and service?

There is, of course, the ecological doomsday answer—if we *don't* cut down on our consumption, then . . . —and it is a powerful one; see, e.g., Ehrlich and Ehrlich. But I am looking for an answer that would be true under any circumstances.

The question cuts deeply, I think, because those of us who do favor love, play, and creativity—those of us who are oriented to life rather than things or death (see Chapter 10)—are in such a minority. It takes much of our strength just to keep on believing in our own values and priorities (or even in our sanity). It doesn't occur to most of us that an entire society can be insane—but see, e.g., Fromm, *The Sane Society*, or Maslow, *Farther Reaches*. Certainly most of us don't try to push our values and priorities onto others.

Marxists, on the other hand, are only too eager to tell us what our values and priorities should be. That's because they're "true believers" in a system of values handed down by an authority that transcends the individual. History, *Das Kapital*, and the top-down state are common examples of such an authority.

The New Age approach is different from self-effacement *and* from "I'm-right-and-you're-wrong." It starts from one simple premise: that we can't help wanting to live. Many New Age writers have pointed out that it's our deepest inner nature to want to live, and it's this that defines us when all else fails.

But wanting to live—being alive—is a dynamic concept. It's the nature of all living organisms to develop or die, and people are no exception to that rule. If you want to live, you're not going to want to stand still or regress, you're going to want to evolve. Being alive and developing our potentialities are, then, one and the same thing (cf. Fromm, *Man For Himself*; Rollo May, *Man's Search for Himself*).

So—to return to our original question—what gives us the right to ask people to live differently is the fact that *we aren't developing our potentialities* by working in order to work, and consuming in order to consume. Life is stagnant under these conditions, and the fact that nuclear or ecological disaster threatens simply bears out the rule that if we cease to evolve we die. Most of us have ceased to evolve. Therefore, all of us might die. And that's not fair.

Moreover, I want to be able to develop my potentialities no matter what the rest of us might want. And that means having some options in society—more than there are now. But I won't have those options until a lot more of us are turned off of the work ethic (work for work's sake) and turned on to love and play, spirituality and service.

Finally, though I don't want to sound like a good samaritan or anything, I'd like people to develop their potentialities because it's the only way they can get to know themselves and life. I think they'd like it better here if they did that. I know I would.

But what are our potentialities, exactly? And how do we develop them? Could there be any agreement here?

In the next section I am going to show that, in the dynamic process of being alive, each of us goes through (or attempts to go through) a series of seven stages of self-development. Many New Agers have referred to the seven stages as a hierarchy of potentialities—a *hierarchy of human needs*. The idea is that we can't go on to the second stage until we've met our needs on the first, can't go on to the third stage until we've met our needs on the second, and so on.

(Some New Agers would disagree with the idea that the stages form a hierarchy. For example: in *Omni-Americans*, 1970, black writer Albert Murray points out that many black people have been able to meet their needs for love and esteem, even without being able to meet their needs for material security. And in one of his posthumously published essays Abraham Maslow says, "I've found some degree of transcendence in many people other than self-actualizers"; and he adds, "It is unfortunate that I can no longer be theoretically neat at this level." Perhaps it is enough, for our purposes, to say that we have to at least begin to meet our needs at each of the seven stages before we can feel whole. If we fail to meet our needs at any one of the stages, then we'll leave that part of our selves undernourished and stunted. We'll feel frustrated and anxious, and we'll take our frustrations out on self, on others, and on society.)

The seven stages represent a synthesis of the work of ten very different persons: Roberto Assagioli, psychiatrist and founder of psychosynthesis; Gopi Krishna, authority on Kundalini Yoga; Ken Keyes, healer and founder of the Cornucopia Institute; Lawrence Kohlberg, academic-experimental psychologist; Michio Kushi, Oriental philosopher and expert on macrobiotics; John Lilly, neurophysiologist and consciousness-explorer; Abraham Maslow, "father of humanistic psychology," grandfather of transpersonal psychology; Ram Dass, formerly Richard Alpert of Harvard and now a well-known mystic; Carl Rogers, the first rogerian therapist; and Chogyam Trungpa, Tibetan Buddhist and director of the Naropa Institute.

I tried to combine the work of Easterners and Westerners, of academics and therapists and spiritual philosophers, because I wanted to come up with a series of stages that could apply to all of us regardless of our individual temperaments and personalities.

The Seven Stages of Self-Development

Stage one: physiological needs. According to many different systems of Eastern philosophy, the invisible but very real "psycho-physiological" energy for this stage is centered at the bottom of the spine, and no wonder: it's the stage where our physiological needs—for food, shelter, warmth, etc.—are most important, and also our need for sex, to the extent that our sex drive is physiologically motivated.

If we've met our needs at this stage and we *keep on* meeting them many times over without even trying to meet any of our other needs—then we tend to be unwilling to talk about our selves, close relationships tend to seem dangerous, we try hard not to pay attention to our feelings . . . and we don't want to change our selves, either. We tend to obey rules only to avoid punishment.

Stage two: security needs. Those of us who are able to gratify our physiological needs reasonably well come to be motivated by our security needs—for safety, order, and so on. The energy center is at the navel, naturally.

If we've met our basic needs at this stage and we "go overboard" with them, meeting them many times over without even trying to meet any of our "higher" needs—then we tend to speak only about things that don't concern us personally ("the weather"). When we do speak about our selves, we tend to speak in the past tense, and our feelings are described as objects and aren't described clearly. We tend to conform to authority to get rewards, have favors returned, and so on. We tend to become concerned with dominating people and with increasing our wealth and our pride—with a million different forms of hierarchy, manipulation, and control. We tend to become overly dependent on things that are safe and familiar; we tend to fear change. But we can never quite get *enough* security—ironically, we tend to spend much of our time feeling bad.

Stage three: love needs. At this stage, whose energy center is in the heart region, we're motivated primarily by our love needs—for friendship, belongingness, and affection, and also for sex, to the extent that our sexual feelings are motivated by love.

At this stage we tend to express our selves more freely . . . though if we never move beyond it we're never really willing to accept our feelings. And we still tend to think of them as shameful, bad, or abnormal. We tend to conform to authority in order to avoid the disapproval or dislike of others. We tend to choose our food according to nutrition (books and charts). We mean well: we really do.

Stage four: need for self-esteem. The energy center for this stage is also in the heart region, for here we're motivated by the need for self-esteem—for a sense of mastery and competence in the face of the world and for a sense of ego control.

We still tend to describe our feelings as objects, but as objects in the present. Sometimes our deeper feelings break through against our wishes, and then we try—not very successfully—to accept them. Mostly, though, our feelings center around our fear that we should be "doing more"—for anyone but our selves, usually. We tend to feel genuine compassion for all those "caught up in the dramas of security, sensation and power" (Keyes). We tend to conform to authority to avoid censure and guilt. If we get stuck at this stage we tend to lose our selves in veritable orgies of self-condemnation.

Stage five: need for the esteem of others. At this point, some of us will pass directly on to stage six. But others of us will come to be motivated by a need for the esteem of others—for recognition and prestige that is honestly earned.

At this stage, whose energy center is still at the heart, we tend to experience and express our feelings fully. There's still more fright than pleasure in this . . . but there's also a desire to *be* these feelings, to be the "real me." And as we become more loving and accepting, the world begins to seem more loving and accepting to us (up to a point of course). We tend to conform to authority to maintain the respect of an "impartial spectator" judging in terms of community welfare—"the law" (if it's fair) or "the masses" will do. If we become stuck at this stage we tend to become obsessed with comparing our selves to others.

Stage six: need for self-actualization. At this stage, whose energy center is at the throat, we're motivated by the need for self-actualization—by the need to be true to our own nature. We try to become what we can be . . . whatever that is. But as a matter of fact, our basic values and priorities at this stage are remarkably similar.

We tend to see reality clearly and to be at ease with it. We tend to be open to new ideas, new data, new experience. We tend to be spontaneous, simple, and natural—to live fully in each moment. And we tend to work at some activity (it may or may not be our job) that allows us to feel competent and self-reliant. (We aren't waiting to have our needs met for us by our husbands or wives or by other monolithic institutions.)

Emotionally, we allow our feelings to flow, and we experience them with great vividness. Our relationships are deep and profound. We obey authority—when we do—in order to avoid self-blame (which isn't the same as guilt); we operate by the morality of individual principles of conscience.

Stage seven: need for self-transcendence. Not all of us who reach stage six feel impelled to go on to this stage. Those of us who do are motivated by the need for self-transcendence (or "self-realization")—the need to achieve a serene or contemplative state of being. "It is 'dying to oneself'," says E. F. Schumacher, "to one's likes and dislikes, to all one's egocentric preoccupations. . . ."

The energy for this stage is centered between the eyebrows or on top of the head, depending on the degree of transcendence. I like to distinguish three degrees. In the first we learn to impartially observe our social games "from a place that is free from fear and vulnerability." In the second we learn to activate and express all of our buried potentialities—selfless service, aesthetic creation, deep mystical love, access to the collective unconscious. In the third we learn to feel at one with everything—we *are* love, peace, energy, effectiveness, etc.

Like those of us at stage six, those of us at stage seven operate by the morality of individual conscience—but we also have a sense that our personal morality fits a larger design.

There are two disadvantages to being at stage seven. First, many of us find it difficult to be at this stage and function competently in the material world. Second, many of us are prone to a kind of cosmic sadness. But it is always possible to return from stage seven to stage six. In fact, six and seven may be thought of as complementary—as complementary dimensions of a whole self (see Chapter 11 for the worldview that comes naturally to those of us who are able to switch back and forth between six and seven).

Some Political Implications of the Seven Stages

Consciousness of wholeness vs. scarcity-consciousness. Why is it so important for us to at least begin to meet *all* our needs? Why is it so important for us to feel whole?

A number of New Age people have recently shown that we think from a *ground* of scarcity or a *ground* of wholeness—and that that profoundly influences the way we see things, and the way we act.

If we're out of touch with our needs, or if we're not able to meet our needs, then we'll always think from what Werner Erhard calls "a condition of scarcity." We'll act *as if* love is scarce, time is scarce, etc. (whether or not we actually *believe* these propositions). Our motto might be, "I'm gonna get mine and to hell with everyone else." Or, conversely, "I'm a selfish, bourgeois oaf, and I've got to learn to forget about my self and 'serve the people'."

Erhard suggests, "Pierce into your own system of beliefs and observe that you do believe in scarcity." And he adds: "While confronting this belief, get that it is not true that hunger and starvation persist on this planet because food is scarce."

If we're not able to meet our needs, says David Spangler, "if we despair of ever being fulfilled, if our consciousnesses have become wholly focused on lack, then our attention and energy are not freed to help others." In other words, "We do not meet the needs of a hungry world because we are all hungry" . . . if not physically, then emotionally, psychologically, and/or spiritually. On the other hand, "There is a willingness to meet other people's needs if we feel our own needs are being met *or that the possibility of their being met exists and can be manifested if we choose*" (emphasis his).

The fact and the promise of wholeness, says Spangler, "offers me a reason for self-development beyond personal needs: that I may become a source of nourishment for my world and a co-creator in the project of the Whole Earth."

Guilt, coercion—or self-development? One of the most important political questions of our time is, How can we get the United States out of the Third World so that insufficiently developed countries can develop their own resources and industries, diversify their economies, and become self-sufficient?

Three answers have been offered.

Liberals would have us get out of the Third World by appealing to our *guilt*: to our feeling that we don't really *deserve* all those resources.

Marxists would have us get out of the Third World by *coercion*: by fomenting a violent revolution here in America and then by insisting that we make do without the resources.

New Age people would have us approach self-development as—in part—a *political strategy*; the idea being that we would no longer *need or want* a disproportionate share of the world's resources if we were fully at home on all seven stages of self-development. We would simply have too many other things to do: love and friendship; arts and crafts; psychic activity, intellectual activity, political activity; spiritual and religious development, appreciation of the world, grounding of our selves in our bodies; community, regional, and planetary service; sex, play, rituals. . . .

Why do we need more and more? The reason we seem to be primarily "economic people" has nothing to do with human nature, as the liberals would have it, or with the notion that we're economically deprived, as the Marxists would. Beyond a certain minimum point, beyond the hard-core poverty level, the feeling of economic deprivation is a relative thing and a subjective thing, and has a lot less to do with our economic assets than our emotional and psychological and spiritual ones. Some families can lead joyful and fulfilling lives on $5,000 a year and others feel deprived with five times as much.

The real political question in the United States today isn't, How can we bring everyone up to a standard where no one feels economically deprived? Since the feeling of economic deprivation is relative and subjective, that's an impossible task by definition. The real political question is (or should be), Why do most people live in such luxury . . . and still feel economically deprived? An answer to that question is desperately needed because the world simply hasn't the resources to give everybody even an American cat's standard of living (let alone an American dog's).

The answer given by New Age politics is that in most cases the deprivation isn't really economic at all. In most cases the feeling of economic deprivation comes from the fact that the monolithic mode of production, and the Prison that's behind it, inevitably blocks our needs for love and esteem—the needs that are important at self-development stages three through five. And that throws us back into stages one and two, onto our physiological and security needs, onto our needs for material things.

So the reason we need so many things—the reason we "need"

maybe ten times more than we really need—is simple. It's that our needs for material things are the only needs that most of us are able to meet in Prison society.

And there's another thing. By blocking our needs for love and esteem, the Prison makes us feel lonely and worthless, weak and inferior. And so we produce more and more in order to win back our dignity, and consume more and more in order to buy back our humanity (see Richard Sennett and Jonathan Cobb, *The Hidden Injuries of Class*, 1972).

Unfortunately (or maybe fortunately!), meeting our material needs isn't enough to keep us happy, or even healthy. For as we've seen, we need to meet our non-material needs if we want to feel whole, and if we want to do more good than harm.

CHAPTER 9

Is Our Main Enemy the Capitalist Economy— or the Stroke Economy?

That's quite a charge to bring to bear on Prison society—that it blocks our needs for love and esteem.

How does it do this exactly? How does it keep so many of us from being loving and self-respecting—from being *whole*—human beings? How does it give us all "Prison-bound personalities"?

It does this by convincing us that there isn't enough affection to go around, by convincing us to make our contribution to what therapist Claude Steiner calls the "stroke economy," a system of emotional control that's more devastating to most of us (in America today) than the material economy.

In an efficient monolithic society like ours, few people die of material hunger—after all, there couldn't be production and consumption if there weren't people. But in every monolithic society, and ours is the most "advanced" in this regard, millions of us are dying slowly inside from emotional hunger—from lack of strokes.

A stroke is a unit of human recognition. A positive stroke is a unit of friendship or affection or esteem; a negative stroke, a unit of indifference or worse. Without strokes we couldn't survive, and when we feel we can't get or give positive strokes, we try to get or give negative strokes (see Steiner).

Some of us have literally died from stroke hunger. Nearly all of us are unable to meet our needs for love and esteem because of the lack of freely given positive strokes. It's an "economic" scarcity—we are indeed living in a depression. And everyone knows that things are getting worse.

On the second level of analysis, there seems to be no reason why we can't give and receive strokes freely. (Liberals may point to "human nature" with a sigh, and Marxists may point to capitalism, but these look more like rationalizations than reasons.) But on the third level of analysis we can see that the Six-Sided Prison *inevitably* makes us feel that there aren't enough strokes to go around. And so we withhold strokes from each other and even from our selves, even though each of us suffers from this.

Here's how the Prison causes and perpetuates the stroke economy:

Patriarchal attitudes convince men that they need to control women. The most effective way that men can do this isn't by physical or economic force but by withholding positive strokes from women. In response, women withhold positive strokes from men. (Men tend to win out anyway, since they tend to be able to withhold strokes longer;

see Slater.) The withholding of strokes is a technique we learn when we're small and our parents use the "withholding of love" technique to control us. (It's an even more prevalent technique in Russia; see Urie Bronfenbrenner, *Two Worlds of Childhood*, 1970.)

Egocentricity convinces us that we're separate, isolated beings, which makes us want to hoard our strokes. It also causes us to feel foolish and hurt when the strokes we offer are rejected, so much so that we can almost never dare to bring our selves to offer strokes freely.

Scientific single vision makes us see the world in hyperrational terms, and it isn't "rational" to give and receive strokes freely . . . is it? Scientific single vision also makes us see the world in quantitative terms, and so we suppose there's only a limited number of strokes we can give or receive.

The bureaucratic mentality encourages and even requires us to withhold strokes from "rivals" (real and potential) and to give strokes in a calculating way.

Nationalism teaches us that there are lots of enemies in the world. And it teaches us that "everyone wants what we've got" and that it's important not to give it to them.

The big city outlook leads us happily to an environment that is filled with dehumanized and dehumanizing structures and is disproportionately filled with people who are suffering from massive stroke hunger. It does not lead us to an environment that is conducive to giving and receiving strokes freely. And so we tend to withdraw, psychically, from the world around us.

As the Prison clamps down on us more totally, it becomes harder and harder for us to give and receive positive strokes—love and esteem. And the consequences of this are all around us. Roderic Gorney puts it simply and well: "We become destructive . . . when our love needs are severely frustrated."

Sometimes when I'm feeling bad I think that the hippies were the last great flash of the dying flame of life (for six months or so back there in '66). But in my better moods I am aware that much of the aimlessness of modern life can be explained as a form of "search behavior" (searching for strokes)—a term coined by rat psychologists. I am able to see that much of the consumption in this country is an attempt to purchase substitute strokes. And I am able to believe that much of the hateful behavior in the world is a way of getting negative but necessary strokes.

Certainly these things are true for me.

CHAPTER 10

Should We Look to the Proletariat— or to All Those Who Love Life?

According to Marx, socialism would be fought for by the proletariat, by the working class, by all those whose basic needs were frustrated by predatory capitalism. In the United States, most members of the working class weren't willing to fight for socialism. But they did change capitalism enough so that they could meet their material needs, their physiological and security needs.

The working class finds it incredibly hard to meet its non-material needs, but so do the rest of us. We're all in the same boat when it comes to these needs, when it comes to the Prison and its institutions.

But we can't expect all the classes to join together and work for New Age society. In fact, we can be almost certain that none of them will. For every social and economic class, *as a class* (as distinct from a collection of individuals), has a substantial stake in monolithic society. What would happen to the industrial proletariat if we wanted fewer goods? To the much-vaunted "professionalism" of doctors if their professional organizations no longer had the power to keep competent "nonprofessionals" from healing us?

No, New Age society won't be brought about by any particular class acting in its interests as a class. But it may be brought about by all those *individuals* who are able to see that Prison society is making it impossible for them to meet their needs as individual human beings.

Or, in more "political" language: if revolution is defined on the third level of analysis, then the potentially transformative class is no longer the proletariat—though it will certainly consist of *members* of the proletariat (and the bourgeoisie and the lumpenproletariat and—yes—even the ruling class!). It will consist of all those who want to change their lives and life-styles in a way that is consistent with the New Age alternative (see Part V).

Or, in more "religious" language: there are no good classes, there are only good people.

Economic Class Analysis—or Psychocultural Class Analysis?

To distinguish the proletariat from the bourgeoisie, Marx devised an *economic* class analysis. To distinguish those who are trying to become whole from those who are not, we need to make use of a *psychocultural* class analysis.

Marx asked, where do you work? We need to ask, are you life-oriented, thing-oriented, or life-rejecting? (Note: I used to speak of my third class as "death-oriented," but I want to get away from the notion of life and death as polar opposites. The term "life-rejecting" is from Dorothy Dinnerstein's book, *The Mermaid and the Minotaur*, 1976.)

But can it be done? Of course it can! In our political work, we've just become so used to thinking of people in terms of their "relationship to the means of production" (even liberals do this) that we've become blind to the fact that there are many other ways of thinking about people—and, in a society where most of us can afford to eat properly, many more useful ways.

For example: many researchers have found that, in the United States today, race, religion, education, birthplace, sex and/or ethnicity are more important than economic factors in determining our political preferences (see, e.g., David Segal and David Knoke, "Political Partisanship," *American Journal of Economics and Sociology*, vol. 29, 1970). Joseph Scott, a black sociologist, has argued that economic class analysis tends to be misleading when it's applied to the black experience—and tends to strip that experience of much of its content and meaning (in Ladner, ed.). And Thelma McCormack, a social scientist, has shown that economic class variables "are not as highly predictive for women as they are for men" (in Millman and Kanter, eds.).

Many New Agers have pointed out that there are now more public bureaucrats than there are industrial workers. . . .

Kenneth Boulding goes so far as to argue that there is no such thing as a working class in the West—"there is a complex stratification of society with many vaguely defined classes." In Boulding's view, the notion of two "distinct and antagonistic classes" appeals just because it makes the modern world seem so much more simple, so much more cut-and-dried than it actually is. In other words, Marxist class analysis appeals not because it speaks to our political needs but because it speaks to our psychological ones.

Other New Agers have argued that there's a *kind* of economic class conflict in America but that it has an overriding psychocultural dimension. Ivan Illich has spoken of it as a conflict between "the prisoners of addiction and the prisoners of envy."

"Status inconsistency theory" has recently made a much more sophisticated attempt to explain our behavior than the old Marxist dichotomies ever could. It examines people's status with regard to at least three socioeconomic variables—generally income, education, and occupational status. And it suggests that if a person's status is different ("inconsistent") in terms of the different variables, if a person has a lot of education, say, but little income, then he or she would be much more open to personal or social change than if his or her status was consistent across the board (consistently high or consistently low or consistently in-between—it doesn't really matter). This theory purports to explain why so many "middle Americans" remain content with their lot—and also why some underemployed B.A.'s turn out to be passion-ate advocates of violent revolution or self-and-social transformation (for more on this see Warren).

But as we saw in Chapter 8, we don't consist primarily of the social and economic roles (or 'games') that we play. We are primarily en-gaged in developing our selves (or in developing substitutes for our failure to do so), and the most important thing about us—the one that determines our behavior more than any number of socioeconomic variables—is the relationship we have with life. Do we love it—or do we love death instead? Or are we somewhere in between, neither im-mersed in life nor "attracted" to the dead, but drawn, more or less, to *things*?

The most meaningful class analysis that we can make today is one that distinguishes among life-oriented, thing-oriented, and life-rejecting people. These psychocultural classes cut across traditional social and economic lines. At the same time, they appear to underlie many of the differences among people that we've noted in this book. Above all, perhaps, they underlie the context out of which we *see* things. For example: if we're life-oriented, seeing a sunset might make us dwell on the beauty or poignancy of life on Earth. If we're thing-oriented, we might wish that we'd taken our cameras along or complain overmuch about the cold. And if we're life-rejecting, we might not want to look out at the sunset for long. We might be afraid of seeing our selves as "impractical dreamers," or as self-indulgent.

A psychologist friend of mine calls these the "being," "having" and "denying" modes, respectively.

And these three class dimensions are precise—they're at least as precise, and therefore as practical to use, as the Marxist dimensions "bourgeois" and "proletariat." They refer to distinct "perceptual worlds" or "universes of sensibility" that are no less real for being internal. What makes them appear less precise is just what makes them deeper and more significant: you can't tell just by *looking* at a person's collar, skin, hair, etc., whether or not he or she loves life. But in one sense this is an advantage, for it keeps us from making snap judgments about people. And in another sense it doesn't matter, since there are at least four clinically precise methods that can be used to find out whether a person loves life, things, or death (see Fromm, *Anatomy*).

Probably the simplest method is by means of a brief questionnaire devised by Erich Fromm, the psychologist, and Michael Maccoby, a social psychologist. This questionnaire has been included in Maccoby, "Emotional Attitudes and Political Choices" (cited in Chapter 27 below), along with the scoring code he used and the results he got among several different groups of people

Fromm and Maccoby broke people's responses down into two cate-gories, life-loving and death-loving. These have the virtue of simplicity, but they're also poles of a duality, and dualistic thinking is Prison thinking nine times out of ten. In real life, people are oriented all up and down a *love-of-life spectrum*, which for convenience' sake I've divided into thirds: hence my life-oriented, thing-oriented, and life-rejecting classes. Because they're segments of a spectrum (fluid) rather than poles of a duality (rigid), my three classes don't imply that anyone is irrevocably cut off from love of life—that anyone's "class interests" are truly irreconcilable with another's (as the ruling class's were said to be with the proletariat's). Instead they're meant to suggest that it's in everyone's class interests to advance up the spectrum toward love of life. This is so because love of death isn't a biologically normal impulse, as Freud assumed. Love of life is biologically normal, but love of things and love of dead things is the result of a crippling process—is "the outcome of unlived life" (Fromm), of the failure to progress beyond the physiological and security needs. However, love of things and love of death, like love of life, probably isn't completely absent in any of us. Consider my example of the sunset. "The dividing line cuts across the heart of every [person]"—Solzhenitsyn.

Psychocultural class analysis is characteristic of New Age political thought. In the 1920s, Ralph Borsodi distinguished among "quality-," "herd-," and "quantity-minded" types, and Waldo Frank distinguished between "Persons" and "persons." More recently, Wendell Berry has said that we are not primarily divided between "conquerors" and "victims," that we are more profoundly divided between two "kinds of mind . . . between exploitation and nurture." Theodore Roszak has distinguished among the person, the possessive individual, and the collective individual. And James Boggs et al. have distinguished among those who are trying to redefine themselves, those who have no self-knowledge "but who are looking for a better reason to live than just changing diapers or demonstrating a Magi-Peeler in the '5 & 10'," and those who are "just out for themselves and don't care about the rest of society."

Life-Oriented, Thing-Oriented, and Life-Rejecting Classes

Now for a description of the classes. It borrows from literally dozens of New Age writers and activists, many of whom tend to think in terms of life-oriented, thing-oriented, and life-rejecting classes though they might never use the words.

Those of us who feel primarily *life-oriented* tend to feel at one with life. We don't have a possessive attitude toward people or things; we enjoy people and things more because we're free from a need to cling to them. We want to *be* more rather than *have* more, we want to construct rather than destroy or retain.

We find it relatively easy to touch each other spontaneously and without sexual overtones; and the sex we have isn't goal-oriented. When we feel exploited we're capable of seeing our exploiter as a "fellow victim of the same puppeteer" (Maya Angelou), namely, of the Prison and its institutions. But what's more important than any of these traits is the attitude we have—a responsiveness to what's most alive and growing in our selves and in others.

It's pretty obvious who the life-lovers are in terms of this book. They're the ones who've managed to break free from the Six-Sided Prison; who aren't fooled by the false promises of the monolithic mode of production; and—since understanding isn't everything—who've *also* managed to reach self-development stages three through seven, or are definitely on their way there. In the United States, probably no more than 10–15 percent of us are primarily life-loving at this point in time. "Little pockets of humanity," in Tom Robbins's bittersweet phrase and in the mystique of the counterculture; but the truth is, life-lovers can be found everywhere, in every social and occupational milieu, and in about the same proportions. LeMaster tells us that many of the construction workers he's interviewed have a more "spontaneous," more "free-flowing" approach to life than a great many middle-class strivers he's known.

If we're primarily *thing-oriented*, we tend to see everything as a commodity—not only all things but all people, not least of all our selves. We tend to feel, "I am what I have"; and we collect injustices done to us (and, if we have a political conscience, to exploited groups) as if these injustices were valuable possessions.

We dream of romance and of power. If we're men we lavish a great deal of affection on our cars and other shiny devices; if we're women we lavish our affections more on our appearance. But we feel more comfortable touching objects than we do touching each other—especially objects that we own. And we tend to feel proud of our sexual prowess, or obsessed with our "performance" in bed.

Those of us who are thing-oriented are trapped by the Prison, though we're capable of seeing that at least some of its sides are neither necessary nor desirable. We're taken in by monolithic institutions, so much so that we don't think the world could go on without them, but we're willing to admit the desirability of alternatives ("if it wasn't for human nature," etc.), especially after sexual intercourse.

The great majority of us (probably 70–80 percent of us) are largely thing-oriented, and being able to see this is being able to see where the political left has made one of its greatest errors. For Old Leftists have always insisted that most of us are life-oriented, and many New Leftists have countered with the assertion that most of us are death-oriented. Both positions can be used to justify dictatorship (to save us from the supposedly death–oriented ruling class or to save us from our selves).

Those of us who are primarily *life-rejecting* tend to be fascinated by the not-alive—not only, or even necessarily, by corpses and decay, but by the many mechanical artifacts that abound in megalopolis. There is, for example, the salesperson who will always add up even two or three small items on the calculating machine, or the person who will always take the car to the corner store. It's like being thing-oriented, only many times more so; our feelings aren't so much repressed as withered. Often they'll take the form of crude passions, such as the passion to win (at other people's expense) or the passion to destroy.

We tend to avoid experience as much as possible, finding it messy or threatening, a "time-waster." We tend to carry our bodies stiffly, like corpses, and we use sex mostly as a tension-reducing device. We tend to feel exploited by nearly everyone, and in response, we project a free-floating *ressentiment* (resentment coupled with anger and envy) out onto the world that would deny everyone—especially the powerless—the right to be happy.

When we're life-rejecting, we tend to be so caught up in the Prison that it's hard to even tell us about it. (Try it and see.) We're so wrapped up in monolithic institutions that we aren't capable of thinking up—or even thinking about—alternatives to them. We're stuck at self-development stages one and two, so we think of work as a duty and pleasure as an immorality. Often we're quite "successful," but we're hell to live with. Maccoby finds that about 10–15 percent of us are largely life-rejecting.

In 1848, Marx saw capitalist society as a battleground between the bourgeoisie and the proletariat. I'd like to suggest (along with Erich Fromm, anthropologist Jules Henry, and many other New Age-oriented writers) that monolithic society is a battleground between those who love life and those who fear life.

Unfortunately for the scientific pretensions of tri-level analysis (i.e., unfortunately for its value as myth), there appears to be nothing inevitable about the outcome of this battle. As we've seen, the Six-Sided Prison is gaining in depth and strength, and the Prison and its institutions are making it harder and harder for us to meet our needs for love and esteem, without which we cannot develop our selves—we cannot *be* our selves—we cannot truly live. In this view, it's only a matter of time before the world becomes unlivable, for one reason or another. But as we've also seen, many of us are managing to escape from the Prison by means of the attack on predefined sex-roles, the rediscovery of the spirit, and so on. And many of us are becoming aware of the perverse effects of monolithic institutions.

If many of us can begin to look at the world in a different, more multifaceted way (Part IV); if a desirable and workable alternative to the Prison and its institutions can be forged out of the ideas that many of us have been coming up with over the last ten years or so (Parts V–VI); and if many of us who are thing-oriented can meet our needs for love and esteem by taking part in the rich and life-giving experience of self-and-social transformation (Part VII)—then, perhaps, the forces of love will triumph.

Part IV
THE TRANS-MATERIAL WORLDVIEW

CHAPTER 11

The Trans-Material Worldview: Metaphysical Basis for a New Age Society

The Prison and its institutions are compatible with two different ways of looking at the world. Both of these ways are so partial as to be dangerous. The first of them, the one we're used to, is so taken-for-granted that probably most of us don't even notice that it's there.

This first way of looking at the world can be called the "materialist worldview." From the materialist point of view, the only way we can know things is by the evidence of our senses (if we can't see it, touch it, smell it, etc., it isn't real). "Reality" is independent of our mental processes. We end at our skins. Our behavior is a product of stimulus-response type conditioning (some liberals may give more weight to genetics). "Man," so called, is the "king of the universe," and the rest of the universe exists to serve "man." And so on . . . and so on.

A second way of seeing the world can be called the "non-material worldview." It can be seen as a kind of protest against the materialist worldview, and, like all protests, it tends to claim just the opposite of what the "official version" claims. The only way we can know things is by looking within. The material world is dependent on our mental processes. We are all One. Our behavior is a manifestation of God's will. And so on. . . .

Marxism and liberalism are political expressions of the materialist worldview. That is why they are based on the ideas of unending economic "growth," unlimited technical "progress," and unceasing personal or social "achievement." On the other hand, in the United States today, the non-material worldview is essentially a reaction against the materialist worldview. It may not be Prison-bound, but it is bound up in a love-hate relationship with the Prison. So it isn't really capable of generating a coherent new politics of its own. In fact, many of its advocates pride themselves on being "apolitical."

Many New Age writers understand how important it is to work out a *new* worldview, a worldview that can serve as the metaphysical basis for New Age society and New Age politics. At least forty books listed in Chapter 27 touch on this theme. Economist E. F. Schumacher sums up their thrust succinctly when he says, "We are suffering from a metaphysical disease, and the cure must therefore be metaphysical." Lewis Mumford—a person not given to overstatement—says, "The achievement of a new personality, a new attitude toward [people] and nature and the cosmos, are matters of life and death."

Some New Age people believe that the new worldview is arising already and that the kinds of insights and understandings that were reported on in Parts I–III are early political expressions of that worldview. This chapter is an attempt to (drastically) condense and synthesize the efforts that New Age writers have recently been making to set this worldview down on paper. I like to call it the "trans-material" worldview because it includes materialism but goes beyond it, too.

The Materialist Worldview

Even in its own terms, the materialist worldview is finding it a lot harder to pose as the "one, true way" to understand reality. Facts keep turning up that suggest that there's more to the world than meets the eye. Research findings keep turning up that show very clearly that the materialist worldview is not so much wrong as narrow—partial—incomplete.

Psychic research. Research into such phenomena as telepathy (extrasensory communication), clairvoyance ("seeing" distant events), and precognition ("seeing" future events) is now being carried out at respectable universities and institutes all over North America. (This research is reported on at length in Edgar Mitchell, ed., *Psychic Exploration*, 1974.) Evidence is mounting that, as Willis Harman puts it, "These sorts of preternormal knowings and abilities are latent in all persons but are typically highly repressed."

Psychic research has been defined as "the scientific study of impossible facts"—those things that *cannot* happen, but do. What are we to do with these facts?

Life after death. A number of studies have recently been published that point to the survival of consciousness after death. Dr. Elisabeth Kubler-Ross, a leading psychiatrist, has studied nearly 200 cases of people who had been declared dead and later spontaneously revived—people of all ages and economic backgrounds, religious and nonreligious alike—and according to her, "All experienced the same thing. They virtually shed their physical bodies, as a butterfly comes out of a cocoon. They describe a feeling of peace, beautiful, indescribable peace, no pain, no anxiety. . . . They were so content that they resented, somewhat bitterly, the attempts to bring them back to life." And she adds: "Not one of them was afraid to die again."

The new physics. It is often said that the materialist worldview is based on the worldview of the sciences and especially that of the "queen" of the sciences, physics. If so, then the least we can say is that the materialist worldview is badly out of date.

For example, according to classical physics, mass is associated with what physicist Fritjof Capra calls an "indestructible material substance." However, contemporary physics tells us that mass is "nothing but a form of energy" which, far from being indestructible, "can be transformed into other forms of energy." The conclusion seems obvious, and has been stated by many: there is no true physical matter ("true" in the sense of being indestructible); there is only energy in motion.

Another example. According to materialist physics, "the fundamental building blocks of matter" are supposed to be solid. But quantum theory has shown us that—as Capra puts it—"the subatomic units of matter are very abstract entities which have a dual aspect. Depending on how we look at them, they appear sometimes as particles, sometimes as waves; and this dual nature is also exhibited by light which can take the form of electromagnetic waves or particles."

And a final example. Classical physics assumes that the world is "out there" and that it's our task to observe it . . . to make reconnaissance raids on it. But a central insight of atomic physics is that observer and observed are not so distinct. We can only take certain factors into account at any one time. Our beliefs and desires will color our data. And the very act of observing will affect what we observe. Physicist John Wheeler concludes that we live in a "participating" universe, and David Spangler concludes, "Reality is a joint creation or product of the participation of observer and observed."

Where are these discoveries taking twentieth-century physics? Sir James Jeans sums it up: "Today there is a wide measure of agreement, which on the physical side of sciences approaches almost to unanimity, that the stream of knowledge is heading towards a non-mechanical reality; the universe begins to look more like a great thought than like a great machine."

My point, remember, is not that the materialist worldview is wrong, but that it's incomplete; that it doesn't fit with what we know about the universe. Unfortunately, it's become so universally accepted as the "one, true way" (to the truth) that the answers it cannot give us are often assumed *not to exist*. And I don't want to have to live with the results. I think of the man from the International Commission on North Atlantic Fisheries, who told the Greenpeace Foundation's harp seal campaign, "These seals should be eliminated because they eat too damn many fish—and what use are they, anyway?" And I think of an article in the prestigious *Journal of Biosocial Science* (vol. 4, July 1972) which states: "Why should publicly financed resources be devoted to preventing infant mortality when the economic worth of such marginal infants is negative? The economy would be better off without them."

We need a trans-material worldview to give us a basis for answering these questions.

The Non-Material Worldview

Sensing the inadequacies of the materialist worldview for our time and place, and appalled by some of its moral and political implications, some New Age writers have begun to promote a non-material worldview that is the mirror image of the materialist worldview.

The non-material worldview certainly has its advantages. We do need to be reminded that there's more to life than our jobs and our possessions. And the non-material worldview opens up vast spiritual horizons that materialism has ignored or ridiculed for centuries. But I just don't believe that the non-material worldview, by itself alone, can give us a basis for healing our selves and transforming our society. Like the materialist worldview, it is simply too narrow.

George Leonard, a founder of the human potential movement, puts it this way: "This train of thought has sometimes created a passive otherworldliness that ignores the problems and play of this world while fostering an elitist devotion to satori or samadhi."

And John Amodeo, a hatha yoga teacher, says (in *Yoga Journal*, July/Aug. 1977): just as the Marxists and liberals "tend to identify with one aspect of their being while neglecting the self-growth aspect, so does one who seeks psycho-spiritual growth tend to overidentify with the sub-personality which seeks spiritual growth, deeper awareness and psychological fulfillment. One example of this is the prevailing myth that we are totally responsible for the reality we have created for ourselves, a point of view which perhaps keeps many Blacks and Third World people away from the growth movement."

The materialist worldview encourages us to talk with a straight face about "the economic worth of marginal infants." But the non-material worldview doesn't do much better. I've heard non-materialists say that the Jews were "responsible" for the concentration camps. Or, when a small child drowned because her daycare center didn't supervise the swimming hole, "Well, that was her karma." The non-material worldview allows us to look at human atrocities like concentration camps with total acceptance and without the feeling that something should be done about a world that allows them.

The Trans-Material Worldview

Many New Age writers believe that both old worldviews are inadequate, that neither of them can give us a basis for a wholistic new politics. Some of these writers are trying to work out a new, trans-material worldview that reflects more accurately what psychic research, twentieth-century physics, etc., are telling us about reality.

If you try to put together what these New Age writers are saying, you'll come up with this: there are at least four valid states of consciousness (or "modes of being" or "separate realities" or "reality stages" or dimensions or aspects or levels of reality). One of them is, indeed, the material state of consciousness. But another of them is the spiritual (non-material) state. And there are two other states, the religious and the mythic states. Each of them is valid or true when used for its own special purposes. And each of them is necessary for us. We need each of them to be healthy, to feel whole: experiential proof that reality is trans-material. (But I think it's also true that each of us—and each of our cultures, too—has a natural or preferred state.

My "natural" state happens to be the material one. But The Farm's is definitely the spiritual state. And Lindisfarne's is definitely the religious. And the Hopi native peoples' is definitely the mythic.)

Four New Age writers have been consciously trying to create a trans-material worldview for us, and the following section relies heavily on their work: Lawrence LeShan, *Alternate Realities* (1976); Philip Slater, *The Wayward Gate* (1977); Huston Smith, *Forgotten Truth* (1975); Charles Tart, *States of Consciousness* (1976). (LeShan is an experimental psychologist, Slater a psychotherapist, Smith a religious writer, and Tart an experimental psychologist at the University of California at Davis.) But they're only trying to systematize what many New Age writers and activists have been saying (or simply assuming!). For example: Jane Roberts, originator of "aspect psychology" as well as a noted medium, says that "the physical senses present one unique version of reality, in which being is perceived in a particular dimensionalized sequence . . . and is the result of one kind of neurological focus. There are alternate neurological routes, biologically acceptable, and other sequences so far not chosen." And David Spangler, a spiritual teacher, says that his own particular tradition, the esoteric tradition, "is simply one container that we have discovered to catch the outpouring of reality. It is undoubtedly more useful than some containers in certain situations and not so useful in others, but no container . . . should be expected to catch all of a limitless truth."

I should also mention that the notion of states of consciousness (or aspects of reality) is a familiar one to many peoples. Sri Aurobindo says that East Indian philosophy speaks of a single Reality with four discrete levels: Matter, Life, Mind, and Superconsciousness. And John Mbiti says that African religion speaks of four "levels of order" in the universe: "order in the laws of nature," "moral order," "religious order," and "mystical order."

Each of the states of consciousness (or aspects of reality, modes of being, etc.) has the following characteristics (according to LeShan):

Each is a totally self-consistent way of structuring what is out there and in here (as a Southern friend of mine likes to put it: when we're in one state, all the other states seem like bullshit).

Each can help us to "accomplish certain goals and answer certain questions. Each is irrelevant to certain other questions and goals."

Each is discrete (Tart), though there may be some overlap (Smith).

"Each satisfies certain parts of our needs, and when [we don't] use one of them with a whole heart, fully accepting its validity and reality, that part of [our selves] remains undernourished and [our] whole being is stunted in its development" (LeShan).

We should also note that when we are very young, we are taught that the material state of consciousness is the *only* true or useful state, that all the other states are "bullshit." In fact, in Prison society, the growing up process consists of our learning precisely this! So it's not going to be easy for us to learn to return to the other states and/or to feel at home in them. It's going to take conscious effort.

States of Consciousness	Objects, Events, Self . . .	Distinctive Categories	Appropriate to	Critical Stage of Development	Essential Need It Fills
Material	. . . are clearly separate from one another	space/time matter brain	crossing the street, etc. "normal" science	to age 7	gives us techniques for living
Spiritual	. . . are seen as One	the One spirit	yoga meditation body therapy	age 14 & up	gives us reasons for living
Religious	. . . are seen as separate but flowing into a larger One	God spirit	prayer "energy re-sourcement" "attunement"	age 14 & up	gives us moral guidelines for living
Mythic	. . . can have any (or all) of the characteristics of the whole	symbol archetype soul	play art dream	ages 7–14	keeps us alive to the wonder of our being

The Trans-Material Worldview: Four Self-Consistent and Necessary States of Consciousness

The Four States of Consciousness

The material state of consciousness. When we're in this state, objects, events, and self are clearly separate from one another. We think in terms of concepts such as space, time, matter, number. All information comes from the senses, everything has a cause, all objects are made up of parts that can be understood and improved separately, and so on. The material state of consciousness is similar to the materialist worldview, but because it exists in conscious awareness of the other states, it is far less rigid, far more modest in its claims.

As LeShan points out, this state is "ideally adapted to asking and answering questions such as 'how' and 'how to'." But it is "completely irrelevant to questions starting with 'why' or to questions of value and moral judgment." It can tell us how to kill and cure, but it can't tell us what is right, moral, good. . . . We need the material state in order to know what LeShan calls the "techniques for living," but we need access to the other states in order to know why and how to live—and if we want to treasure life.

The spiritual state of consciousness. This state and the next one, the religious state, are lumped together by Smith (as the "infinite" state) and in popular thought, but there are some important differences between them.

When we're in the spiritual state, everything merges into one great unity: the unity of the cosmos. The senses can't be trusted; events don't "happen," they "are"; all desires and beliefs must be given up, because they separate us from the One; all categories must be given up, even the categories of "good" and "bad," for the same reason; and so on.

Within its frame of reference, the spiritual state of consciousness is just as valid or true as the material state. And it enables us to meet needs that are equally vital. LeShan states, "It is our need for a sense, a knowledge, of our solid connectedness with the totality of whatever is. . . . Without this, there is always somewhere a sense of alienation and a need to somehow act to strengthen and cement our anchor ropes to the world." If we can't achieve a sense of oneness with nature, or the human race, or the cosmos, then chances are good that we'll try to "leave a mark on history" by following the path of least resistance to growth, or by advocating violent revolution, or by having lots and lots of children.

The religious state of consciousness. In this state, objects, events, and self are neither separate, as in the material state, nor identical, as in the spiritual. Objects, events, and self are seen as separate *and* as flowing into a larger unity. As David Spangler puts it, difference is seen "as really an enriching manifestation of this unity rather than a fragmentation of it."

One way of getting in touch with the religious state is through prayer. Another way, reported on by Sally Gearhart (in *WomanSpirit*,

Winter '76), is through the process of "energy re-sourcement." In this process, women get together for substantial periods of time—often in the country, but also in quiet and sheltered places in the city—'to re-touch their inner channels of energy and to join those channels with those of other women." A third way is through the process of "attunement" as developed by the Findhorn community in Scotland. In this process people hold hands and "attune to"—get in touch with—each other's energy, their own energy, and also, if they wish, the energies that are said to emanate from devas, nature spirits, and greater Beings.

The religious state of consciousness is as valid as the others and as necessary to us, for without it we could have no morals, no guidelines for living. In the material state, morality is meaningless. An action works or it doesn't work, and that's that. In the spiritual state, morality is impossible; if you wish for something for your self, even guidelines or principles, you've already separated your self out from the One (and besides, everything is as it should be). But in the religious state, a moral principle is inherent in the universe, since *whatever is done to one part affects the whole*. As LeShan puts it, "if one part moves another toward greater harmony with the whole, all of the whole—including the part that took the action—benefits"; and the reverse is also true. Therefore, "anything that moves a part toward its fullest development and fullest integration with the whole is good," anything that does the reverse is evil.

The mythic state of consciousness. In this state, objects, events, and self "can become identical with anything else or stand for anything once the two have been connected. . . . If you treat the flag of a country reverently, you are treating the country reverently. . . . If you were born at a particular time, that time and you are permanently associated . . ." (LeShan).

The mythic state is expressed in play, art, dream. In play—real play—anything can be anything and new combinations are always being arrived at; similarly in poetry and in the dream. The mythic state is reflected in the myths and legends of a culture, and in his book *Festivals in the New Age*, David Spangler urges that we begin to reinfuse the seasons with rich symbolic meanings. Winter, for example, might be given over to celebrations of identity, celebrations of renewal, celebrations of the birth of Jesus, rather than Christmas.

The mythic state is a valid way to construe reality—as valid as the others. LeShan sums up its special usefulness very nicely when he says, "As the material [states of consciousness] tend always to the general, to the understanding of the general laws that underlie each separate event, the mythic [states] tend toward the individual. Each thing and each event is charged with meaning, is unique and important. The world is full of specialness and newness due to this uniqueness. The child's eye is filled with wonder and possibility as long as this [state] is perceived to be as valid as any other. When we teach the child that play is inferior to work, that the mythic [states] are invalid, [he or she] becomes blasé, the shining newness goes out of things, and the colour and possibilities that underlie [his or her] creativity are lost."

The mythic state is a kind of "psychological adrenalin" for us. Without it we run the risk of becoming bored with our selves and with life. Without it we can undergo serious psychological deterioration. In laboratory experiments, when people are prevented from dreaming, most of them undergo profound negative personality changes and become psychologically quite ill. Without our psychological adrenalin we are liable to look for a "fix" in the endless buying of things or in the "high" we get from one-upping other people.

The materialist worldview demands that we rely wholly on *rational control*—on what Philip Slater characterizes deftly as a "detached and risk-free state of mind and being." The non-material worldview demands that we rely wholly on *intuition*—"even in the face of negative feedback." But the trans-material worldview allows us to rely on what Slater calls *mobile balance*. "[Mobile balance] involves trusting your internal harmony with the [E]arth, feeling your way, reacting fully, committing yourself to people and situations, allowing yourself to sort things out through trial and error. . . ." Mobile balance allows and even requires us to immerse our selves fully in life. The trans-material worldview is for those who love life.

We Are More Than Our Conditioning

According to the materialist worldview we are completely determined by our social conditioning. According to the non-material worldview, only our most superficial characteristics are determined by our conditioning. The trans-material worldview is able to give us a much more rounded sense of who we are than either of our old worldviews. It sees us as existing in both material and non-material dimensions—therefore, it sees us as made up of both matter and spirit; part socialized and part spirit. Many New Agers say that the point is to infuse our socialized selves with spirit (see, e.g., Berdyaev or Noyes).

Even in the material dimension there's now much evidence to show that awareness can't be reduced to brain functioning, the implication being that we aren't completely determined by our conditioning, that there's a "space beyond conditioning." Some of this evidence comes from neurophysiology: "there is no brain-spot which, if electrically stimulated, will induce [people] to believe or to decide" (Smith). Other evidence comes from people's experiences in altered states of consciousness: "experiences of feeling that one's mind leaves one's body, of supernormal knowledge directly given [etc.], fit more comfortably into schemes that do not assume that awareness is only a function of the brain" (Tart). Still other evidence comes from psychic research (see above).

The fact that there is in each of us a "space beyond conditioning" has tremendous political importance. For one thing, it means that there is, or at least there can be, "freedom of choice"—and so it gives the lie to all those Marxists (and Skinners and Delgados) who find it convenient to deny that there is such a thing. For another thing, since the space exists *within* us, it follows that the individual is to be treasured—not suppressed—in New Age society. If we have another violent revolution in which the person is "compressed into being a unit in the mass," says William Irwin Thompson, "we will lose the unique opening to the universal that is contained in the self."

The materialist worldview says that we're totally determined by our genes and social conditioning; therefore, we lack free will (not to mention personal identity!); therefore, we can't be held responsible for our actions and situations. The non-material worldview says that we bring our social conditioning (and even our genes) onto our selves and are therefore totally responsible for our actions and situations. The trans-material worldview is careful to distinguish between what we can and can't be held responsible for *in the different states of consciousness.*

New Age people disagree over how responsible we should consider each other to be in the material state of consciousness. Probably most New Agers would consider us to be partly responsible for our situations—for who and what we are—and ultimately responsible for what we do. Edgar Z. Friedenberg, educator and gay activist, says, "However pitiable their own lots may be, the poor whites of Texas and the blue collar workers of Detroit must be held responsible, by anyone who defends the democratic state in principle, for what was done to the peasants of Indochina. To refuse to hold them responsible for what they have endorsed is to deny them exactly the dignity as persons that citizenship in a democracy is supposed to confer."

Still in terms of the material state, many New Age activists choose to go further—not for philosophical reasons but for political ones, in order to get *results.* Mimi Silbert, counsellor at the Delancey Street Foundation (for ex-felons), puts it this way: "If someone has been blaming the system all their lives, you have to say to that person, 'No—it's *your* fault.' Whether or not that is empirically correct, it is the correct *antidote* for his chronic dependence. It is by going to the 'extreme' of self-determination that he breaks the chain."

In the *spiritual* state of consciousness, New Age people find it useful to go further still. We recognize that we're responsible for choosing everything—our parents, our personalities, everything. We even experience events as if we've created or willed them in some way. In the *material* state of consciousness this experience is of course not "true," it is only a way of experiencing the world; but it's often an extremely valuable and stimulating one. It takes us out of the powerless feeling of being "done to" since, no matter how disastrous a situation may be, we also look for what we can gain from it. (We might ask: Why is this happening to me, at this particular point in my life? What is it trying to teach me, meant to teach me? Or we might ask: Why am I causing this to happen to me?) It's kind of like confronting every situation with the old pragmatic American question, "What's in it for me?"—except we're looking not for material benefits but for consciousness-and-growth benefits.

Jerry Rubin says, "Whenever I come into any situation in my life, whether it's an auto accident, an upset, anything extremely oriented that causes me pain, if immediately I choose it and act as if I was responsible for it, all of a sudden I have increased power." Where does this power come from? According to Patricia Sun, a healer, it is our own power, freed at last from the shackles of the "anger and grief and remorse and hatred and sadness" that we feel when we *don't* experience the world from a position of total responsibility.

CHAPTER 12

New Age Ethics and Values

In America—and in the world at large—we no longer have a guiding series of ethics and values. Just look at our art, says Rollo May. All the "great art" of the early twentieth century merely coasted on the ethics and values of the past; and all the "great art" of our time merely laments the loss of those ethics and values. It cannot identify and it does not propose new ethics and values.

This is *politically* important because—as Robert Nisbet and many others have told us—coercive power exists "in almost exact proportion" to the absence of internalized and institutionalized ethics and values. Unless we are able to work out a new and/or believable series of ethics and values—and then write them into law, base our institutions on them, base our expectations of one another on them—the world is doomed to chaos, or to top-down authoritarian control. Ali Mazrui, an African expert on "world order," puts it well (in Mendlovitz, ed.): "The world of tomorrow can be tamed either through outside force or through shared values." He goes so far as to contend that "the transmission of [values] and their internalization are more relevant for world reform than the establishment of formal institutions for external control." Wendell Berry is getting at much the same thing when he says, "To think or act without cultural value, and the restraints invariably implicit in cultural value, is simply to wait upon force."

Fortunately, this is where the trans-material worldview comes in. For the trans-material worldview is more than a satisfying intellectual construct. It implies a whole new way of looking at people, and a whole new set of ethics, values, goals, priorities. And since the trans-material worldview is *natural* to us when we've begun to transcend the Prison, New Age society would be based on the ethics and values that are embedded in this worldview. (But it is important to note that these "New Age" ethics and values are not foreign to any major culture or ideology or religion. The very same ethics and values took some of our first colonies—Connecticut, Rhode Island—through their first couple of winters. The very same ethics and values are embedded in the writings of some of the founders of all of the great religions; and in the writings of some of the founders of most of the political "ism's." (See esp. Laszlo, *Goals*, 1978.)

Four New Age Ethics

The self-development ethic. The trans-material worldview says that there are at least four valid and self-consistent states of consciousness and that each state satisfies certain parts of our needs. If we're not able to get in touch with one or more of these states, then we'll be dangerously out of balance. And we'll be sure to compensate by doing harm to our selves and/or to others.

In order to get in touch with all four states—in order to be at least *comfortable* in each of them—we are going to have to develop our selves. We are going to have to go beyond our obsession with material things and learn to desire the non-material "things" that the spiritual, religious, and mythic states of consciousness can give us. We are going to have to come unstuck from self-development stages one and two, from our physiological and security needs.

So. Getting in touch with our selves would appear to be, not just fun (though it can be that), and not self-indulgence at all, but an imperative for survival that's built right in to the structure of the universe. (Maybe even an evolutionary imperative.)

The ecology ethic. Each state of consciousness speaks to us here. In the material state, scientists of wildly different political persuasions have been urging us to learn to work *with* nature's resources rather than merely to use them up. The consequences, if we don't learn this, are too terrible to contemplate (in the material state). More mundanely, one of our commonest adages is the one about not fouling your nest; and you don't need the least bit of "non-material" awareness to grasp that the nest is now our planet, and always has been really.

The spiritual and mythic states of consciousness both suggest the interdependence and interpenetration of all things. And the religious dimension has its own built-in ecological principle in that it implies that "if one part moves another toward greater harmony with the whole, all of the whole—including the part that took the action—benefits" and vice versa. (Hazel Henderson tells us that her mother's "brand of pantheism [was] in retrospect . . . a fairly useful basis on which I developed my particular ecological model of reality.")

The self-development and ecology ethics are closely connected. Willis Harman says, "These two ethics, one emphasizing the total community of [people] in nature and the oneness of the human race, and the other placing the highest value on developing one's own self, are not conflicting but complementary—two sides of the same coin. . . . Each is a corrective against excesses or misapplications of the other." Stephen Gaskin, founder and spiritual leader of The Farm, in Tennessee, speaks to the politics of the two ethics: "We have it within our power to voluntarily assume a simpler lifestyle which can be so graceful and so much fun that it will just naturally spread of its own accord. . . . Whether we like it or not, we're all going to have to assume that simpler lifestyle anyway [for environmental reasons—M.S.]. . . . It's just that some of us are going to be dragged into it kicking and screaming, and some of us are going to adopt it beforehand, on purpose, and enjoy it and make it a nice way to live."

The self-reliance/cooperation ethic. Self-development makes it possible for us to be self-reliant and cooperative at the same time, and makes us *want* to be both at once. Individually, and as communities or regions. Truly self-reliant behavior would be impossible without our ability to act cooperatively in many ways, and truly cooperative behavior would be impossible if one of us were leaning on the other. (See "Autonomy and community" below.)

The nonviolence ethic. "If one part moves another toward greater harmony with the whole, all of the whole—including the part that took the action—benefits." Is there any need to show, at this late date, that only nonviolent behavior is harmonious with the whole? (In fact, violence can be defined as disharmony at its most extreme; though nonviolence should never be confused with lifelessness or indifference.)

The self-reliance/cooperation and nonviolence ethics are connected. Richard Gregg, nonviolent strategist and activist, has found that only those of us who are self-reliant *and* cooperative can practice nonviolence successfully. And it's obvious that violence or the threat of violence would make "cooperation" pretty shallow.

If the trans-material worldview is the emerging shared worldview for the New Age; and if the four New Age ethics are implicit in the trans-material worldview; then quite a few of us should be discovering and acting according to the four New Age ethics.

And it's happening. For example, James Robertson's remarkable introduction to New Age politics, *The Sane Alternative*, published in Britain in 1978, speaks of the emerging "ethic of ecology, social responsibility, and self-realization"—and speaks of the "central . . . concept of non-violent power." Or, for example, the Stanford Research Institute recently completed a report on the "Changing Images of Man," and their findings were that a "new image" of the person is definitely arising, an image that "reinstates the transcendental, spiritual side of [people] . . . [while denying] none of the conclusions of science in its contemporary form"; in other words, an image based on the trans-material worldview; and that the "ecology" and "self-realization" ethics are inherent in the new image. In addition, consider that there are now literally dozens of groups and magazines whose purpose is to promote one or more of the New Age ethics (see Chapter 27).

Six New Age Political Values

The four New Age ethics translate themselves fairly easily into six basic political values—like this:

To maximize the *self-development* ethic we need (1) maximization of social and economic well-being. We need (2) maximization of social and political justice—prevention of genocide; elimination of colonial regimes; elimination of torture and cruelty; equality of treatment for people of all ages, races, sexes, religions. . . . And we need (3) maximization of cultural, intellectual, and spiritual freedom.

To maximize the *ecology* ethic we need (4) maximization of environmental quality—including maximization of the well-being of all creatures.

To maximize the *self-reliance/cooperation* ethic we need (5a) maximization of self-reliance of communities, regions, and nation-states, and (5b) maximization of the cooperative *potential* of communities, regions, and states (which they can choose to take advantage of if they wish).

To maximize the *nonviolence* ethic we need (6) minimization of violence between individuals, groups, and governments.

In the short run, some of these values may conflict with one another (e.g., 1 and 4); in these cases people and politicians should—as Richard Falk advises—judge proposals according to what they think might be their *net* effects. In the long run I suspect that all six political values are interconnected and interdependent.

Some radicals have argued that "maximization of cultural, intellectual, and spiritual freedom" is a Western cultural value and not a "primary" political value at all. But in the New Age perspective, with its stress on self-development, we are able to recognize this value as a *precondition* for all genuine culture and for the life of the mind and spirit; just as "minimization of violence" is a precondition for the continuation of physical life.

Some New Age Social Values

New Age ethics and political values are suggestive of a great many other values that New Age communities might want to adopt in some way. After all, as Robert Nisbet tells us, "A culture is required for great individuals, good or evil, in life or art, to flourish"; and "the basis of any culture is the presence of values which have external force in the individual's life. . . . In the fusions of such values we get the 'patterns of culture' the late Ruth Benedict wrote of so eloquently. . . ."

The Synergy Power Institute has recently drawn up a list of thirty New Age values that are consistent with the New Age ethics and political values as I've described them. Among these values are: "security (survival necessities assured for everyone)"; "respect for people, their ideas, and their feelings"; and "joy and pleasure." The Twin Oaks community is trying to implement its own "core values" which are also consistent with the New Age ethics and political values: "cooperation," "sharing," "treat people in a kind, caring, honest, and fair manner. . . ."

What follows is far from being a complete list of New Age social values—even the Synergy Power Institute's list is less than complete—but it is meant to be representative and suggestive.

Enoughness. In Prison society we usually think of "enough" in a negative sense—as in "That's enough of that!" And "more" is usually considered "better." But in New Age society we would be free of the Prison, and so we would find that our needs for things were actually quite limited. (Many of the goods we would need would actually be *tools* we could use to make our own goods with. That's the point of the *Whole Earth Catalog*, whose subtitle is "Access to Tools," and of Ivan Illich's book *Tools for Conviviality*.)

"We are learning," says Tom Bender, "that too much of a good thing is not a good thing, and that we would often be wiser to determine what is enough rather than how much is possible. . . . The fewer our wants, the greater our freedom from having to serve them."

Stewardship. "Progress," says Tom Bender, "assumes that the future will be better—which at the same time creates dissatisfactions with the present. . . . As a result, we are prompted to work harder to get what the future can offer, but lose our ability to enjoy what we now have. We also lose our sense that we ourselves, and what we have to do, are really good. . . . Stewardship, in contrast to progress, elicits attentive care and concern for the present—for understanding its nature and for best developing, nurturing, and protecting its possibilities. Such actions unavoidably insure the best possible future as a byproduct of enjoyment and satisfaction from the present."

Autonomy and community. Marxism stresses community at the expense of autonomy, and liberalism does just the reverse. But each of these values requires the other, and is the logical extension of the other, like the light and dark sides of the moon. By stressing the one and repressing the other, we don't come to know either, since the one that's stressed gets exaggerated and distorted: autonomy becomes isolation and community becomes conformity. In New Age society we would learn to make our own decisions and not to hang on others. But that wouldn't isolate us from others; as Claude Steiner points out, it would make us more attractive to others and more confident about being in community with them.

Diversity. New Age people aren't interested in creating a "perfect" or "utopian" America run according to the "correct" political principles. Instead, *diversity* would be treasured—partly as a safeguard against authoritarianism, and partly as an enrichment of life.

The Twin Oaks community is run along these lines. Vince, who lives there, writes (in *New Directions*, no. 21) that at Twin Oaks there are people "with endless interests and paths and approaches to what is best for each. This is one of my reasons for being here. . . . In the process of close cooperation with people of varying attitudes, it is important to be open to many approaches and points of view regarding decision-making, priorities, resolving conflicts, and ways to express our growth. . . . The ego is constantly being tested. What a wonderful opportunity for expansion of consciousness!"

Many-sidedness. Diversity would reach in to our inner lives. Maslow selfish, Dionysian and Apollonian, individual and social, rational and tells us that self-developed people "are simultaneously selfish and un-

irrational, fused with others and detached from others. . . ." Michael Rossman figures that most of us would choose to lead "a way of life which cycles harmoniously between travel and indwelling, between city and country, between community and isolation . . . [between] the polarities of engagement-retreat, creation-reception, etc." Probably more of us would—most of the time—be more receptive than active, since the world would no longer be seen as a project, and a receptive attitude would allow us to see the world more clearly.

The multidimensional person. Gustavo Lagos and Horacio Godoy, in *Revolution of Being: A Latin American View of the Future* (1977), say that the person in the new society "will seek to be multidimensional, perpetually in the process of inward and outward self-fulfillment." The multidimensional person will want to develop his or her paths in many spheres, "the absence or underdevelopment of which may deplete him or her." James Ogilvy goes so far as to claim that the "many-dimensional" person—the "decentralized self"—is an absolutely necessary component of any "decentralized society" or decentralized theology.

Desireless love. Today we often love because we need something from the other, praise, approval, vindication of our being, whatever. In New Age society we would love other beings in a desireless way, not because we needed something (some thing) from them but because—out of our fullness—we wanted to share our time with them. Anne Koedt writes, "In reality there can be no genuine love until the need to *control* the growth of another is replaced by love *for* the growth of another."

Reverence for life. This has two aspects, equally important. To Erich Fromm it means, "Valuable or good is all that which contributes to the greater unfolding of [our] faculties and furthers life. Negative or bad is everything that strangles life and paralyzes [our] activeness." On the other hand, here is Wendell Berry on the poet Gary Snyder: "His realization of the smallness and shortness of his life in relation to the world's life is of such intensity as to make him virtually absent from the place and from his own sense of things. He is present in the poem finally only as another creature, along with moon and rock and juniper and the wild animals. And in proportion as he withdraws himself and his human claims, his sense of it grows whole and grand."

Species modesty. If we felt the kind of oneness with nature that Snyder and Berry describe, we would find it hard to think of our selves as "kings" of the universe. Black Elk teaches that we "two leggeds" are *sharing* in life "with the four leggeds and the wings of the air and all green things. . . ." We would also find it possible to learn from other species. John Lilly notes (in *Seriatim*, Spring 1977) that whales, dolphins, and porpoises have "shown a hell of a lot better survival record than we are showing today," and he asks, "What kind of interpersonal relations, ethics, philosophy has led to their survival over the last 15-million-year period? What is this mysterious business that they can do and we can't?"

Quality. Many good people feel that reverence for life is the highest

New Age value; however, I feel that beneath it and beneath all things lies what Robert Pirsig calls "Quality."

Quality is both a noun and an adjective. As an adjective—as quality behavior (or "high-quality behavior")—it refers to what Esalen's George Leonard calls the "Zen strategy of seeing equal 'religious' significance in every aspect of life, not holding ceremonial meditation to be any more or less crucial than eating or sleeping or building a wall." In Pirsig's book *Zen and the Art of Motorcycle Maintenance*, fixing a motorcycle turns out to be a higher-quality activity—for Pirsig—than attending the University of Chicago.

As a noun. Quality is much harder to define—exactly; and according to Pirsig, it can't and shouldn't be defined. It is whatever *feels* right and good to us when we're at self-development stages six or seven. If, as Erich Fromm says, reverence for life is the basis for the art of loving, then reverence for the good is the basis for the art of living, for the art of self-development.

For thousands of years people felt no need to define Quality, it was so natural a concept. But in civilized society, in order to defend the concept from the Prison (which had begun to descend), Phaedrus did try to define it. And then Aristotle redefined it as being less important than reason. And from that time on, we have been willing to do things that are "reasonable" even when they aren't any good.

Be kind to your self. Some people like to say (usually sanctimoniously), "I won't get a massage until every single person can afford one." Or they'll say that people who take yoga classes are being "self-indulgent." But if you say, "I've had a rotten week, I need a stiff drink," you probably won't be criticized. Same if you say, "Thank God it's Friday, tomorrow I can go to the football game."

The implication is that if you spend your dollars on alcohol, that's okay; but if you spend them trying to feel better in a healthy way, like with massage, that's not okay. If you spend your dollars sitting passively in a stadium, watching football, that's "relief"; but if you spend them on a yoga class, trying to get in touch with the non-material states of consciousness, that's "self-indulgence."

In Prison society we practically consider self-abuse to be a moral virtue. And a virtue that somehow makes us "one of the folks." (Philip Slater goes so far as to suggest that we *collect* tokens of suffering—because they make us feel so good.) In New Age society, kindness to self would follow naturally from the self-development ethic. It is, or was, already the basis for one of our most profound religious truths, "Love thy neighbor as thyself"; the idea being that you can't love your neighbor if you don't love your self.

Part V
NEW AGE SOCIETY

The chapters in this part are about the way we might want to live after we've begun to get free of the Prison and its institutions; after we've begun to use, and not just intellectually understand, the transmaterial worldview; after we've begun to live by the New Age ethics and values. It covers quite a bit of ground: alternatives to the Prison, biolithic institutions, synergic power, community self-reliance, and the planetary guidance system (the New Age economy—and the emerging New Age economic theory—are dealt with in Part VI).

Some of the alternatives proposed here could be implemented tomorrow (some are being implemented now, if you know where to look), others not for a hundred years or more. But all of them have this in common: *all of them are rooted in present trends*, are extrapolations based on present trends. Minority trends, to be sure, but we *could* go in the direction set forth below—that's my point. It is not a utopian dream.

CHAPTER 13

New Age Alternatives to the Prison

Androgynous Attitudes: the New Age Alternative to Patriarchal Attitudes

In Chapter 3, we saw that patriarchal attitudes turn us into half-people, into "men" or "women." In New Age society, our attitudes, values, and beliefs wouldn't be based on our sexual identities. They would be sex-free, or "androgynous."

Androgynous attitudes cannot be typed. They are simply the attitudes that are natural to us, to our temperaments and personalities, after we've begun to get free of sex-roles and after we've begun to meet our needs for self-actualization and self-transcendence. Certainly men would learn to be more in touch with their feelings and their bodies, to be less aggressive, and so on; and women would learn to feel more independent, more assertive. But beyond that, our androgynous attitudes would be as varied and as protean as New Age society itself.

June Singer, a Jungian psychologist, puts it nicely when she says, "We need to think of ourselves as no longer exclusively 'masculine' or exclusively 'feminine' but rather as whole beings in whom the opposite qualities are ever-present." The power of androgyny "lies in the openness to the opposites within oneself—not by an effort to integrate that which is strange or foreign, but by awakening to the reality that the opposites have been there all along, and would coexist in harmony if only we did not drive a wedge between them." Singer's conclusion: "We do not become androgynous; we already are. It is necessary only to let ourselves be ourselves. . . . This may seem like the easiest thing in the world, but . . . there may be much to *unlearn* in the process."

Why is it important to become androgynous? Why is it a New Age goal? Simply because we can't become whole without becoming androgynous. If we want to become whole, then we're going to have to get back in touch with that part of our selves that has been lost to us through sex-role training and patriarchal attitudes.

Matriarchal attitudes are occasionally proposed as the New Age alternative to patriarchal attitudes (see, e.g., Jane Alpert, "Mother Right," *Ms.*, Aug. 1973). Androgynous attitudes would—or could—include many traditionally matriarchal attitudes (among them compassion, unconditional love, supportiveness, and generosity), but they would—or could—include much else besides. The point is simply that they be free of patriarchal attitudes (and that they embody Quality, that is, the good as we perceive it at self-development stages six and seven). For example, many religious mythologies provided a "primal androgyne" that managed to combine male and female energies in a synthesis that was greater than the sum of its parts; even the symbols of Yin and Yang were united at one time in the holy woman T'ai Yuan, who was an androgynous figure; and I am sure that many of us would try for such a synthesis in our own lives.

Spirituality: the New Age Alternative to Egocentricity

At least sixteen people in Chapter 27—community organizers and political scientists among them—have called for the creation of a new spirituality. We need a new spirituality if we want to get beyond the isolation, pride, and guilt that egocentricity imposes (see Chapter 3), and if we want to have a foundation for constructing a new theodicy, a new and more believable rationale for life's suffering that can give us back our sense that life is worth living—and worth preserving (see end of Chapter 6). We need a new spirituality if we want to get in touch with the spiritual and religious states of consciousness.

But why do New Age writers and activists speak of a "new" spirituality? Surely the Judeo-Christian tradition isn't dead?

Wendell Berry has found in John Collis's *The Triumph of the Tree* an almost perfect statement of what is "new" about New Age spirituality: "Both polytheism and monotheism have done their work. The images are broken, the idols are all overthrown. This is now regarded as a very irreligious age. But perhaps it only means that the mind is moving from one state to another.

"The next stage is not a belief in many gods. It is not a belief in one god. It is not a belief at all—not a conception in the intellect. It is an extension of consciousness so that we may *feel* God, or, if you will, an experience of harmony, an intimation of the Divine, which will link us again with *animism*, the experience of unity lost at the in-break of self-consciousness."

It is of course that "experience of unity" that can break down our egocentricity. And introduce us to the spiritual and religious states of consciousness.

There are a number of paths that can help us return to that experience of unity, that can help us feel at home again in the spiritual and religious states of consciousness. In *Unfinished Animal* Theodore Roszak lists over 150 such paths! Here I just want to mention eight general *kinds* of paths—and make one general observation. A spiritual path is valid *for us* if it is appropriate to *our* needs as *we our selves* define them. Whether or not it seems "glamorous" or "sophisticated" to others is not the point at all. (In this sense, a spiritual path is just like any other "appropriate technology!") Still, Collis is right; for most of us the old images *are* broken, forever. And so most of us are going to have to follow a path that is—for Americans, at least—genuinely new.

For example:

Judeo-Christian revivals. Chassidic Judaism; contemplative Christianity; "charismatic" or "evangelical" congregations in mainstream churches. . . .

The Eastern philosophies and religions. Zen, Tibetan Buddhism, Tantra, Vedanta, Yoga, Sufism, Subud, Baha'i, Taoism, Sikhism. . . .

Mass movements. Transcendental meditation ("TM"), Kundalini Yoga ("3HO"), Krishna Consciousness, Integral Yoga, Ananda Marga. . . .

Spiritual teachers and healers. Rabbi Shlomo Carlebach, Earlyne Chaney, Sri Chinmoy, Bubba Free John, J. Krishnamurti, Bhagwan Shree Rajneesh, Ram Dass, Jane Roberts, David Spangler, Patricia Sun, Vimala Thakar, Chogyam Trungpa. . . .

The trans-material therapies. Jungian psychiatry, Psychosynthesis, est, Arica, Mind Dynamics, the Living Love Way, Actualizations. . . .

The body therapies. Many of us have found that shiatsu massage, ta'i chi, "sensory awareness," rolfing, etc., can put us in touch with the spiritual and religious states of consciousness. Stanley Keleman, a teacher of "bioenergetics," writes, "I understand spirituality as a heightening of the excitatory processes of the human animal. The religious experience . . . is our vivid experiencing, and it is the vividness of what we experience. Its depth and intensity correspond with how deep and intense our [bodily] streamings are. . . . To experience our streamings is the spiritual experience."

Native people's religion. North American Indian spirituality has inspired many of us and has a lot to teach us. Doug Boyd, who has studied the Hindu mystic Swami Rama and the Shoshone medicine man Rolling Thunder, reports that "Swami Rama's method is to work internally, to withdraw the mind's attention from external perceptions. . . . Rolling Thunder's way is to work externally, to sharpen the senses, to embrace the world. . . . Through interaction with his environment [Rolling Thunder] learns about the natural world and then comes to understand his own nature. He becomes one with nature, one with himself, one with the Great Spirit." Vine Deloria, Jr., well-known native writer and activist, has argued that Christianity, like Marxism and liberalism, is a European import, and that North Americans must seek God here, within their own land. All true religions, he says, are intimately connected with the land of their people, and the North American religion should be no exception. "It is the spirit of the continent . . . that shines through the Indian anthologies and glimmers in the Indian communities in grotesque and tortured forms. . . ."

The new paganism. Deloria calls Christianity a European religion; Tom Robbins calls it an *Eastern* religion, and argues that it was imposed on Western Europe by the Church—imposed on our own, natural, pagan religion which we had been celebrating for thousands of years.

"The Old Religion," says Andrea Dworkin, "celebrated sexuality, fertility, nature and women's place in it. . . ." Its central figure, says

Robbins, was "a hairy, merry deity who loved music and dancing and good food." It was nature-centered and woman-centered. There were priestesses, wise women, midwives, goddesses, sorceresses. "There was no dogma; each priestess interpreted the religion in her own fashion."

The Old Religion couldn't be reestablished in New Age society, but we *could* adapt its nature- and woman-centeredness to our own new priorities and concerns. In fact, both these things are already happening.

Nature-centeredness has an obvious parallel in our growing recognition that the quality of our connection to the environment—both natural and people-made—has a lot to do with our spiritual health and spiritual growth. Tom Bender would have us "spiritualize" our surroundings by building things that are in harmony with nature and with natural forces. In his novel about a New Age society (which he calls "Ecotopia"), Ernest Callenbach has his narrator see "a quite ordinary-looking young man, not visibly drugged, lean against a large oak and mutter, 'Brother Tree!'" (And across the sea, in monolithic Russia, in a film called *The Red Snowball Tree*, Vasily Shukshin has his hero kiss the Russian birches, while the camera "lovingly caresses the flowing rivers and rambling fields of the Russian countryside." See Hedrick Smith.)

Significantly, among those of us at self-development stages six and seven, religious worship has already begun to rely less on the tradition of the sky god and more on the tradition of the earth goddess. As sociologist Robert Bellah sees it, "The sky religions emphasize the paternal, hierarchical, legalistic and ascetic, whereas the earth tradition emphasizes the maternal, communal, expressive and joyful aspects of existence. . . . The earth tradition is tuned to cosmic harmonies, vibrations and astrological influences . . . [and it] expresses itself not through impersonal bureaucracy or the isolated nuclear family but through collectives, communes, tribes and large extended families."

Mary Daly, a Boston feminist, believes that the new spirituality can learn even more from the feminist movement, that the current "unfolding of woman-consciousness is an intimation of the endless unfolding of God." In this view, God isn't a noun (let alone a gender) but a verb, an endless Being; and those of us who are trying to develop our selves are at One with God, because we are challenging our own non-"Being" in Prison society and actively participating in God the Verb.

Multiple Vision: the New Age Alternative to Scientific Single Vision

In Chapter 3, we saw that our narrowly scientific way of seeing the world requires us to ignore many of the insights of the Eastern philosophies, and many of the signals that are coming to us from the right side of our brains. And in Chapter 11 we saw that the emerging trans-material worldview recognizes that there are at least three other *essential* states of consciousness besides the material, and that the material state itself is far too narrowly understood. In light of all this, it isn't going too far to say—as many Eastern philosophers do—that the "reality" that scientific single vision reveals to us is so narrow as to be an illusion.

In New Age society, scientific single vision would be replaced by "multiple vision"—by a way of seeing the world that takes all four states of consciousness into account. Different New Age thinkers have proposed different versions of this "multiple vision" science, but all of them would agree on the main point: that we need to learn to combine the functions of the left and right sides of the brain. We desperately need to learn to be intellectual *and* intuitive, analytic *and* holistic, active *and* receptive, etc.

Beyond that, there seems to be a wide measure of agreement with some other points, recently summed up succinctly by psychologist Robert Ornstein. He says that we need to recognize the "importance of consciousness itself as an object of inquiry"; that we are "sensitive and permeable to subtle sources of energy from geophysical and human forces"; and that we need to greatly expand our concept of the normal. Until recently, for instance, it was considered "paranormal" to be able to control our nervous systems, despite the fact that yogis had been doing it for thousands of years.

But beyond these points there are some important differences of opinion, and they seem to be rooted in this: Fritjof Capra believes that there can be no synthesis between science and what he insists on calling mysticism, that science and mysticism are "two complementary manifestations of the human mind. . . . Science does not need mysticism and mysticism does not need science; but [people] need both." On the other hand, Theodore Roszak, Willis Harman, and many other New Age thinkers, would change the scientific enterprise itself: would change its *purposes*, its *methods*, and its *scope*. Multiple vision, says Roszak, "can never be achieved . . . by processing young scientists through an additional course of study in Taoist nature mysticism. It's a matter of changing the fundamental sensibility of scientific thought."

Purposes. The task, says Roszak, is to "deepen the personality of the knower" rather than merely or primarily to "increase what is known." Harman adds that multiple vision science "would aim to . . . guide individuals and society in their efforts to discover new realms of experience and potentiality and to foster actively the growth and evolution of society and individuals."

Methods. According to Harman, multiple vision science "would foster open, participative inquiry; it would diminish the dichotomy between observer and observed, investigator and subject. Investigations of subjective experience would be based on collaborative trust and 'exploring together', rather than on the sort of manipulative deception that has characterized much past research in the social sciences." According to Roszak, multiple vision science "would surely end some lines of research entirely out of repugnance for their reductionism, insensitivity and social risk."

Scope. To Harman, multiple vision science would encompass "objective experience," "religion," and "philosophy, literature and the arts." To William Irwin Thompson, it would encompass "math," "spirituality," and "music." To Robert Pirsig it would encompass "conventional science," "religion" and "art." To each of these writers, then, multiple vision science would be based on a *fusion* of the material, spiritual/religious, and mythic states of consciousness.

There have already been at least three carefully thought-out proposals along these lines. In 1972 and again in 1975, Dr. Charles Tart called for the development of what he likes to term "state-specific sciences." According to Tart, single-vision science is a state-specific science, specific to our ordinary state of consciousness; and each of the other states of consciousness would require its own state-specific science. "Scientists might want to investigate . . . internal phenomena of the particular [state], the interaction of people in that [state], the interaction of that [state] with other [states], and so on. . . ."

In 1977, Philip Slater observed that single-vision science tends to assume that everything is "separate, independent, and unrelated to everything else until proven otherwise." He proposed that New Age science begin with the opposite assumption—"accept every relation as self-evident unless proven otherwise." In other words, assume the unity of things as postulated by the spiritual and religious states of consciousness, but also leave room for sorting things out by material-state trial and error. "[This assumption] would force science to abandon its current disputatious style and concentrate on the *quality* of the various influences. . . . It would also make for a different kind of technology—one less concerned with trying to push the environment around."

In a speech at Georgia State University in April 1978, Dr. Willis Harman made his boldest proposal yet for a "noetic" science (defined as a "science of subjective experience"). Harman stated that conventional science assumes that "whatever can be known about the human mind will ultimately be learned by studying the physical brain. In a science of subjective experience, on the other hand, consciousness is the primary datum. Mind is not brain. The strong implication of the range of psychic phenomena . . . is the unlimited potentiality of mind. The same principle is implicit in all the world's religious traditions, ancient and modern, Eastern and Western. Mind and spirit are ultimately dominant over physical reality."

What might our new multiple-vision science produce in the way of insight? Thompson summarizes what might be called the conventional wisdom of multiple-vision science: (1) "There is intelligent life in the universe beyond earth"; (2) "The Gods do not talk *to* us, they play *through* us *with* our history"; (3) "Our religious myths are the detritus of the lost history of earth"; and (4) "Matter, energy and consciousness form a continuum" (as in the worldview of the Hopi Indians). Alyce and Elmer Green, a pair of psychologists who have come as close as anyone to working in this new mode, hypothesize (see Boyd) that a "unique energy field, a 'field of mind', must surround the planet"; that "each individual mind with its extension, the body, must have the inherent capability of focusing energy for manipulation" of both internal and external "events"; and that "the individual mind and the general 'field of mind' meet in the unconscious."

The Cooperative Mentality: the New Age Alternative to the Bureaucratic Mentality

In Chapter 3, we saw that our bureaucratic mentalities and our large, bureaucratic-hierarchical organizations are doing us all a lot of harm. It should not be surprising, then, that New Age thinkers and activists have been experimenting with a number of attitudes and organizational forms that can take us "beyond bureaucracy."

I-You attitudes. In Prison society most of our relationships are of the I-It type: the other person becomes an object, a means, a number. This is especially true in the work world (and helps to explain why some New Age people are in favor of replacing, e.g., supermarket tellers with computers—a supermarket teller could probably *never* escape being treated like an object). The anarchist alternative to this situation is to convert as many relationships as possible to the I-Thou type: relationships of intimate friendship. In the "real world," however, as Ruben Nelson points out, "there simply is not enough time to develop, test, and sustain friendships with the large number of people whom we know and with whom we deal." Therefore, Nelson and many other New Age writers have suggested that we convert most of our relationships with people to the "I-You" type. In I-You relationships, says Nelson, "we acknowledge that the other is a person and potentially a friend, although for a variety of reasons, he/she will not be so with us."

David Spangler would have us learn to share "a spirit of familiarity, a spirit of shared personhood, a spirit of the presence (and the potential) of connections and bonds beyond the functional." And he would have us learn "to see the 'personhood', the divine potential, of things, thus seeing things as persons rather than persons as things."

The win-win model. In Prison society we assume that those who disagree with us must necessarily be in conflict with us, and we spend a great deal of time arguing with them in order to show that "we're right" and "they're wrong." In New Age society we would acknowledge that, as economist Robert Theobald puts it, "It is possible for everybody to gain from an interaction rather than for some people to win and others to lose." We would develop "an inclusionary, win-win model," where we recognize that those who are not against us are for us. We need to understand that all of us can be better off if we share our divergent perspectives. "People are rarely wrong; rather, each person focusses on different parts of the truth, which can then be pieced together to produce a larger vision of reality. Once one understands that subjective diversity is inevitable, then one can consider differences of opinion as healthy and productive and a way of learning more rapidly."

Synergic principles. Synergic principles are those that make it possible for us to produce *more and better* when we're working together than when we're working apart—and to enjoy our selves more—and to grow. The Synergy Power Institute has recently drawn up a list of eighteen basic synergic principles that New Age organizations might want to follow and build on. Some examples:

- Embrace a set of New Age values agreed upon by members;
- Use ritual or other planned processes to keep the values in members' awareness;
- Give equal attention to the organization's external mission and to the fulfillment and growth of its members;
- Involve affected persons from the larger society in designing the organization's external mission;
- Design your organization's impact (products, services, education, etc.) upon the larger society so as to make it more receptive to New Age transformation;
- Make policy changes only after involving or at least consulting *everyone* who might be affected;
- When conflict arises, substitute "joint problem-solving" for adversary negotiations and aim for full satisfaction for all parties rather than compromise.

Synergic interactions. New Age organizations would introduce into their day-to-day functioning many of the techniques that are currently being used in the human potential movement. According to the Synergy Power Institute, members of New Age organizations would "share power and build trust by regularly and openly sharing information, feelings, desires, intentions, reservations, objections, fears, options and choices." And members would "employ rituals and-or other activities to build cohesion and intimacy within the organization." Abraham Maslow would like to see the "most basic module of social organization . . . be the equivalent of a T-group, that is, a face-to-face group moving toward intimacy and candor, valuing self-disclosure and caring feedback."

Jim and Marge Craig, co-directors of the Synergy Power Institute, tell us that human potential techniques would have many advantages. Partly for our selves alone—e.g., they would help to put us in touch with our selves—but partly for our organizations as well as our selves. For example, members of New Age organizations would learn to expand their awareness and understanding of all the needs and desires and fears that are at work in any group process; and the efficiency of the group would—in the long run—definitely increase.

The "consciousness business model." Hawthorne/Stone, a New Age-oriented real estate firm in San Francisco, says that the most important thing is to create a company environment that is conducive to raising your consciousness—about who you are, about those you work with, and about the community/country/planet that your work is serving. "If we can create an environment that's supportive, loving, fun and successful," says Marshall Thurber, president of Hawthorne/Stone, "I think other . . . companies will choose to follow suit."

By all accounts, H/S has succeeded in creating such an environment (see, e.g., David Brown, "Consciousness in Business," *New Realities* no. 3, 1977). And it has succeeded in the "other" direction too: H/S is probably earning more money per capita than any other company in America! Some of the highlights of the H/S "consciousness business model" are:

- "Begin by defining the 'purpose' of the organization. . . . H/S Purpose is 'to create and play games together transcending economic limitations in a satisfying environment'."

- "Define the common goal. A fixed goal to be achieved within a certain period of time. . . ."

- "Establish the ground rules of the organization. H/S ground rules include: to be honest in communication; to keep agreements once they're made; . . . to take responsibility for creating and supporting an abundant environment; . . . to be willing to share and support so that everyone succeeds (every act is a contribution to the whole); . . . to choose and re-choose to be together. . . ."

- "Players define their personal goals for the same period of time as the organization's overall goal. The organization then agrees to support the players' individual goals. At H/S all salaried people are required to take one 'Goals day' a month off (with full pay) to work on their personal goals (this is in addition to abundant vacations)."

Sapiential authority. The bureaucratic mentality holds that only certain people are capable of making the decisions. The cooperative mentality holds that, not only are most people capable of making the decisions, but that we should be held responsible for those decisions that we do make—and even for those decisions that we "merely" carry out (no more "I was only following orders"). Therefore, in New Age society, we would have to create institutions in which we could *refuse* to "follow orders"; in which we could exercise what Robert Theobald calls "sapiential authority."

Sapiential authority as I understand it would hold us *personally and legally responsible* for our actions in an organization—its effect would be to keep us from falling into the "agentic state of mind" that was reported on in Chapter 3. At the same time, it would give us the right to refuse to follow orders, rules, guidelines, standards, whatever—not on a whim, but if they didn't seem good and right to us (if they didn't seem like Quality orders, rules, etc.).

Theobald points out that we've already begun changing over to a system of sapiential authority here and there—e.g., a soldier is now told that he or she should refuse to obey an order "when on the basis of [his or her] own judgment, [he or she] believes it to be unlawful." He also points out that the first glimmerings of the transition to sapiential authority has made many of us fear, wrongly, that we're experiencing the end of *all* authority.

Still, that fear makes a lot more sense when it's put this way: if New Age institutions really did give us the "right to say no," how could a New Age society survive?

New Age institutions would have to agree not to fire or otherwise punish their members for exercising their sapiential authority. Their only alternative, then, would be to accommodate themselves to the special needs and perspectives of their dissident members. For their part, members would have to be willing to engage in "give and take" with their institutions; to share their views and change their views; to feel responsible not only for their own development, but for that of their institutions as well.

An easy death. As organizations get older, Kenneth Boulding observes, they tend to "harden" no matter how democratic or open-ended they might have been in the beginning. He sees only one remedy for this, the "constant death of the old. . . . The less existing organizations are protected and the easier it is for them to die," the more likely it is that the old will give way to the new, to new organizations that are sapiential and synergic and humane.

Patriotism—and Planetary Consciousness: the New Age Alternative to Nationalism

In Chapter 3, we saw that it is natural for us to identify with our communities and regions and with the planet as a whole, but not with the giant nation-state. And we mentioned some of the harm that has come to us because of our rampant nationalism.

In New Age society, community-districts and regions (contiguous community-districts) would be able to achieve as much autonomy as they liked (see Chapter 16). And governments, *all* governments, would be encouraged to cooperate on a planetary basis—to cooperate in a kind of "planetary guidance system" whose purpose would be to implement the New Age ethics and political values (see Chapter 17). And just as important: we wouldn't want or need to live vicariously through the triumphs and tragedies of our particular nation-states. Life would be too rich, too full for that.

We might then be in a position to appreciate Herbert Agar's distinction between patriotism and nationalism. Patriotism he defines as "an unselfish affection for the land of one's youth and for the people who inhabit it"; nationalism, as "selfishness glorified." And he adds: "Patriotism is like family memories and family loyalty; nationalism is like a bitter business rivalry among giant monopolies which are uncontrollable by law. . . . The more a [person] is relaxed and happy in [his or her] patriotism, the less quarrelsome [he or she] will be; but the more a [person] worships [his or her] 'national interest' the more likely [he or she] is to make war."

We might also be ready and willing to finally understand that there is no necessary conflict between national patriotism and planetary consciousness, planetary loyalty. Everyone can love the land of their youth, and everyone can at the same time "declare their allegiance to the oneness of the human family," as Planetary Citizens likes to put it. I would go so far as to say that one cannot really love the general (the human family) without also—and first—loving the particular (one's own subfamily).

The Human-Scale Outlook: the New Age Alternative
to the Big City Outlook

In Chapter 3, we saw that our big cities—cities of maybe half a million people or more—are destructive to those of us who live in them (a majority of us) by their very nature. And we saw that our big cities reinforce and perpetuate a "big city outlook" in us, a fearful and withdraw-ful way of looking at the world. In New Age society, therefore, we would want our big cities to be drastically reduced in size—and to be utterly transformed as places to live in.

This would be easily possible for two reasons. First, our big cities no longer serve any necessary purpose; Buckminster Fuller points out that big cities have been our warehouses and our factories, and neither of these functions needs to be centralized any more—if indeed they ever did. Second, in New Age society we would no longer be Prison-bound, and so we would no longer be driven to big cities for psychocultural reasons.

There would, of course, still be cities of half a million people or slightly fewer. New Age society would be nothing if not diverse, and merchants, drifters, and intellectuals would probably always prefer large cities to small ones. But most of the rest of us would probably not choose to live in cities of even this size (except for brief periods), since self-development can take many forms, and most of them require not the passionate anonymity of city life but the rootedness and warmth of human-scale community.

There would be no standard city size—though many New Age writers have said that the "ideal" city size is around 100,000 people. They have arrived at this size partly for negative reasons (the crime rate tends to take a big jump around 100,000 population) and partly for positive ones—e.g., Barbara Ward tells us that a community that's much smaller than 50–100,000 wouldn't be able to sustain the "shops, schools, entertainment, recreation and special events" that are necessary to attract visitors from elsewhere (to keep the place lively) or to satisfy the more mobile members of the local society. "It is also the scale needed to allow for smaller cultural groupings . . . to join [together] in a shared [subculture]." Still, there's nothing magical about the 100,000 figure—for example, cities don't become conspicuously more expensive, per person, until they've reached a population of 250,000 or so.

The more important question is, what would our new Prison-free dwelling places be like? And the answer is simple: they would take on every form under the sun—and I mean that literally. Just so long as the form was able to foster the New Age ethics and values. Here are some of the most talked about proposals:

Intentional communities. Some of them, certainly many more than today, would be "intentional communities"—country communes and the like—dwelling places whose purpose was to demonstrate a particular truth, reveal a particular vision.

Anthropopolis. Probably most of our New Age communities would try to break down the distinction between city and country altogether. Constantinos Doxiadis, the Greek city planner, has proposed a number of "extended cities" that would blend farms and factories, gardens and homes. Extended cities would be made up of many different-sized and independent or semi-independent communities strung together by public transit. Communities would be multidimensional and human-scale (few or no high-rises; few or no cars), but beyond that, as diverse as possible: "continuous streams of fairly intense neighbourhoods of the human scale" is how Doxiadis likes to put it. The point is that the extended city would then truly be an anthropopolis—"city of all the people"—and we could enjoy an environment of maximum community *and* maximum contact with other communities, other cultural groupings. Margaret Mead, an advocate of this approach, adds, "We rebuilt this country after World War II, and we can rebuild it again very easily."

Arcologies. Paolo Soleri, an Italian architect and student of the evolutionary thinker Teilhard de Chardin, believes that human evolution is characterized by increasing "complexification," and increasing "miniaturization." His "arcologies" (literally, architecture plus ecology) are designed to help us in our evolutionary journey; they are, therefore, cities in which everything contracts, intensifies. "Miniaturization," Soleri explains, isn't a "scaling down" or "piling up" of things so much as it is "the expulsion of those elements that go for the chastening of the urban landscape and the punishment of its dwellers. . . . By expelling, for instance, the car and the paraphernalia of its demands, 50–60 percent of the urban topography" could be "miniaturized" out of existence.

"The bridge between matter and spirit," says Soleri, "is matter becoming spirit"—becoming more complex, more condensed, more dense.

In practice, Soleri's arcologies would be medium-sized (population 3,000 and up), multileveled "cities in the image of [people]"; cities that were physically, ecologically, and to some extent economically self-contained . . . and carefully designed to promote face-to-face encounters. Too carefully designed, too totally planned, say some New Agers. At any rate, you owe your self a couple of hours paging through Soleri's lovingly intricate designs for these arcologies (*Arcology*, 1969). Or for $440 for five weeks you can work as a laborer-apprentice with Soleri in Arizona, where he's building the first arcology (see Chapter 27).

Tetrahedronal cities. Buckminster Fuller has proposed building floating "tetrahedronal cities," pyramid-like structures that could be "symmetrically growable as are biological systems. They may start with a thousand occupants and grow to hold [hundreds of thousands] without changing overall shape though always providing each [household] with 2,000 sq. ft. of floor space"—including 1,000 sq. ft. for a garden. "Withdrawal of materials from obsolete buildings on the land [could] permit the production of [many] of these floating cities."

The small community reborn. The movement out of our biggest cities has already begun, and surveys have shown that many more people would leave if they felt they had the chance. But New Age people hope to do more than *return* to smaller places. As Arthur Morgan, founder of Community Service, Inc., puts it, "The small community of the future will be . . . a new creation, uniting the values of both [the small town and the city], and largely avoiding their limitations."

Why would the small community be a "new creation"? Largely because of the "new expectations" of those who would move there, say James and Carolyn Robertson in their book, *The Small Towns Book* (1978). There would be a move away from the values of efficiency-for-efficiency's sake, growth for growth's sake, etc., and toward such values as enoughness, self-reliance/cooperation and personal responsibility. Peter van Dresser, an advocate of the "human scale" whose writings predate Illich's and Schumacher's by at least two decades, puts it this way (in *Solar Age*, Nov. 1976): "We [would] not only . . . decentralize, but . . . recentralize in effective smaller communities capable of organizing their resources and exchange patterns within defined regions of natural resources. I think of these as micro-urban centers, . . . urban in the sense of representing a great deal of knowledge and great ability in a small scale—as opposed to the conventional small town . . . which is nothing but a distributing center for products produced elsewhere" (see Chapter 16).

CHAPTER 14

New Age Alternatives to Our Monolithic Institutions

In Part II we saw that the Prison is institutionalized by means of monolithic institutions that establish a monopoly not of brands but of products and processes: in healing there's a monopoly of "professionalized" medical care; in transportation, of rapid transit; in education, of universal and compulsory schooling; and so on. In New Age society, we would be free of the Prison, and so we would want to replace our monolithic institutions with what I call biolithic institutions.

Biolithic institutions would not require us to "do things their way," would allow for the existence of institutional and technological alternatives—we would enjoy, as Ivan Illich puts it, "freedom from monopoly in the satisfaction of any basic need." Biolithic institutions would offer us the widest possible choice of goods and services, information, and technology. They would allow us—Illich again—"the freedom to make things among which [we] can live, to give shape to them according to [our] own tastes."

Biolithic institutions wouldn't do away with professional medical care, cars, etc. (not necessarily, anyway), but in a biolithic society these things—because they tend to be monolithic—would have to be definitely subordinate to products and processes that fostered diversity (by fostering self-reliance, say, or by being ecologically more sane). Each New Age society would have to determine its own *point of maximum synergy* between industrial-era institutions and technologies and those institutions and technologies that fostered individual and community self-reliance (for an introduction to the concept of synergy, see Chapter 15).

Biolithic institutions would increase our ability to develop our selves and our self-reliance, would encourage our capacity to cooperate with others, would be ecologically more sane, and would only be compatible with a non-nuclear defense. Biolithic institutions are obviously necessary if we hope to live by the New Age ethics and values! Necessary but not sufficient: for we would also have to want to *use* the opportunities that our biolithic institutions would give us. And no institutional arrangement, no matter how life-oriented, can ever give us that.

Biolithic transport wouldn't eliminate cars altogether, though some *communities* might. But if we wanted a diverse society we would have to devise a form (or forms) of transportation in which the car was definitely secondary. These might be as diverse as the communities that adopted them. Probably one alternative form would be a much-improved system of rapid transit—but as we saw in Chapter 7, rapid transit doesn't really get us away from the Prison-bound needs for speed and efficiency. So I would suspect that a more popular substitute for reliance on the automobile would be a system of bicycles and pedicabs, complemented perhaps by a system of busses to bring people in from beyond the city limits (see Greater Philadelphia Bicycle Coalition).

According to Barbara Ward, a telecommunications system would make it possible for us to do away with much of our transport—including most long-distance transport. A telecommunications system would also make it possible for us to radically decentralize our work places—again, making it more possible for us to come to work on foot or by bicycle. (If we were free of the Prison, it wouldn't much matter if we came to work with wind-blown hair, or rain-spattered pants—we might even enjoy bicycling through the rain and cold.)

I also suspect that a maximum speed limit would be set on travel between cities (say, 35 mph)—partly to save on energy, but mostly to get the pace of life back under control. In his new book Charles Reich writes, "I learned that if I slowed down, things in my immediate surroundings became more interesting, more capable of giving me good feelings."

Biolithic healing wouldn't do away with professional, institutional care, but basic medical information would be made available to all of us—and so would the tools that we might need to care for our selves and to cure our selves of most diseases. Paramedics might be trained to make house calls or to set up shop in local communities (possibly through neighborhood "health centers"). Oriental and herbal medical practices would be fostered and encouraged (for the extraordinary possibilities of these, see—respectively—Naboru Muramoto, *Healing Ourselves*, 1973, and Jethro Kloss, *Back to Eden*, 1971).

Just as important, health would be *redefined*. Toward the end of his life Abraham Maslow spoke of "full humanness" rather than health, and Eric Utne states (in *New Age*, Sept. 1974), "Health lies in the presence of something rather than in the *lack* of physical disease or pain." What is this something? To Utne it's our ability to be fully in touch with body, heart, and mind; to Philip Slater it's our ability to connect with others. Utne says that "we are all healers," that we should look to see what's right with self and others and give it recognition. Elisabeth Kubler-Ross would have us redefine tragedies as "gifts, virtual gifts, which help you understand the meaning of life."

One of the directors of Innerface, Rick Ingrasci, has drawn a useful distinction between the "medical establishment" and the "holistic health movement." Established medicine, he tells us (in *New Age*, May 1978), is a product of the "dualistic, mechanistic worldview which has dominated western thought for the past 2,000 years." The holistic worldview, on the other hand, "sees humankind as an integral part of nature," and health "as the dynamic, creative process of living in harmony with nature. . . . In holistic health the emphasis is on the functional relationships among the various aspects of the whole person. Disease is understood to be a signal of disharmony or imbalance among the aspects of our being; it is looked upon as a teacher, a form of feedback which allows us to self-correct our life course and choose to grow in more positive, wholesome directions." Incidentally, a recent "Report on the Health of Canadians," by the Canadian Minister of Health, has concluded that life-style changes are the most important single factor in reducing a disease—for all major age groups and in all major diseases studied. The second most important factor is change of environment. Less importance is placed on health services, and the least significant factor is medical research. (See *New Realities,* no. 6, 1978.)

Biolithic learning wouldn't do away with all schools—but their nature and their purposes would be totally transformed.

New Age schools wouldn't be compulsory, wouldn't rank students, and wouldn't lock students into, as John Holt puts it, "a prescribed sequence of learning determined in advance." Moreover, laws would have to be passed stating that no one would be denied an available job solely on the basis of school credentials, and whenever a credential was needed for a job there would have to be a way to get this credential without going to school. (One way might be by extending the idea of apprenticeship; another, by extending the idea of the equivalency exam.)

At the same time, the curriculum of our schools would have to be transformed. Monolithic schools, true to the materialist worldview, focus on what they like to call "the basics"—the three R's. Biolithic schools, true to the trans-material worldview, would focus on *their* basics: would focus on the development of the personality as a whole (body, emotions, imagination, intuition, will, *as well as* mind) and would help us get in touch with what Roberto Assagioli has called our "transpersonal essence" and I earlier (Chapter 11) called our "space beyond conditioning."

According to Jack Canfield and Paula Klinek, co-directors of the Institute for Wholistic Education, our schools could nurture the whole self by making systematic use of "humanistic" and "transpersonal" methods of teaching that are already in use here and there.

The field of humanistic education has developed techniques "to help people validate themselves, to communicate more effectively with others, to enhance their self-concepts, to ask directly for what they want, to clarify their values, to express their feelings, to celebrate their bodies, to use their will, and to take responsibility for their lives." The newer field of transpersonal education acknowledges and fosters our non-material states of consciousness through working with forms such as dreams, meditation, "guided imagery," chanting, centering, and fantasy literature. Canfield and Klinek state, "Now is the time to combine both of these focuses, for the New Age means integrating the soul and the personality" (see *New Age,* Feb. 1978).

According to Jerry Fletcher, a New Age-oriented "Education Policy Analyst" at the Department of Health, Education and Welfare, our schools might want to encourage their students to develop a personal set of goals, "a personal life through-line for themselves," and—just as important—our schools might then want to help their students "work through what is between themselves and the goals." In a paper presented to the American Educational Research Association annual conference (March 1978) Fletcher stated: "The goals established by students would be related to blocked areas of their lives: developing, improving, or repairing relationships; accomplishing something such as getting a job (or making a present job more fulfilling), making an athletic team, or doing well on a college entrance examination.

"Once the statements of intention were developed, students would set about to create those things in their lives. For most, the next step would be some form of stretch: actually taking the first move toward dealing with an aspect of their lives that was less than satisfactory. Each stretch would be worked out in conjunction with, and would be acceptable to, the teachers. Then support groups would be formed to assist each other in accomplishing the stretches. In particular, failure would be O.K. The student would just be encouraged to learn whatever the lessons were, and try it again."

Despite these institutional transformations, many New Age people might choose to rely primarily on self-motivated learning (after all, many New Age families might themselves be producing well-developed young people). At different times in their lives, whenever it felt right (made sense) to them, many New Age people might choose to enter into what Ivan Illich calls a "learning web"—a series of community-based educational networks that could help us gain access to information and understandings *outside* of the regular school system. Networks might be run at one-hundredth the cost of public schools and universities if they consisted simply of (a) bulletins that would allow us to describe the learning activities we wanted to engage in (would help us find partners); (b) bulletins that would allow us to list our skills and experience and the conditions under which we were willing to share our skills; and (c) bulletins that would allow us to find the things we were interested in—things stored in museums, laboratories, etc. (Call it premature, but The Learning Exchange, P.O. Box 920, Evanston, Ill. 60204, has been running something similar to Illich's learning web since 1972.)

According to Michael Rossman, some of us might go so far as to create "learning families," supportive groups "flexible enough to be seminar, action group, economic collective, playground and hospital."

Biolithic housing would be characterized, above all, by its diversity. Yes, some buildings might still be put up by "developers" (following stringent community guidelines). But those of us who wanted to make our own homes would be encouraged, not hounded—Ivan Illich suggests that all self-builders be given "access to some minimum of physical space, to water, some basic building elements, some convivial tools ranging from power drills to mechanized push-carts, and, probably, to some limited credit." "Making our own"—as River, a rural self-builder, likes to put it—would come to be seen as a process of healing and growth, and the home would come to be seen "as a natural extension of the creative vision . . . of those who will live within its walls" (among some New Agers this is already happening—see River's remarkable book, *Dwelling*, 1974, and see Cornerstones, Inc., in Chapter 27).

At the same time, *community* building would take on a life of its own. New Age architect Hassan Fathy has proposed a system of co-operative design and construction that would cut present-day construction costs by up to 85 percent—and have many other advantages besides. Architects would be trained to help people design their own structures; contractors, subcontractors and imported labor would be replaced by community labor at the standard minimum wage; buildings would be made of cheap, readily available local materials; and emphasis would be placed on intuitive decision-making rather than on "rationalization" of the building process, and on the creation of beauty.

An elementary school was recently built along these lines in northern California, despite stiff opposition from the construction and teamsters' unions. According to Colin Kowal (in *Seriatim*, Spring 1977), "The actual construction of the school was an epic story of community participation. . . . Hundreds of people with a great diversity of skills worked on the school and taught others their know-how. . . . Children dug ditches, planted flowers and fruit trees, and seeded and mulched the grass. . . . Highlights of the building include . . . stained glass windows, hand-crafted tiles, hand-carved beams . . . and a massive stone fireplace." Cost of the building? Twenty percent *less* than the next lowest bid received by the school board.

Biolithic religion would retain our churches—but most New Agers would supplement or even replace their church-going with many other religious and spiritual activities.

Ivan Illich foresees "the face-to-face meeting of families around a table, rather than the impersonal attendance of a crowd around an altar," and would have many, possibly millions of laypeople be ordained for this purpose. The Findhorn community has developed a spiritual practice called "attunement," and the people around *Woman-Spirit* Magazine, a practice called "energy re-sourcement"; both these practices would probably become common (see Chapter 11). Most important of all, perhaps, our surroundings would become "spiritualized" as we learned to see things through the trans-material worldview—the world would once again be seen as a sacred place (but not, this time, *only* as a sacred place!).

The biolithic economy would provide alternatives for those of us who wanted to do things that could not be structured into jobs. Some New Age economies might provide free essentials for all, or nearly-free essentials along with easily obtainable day-a-week-type employment; other New Age economies might provide free access to land and easy access to tools; still other New Age economies might provide a guaranteed subsistence income.

Even now—as Tom Bender has recently pointed out (in deMoll and Coe, eds.)—we "can work for ourselves (self-employment). . . . Or we can demand less and work less (self-restraint). . . . Self-employment avoids the division of interest between worker and management. You've no one to get mad at but yourself, and there's no profit in trying to pull one over on yourself. . . . Self-restraint takes us another important step towards surmounting divisive conflicts of interest. Demanding less and thereby avoiding unnecessary production and consumption lessens our demands upon our resources and each other," and upon our grandchildren.

Biolithic sexual relationships and commitments would be incredibly diverse. Monogamy, heterosexuality, and two-person marriage would remain—but no longer as the only "normal" relationships, or even (in some communities, anyway) the most common ones.

Compulsive heterosexuality would give way to androgyny, and so there would be room for a wide range of love-sex relationships—finding a good person (or persons) would be all that mattered. Compulsive monogamy would give way to many different kinds of sexual patternings—the one(s) we chose for our selves would depend entirely on our own needs and wants, which would probably vary over time. Conscious monogamy would remain, as one choice among many. Similarly, compulsive marriage would give way to many different kinds of union between (or among) people, some permanent, some temporary; some exclusive, others "open"—but all would be consciously chosen, and all would be in keeping with the New Age ethics and values!

Formal marriage might remain, but its content would change substantially. For example: Anaïs Nin says that men and women would stop struggling against each other for power, and learn, instead, "the subtle art of oscillation. . . . Neither strength nor weakness is a fixed quality. We all have our days of strength and our days of weakness."

At one point on the New Age spectrum, Ananda Cooperative Village has been developing "spiritual marriage." In open marriage, says Nalini (in *Communities*, Nov./Dec. 1975), growth is defined as the process of learning to relate to more and more people; in spiritual marriage growth "is defined inwardly, in terms of *depth*—the depth of one's relationship with one other person and with [his or her] higher Self, or God."

Other unions among people might dispense with "marital ties" altogether; some communities might not even issue marriage licenses. Robert Thamm believes that, in the long run, the communal or cooperative family is the only real alternative to the "ultimate fragmentation of the nuclear system," that is, to living alone. (It's already happening—between 1960 and 1971 the number of people living in unrelated groups jumped by over 40 percent.) "As the importance of our marital ties diminishes," says Thamm, "groups of adults and children will form living units based upon friendship ties. These ties may or may not include sexual involvement."

The cooperative (or "polycentric") family would have many advantages, according to Thamm. "Total sexual-emotional involvement between two people will be modified to partial involvement among a few. This pattern will prevent both our restricted gratification and our overdependence on one person, . . . and jealous possessiveness will evolve into a loving concern." Sex and age roles would (or at least, could) be completely broken down. And if we wanted to leave for some reason, whether temporarily or permanently, the stability of the family wouldn't be threatened—its continuity could be maintained.

The Kerista group, in San Francisco, is setting up experimental "superfamilies" of twenty-four adults each. In their introductory book- let they write, "The adult members of a superfamily have equally deep relationships with each of their twenty-three partners"—23 primary relationships! (For more information write: Storefront Classroom Community, P.O. Box 1174, San Francisco 94101.)

The biolithic family would be very different from the monolithic family, as you can see from the above. And so would its "product," our children.

If the *quality* of the nuclear bond were altered in a New Age direction, we would be better models for our kids, and we wouldn't need to use them as love or help or hate objects. Better yet, we would feel good about giving them as many "adult" responsibilities as they wanted—about giving them the opportunity to explore the world on their own (see Chapter 24.) At the very least, we would be willing to hold them and to openly express our affections for them . . . partly to keep them from falling into the "stroke economy."

If the *bond itself* were altered—expanded—so that there were many nurturers, not just one or two, then we would have an even greater opportunity to give our young people Prison-free and stroke-economy- free upbringings. If we felt unhappy or upset, our young people would have many other sources of love to turn to—so they wouldn't grow up fearing the loss of love (according to Philip Slater, that fear leads directly to the stroke economy). And if we were sharing our nurturing duties, we would find it relatively easy to offer unconditional love and respect to our young people, and that would make it even more pos- sible for them to grow up free of the fear of the loss of love, free of the "withdrawal of love" technique of child-rearing. (Psychologists like Abraham Maslow and Carl Rogers are convinced that unconditional love and respect are the absolutely necessary prerequisites for self- development.)

Biolithic technology wouldn't necessarily do away with all large- scale, complex, capital- and resource-intensive technologies. "Biolithic" means "oriented to life," and biolithic technologies would be all those ways of doing things that were able to help New Age communities meet what they considered to be their life needs. Some New Age communities might define their life needs in such a way as to exclude all large-scale production. But probably most communities would hold, with Ivan Illich, that small-scale production can be "supplemented by industrial outputs that will have to be designed and often manufac- tured beyond direct community control. Autonomous activity can be rendered both more effective and more decentralized by using such industrially-made tools as bicycles, printing presses, [tape] recorders, or X-ray equipment. . . ." Not to mention computer typesetters! In the same vein, social philosopher James Ogilvy likes to distinguish between "paratechnology" and the technology of "totalitarian limitation." Ogilvy writes: "The rape of technology is no answer to the rape of nature by technology misused. To transcend one-sided dependence on either technology or nature a paratechnology is necessary . . . to work *beside* technology in order to make use of its real gains and . . . to work *against* the gross defects that obscure those gains." *Rain* co-editor Lee Johnson has an interesting term for the ideology behind a sharply limited/limiting technology: "technological Jeffersonianism."

Biolithic technology would, then, most usually be a balance (or synergy) between certain kinds of "high" technology and what is currently known as "appropriate" or "alternative" technology (A.T. for short). There have been a number of attempts to list the central characteristics of A.T., and my attempt, below, is based on previous lists by: Tom Bender (co-editor of *Rain*), Jim Benson (of the Institute for Ecological Policies), David Dickson, William Ellis (editor of *Tranet*), Karl Hess, Amory Lovins (of Friends of the Earth), E. F. Schumacher, and John Todd (of the New Alchemists).

Appropriate technology should:

- be small scale;
- be low cost;
- be easy to understand;
- be durable;
- be easy to maintain;
- be nonviolent—not even potentially dangerous to people;
- be sustainable with renewable energy resources and materials recycling;
- protect the existing natural habitat and the viability of existing ecosystems;
- enrich the human habitat;
- reduce dependency among individuals, communities, regions, nations;
- substitute human resources for energy and material ones;
- generate meaningful employment; be skill- as well as labor-intensive;
- be designed on the basis of ecological and social considerations rather than those of economic efficiency;
- be operated nonhierarchically;
- be operated in consultative conjunction with anyone affected by it;
- provide support for our social, emotional, psychological, and spiritual growth;
- reduce the need for centralized government and other politically remote institutions;
- permit the evolution of small decentralist communities;
- be diverse;
- be genuinely preferred to other kinds of technology by workers and society alike.

This list represents something less than a perfect synthesis, since the eight writers manage to contradict each other in various ways—some of them might even claim that my definition of biolithic technology is the "real" definition of A.T. Certainly there's no difference in the sense that, as David Dickson puts it, "The main importance of [A.T.] does not lie in the particular solutions which may be offered to certain problems. Rather it is in the approach that they represent, that technology should be designed to meet human needs and resources—and not the other way around."

New Age communities would be responsible for choosing their own particular mix of technologies according to what they felt were their own needs and priorities—but always in the context of the New Age ethics and political values. Specifically, if a community wanted to charter or develop a "high" technology industry, it would also have to adopt an extremely frugal life-style, to cut down on energy and resource use, or pay a special tax to an appropriate planetary body for using up more than its fair share of the world's energy or resources. The tax might be paid in the form of a certain percentage of whatever the energy- and resource-intensive industry produced—thereby helping to make it possible for other communities to obtain the printing presses, tape recorders, X-ray machines, etc., referred to above.

Biolithic energy could *not* include nuclear, which would unavoidably threaten both the ecology and the nonviolence ethics. Nor could it involve anything more than a transitional dependence on fossil fuels. Consultant physicist Amory Lovins states that the commitment to a long-term coal economy would make "the doubling of atmospheric carbon dioxide concentration early in the next century virtually unavoidable, with the prospect then or soon thereafter of substantial or perhaps irreversible changes in global climate."

There is, however, one energy strategy that is not only consistent with the New Age ethics and values but is in some ways dependent on them, on our learning to live by them. That is what Amory Lovins calls the "soft technology" energy strategy, combining rapid development of renewable energy sources (especially solar), special transitional fossil-fuel technologies, use of thriftier technologies ("technical fixes"), and a much greater commitment to "simple living"—to car pooling, walking, opening windows, dressing to suit the weather, recycling materials, etc. Lovins suggests that in the long term, technical fixes alone—thermal insulation, more efficient furnaces, less overlighting in commercial buildings and the like—could improve our energy efficiency *by up to 80 percent*, and that even by the turn of the century we could nearly double the efficiency with which we use energy.

If we cut our energy consumption in half by becoming even slightly more New Age in our living habits, then we could construct a largely or wholly solar economy in America by the year 2025—using only those technologies that are now economic or nearly economic. And, according to Lovins, a solar economy would have many advantages over a nuclear or fossil fuel economy, or combination of the two. For example: a solar economy would cost less because of its technical simplicity, small unit size, scope for mass production, and so on; its environmental impacts—unlike those of nuclear energy or coal—are relatively small, and reversible; coal and/or nuclear energy relies on a very few high technologies whose success is by no means assured—solar distributes the technical risk among many diverse small-scale technologies, most of which are already known to work well; and unilateral adoption of solar energy by the United States could help to control nuclear proliferation—the power of the American example is still very great.

A number of New Age people have recently pointed out that a largely solar economy would not be a monolithic mirror-image of the monolithic nuclear-oil-and-coal economy. William Ophuls tells us that "the Great Plains may depend heavily on wind; New England on water, as it did in Colonial times; California on eucalyptus-tree energy plantations and offshore kelp beds; Florida on ocean currents and thermal gradients; and so on." Ophuls also suggests that a biolithic, as distinct from a merely "reactive" or "alternative" energy path, might very well lead to "a kind of multiplex, two-tier energy economy in which centralized, industrial power production will support certain key sectors but in which individuals and localities, employing a . . . combination of pre-modern and post-industrial means, will be more or less self-sufficient in the energy needed for basic subsistence."

But it can never be said too often: the point is not to *prescribe* energies or technologies for the different communities and regions. The point is merely to suggest the range of energies and technologies that might be compatible with the New Age ethics and political values.

Biolithic defense would have to be compatible with New Age society: with the New Age ethics and values (including the nonviolence ethic!), with other biolithic institutions, and with people who were oriented to life rather than things or death. And it would have to be accessible to communities and regions that wanted to put some distance between themselves and the national government (i.e., it would have to be cheap and decentralist).

New Age defense strategists have come up with at least two schemes that fit these criteria—and that promise to be at least as effective as our current "defense" strategy.

Gene Sharp, a Boston-area defense strategist, and many other New Age activists, have proposed what they call a "civilian" (not "civil") defense strategy—"civilian" because it relies on people's own sense of responsibility and worth rather than on guns. I like to call it a system of "cooperative nonviolent defense" because it relies on our ability to work together as well as responsibly, and because it would be completely useless if we were to engage in any kind of interpersonal violence.

The first thing to realize is that civilian defense does *not* mean the reduction of defense capacity. Instead, as Sharp puts it, "the changeover to civilian defense is *transarmament*—the substitution of a new defense capacity that provides deterrence and defense without conventional and nuclear military power. It also contributes to world peace, since unlike military means civilian defense cannot be used for, or be misperceived as intended for, international aggression." Mulford Sibley, a well-known exponent of "nonviolent resistance," adds that a government committed to civilian defense would, indeed, "surrender" some things—"would surrender everything likely to incite others to violence or apparently defensible only by violence. Thus, grossly disproportionate economic power, military bases and threats, . . . and imperialist control of other peoples would have to go."

What would civilian defense look like in action? If a New Age community were invaded, we could wear mourning bands, stay home, defy curfews, etc. All these actions would let the invader know that we meant to resist the occupation of our community—forever if need be. The invader's soldiers could be told that the resistance wasn't being directed against them personally, but against their attempt to take control. (That might encourage them to be less brutal than they would be if they thought they might be killed.)

Eventually there might have to be more substantial forms of noncooperation. For example, we might simply refuse to carry out the invader's orders. Or, for example, attempts to exploit our (relatively paltry!) economic capacities might be met with limited strikes, the "disappearance" of New Agers who were in positions of authority, etc.

Sharp acknowledges that, in the long run, injuries and deaths in retaliation for such behavior might be common. But he is convinced that they would be less common than if we were to take up arms ourselves.

The main point would be to keep the invader from getting control of our institutions. For in civilian defense, keeping a free press, or keeping the invader's propaganda out of our educational networks, would be a more important strategic objective than the possession of, say, a given mountain. And since our institutions would be biolithic—incredibly diverse—getting control of them would be an almost impossible task in the first place.

In civilian defense, then, even under the worst of circumstances, we could still hang on to a measure of autonomy for our community and its institutions. And as the invader failed to break the resistance down totally—because he failed to break *us* down totally—there would be unrest within his country, and international pressures would mount. Even the invader's soldiers would begin to wonder what they were fighting for (or rather, not fighting for).

A second biolithic defense strategy has recently been proposed by Adam Roberts, a British strategist and a convinced civilian-defenser until the Russian invasion of Czechoslovakia. That event (the Czechs made a heroic, but largely futile attempt to defend their country nonviolently) caused him to think twice: and he has since worked out a possibly more effective system of defense which he calls "territorial defense."

Territorial defense is a method of defending a community or region, not a large country, by force of arms—but with a difference. First, the arms would be small—too small to use effectively for offensive purposes, and cheap enough to give to everyone ("only by democratizing the distribution of armed force within a state can the danger of domination by a small military clique be overcome"). Second, there might or might not be professional soldiers, but the bulk of the defense would rely on a citizen army, including local units of a militia type (these could be easily run on a volunteer basis—if the militia were purely for defense, many New Age people would *want* to join). Third, the militia might make a tactical defense of the borders of the community or region, but the larger strategy would be to allow the invader to enter— and to harass him or her continually while he or she was there. In part this harassment might consist of the kinds of noncooperation Gene Sharp talks about above (the militia might train people in this). In part it might consist of military retaliation (which might be carried out by specially designated forces, to keep the invader from feeling threatened by the population-at-large).

Territorial defense is, then, a kind of synthesis of the neopacifism of Sharp and the various guerrilla movements that have been so successful in so much of the Third World. (It does have some precedents though—for example, something very much like it was used by the Iroquois Indians.) It could be used not only for defense against invasion, but for defense against any undemocratic regime. And it could be used as a transitional strategy—as a kind of bridge between nuclear and civilian defense. It would be compatible with the New Age ethics and values in communities where nonviolent behavior was defined in such a way as to include defensive violence. (See Chapter 24 where I call for the establishment of the military draft to train us in the arts of civilian and territorial defense.)

The biolithic state would allow—encourage—communities to determine how decentralized, how powerful, how autonomous they wanted to be (see Chapter 16). At the same time—as Jacques Ellul emphasizes—faith would be restored in other avenues of human effectiveness than the traditionally political. As a result, we would no longer want or need the monolithic state.

The biolithic governing elite—a contradiction in terms. In many New Age communities, policy decisions would be made by a series of self-selecting, task-oriented work groups, from the bottom up; see Chapter 15. And yet, there would probably be some people who were much more active than others. According to social planner John Friedmann, no more than one-third of the adult population has *ever* been willing to involve itself in the decision-making process. But a self-selecting 33 percent of the population is not a governing elite. It is a governing people.

The biolithic corporation might not *have* to be small, but if it weren't small it might end up being completely frozen out of some New Age communities and regions. (Loss of some critical markets might force all large corporations to reduce their size.) Other communities and regions might insist that corporations adhere to strict community and regional charters on pain of expropriation (see Chapter 18). At the same time, many New Age communities and regions, worker collectives, and local businesspeople might be starting their own small corporations—and communities and regions could obtain the authority to tax all competing corporate goods at the border.

Self-images would, to a great extent, replace roles in biolithic society. "Self-images," says Stanley Keleman, "grow out of our individual living process. Our unique livingness initiates each of our self-images. Each self-image reflects our own unique self-forming."

We would probably continue to have *some* expectations about how we should act as, e.g., parents, lovers, workers; but our expectations would come primarily from our own sense of our selves, from our own understanding of our wants and needs, and from the New Age ethics and values as our communities and regions and we our selves defined them. Keleman states, "I do not have a fixed role, nor am I everybody in the world [as someone who was only concerned with the spiritual state of consciousness might think—M.S.]. I don't have to be a fixed thing and I don't have to be everything. I'm always forming, expressing that which shapes me, that which gives me an identity."

At the very least we would strive to put some distance between our selves and our roles. Peter Berger reminds us that in ancient Greece the word "ecstasy" referred to "the act of standing or stepping outside the taken-for-granted routines of society," and he says, "As soon as a given role is played without inner commitment, deliberately and deceptively, the actor is in an ecstatic state with regard to [his or her] 'world-taken-for-granted.' What others regard as fate, [he or she] looks upon as a set of factors to reckon with in [his or her] operations. . . . In other words, 'ecstasy' transforms one's awareness of society in such a way that *givenness* becomes *possibility*." A well-known technique in psychosynthesis called "dis-identification" has helped some New Agers move from an overidentification with their socially assigned roles to the recognition that we are, each of us, "a center of awareness and of power."

The biolithic mind would rather see clearly than be right; would rather heal society than prove others wrong; would rather help the person "experience experience" than go on and on endlessly with its positions, points of view, beliefs, attitudes, justifications. . . .

The mind is not, however, "naturally" biolithic—its natural tendency is to forever try to escape from what Krishnamurti calls "that fear of emptiness, that fear of loneliness, that fear of stagnation, of not arriving, not succeeding, not achieving, not being something, not becoming something. . . ." The biolithic mind is a product of the kinds of therapies that are reported on throughout this book and in the *Journal of Transpersonal Psychology*.

Freedom to give all we wanted to give: The New Age alternative to the stroke economy. In Chapter 9, we saw that the Prison gives us "Prison-bound personalities" by convincing us that there aren't enough positive strokes to go around (positive strokes are units of friendship or affection or esteem). As a result, we are fearful of giving or even receiving strokes. In New Age society, the Prison and its institutions would be collapsed by their New Age alternatives, and as a result we would find it much, much easier to give positive strokes if we had them to give; to ask for strokes if we needed them; to feel free to accept them if we wanted them; to feel free to reject them if we didn't want them; and to feel free to give *our selves* strokes (see Steiner).

If we were more willing to give each other strokes, we would probably also be willing to touch each other more (as the term implies). Many New Age people have argued that touching not only makes us feel better but that it might actually be necessary to us—to our physical and emotional well-being and to our intellectual development. Joseph Chilton Pearce reports that Kenyan and Ugandan babies are the happiest in the world—and are more *cognitively* advanced than American babies—primarily because their mothers stroke them constantly.

The fear that a society of "touchers and feelers" (as we put it so priggishly) might be oppressive and forced is a fear that comes right from the "stroke economy": from our assumption that we'd have to give more than we wanted to give. As one woman puts it (in *The Hite Report*), "Perhaps if we all had more people we related to with physical affection and touching, . . . we wouldn't necessarily feel that every contact points in the direction of intercourse so that you don't feel free to take Step A unless you are willing to take Step B, C, D, etc. . . . [Perhaps] we'd have a generally more loving atmosphere in which to dwell."

Decentralization and decriminalization: the New Age solution to most criminal behavior. New Age politics believes that most crime is caused by our lack of shared culture and common purpose. According to Richard Cloward and Lloyd Ohlin (in *Delinquency and Opportunity*, 1960), the criminal subculture appeals precisely because it is able to provide us with a tangible set of goals that we can achieve. It is definitely not caused by economic deprivation. Several studies have shown that crime and delinquency do not vary significantly from one socioeconomic group to another—only the kinds of crimes change. The poor steal, the rich embezzle.

The lack of a common bond among us is not only the leading cause of crime, it has also made us *need* a criminal population in our midst. Eugene Doleschal and Nora Klapmuts (see Dodge, ed.) argue that the identification of acts as criminal "allows a harmless channelling of aggressions, while at the same time reinforcing group solidarity," and that the public denunciation of criminal acts helps to reinforce the norms on which the society is based.

New Age politics has no illusions that a New Age society would do away with all crime, but New Age society could certainly do away with, say, 90 percent of all crime. George Leonard points out that half of it—literally, 50 percent—could be done away with tomorrow by eliminating all laws against "non-victim" behavior—gambling, drunkenness, vagrancy, drug use, sex "deviancy," and the like. And most of the rest of it could be eliminated by the kind of drastic decentralization of our society envisaged in Chapter 16. If communities became coherent, self-reliant, human-scale; if communities were based on the New

Age ethics and values and were allowed to interpret them in their own way; if communities were encouraged to be as open or as exclusive, as fluid or as purposive as they liked; if it were possible for us to choose to live in a community that suited our particular temperament and interests—then we would no longer suffer from a "lack of shared culture and common purpose." And society would no longer need the "social glue" that a criminal element provides.

How realistic is this? According to Klupmuts, most post-1960s criminology theory "views crime and delinquency as symptoms of disorganization of the community as much as of individual personalities—*or even as a product of an inadequate mesh between the two*" (emphasis mine).

As for those of us who were still driven to criminal behavior: the traditional prison or training school is ineffective (in fact there's now much evidence to show that the prison does more harm than good—to all concerned), not to mention that it costs upwards of $15,000 a year to keep one criminal in jail! On the other hand, a New Age community setting—human-scale, life-oriented—would make "community-based alternatives" to prison far more likely to succeed than they are at present. Even in Prison society, numerous studies have shown that community-based alternatives can handle the offender at least as effectively as prison and at a fraction of the cost.

CHAPTER 15

Synergic Power: the New Age Alternative to Coercive, Competitive, and Anarchic Kinds of Power

Definitions

For many of us, says Kat Kinkade of the East Wind Community in Missouri, "power is a dirty word." And no wonder. If asked to define the word "power," most of us would probably say something like "being able to tell other people what to do."

We are all familiar with that kind of power. It is what the boss has; it's what our parents had before the boss took over; for women, it's all too often what their husbands have. Most of us are locked into power struggles at home and at work and, if we have strength left over for it, in society, too. The Biblical injunction to "do unto others as you would have them do unto you" has become translated to "do unto others before they do unto you."

The choice seems either to be power-full or power-less—and nobody likes to feel powerless. At best we hope for some kind of uneasy truce where the power is "equalized."

New Age people have begun to realize that there are a number of different *kinds* of power, and that power doesn't necessarily mean coercion or manipulation. To Jean Baker Miller, feminist psychologist, power is basically "the capacity to implement." To Leroy Pelton, psychologist of nonviolence, it's "potential social influence." To Rollo May, it's "the ability to cause or prevent change." To David Spangler, it's "the capacity to act." Patricia Mische sums up the thrust of these definitions very nicely when she tells us that, "in point of fact, power is neither good nor evil, although it may be an instrument of both." And power is absolutely necessary to us; "power is essential to all living things. . . . We need power to live, to survive, to stay healthy, to love, to create, to become who we can be. . . ."

But power of a special kind. In their book *Synergic Power*, which is an attempt to synthesize many New Age ideas about power, James and Marguerite Craig call our commonly accepted notions of power, "directive power." According to the Craigs, directive power "includes any form [of power] in which the initiator intentionally makes people act against their will, their judgment, their interests, or leads them to act blindly without considering their interests and those of others." This is not the kind of power Patricia Mische has in mind.

The emerging New Age definition of power, according to the Craigs and others, would mix the concept of "synergy" with the concept of power-as-the-ability-to-cause-or-prevent-change. Synergy is another awkward but indispensable New Age word; to the Craigs it means "working together to benefit myself and others at the same time" or "the working together of unlike elements to create desirable results unobtainable from any combination of independent efforts."

Synergic power, then, according to the Craigs, means "the capacity of an individual or group to increase the satisfactions of all participants by intentionally generating increased energy and creativity." And they add: "Synergic power differs radically from directive power in the concern it expresses for other people and the roles it affords them. Any application of synergic power accords with the will, the judgment, and the interests of the other human beings, and it is fully effective only when no energy or creativity is wasted in domination and resistance to domination. For example, we will have exercised synergic power if other people's behavior becomes more in tune with ours after we have shared information and feelings with them in non-manipulative, non-coercive ways, and have creatively cooperated with them to discover new solutions to problems or conflicts. . . . The more synergic we observe [a person's] power to be, the more fully does [he or she] seem to display the same positive attitudes toward his adversaries as he does toward his followers and allies."

That's probably the key to seeing if a person is wielding (trying to wield) directive or synergic power. Watch how he or she handles those who disagree. Patricia Mische puts it well when she says, "[Synergic power] is aware of and responsive to the *other*. It is not men versus women or women versus men or women versus women. Nor is it surrendering self or values in a false cooperation. The identity and the dignity of all parties is respected—one's own and that of the other. [Synergic] power is non-harming, even when the other stands in opposition. . . .

"[Synergic power] is a caring form of power. It is power aligned with love. It is the combination of both power and love that makes a good marriage or family life workable. . . . [And] it is this alignment of love and power that is essential to shape a humanizing future—on a personal level and in the world."

The Craigs give a nice example of using synergic power. If I want to plant a vegetable garden and you want to plant a flower garden on the same plot of land, how do we settle the matter? The "fair" way, according to the directive power approach, would be to split the land 50–50 between us. But that wouldn't really satisfy either of us. From a synergic power perspective, say the Craigs, "every initial request or demand is seen as a proposed solution to a usually unstated problem." And the point is to explore that deeper level.

With regard to the garden, we might find that behind my desire to plant vegetables is really a desire to do *anything* creative, and/or that behind yours is a desire to grow the most luxuriant flowers possible. So I might end up writing *New Age Politics* and shopping at the local health food store. Or you might end up growing even more luxuriant flowers in a greenhouse on the roof. Or we might find a neighbor who might let one of us plant our garden in his or her yard (because he or she liked flowers, or in exchange for some of the vegetables). As the Craigs put it, "The search for new solutions becomes an adventure in openness and creativity that is far more satisfying than attacking or resisting each other's initial proposals."

Implications

The concept of synergic power has some extremely far-reaching political implications. Especially, it means that our traditional ways of deciding things—by voting and by collective bargaining—may be less constructive than the small-group decision-making process, so long as the small groups are open and representative, and based on synergic power. For in voting, however "fair," the winners, ostensibly the majority, are able to force the minority to give in to their wishes, thereby making them "losers." And in collective bargaining (which is not confined to the conference table but goes on all the time between lovers, friends, and political associates), two or more "adversaries" face each other, each of them claiming to be right, each of them unwilling to give an inch . . . until the process of bargaining begins; and this is often a swapping of point for point without regard for the rightness or wrongness of the individual points.

Many New Age thinkers would put small, synergic groups at the heart of the decision-making process. For example, Frederick Thayer, a political scientist, has worked out a "theory of extended face-to-face discussion within an almost infinite number of small groups." Similarly, John Friedmann, a sociologist, would organize communities according to the principle of "cellular structure." Communities would have as their smallest unit the "task-oriented working group" of maybe fifty members each, and these groups would come together in "working group assemblies" to exchange information and set policy.

New Age activists believe that we should be able to do more than just advise decision-makers of our views (at public meetings, say). This type of "citizen participation," which is common now in North America as well as in the socialist countries, still puts us in the role of petitioners (for the redress of grievances), of people asking someone else to solve our problems for us. It doesn't allow us to assume any real responsibility.

On the other hand, most New Age activists believe that we shouldn't *all* get to decide on *all* issues through a kind of continuing referendum system (a scheme advocated by many "futurists" and anarchists). As Robert Theobald points out, it simply isn't true that all of us are equally able to make decisions on all issues or that all of us are willing to spend a great deal of time in thinking about each issue. Probably most of us will always be oriented to private life, not to public life at least for the greater part of our lives; after a while even Castro recognized that the revolutionary is a personality-type, not a valid model for the new "Socialist Man." In New Age society, socially committed people would also be regarded as a personality-type—a necessary type, but no more noble a type than the others.

It isn't hard to see that the choices we've been considering, no-final-decisions-by-us and all-final-decisions-by-all-of-us, are products of the Prison (of its tendency to dichotomize). New Age activists believe that everyone should have the opportunity to make decisions but that our commitment to an issue and to the decision-making process itself should carry some weight. Therefore, most New Age activists believe that those of us who are informed about, or concerned about, a particular issue should have the opportunity to take part in the decision-making process—maybe even the final decision-making process—on that issue.

One kind of New Age community, then, might be organized as follows. Decision-making units might be made up of groups of all those people who were informed and/or concerned about an area, problem, issue, crisis, etc. One group might be in charge of housing policy, a second group in charge of medicare policy, a third group in charge of New Age festivals, and so on. And there could be ad hoc groups formed around passing issues, and groups formed to *prevent* issues from arising. The point is that the groups themselves would be making the actual decisions about housing policy, the rites of spring, and so on.

If a group felt it was becoming too big, it could, among other things, divide into sections and have sectional representatives come to a final decision.

Some New Age communities might choose to have these groups present their decisions to an elected governing body or to a general assembly. Other communities might choose to have group leaders come together in a community congress. Still other communities might allow final decision-making power to rest with the groups—though a governing body would have to decide how much money to give each group. All kinds of variations could be worked out.

It hardly needs to be added, though, that this form of government could only work if we were committed to using synergic power rather than power based on the force of money or numbers. Without a firm commitment to discovering and then meeting each other's deepest needs, there could be no open discussion in groups, and we wouldn't be able to learn and grow and change through the process of group discussion. Without synergic power, there would be a multitude of hostile and competing groups.

On the other hand, the fact that we were free of the Prison would make the success of this genuinely democratic form of government a real possibility. Versions of it are being used successfully now at Findhorn, at Twin Oaks, and at several other intentional communities.

CHAPTER 16

Localization:
Celebration of Diversity

Localization is decentralization with a positive focus. Localization is decentralization as seen from the perspective of the New Age. Let me attempt a formal definition: localization is the process of the continent evolving in the direction of its natural diversity by means of the spread of community consciousness and the evolution of various forms of community and regional self-reliance.

Community and Regional Consciousness

Most of us have lost our sense of community, and no wonder. The average North American moves once every four years, and those of us who are under forty tend to move more often than that. With predictable results: on the one hand, the transient society encourages a concern with narrowly defined property values. We buy and keep our homes, etc., with an eye to their expected resale value rather than with a desire to turn them into really unique and interesting expressions of who we are. Our neighborhoods are equally "unsullied," equally bland. On the other hand, we are more prone to abuse and eventually destroy our living places, because the transient society leaves us without what Wendell Berry calls "the comfort and the discipline" of old memories and associations. "Without a complex knowledge of one's place," he warns, and without the "faithfulness to one's place" on which such knowledge depends, "it is inevitable that the place will be used carelessly, and eventually destroyed."

Many of us feel that our "networks" have been able to replace community. Network is Philip Slater's term for a group of people who think like we do, who have common interests, and who have no territory. There can be networks of friends, political activists, poker players, professionals. By contrast, a community has people—many people —who don't think like we do; who we may think of as boring or prejudiced or even slightly crazy; who may remind us of those parts of our selves that we do not like. "But it is community that heals," says Lee Swenson (in *Simple Living*, no. 7), "while a network cannot sustain us for long. We are healed by the fresh air of life diversity brings us—others who are different from us can help us fill out, round out ourselves. We need both network and community, but we would do well to know the difference, and get on with living in our community as well as our network."

Community heals—that is the point. Community tells us things about our selves that we could never learn any other way. Community nourishes many parts of our selves that need to be nourished. According to Philip Slater, "Humans deprived of community can become in a sense 'imprinted' on rules, machines, ideologies and bureaucratic structures." Rene Dubos goes so far as to suggest that we have a "biological need . . . to be identified with a place," that traditional societies functioned in small groups for so long that a need for community has been stamped onto our genetic code.

What is this "community" exactly? As a physical place it could be a rural district, a small town, an "intentional community," a city, or a big-city neighborhood. David Morris and Karl Hess say that their "homeliest test" for a big-city neighborhood is whether or not a person "can easily walk its boundaries." But even these hard-nosed political economists recognize that a neighborhood is more than the sum of its physical parts. "You or we probably would be hard pressed to define any neighborhood. Yet, once in one, we would know it." (In *Planet/Drum*, no. 4, Eric Bookhardt and others discuss a New Age science called "geopsychics" whose subject is the "phenomena that may be seen as an expression of the consciousness of a locale in its most unique . . . manifestations.")

To New Age people, community has to do above all with people's *experience* of a place. According to Wendell Berry, community is "local life aware of itself." According to David Spangler, community is "a spirit of the presence (and the potential) of connections and bonds beyond the functional." According to Arthur Morgan, community is a "quality of society" present when many of its members have such "traits of mutuality" as "intimate acquaintance," "mutual confidence," and a "feeling of oneness." (*Zen and the Art of Motorcycle Maintenance* might say: community is Quality-in-a-community-district.)

Many New Age people have begun to say that our experience of a place can and should run so deep in us, that to consciously create and nurture that experience is to go through a process of "reinhabitation." Regional reinhabitation, say Peter Berg and Raymond Dasmann (in Berg, ed.), "involves becoming native to a place through becoming aware of the particular ecological relationships that operate within and around it. It means understanding activities and evolving social behavior that will enrich the [human and natural—M.S.] life of that place. . . . Simply stated, it involves becoming fully alive in and with a place. . . .

"Reinhabitation involves developing a bioregional identity, something most North Americans have lost, or have never possessed. . . . [Bioregion] refers both to geographical terrain and a terrain of consciousness—to a place and the ideas that have developed about how to live in that place."

Robert Curry puts it well when he says (in Berg, ed.) that reinhabitation "is a process of becoming 'terrate'," in addition to literate and numerate.

Today, regional development calls for the formation of an infrastructure of multimillion-dollar dams, power networks, and superhighways. This infrastructure then leads (hopefully!) to the development of extractive industries, huge farms or ranches, a tourist industry, and urban areas, as well as to the establishment or "upleveling" of all the monolithic institutions that I dealt with in Chapter 7. You don't have to be a committed New Age activist to see that this process displaces many people (often to the urban slums), consumes terrible quantities of energy, minerals, water, and land, makes us almost completely dependent on faraway markets, imported necessities, mass transportation and the like, and destroys the integrity of the regional culture.

Fortunately, there is an alternative.

Those of us who take the New Age ethics seriously are more and more coming to believe in what has been called "watershed politics." Watershed politics, says Lee Swenson (in *Simple Living*, no. 7), "could be seen as linking the size and scale of your political and cultural community to the biology of the place. It means adopting a bioregional process of working from the ground up, letting the culture flow from the natural base. When this happened organically, all over the world, it was what gave us the rich, rich diversity of culture" that we're now in danger of losing, thanks to the descent of the Prison and its institutions.

The clearest and most practical single expression of watershed politics to date has come from Peter van Dresser, economist, tax refuser, and lifelong simple liver. Van Dresser's thesis is that the essential infrastructure for a region isn't dams, power plants, and superhighways but "a thriving permanent population sustaining a way of life ecologically adapted to the regional environment."

Central to van Dresser's argument, and to the watershed politics philosophy, is a redefinition of the concept of natural resources. The monolithic mode of development defines natural resources as anything that can be sold on the continental market for a profit. Peter van Dresser defines natural resources differently, as all those resources that can "fill the bulk of human needs." And he claims that most of our bioeconomic regions contain enough arable land to raise a region's food; enough timber and minerals to construct a region's buildings, equipment, and tools; enough plant and animal life for meat and fuel and textiles. "Out of such taken-for-granted factors," he says, "an ingenious and intelligent people can fabricate most of the necessities and many of the embellishments of a good society."

Community and Regional Self-Reliance

As we become more self-reliant, it makes sense that we'd want our dwelling places to become more self-reliant too. As we become more cooperative, it follows that we'd want our communities to cooperate with other places consciously and voluntarily, rather than because they had to, as they have to in the traditional nation-state.

Most New Age people believe that the most important unit of government should be, not the nation, and not the state or province, but the "community district." Community district is a New Age term for: counties, intentional communities, cities, and big-city neighborhoods (or any self-chosen combination of same). On the other hand, most New Age people also believe that you don't make nonviable people viable simply by splitting a nation into a number of community districts. The initiative has to come from the district itself. Otherwise the district is in danger of being controlled by a tiny minority of "true believers," or a smaller, more competent, and so less vulnerable bureaucracy.

As New Age society evolves, New Age people would want community districts to have the right to redefine their relationship to the nation-state. Some community districts might opt for complete independence. Still, probably most community districts would choose to retain some kind of formal association with the nation-state (economic common market, open borders, etc.). Community districts might redefine their association in such a way as to obtain full power to decide on such things as levels of taxation (if any), kinds of social services (if any), kinds of institutions, housing and employment policies, income distribution, foreign policy, defense policy. Regardless of how each district defined its relationship to the nation-state, just having the power to do so would make it possible for us to take real responsibility for the decisions that affected our lives.

Just as the American colonies felt it was necessary to separate from England at the end of the eighteenth century—partly for economic reasons and partly, I would say primarily, in order to become themselves—so many community districts that prized the New Age ethics and values might want to enter into a different relationship with the nation-state. Partly to eliminate a number of monolithic institutions, and partly to become themselves, to become more specific manifestations of themselves, of the collective identity of their residents.

In Quebec they have a name for this kind of limited sovereignty: "sovereignty-association." In western Europe, the new localists (or "new nationalists") speak of "devolution" or "autonomy" or "federalism on the Swiss model," rather than complete independence. What is "federalism on the Swiss model"? Very much like what America might have been had we modified—rather than replaced—the Articles of Confederation. Michael Zwerin, an American businessman and jazz musician who has written an interesting book on the "new nationalism," tells us that the Swiss are citizens of their cantons first, of Switzerland second. (There are twenty cantons—in a country of seven million.) "Direct taxes are paid to the cantons which keep 80 percent and pass along the rest to the federal government to pay for defense, customs, post, the diplomatic service, and so on. The rich cantons subsidize the poor."

Zwerin complains that the new nationalism "does not go far enough.

I would rather see twelve autonomous counties than an autonomous Wales, five autonomous departments than an autonomous Brittany. . . ." In the New Age perspective, however, with its stress on diversity, we would treat this as a matter for the individual localities to decide for themselves. It would not become a "problem" for national planners to "solve"—not even New Age-oriented planners.

Here are the relevant options:

● complete independence for a community district (possibly, e.g., Las Vegas);

● complete independence for a region (state or contiguous states or states-and-contiguous-counties) (possibly, e.g., Puerto Rico);

● sovereignty-association for a community district vis-à-vis the government in Washington (possibly, e.g., Harlem);

● ditto for a region (possibly, e.g., the Pacific Northwest—"Ecotopia");

● sovereignty-association for a community district vis-à-vis the *regional* government (possibly, e.g., Takilma, Ore., vis-à-vis Ecotopia);

● no change in present political status for counties, neighborhoods, cities, states (possibly, e.g., Dallas, Texas).

With these six options for our communities and regions to choose from, the life-giving diversity of the society would increase a hundredfold, or rather, the underlying richness of this country would finally be permitted and encouraged to blossom forth (see Chapter 24 for some specific proposals along these lines).

CHAPTER 17

Planetization: Celebration of Unity

"Planetization" is a process that is complementary and *necessary* to localization. After all, if communities and regions and small nation-states want to be more self-reliant, then they are going to have to learn to cooperate together in an effective way.

Here is a formal definition: *planetization* is the process of our species evolving in the direction of its natural unity by means of the spread and deepening of what many New Agers have begun to call "planetary consciousness" and the evolution of an effective system of "planetary guidance." (But don't forget that "union differentiates"— Teilhard de Chardin.)

Or, more simply: planetization is the effective application of the New Age ethics and political values to planetary problems.

New Age people prefer to say "planetary" rather than "world" for a number of reasons. "World" implies a system of nation-states, "planetary" implies a kaleidoscope of communities, regions, and nations. "World" implies a place where people dominate the ecosphere and dominate each other, "planetary" implies a place where people cooperate with the ecosphere and cooperate with each other. "World" implies that the Earth is the center of the cosmos, "planetary" that the Earth is an integral part of the cosmos.

Planetary Consciousness

International consciousness sees the world whole, but from the perspective of a particular nation-state or ideology, whose interests are held to be *separate from* and *prior to* those of the whole. International consciousness believes very strongly that the Prison and its institutions represent "modern" consciousness (a hundred years ago it might have said "civilization itself") and that "progress" or even "survival" depends on spreading the Prison and its institutions as fast and as far as possible.

Planetary consciousness recognizes that the world is full of dread and danger—but also promise and possibility. Both recognitions— danger and possibility—are inherent in the often repeated planetary perception that, as Margaret Mead put it, "Our technology has increased the size of interdependent units to include the entire planet."

Planetary consciousness recognizes our oneness with all humanity and in fact with all life, everywhere, and with the planet as a whole.

Planetary consciousness recognizes the interdependence of all humanity, of all life, and of all our nation-states.

Planetary consciousness sees each of us as "cells in the body of humanity," as Planetary Citizens puts it—with all the obligations that implies. (Rolling Thunder conceives of the Earth as a body, "a gigantic body of a conscious, struggling, living being," and says that we "have to learn to be within it—like cells.")

For some of us, planetary consciousness may come as the direct result of an experience, even so simple an experience as stalking the halls of the U.N. or canvassing a neighborhood for a community project. For others of us it may come from a simple intuitive understanding of all people as brothers and sisters with a common destiny. Margaret Mead says that it comes from being a part of a multigenerational community—"All you need is your child, grandchild, or someone in front of you that you care about and a little bit of imagination." I think it's obvious that it comes (or can come) from the transmaterial worldview, from learning to be at home in all four states of consciousness. (Just look at the last four paragraphs above. They correspond to—they are products of—the material, spiritual, religious, and mythic states of consciousness, respectively.)

Planetary events are, in a sense, *conspiring to inspire* us to recognize our oneness and interdependence. Our modern means of transportation and communication have recently put us in touch with each other—continuously and totally—for the very first time. Then there was the race to the moon, which for all its surface irrationality, did cause us—for the first time ever—to see our planet from outer space. "In an instant of space exploration," says a Planetary Citizens publication, "we became increasingly aware that life is precious in the universe. And somehow, we began to see the inhabitants of the earth as one family—no longer 'we and they'—but interdependent." The feeling of oneness and interdependence had some obvious political implications. "Almost spontaneously, the need was recognized by concerned people in many countries: the human family must find a way to work together if human life on earth is to be preserved and improved."

The Planetary Guidance System

Internationalists tend to believe that our problems can best be solved by a strong world government, by a kind of nation-state writ large. (One that would be based on their own political philosophies.) Many planetarians have begun to speak out *against* the concept of world government as it has been traditionally understood. Ervin Laszlo, of the Club of Rome, notes that even the large nation-states are too richly diverse to govern by a single political philosophy, "yet diversity on the global level is incomparably richer still. If a kind of world government would head it which we now know from national political experience, it would almost certainly need to exercise highly coercive policies to stay in power." Richard Falk, of the Institute for World Order, adds,

"There is nothing intrinsic about the idea of world government that precludes elitism, mass poverty, ecological decay, or even large-scale violence."

Many other planetarians have made the point that our problems aren't really institutional at all, but are problems of will (and therefore ultimately of ethics and values). Barbara Ward, for example, claims that we would have no difficulty in working out a "just political framework" *if we wanted to*—"What is lacking is political will." Similarly, Donald Keys, president and registrar of Planetary Citizens, says that there is "no dearth of possible blueprints [for world order], and that the logic in most of them is impeccable," but that the real or at least the deeper problems have to do with the lack of a shared set of values on the basis of which we could solve our problems.

In response to these understandings, some New Age people have begun to argue for the polar opposite of a world government. In their view, all we really need is a "maximally functioning communications system"; once we devise an adequate set of values and an adequate philosophical basis for them, access to relevant information should be enough; and setting up a world "authority" that could wield any kind of power would almost certainly do more harm than good.

I believe that the New Age ethics and political values imply some commitment to working in the world as we know it. And I have no trouble agreeing with Laszlo that it "appears unreasonable to assume that a dependable form of mutual accommodation could evolve among the world's peoples" without some form of institutional guidance— especially since our situation is so unprecedented (planetary constraints have never limited growth before) and so dangerous and urgent.

So what we need to evolve is a kind of institutional system that falls between the extremes of monolithic world government and power-less communications. An institutional system that would allow us to deal with the world's problems; have as its main, acknowledged purpose the furthering of the New Age ethics and political values (however these might be described); and allow us to plug into it gradually and voluntarily. Following Laszlo and others, I'll call it a system of "planetary guidance" (it would, after all, seek to be the "central guidance mechanism" for Spaceship Earth).

A planetary guidance system, as opposed to a world government, could exercise some control over global processes without having to deny different ideological systems the right of existence. As Laszlo points out, a guidance system would recognize that different political and economic structures may have the same effects on the environment—for example, a socialist steel mill pollutes neither more nor less than a capitalist one—and it would focus its attention on those effects.

In other words, the planetary guidance system would *regulate* society, not *organize* it. It would inform governments and corporations of the potentially harmful effects of their activities (especially with regard to the New Age ethics and political values) and make recommendations to them. If the harmful behavior continued, the regulation system would have the power to impose political and economic sanctions—sanctions that, in an increasingly interdependent and co-operative world, would probably be decisive.

Planetarians tend to be extremely pragmatic about the shape of the future guidance system. Probably most planetarians see it as an outgrowth of the U.N. The U.N. doesn't really fail in conception, says Donald Keys, "it fails from lack of support by the member states who are so reluctant to allow any world organization to assume rival authority, rival jurisdiction to what they wish to retain for themselves even if it means the death of humanity." Certainly few planetarians would deny that the U.N. mirrors the actual state of the world's readiness to cooperate—that it is a "reality-mirror," as Planetary Citizens puts it—and that our main task must therefore be, not to change the mirror, but to change the values and priorities that the mirror reflects.

Richard Falk would like to see the planetary guidance system evolve in the directoin of a "wide dispersion of authority and distribution of power." Similarly, Margaret Mead says, "For the planet to work as a whole system, you need a series of systems, not just one system. Any one system can crack." According to Keys, these views are more or less shared by the U.N., which has for some time now been establishing a series of "departments of planetary management" in the fields of, for example, health, education, agriculture, energy, economic development, population, and environment. "Almost without public awareness, a pattern has emerged: There will not be a unitary 'world state' with centralized powers. Instead there will be a system of interrelated departments each with its own area of competence and mechanisms for governance, as well as a system of representation from the world community. They will remain ultimately responsible to the main Organs of the United Nations—the General Assembly and Security Council."

Despite these positive changes, nearly all planetarians are hopeful that the U.N. will evolve more speedily than it has so far; and many have their own ideas as to where it should go. For example: Gerald and Patricia Mische would like to see the so-called departments of planetary management be given "adequate means and the authority of effective law to manage problems beyond the ability of [the] individual nation-states"—especially in the areas of monetary authority, law of the seas, food, environment, and disarmament. Falk would like to see the U.N. evolve into or be replaced by a "World Assembly" made up of three chambers: an Assembly of Governments (roughly equivalent to the present General Assembly); an Assembly of Peoples (kind of like the American House of Representatives or the Canadian Parliament); and an Assembly of Organizations and Associations. Ali Mazrui (in Mendlovitz, ed.) would like to see the U.N. evolve into a "World Federation of Cultures" where representation would be "not only on the basis of nation-states but also on the basis of allegiance to a particular world language and on the basis of regional location."

Mead would like to see the guidance system work without reference to the system of nation-states. And Frederick Thayer and John Friedmann would have their small, synergic, face-to-face groups at the community level, send representatives to similar groups at the regional level, and so on up to the planetary level.

World Problems and Planetary Solutions

With planetary consciousness and a planetary guidance system, we could make a lot of headway against the planetary problems that most of us consider to be basically insoluble, or soluble only by force of arms. Here are some problems that result from the Prison and its institutions, and some ideas and solutions that planetary thinkers and activists have been coming up with—ideas that are rooted in the New Age ethics and political values. (See also Chapter 24.)

Food. *Problem*: One-quarter of the human race experiences severe hunger or famine during some part of every year (Shurtleff and Aoyagi). Seventy percent of children in the insufficiently developed Third World countries (IDC's) are suffering from malnutrition (Tinbergen). Between 10 and 20 million deaths a year—about 40,000 a day—are directly or indirectly attributable to starvation or malnutrition: diseases that are only nuisances to most of us are devastating to the malnourished (Ehrlich and Ehrlich).

Solution: Every society should try to be self-sufficient in food production. Rather than going abroad for luxury produce, societies should seek to improve the quantity and quality of their own produce. "A native rice-bean-fish standard would become a better rice-bean-fish, not a foreign and dearer meat-carrot-pea" (Kohr).

For the IDC's to become self-sufficient food producers, *they* are going to have to carry out thoroughgoing programs of agrarian reform. At the same time, *we*—the MDC's (monolithically developed countries)—are going to have to agree "not to strengthen the powerful vested interests that have been delaying, distracting, or stopping those reforms" (Myrdal).

Population. *Problem*: The earth's population is doubling now every thirty-five years (Shurtleff and Aoyagi), and what is now being discussed with *hope* is the achievement of a "reasonably stationary population" somewhere in the middle or latter half of the twenty-first century, at a level of *12 to 20 billion* (Tinbergen). (Today we are "only" four and a half billion.)

Solution: Theoretically, the planet can feed many more people than it does today, and materialists often use this fact to "prove" that we are not overpopulated. I think most planetarians would define overpopulation somewhat differently, would say that it has to do with how many people we feel comfortable sharing the Earth with, and how many people the Earth can safely carry. I agree with the Ehrlichs that our rapidly expanding population has already begun to have disastrous, if subconscious, psychological effects on us, leading to the cheapening of life everywhere; I believe that the "material limits to growth" argument is more than a "capitalist plot"; and I believe that an enormous population would require an enormously high degree of social organization. Therefore, I believe that our planetary guidance system should strive to bring the planet down to about two-thirds its present population—down to about three billion people. Since there are at least *eight times* as many people on Earth today as there were in 1800, I don't think three billion represents an "unnaturally" low figure. (At the same time, I think that many other endangered species should be encouraged to multiply—cougars, wolverines, osprey, lynxes, whooping cranes, polar bears and grizzly bears, prairie dogs and prairie chickens, walruses, bison, antelope. . . .)

The most important step that our planetary guidance system can take with regard to population control is to help make economic conditions more secure in the IDC's. The most important step that we can take is to set a good example.

Income distribution. *Problem*: Today about a billion human beings try to live on an annual per capita income *of $75 or less* (Ward). Over the next fifty years, the average income gap between the market economy (MDC's) and Latin America is expected to *increase* from 5:1 to about 8:1. The gap between the MDC's and South Asia and tropical Africa will, however, remain about the same: 20 to 1 (Mesarovic and Pestel).

Solution: In the short run, there should be an increased transfer of wealth from rich to poor countries, and, just as important, an increased transfer of income and resources from the rich minority in the IDC's to the poor majority. (Development strategies in the IDC's should be designed *first of all* to meet people's basic and immediate needs in the areas of food, shelter, clothing, and health.) In the longer run, but as soon as possible, a kind of Planetary Treasury should be set up whose purpose would be to promote planetary equity and eliminate planetary poverty. An internationally recognized definition of (degrees of) poverty would have to be worked out.

Trade. *Problem*: With 71 percent of the world's population, the IDC's account for only 7 percent of world industrial production. Therefore, their annual deficits are going up at an astronomical rate, and their share of world trade is actually decreasing due to deteriorating terms of trade (in 1974 the IDC's paid 65 percent more for their imports, though they bought only 20 percent more goods) (Tinbergen).

Solution: The IDC's should be encouraged to be more than hewers of wood and drawers of water for the MDC's; to be more self-reliant industrially as well as agriculturally; to be biolithically developed Fourth World countries (BDC's), in effect. Nations should join together to work out a planetary industrial strategy that could help them in formulating their own self-chosen industrial policies within the limits of planetary energy and resource capacities. These strategies could serve as a basis for negotiation with other parties, for example, with multinational corporations.

Aid. *Problem*: In 1961, the market economy MDC's agreed to target

1 percent of their Gross National Product (GNP) to the poor nations, with 0.7 percent to be spent in the form of "development assistance" (outright grants). By 1975 the flow of development assistance from the MDC's had *fallen to less than half* that figure, and was expected to fall to 0.28 percent by the end of the decade.

Solution: Aid is no substitute for the social and economic reforms that can only be carried out by the IDC's themselves. Therefore, aid should *not* be given to regimes that are resisting important reforms (except in emergencies, for humanitarian purposes). Also, aid should not be given "bilaterally," from one country to another; instead it should be channeled through the guidance system. This would have the effect of restricting the role of national interests in decisions on aid.

Resources. *Problem*: "To raise all the 3.6 billion people of the world of 1970 to the American standard of living would mean . . . the extraction of some 75 times as much iron as is now extracted annually, 100 times as much copper, 200 times as much lead, 75 times as much zinc, and 250 times as much tin. The needed iron is theoretically available, . . . but a serious limit could be imposed by a shortage of molybdenum, which is needed to convert iron to steel. Needed quantities of the other materials far exceed all known or inferred reserves. . . . Of course, to raise the standard of living of the projected world population of the year 2000 to today's American standard would require doubling all of the above figures . . ." (Ehrlich and Ehrlich).

Solution: "Mineral resources [should] be viewed as a common heritage of mankind. This concept implies . . . a system of world taxation [on resource use]" (Tinbergen). Also, a Planetary Energy Authority should be set up to stimulate research on solar and geothermal energy and to make this research available in the form of technical assistance to all governments.

Multinational corporations. *Problem*: The multinational corporation doesn't train people in entrepreneurial skills (which the IDC's need badly), and the much-vaunted "transfer of technology" is often mini-mized because research and development is generally carried out by the parent company, and because the technology itself is often closely held (Falk). Net foreign direct investment into the IDC's tends to be *one-third or less of the investment income outflow*—so much for the much-vaunted "transfer of capital" (U.N. report).

Without changes in present trends, multinational corporations will control more than 40 percent of planetary production by the end of the 1980s (Tinbergen).

Solution: Multinationals can be useful *under certain circumstances*. For example, a foreign multinational could contract with the government of an IDC "to set up and manage a new plant for a limited period, say ten years. The foreign concern could either make a direct investment for the period agreed upon, or could make it a joint project with the state or an indigenous firm. . . . In any case, the contract should assure the foreign concern a management fee and, in the end, the return at fixed dates of any capital provided, as well as a normal profit on it until then. On its side, it should provide the needed technology and management, but undertake to train and gradually employ personnel from the country itself" (Myrdal).

As a result, the IDC "would be assured of an industrial start and the needed skills" and would eventually get the plant itself (to manage or pass on to a group of its nationals, or the community, or the employees). And the multinational corporation would make a "fair" profit.

Arms. *Problem*: In 1948, worldwide expenditures on defense budgets totaled $65 billion in constant (1970) dollars. In 1976 they totaled $334 billion (Robert Anson, in *New Times*, Aug. 5, 1977). That's about twenty-five times the amount that's spent each year by everyone, everywhere, on development assistance (Inge Thorsson, in Tinbergen).

Between 1965 and 1974, the IDC's increased their share of world military spending from 6 percent to 17 percent. There was no increase in their share of world financial resources during that time (Tinbergen).

The MDC's spend about $20 billion annually on military research. Close to *half a million* scientists and engineers are involved in this research (Donald Neff, in *New Times*, ibid.). One of the promising new fruits of this research is the neutron bomb. Technically speaking it is an "enhanced radiation warhead," not a nuclear weapon, so it's much more likely to be used in the next war. It is designed to kill people slowly, over days or weeks (your cuts won't heal, your hair will fall out, your breathing will become heavier and heavier, you'll begin to spit blood, you'll fall into a coma) but buildings, *things*, will be left intact (Anson).

Solution: Complete military disarmament is the final goal. But there can be little real progress along these lines until people are free of the Prison. As we work against the Prison and its institutions, we should also be trying to establish a negotiated timetable for reductions in military budgets; regulate and then prevent altogether the enormous and expanding trade in arms (a $20-billion-a-year business); ban the use of unnecessarily cruel conventional weapons and of chemical weapons; and begin genuine nuclear disarmament.

Human Rights. *Problem*: In Indonesia there are 100,000 political prisoners (people who've been imprisoned for their race, religion, or beliefs). Most of them have never been tried—and most of them have been in detention for ten years or more (Amnesty International; International League for Human Rights). In China, possibly sixteen million people are in "reform through labor" camps where people are kept indefinitely or until they're considered to be "remolded"; and an indeterminate number are in "education through labor" camps where sentences are at least set (Jean Pasqualini, *Prisoner of Mao*, 1973—a book that's not unsympathetic to Mao, despite its title). In Uruguay, one out of every 500 persons is a political prisoner, and Amnesty International has documented evidence of literally hundreds of cases of death by torture there. Many Uruguayan officers volunteer to work even on their days off so they can witness the "interrogation" of women prisoners (AI).

Solution: The planetary guidance system should withhold some agreed-upon percentage of funds from governments that are abusive of human rights. (Like poverty, human rights would have to be very clearly defined.) Priority should be given to human rights abuses that involve actual physical violence or coercion or are clearly unacceptable to a majority of people in the country concerned.

National Security. *Problem*: "There are three new national security motors," say Gerald and Patricia Mische, "balance-of-weapons competition, balance-of-payments competition, and competition over scarce resources. The ability of a nation to compete in all three of these areas is vital to the security and well-being of its citizenry. Lacking global institutions capable of providing individual countries with security in these areas, [all] nations . . . must mobilize themselves according to the priorities of national security rather than the priorities of human development."

Solution: A functioning planetary guidance system would allow the centralized "national security state" to decentralize. "In a world order that has eliminated competition over armaments and regulates competition over scarce resources and international payments, much power presently centralized in federal national security bureaucracies . . . *could* become decentralized" (Mische and Mische).

Part VI
NEW AGE ECONOMICS

CHAPTER 18

The New Age Economy

New Age politics cannot be defined by an economic *system* in the same way that, say, liberalism can be defined by capitalism or Marxism by socialism. As a matter of fact, New Age politics is compatible with either capitalism or socialism—with private or public ownership of the means of production. Probably most New Age governments would favor some mixture of the two, since New Age society would favor diversity more than purity; and probably some New Age governments would, over time, evolve several new economic "ism's." But economic system—economic "ism"—is not what makes an economy "New Age."

A "New Age economy" as I understand it is any economy that organizes its production and distribution in a way that is compatible with New Age ethics and political values (see Chapter 12). Within the limits of these ethics and values there is, again, plenty of room for diversity, much more than there is now. But some things would be crystal clear:

- Life-oriented behavior would be promoted, and thing-oriented behavior would be discouraged, or at least not promoted.
- An alternative to the "job economy" would be provided, possibly in the form of a guaranteed subsistence income or guaranteed access to basic products and services.
- Biolithic institutions (environmentally benign, etc.) would be preferred to monolithic institutions; or a national or planetary tax would be levied.
- Local and regional self-reliance would be promoted—at least to some extent.
- Planetary cooperation and sharing would be promoted—and would be engaged in, regardless.
- Synergic and appropriately regulated economic competition would be preferred to cutthroat and exploitative economic competition. Voluntary or induced economic cooperation would be preferred to top-down economic coercion.

Four New Age Economies

Within the limits or, better, framework of New Age ethics and political values, there are at least four ways that New Age governments could organize their economies. (Some of these ways overlap, and in practice I'm sure that New Age governments would develop a hundred variations on these ways.)

The crafts economy. "The human being," says economist E. F. Schumacher, "enjoys nothing more than to be creatively, usefully, productively engaged with both [his or her] hands and [his or her] brains." The result of this process he calls "real production" (to distinguish it from, e.g., planning and paperwork). Monolithic technology has reduced the amount of real production time down to about 3½ percent of all our time, and Schumacher's New Age economy would seek to increase real production time sixfold, partly by reducing the scale (though not necessarily the sophistication) of our technology. "An incredible thought!" he says. "Even children would be allowed to make themselves useful, even old people. . . . There would be six times as much time for any piece of work we choose to undertake—enough to make a really good job of it, to enjoy oneself, to produce real quality, even to make things beautiful. Think of the therapeutic value of real work; think of its educational value."

The purpose of the crafts economy, then, would be to offer maximum opportunities for life-oriented productive work for all. Most of the work would take place in workshops of a human scale, rather than in factories; would be performed with tools that people could understand; would proceed at a pace set by the rhythms and needs of human beings; and would often take place in a cooperative or collective context.

William Irwin Thompson likes to say that the crafts economy is really a kind of "metaindustrial" economy that recapitulates "the four classical economies of human history, hunting and gathering, agriculture, industry, and cybernetics." The hunting and gathering economy is recapitulated in the "gathering of wood, wind and sun"; the agricultural economy, in the rise of organic gardening and farming (many of the people in a crafts economy would be farmers); the industrial and technological economy, in the rise of the workshop (small, but often quite sophisticated); and the postindustrial or cybernetic economy, in the "emphasis on research and development and education. . . . The entire community would function as a college. . . ."

Schumacher says that the crafts economy would not mean "an enormous extension of working hours," and he gives four reasons why: many paper-pushing jobs, jobs that are a result of our monolithic technology, would disappear; "there would be little need for mindless entertainment or other drugs, and unquestionably much less illness"; we would no longer make a hard-and-fast distinction between "working hours" and leisure; and everyone or nearly everyone would *choose* to work.

Economist Hazel Henderson has said that we could hire a million new postal workers *right now* if we'd "put them to work handling the mail carefully and lovingly by hand" and if we'd go "back . . . to the twice-a-day mail service which our forefathers used to take for granted."

The service economy. "Instead of devising employment policies aimed at putting people back into precisely the same jobs they have left behind," says futurologist Alvin Toffler, "it would be far more intelligent to design selective re-employment policies that continue our conversion to a service-oriented society."

Millions of socially necessary jobs could be created *right now* in a variety of fields: reforestation, rat control, work with the mentally ill, work with convicts, work with alcoholics, child care, community health, and so on. All of these jobs could conceivably be carried out in biolithic institutions (even though some service economy advocates, such as Toffler himself, would retain some of our monolithic institutions). Policy analyst Michael Marien (in *Futures*, Oct. 1977) says that a service-oriented economy could do away with monolithic institutions so long as we were willing to reduce our workweeks and live simple life-styles, and 10–20 percent of us were willing to become small farmers.

A service economy would have two great advantages, Toffler explains. First, it could "help us solve many accumulated social, community, and environmental problems" bequeathed to us by our "unrestrained economic growth policies"; and, second, "a service-oriented society is less dependent on high inputs of energy and resources than is a traditional industrial society."

The leisure economy. Political scientist Sebastian de Grazia argues forcefully and, to some New Agers, convincingly, that the 40-hour workweek is debilitating to us (partly just because it's no longer necessary) and that only an economy that maximized leisure would allow us to live "lives of quality" (Quality). "Tomorrow's city," he writes, "slightly mad, not too neat, human, will become a place to stroll, to buy and sell and talk of many things, to eat and drink well, to see beauty and light around. . . . Work, we know, may make a [person] stoop-shouldered or rich. It may even ennoble [him or her]. Leisure perfects [him or her]."

The problem with the leisure economy is that it would—to some extent—have to be based on an energy- and resource-intensive technology. And the United States is already using six times more than its fair share of the world's energy and resources. However, this problem would disappear if a New Age society wanted to live at a subsistence level. In their book *Communitas*, Paul and Percival Goodman point out that we are actually producing *ten times more than we need* to survive at a reasonable subsistence level (and Philip Slater has revised that figure upward, to fourteen times). Therefore, if we cut back on production by a factor of 10 or more we'd be able to live in a leisure society *without* being abusive of the New Age ethics and values. Or the leisure society could pay a certain agreed-upon percentage of its mass-produced goods to the planetary guidance system, as a kind of resource tax. Everyone could then benefit. (And it's possible that we'll be able to automate our factories someday using renewable energy sources. It *may* be possible—depends on who you read.)

There are so many ways that our jobs could be reduced in *scope* and therefore in time. For example: rather than being hand-delivered, our mail could be put into neighborhood post-office boxes. If the neighborhood post offices had lounges and coffee shops, picking up our mail could be an enjoyable social experience. Like going to the well in the old days.

The household economy. Economist Scott Burns estimates that we could meet 70–80 percent of our needs *in our homes* by learning to do our own carpentry work, gardening, sewing, etc., and by making use of small-scale, often quite sophisticated technologies that we could share with other members of the community. Burns further estimates that if everyone in the community agreed to work two or three years at jobs that went beyond the scope of what he calls the household economy— for example, if the community instituted a kind of labor-draft—we could then sustain our selves through household work, voluntary work, sharing, and barter for the rest of our lives. (For more on the household economy, see Chapter 19.)

A variation on the household economy is what I like to call the "homestead economy." The basic principle is the same, but whereas the household economy could be actualized anywhere, the homestead economy is specifically rural. It is based on the *additional* premise that, as Wendell Berry puts it, "as many [people] as possible should share in the ownership of the land and thus be bound to it by economic interest, by the investment of love and work, by family loyalty, by memory and tradition."

The household economy differs from the crafts economy mainly in that the latter would create workshops and factories to do many of the things that we could do for our selves, or that we could obtain for our selves through barter. The household and crafts economies differ from the service economy mainly in that the former are convinced that, as policy analyst John McKnight puts it (in *CoEvolution Quarterly,* Fall 1977), "there is a hidden dilemma in the growth of our services. In order to provide universal work by serving each other, we will need *more* clients who need help, or clients who need *more* help. . . . To develop a serving economy we depend upon more crooked teeth, family disarray, collapsing automobiles, psychic malaise, educational failure, litigious conflict and underdeveloped human potential. . . . A service economy needs people in need." The household economy differs from the leisure economy mainly in that the latter would remain dependent on many more of our mass production facilities.

Beyond Corporate Capitalism

New Age people are critical of our big corporations for basically three reasons. First, they are ultimate expressions of the bureaucratic mentality. Second, their very size allows and encourages them to set prices, bribe foreign governments, absorb or destroy domestic competition, etc. And third, they are losing their legitimacy as more and more of us are asking, what gives them the *right* to do what they do?

Socialists and anarchists aren't stumped by these difficulties. At least as a first step, they would have the government take over ("nationalize") the corporations. New Age writers and activists are more inclined to see government ownership as a false solution to these problems, false because it fails to address the problem of the Prison and the problem of size, and false because it fails to address what New Age business theorist George Lodge sees as the real or underlying question. That question is, as Lodge puts it, "What are to be the criteria for and means of controlling large bureaucratic entities, whether corporate or governmental?" In Lodge's view, nationalization "merely pushes our problems from one inadequately controlled bureaucracy to another" and can all too easily become a substitute for our really figuring out what we want from our corporations.

In a similar vein, but from a different point of view, New Age economist Jaroslav Vanek—a specialist in workers' self-management—says that the question, "Who owns the capital?" isn't nearly so important as the question, "Who controls and manages the firm?" The first question implies that the difference between public and private ownership is the really important one. But the second question is able to take us beyond the second-level differences between capitalism and socialism. After all, a community- or worker-controlled firm is possible under capitalism *or* socialism—and is maybe even more genuinely possible under capitalism, since there aren't any central economic planners under capitalism to tell firms what to do.

The New Age economy would have its own way of dealing with the problem of the "bureaucratic corporation," with the problem of size, and with the problem of corporate responsibility and legitimacy.

In Chapter 13, I described a number of attitudes and organizational forms that are products of the "cooperative mentality," as distinct from the bureaucratic mentality.

So far as size goes, there appear to be only two ways of dealing with it. One way is by setting up a vast government apparatus in order to monitor and control key prices and profit margins. That is the solution favored by the left wing of the Democratic Party and by most socialists today. The other way is by breaking up the monopolies and ending price-fixing in restraint of trade. That is the way that has always been favored by the "third strain" in American politics. It would restore genuine competition to the American economy, and it would set the stage for the "New Age capitalism" that I describe in the following section.

With regard to the problems of corporate responsibility and legitimacy, New Age governments (both community and national governments) would acquire the power to *charter* all businesses and industries operating within their territory. These charters would be as general or as detailed, as restrictive or as permissive, as the various governments chose to make them. Probably most community charters would say something specific about such questions as: the amount of money that investors would be allowed to make on their investments; the maximum size of firms; the number of community representatives that would sit on each firm's board of directors; and the kinds of corporate issues that would have to be submitted to the board (a crucial point, according to Barnet and Muller). Most charters would undoubtedly allow communities to start their own competing businesses and industries and to engage in joint investments with private or outside investors. And probably most community charters would give employees the right to at least participate in some of the decisions that were made.

Recently some American firms have been experimenting with limited degrees of worker participation in management. A number of studies of these experiments have been carried out, and are summarized by Frederick Thayer as follows: "If the objective is to increase productivity, participation helps; if the objective is to increase quality, participation helps; if the objective is to transform work into something which does not alienate the individual performing it, participation helps."

Men's liberationist Marc Fasteau is particularly excited by the achievements of a new General Foods plant near Topeka, Kansas. This plant had been divided into "self-governing" work teams of 8–12 members each; and each of these work teams had been given collective responsibility for large parts of the productive process. Individual assignments were made by the teams themselves. Pay increases were geared to the number of jobs a worker could master—in effect, workers were paid for learning about their work. "No plant rules were laid down by management; instead a commitment was made to let rules evolve through collective experience."

Even without profit sharing, the results were impressive. Industrial engineers had estimated that 110 workers would be needed to run the plant, but only 70 were needed; greater productivity, minimized waste, and avoidance of shutdowns brought major cost savings; and outside the plant an unusually high percentage of workers became involved in community projects.

Some community charters might go so far as to insist that *all* community businesses (or at least, large businesses) be fully participatory. The fully evolved "participatory economy" would have five defining characteristics, according to Vanek, who sees it as an alternative to capitalism and socialism:

Genuine participation. Everyone would have the right to participate in management, on the basis of "one person—one vote." Some work groups might choose to make all decisions collectively; others might choose to let the "owners" structure the decision-making process; still others (Vanek feels this might be the norm) might elect officers and a body of representatives and hire an outside manager.

Income sharing. All participants would share in the income of the enterprise. Workers would have to agree on an income distribution scale. "A collectively agreed-on share [could] be used for reserve funds, and various types of collective consumption, or investment."

Ownership separate from control. The working community would have the right to control and manage the firm, but only in rare cases would it own the capital assets. The working community might pay a contractual fee to investors, or an agreed-upon percentage of the net income, or rental-and-interest plus—some scheme would have to be worked out.

Genuine decentralization. All decision-making units—firms, households, associations, and the "public sector"—would decide freely on their actions. (This defining characteristic is meant to ward off the possibility of an authoritarian socialism with its top-down economic planning.)

Freedom of employment. A person would be free to take, not to take, or to leave a particular job.

The trouble with Vanek's scheme—the trouble with the New Left idea of "workers' control" in general, when taken to its extreme and when made into the only "correct" or acceptable way to do things—is that it would merely be standing today's corporate decision-making process on its head. For sure, the workers would be making the decisions; but after all, the workers are not the only ones whose interests are affected by an enterprise, just as the investors are not the only ones. Besides the workers *and* the investors, there are the customers; there is the community; there is the general public; and there is the "environment" of other living things. Economist James Robertson makes the essential point (and beautifully distinguishes the New Age approach from the New Left position) when he tells us that the business enterprise of the future needs to be based on the principle of *balance*, and not on the "aggrandizement" of *any one* of the groups whose interests are bound up with that enterprise. He writes, "The first aim of business enterprises, financial institutions, and economic agencies of government, would not be to grow or expand or maximize, but to balance the interests of their main stockholders—workers, customers, investors [etc.] . . . This balancing of interests of *all* the various stockholders will provide a more genuine form of economic democracy than worker-management—and also a more effective way of bringing inflation under control."

New Age Capitalism

Especially in the United States, many New Age communities might want their economies to be "based on capitalism." But it would be a very different capitalism from the one we know today. The capitalism of the New Age—a capitalism that's evolving already in the cracks and on the margins of our society—would reflect the values of a human-scale, life-oriented society, just as today's capitalism reflects the values of a monolithic, life-rejecting society.

But why capitalism at all? Isn't socialism the aim of radicals everywhere?

Not at all. Many New Agers are more drawn to capitalism (as a theory) than to socialism (as a theory). Three of our main reasons are:

(1.) There's been a historical connection between the economic market and political democracy—between economic and political choices. Precisely *because* of capitalism's greater economic competitiveness, it tends to have "a strong pluralistic thrust" while socialism tends to have "a built-in tendency to contain plurality" (Peter Berger). Which isn't to say that competition is absent from socialism, only that it's expected to take a different (and less open) form. In socialism, the competition is "an endless maneuvering for position within the bureaucratic hierarchies."

(2.) Capitalism is often spoken of as a way of concentrating economic and political power. But New Age entrepreneur Robert Schwartz states, "Capitalism is a method of spreading the power, not concentrating it. Private property and individual production are *systems for the dispersal of power*. The absence of private property almost universally leads to the concentration of power in the state—with an attendant deadening of individuality. . . . The principal pay-off of capitalism is not that it produces goods but that it produces islands of independence." Schwartz concludes, "Capitalism, for all its faults, creates a feisty, independent citizenry with private property and local power bases."

(3.) Socialism is often said to be more *moral* than capitalism, because socialism is supposed to make it harder for people to take advantage of one another. But according to Nikolai Berdyaev, the greater degree of constraint in socialism represents no moral victory. Instead it suggests that socialism has a rather pessimistic view of human nature, even a cynical one; whereas the optimism behind the assumptions of free-market capitalism is great indeed.

Basically, capitalism can work well in a society where people are free of the psychological need to control and exploit one another, and realistic enough to write their ethics and political values into law. I wouldn't be surprised if some New Age communities move from a kind of socialism to a kind of New Age capitalism as their members get more and more free of the Prison—thus reversing the "dialectical movement" that Marx felt was taking us "inevitably" to communism.

So—back to New Age capitalism.

Robert Schwartz believes that the emerging New Age entrepreneur —a species that his School for Entrepreneurs is helping to bring about (see Chapter 27, listed under Burklyn Humanistic)—may be "the ultimate agent of change in making the transition to a new way of living." (Just as a different kind of entrepreneur was the "ultimate agent" in bringing the present society about.) The new entrepreneurs differ from the old in at least three ways, according to Schwartz: in their motivation, in the kind of product they offer, and in their relationship to the market.

The new entrepreneurs are motivated not only or even primarily by a desire for money, but by a desire to express themselves in some creative and healing way. "Right livelihood," says a pamphlet put out by the School for Entrepreneurs, "means that work should not only provide a living but also develop selfhood, foster companionship and nourish the earth. If a business makes money but alienates its members from one another, from themselves and from nature, it is a livelihood —but it is not a Right Livelihood. . . ."

The new entrepreneurs want to produce a new kind of product, not "services" in the traditional sense so much as what Schwartz calls "problem-solving things of a subtler nature." Transactional analysis and Actualizations and recreation-learning packages, for example, are "products in a sense, but they actually are problem-solving or growth services. They're part of a new kind of education. . . ." In the same vein, James Robertson speaks of the new "entrepreneurs of social change" who are "facilitating new types of social and psychological growth and helping to bring social and psychological innovations into widespread use."

Finally, the new entrepreneurs want (or strive or dare) to approach the market in a new way. In capitalism today, money is the primary thing; then the idea; then the entrepreneur. It's like businessman Carl Frederick says in his book about est: first you have, then you do, then you are. In New Age society, this sequence would be reversed. As Frederick says, first you are, then you do, then you have. If what you are is *really you*, the rest will follow.

Similarly, Schwartz says that "the quality of the person, the integrity of the idea, and the person's relationship to it" will determine which entrepreneurs are successful in the future. Even today, "Nothing is as irresistibly attractive to a potential investor as a person with conviction about [his or her] vision." Investment counselor Michael Phillips goes so far as to advise, "Do it! Money comes to you when you are doing the right thing."

A "New Age capitalist" business institution would have dramatically different goals from those of a corporate capitalist (or state-capitalist) business institution. Some of the goals that have been frequently mentioned are:

• "To carry on activities that contribute to the self-fulfillment of the persons involved" (Willis Harman);

• "To carry on activities that contribute directly to satisfaction of social needs and . . . social goals" (Harman). Or, as William Irwin Thompson likes to put it: "The purpose of business will not be seen as the maximization of profit, . . . but simply as an act of service";

• "To earn a fair profit on investment, not so much as a goal in itself but rather as a control signal monitoring effectiveness" (Harman);

• In the long run, not to encourage us to buy MORE, MORE, MORE, but to help us buy less, by helping us to become more self-reliant (James Robertson). In his novel about a New Age society in the year 1999, Ted Cox has a washing machine firm rewrite its Statement of

Purpose as follows: "To cut sales and production to the level of actual need and seek optimum conservation of human and natural resources."

How realistic is this New Age capitalism? After all, it's easy to motivate people to be greedy, and it's easy to motivate people to attack the greedy. But why would people become life-oriented capitalists?

The answer, I think, is that it is ultimately more satisfying to be life-oriented than greed-oriented—even in business. Or rather, *especially* in business. One thing people need now is to *see* the New Age capitalism at work. And it's possible to do so, even today.

In the San Francisco Bay area, many New Age entrepreneurs and businesses—300 at last count—have joined together to share ideas, services, experiences in a network called the Briarpatch. Briars tend to do exactly what they want to—stuff chairs, teach yoga, fix trucks, make windmills, run health resorts, etc.—and their life-styles and political outlooks are incredibly diverse. But despite or even because of this, they are working out many of the "vital principles" of the emerging New Age capitalism. In practice!

Some of these principles are listed below.

Social purpose rather than profit. "When I went to the bank," says Paul Hawken (in *Briarpatch Review*, Fall 1976), "I had to pretend that I was really in it [his natural foods company] for the money or they would have jumped out of their shoes for fright. We simply wanted to 'stay' in business in order to accomplish our goals. That was reward enough." What were their goals? "We were all motivated," says Hawken, "by the vision of growing and distributing natural foods, rather than by profit."

Sharing rather than greed. "Greed," says Hawken, "is condemned not for moral but for practical reasons: it doesn't work. . . . Briars have decided to abandon that game in favor of a new game, an open-ended game, a game which is evolutionary and noncompetitive." This "game" is called sharing. "We can't imagine . . . Coke cheerfully sharing with Pepsi, but Briars can because they don't see size as a goal, nor sales as a ranking."

Appropriate pricing. "When a business is just starting up," says Gary Warne (in *Briarpatch Review*, Fall 1975), "prices should be high enough to allow for contingencies such as taxes, recessions, and unexpected foul-ups. Later, as the entrepreneur learns to use resources more effectively . . . prices could be lowered. . . . If [my store] makes more money than I need, I'll lower my prices."

Learning rather than acquiring. "If a Briar business fails economically," says Hawken, "but the people involved have learned a great deal, then that is seen as success enough . . . [If] we are a learning-based society and think of our roles as a continuous learning process, we will naturally have a sound economy as a result."

Openness rather than secrecy. In a long article in the *Briarpatch Review* (Spring 1977), Kristin Anundsen and Michael Phillips say that openness of books—and openness in general—"is a keystone of Briarpatch operations, for it promotes community and learning, two other

Briarpatch values. Openness leads to trust, responsibility, new ideas, greater awareness. . . ." Anundsen and Phillips argue that the value of information "increases with its abundance" and "if I give information to you, both of us are better off. . . . Sharing of information often leads also to sharing of material things such as trucks, houses, and tools." Briars are expected to share information even if it means giving help to a potential "competitor."

Networking rather than separateness. Briars keep in touch with each other with two full-time coordinators, an excellent quarterly magazine, and lots of personal contact—especially at parties. (At the same time, most Briars have deep mistrust of anything more formal than networking.)

Concern for the people you do business with. "I like to find out whether the person needs the product or service I'm selling," says Gary Warne, "or something else entirely. . . . Consumption is habitual and impulsive; what people are feeling is not always directly related to what they are buying. . . . If the medium is the message, the *way* people are dealt with is as important—maybe more important—than the product or service they are dealt."

Community involvement. "The business and the customers share the same environment," says Warne. "The money that is spent on the goods and services is part of the community's—the neighborhood's—resources. So the business person has a responsibility to be an integral part of that community, to understand it and to contribute to it."

Fun rather than solemnity. Anundsen and Phillips state that "historically, in cultures not so specialized as ours, fun has been an important part of the business scene"—in Africa, for example, the marketplace is the "one place to come for fun," with clowns, jugglers, singers, and comedians—and in the Briarpatch, they say, this tradition has resurfaced. Partly because Briars hope to integrate their lives ("business with pleasure") and partly because fun is "part of the way we learn." You can see their sense of fun in the names they choose: Raskinflakkers Divinely United Ice Cream Organization, Lifestyle Restructurers, Rare Earth Real Estate Brokers of Remote Retreats, etc. The slow pace and unpretentious quarters of most Briar businesses actually gets people talking to one another. . . . "If you take 'making a lot of money' off the list of reasons for being in business you can pretty easily replace it with 'fun,' since you then have time to enjoy yourself by interacting with others."

Continuity of values. "If and when I should decide to sell my [store]," says Warne, "I would sell it only to someone who shared my own standards and values."

Money as a Dense Tool

Some New Age people believe that money is a product of the Prison and should be gradually done away with in New Age society. One New Age editor writes, "The existence of money implies centralization, competition, theft, bureaucracy. . . ." Other New Age people believe that money is essentially a mirror and that our relationship to money tells us not so much what money is but who and what we are. Michael Phillips says that we'll always want to exchange our services and that "keeping score with currency" is the simplest and the cleanest way we have for doing this.

We can expect, then, that New Age communities will take many different approaches to money and to the question of economic exchange.

Lee Swenson, an editor of *Simple Living*, takes a representative position. He writes (in *Simple Living*, Summer 1976) that money is not *intrinsically* destructive so much as it is *simplistic*. "If the only tool you have is a hammer, you tend to treat everything as if it were a nail. Money is a dense tool, limiting our vision of the way we can exchange with one another. . . . It cuts down relationships to a narrow exchange. It's a lean way to deal with one another."

Swenson believes that the transition to a New Age society is going to have to involve a transition to a "more mixed economy," mixed in the sense of the money economy being mixed with other systems of economic exchange. With a system of barter of products and services. With a system of labor exchange (or "intergroup service"). With a vastly increased number of what futurologist Burnham Beckwith (in *Futurist*, Dec. 1978) calls "collective free goods," such as public health care. With a vastly increased number of what Beckwith calls "noncollective free goods," such as free transportation. And—not least with a lot more selfless service.

Planning

Suddenly, national economic planning has become as American as maple syrup. Liberals (most of them) and Marxists alike are in favor of it, and according to George Lodge, the biggest corporations are in favor of it too. Even the Movement for a New Society advocates an overall planning system (though they stress that at various points the plan would be "resubmitted to the local unit for approval." Like in China?).

On the other hand, most libertarians and anarchists are unalterably opposed to planning. E. F. Schumacher is speaking out of his libertarian/anarchist sympathies when he tells us that "genuine planning is coextensive with power" (meaning: the more planning you have, the less control of your life you'll have—period). He goes so far as to say that a planned society—exactly to the extent that it was planned—would "imply the end of freedom."

New Age politics takes what I like to call a biolithic approach to planning. This approach accepts that there is going to have to be *some* kind of planning—otherwise we are not going to be able to shape the future according to New Age ethics and political values. On the other hand, it is relentlessly aware of the dangers of planning; and is prepared to meet those dangers.

New Age-oriented people have done basically two kinds of critiques of planning. One is of specifically economic planning, the other is of the whole concept, the whole metaphysic of planning. The critique of economic planning is well represented by economist Eugen Loebl's extensive survey of the planned economies, which comes to the conclusion that "in most cases target figures express quantity whereas qualitative aspects cannot be, as a rule, expressed in target figures. Consequently . . . the primary concern of both management and labor is quantity rather than quality." Another conclusion is that "no one would dare take responsibility for something that was not explicitly assigned to [him or her] by the target figures."

A broader kind of critique has been done for us by Tom Bender. "Planning," says Bender, "prevents us from experiencing, enjoying, and acting rightly in the present, as we attempt to keep events in line with our projections of the future."

New Age-oriented planning—which I prefer to call "design," following political scientist William Ophuls—proposes to meet these dangers in at least seven ways: by emphasizing local and regional self-reliance and self-determination; by simplifying our technological configurations; by ensuring that people, laypeople, have a significant role in the design process; by focusing on the lessons learned by the designers themselves; by setting qualitative social goals rather than quantitative target figures; and by seeking to change our Prison-bound mentalities.

Community activist Karl Hess speaks of decentralism as an alternative in itself to "big central planning and control systems." He says that "self-reliance, community, and creative diversity" would get us away from "massive plans and even cities."

Economist Hazel Henderson is a forceful advocate of simplifying our "technological configurations" rather than "simplifying by control." She writes, "The [New Age] path requires simplifying the hardware itself, i.e., the technological interlinkages which are so vulnerable to breakdowns, sabotage, and supply bottlenecks. Reordering the scale and interlinkage of our technologies . . . will be very difficult. However, it may be easier than trying to increase our computer modeling skills and capabilities for control."

Futurologist Alvin Toffler has coined the term "anticipatory democracy" to describe a "process for combining citizen participation with future consciousness." This process would be an integral part of any New Age-oriented design strategy. According to Toffler, "We certainly need experts and specialists; they are indispensable, in fact. But in anticipatory democracy, goals are not set by elites or experts alone. Thus, where futures activity exists, we need to open it to all sectors of society, making a special effort to involve women, the poor, working people, minority groups—young and old—and to involve them at all levels of leadership as well. Conversely, where participatory activities exist . . . we need to press for attention to longer-range futures."

Social designer Donald Michael has argued that social design can be "a means for societal learning rather than . . . a means for social engineering." In fact, according to Michael, we can't do long-range design effectively unless we are willing to learn to live with great uncertainty; embrace error; "accept the ethical responsibility and the conflict-laden circumstances that attend goal-setting"; "evaluate the present in the light of anticipated futures"; "commit ourselves to actions intended to bring such futures about"; live with role stress; and be open to changes in commitments and direction.

A number of New Age-oriented authors have emphasized the importance of the availability of accurate and up-to-date information. Anthropologist Jeanne Scott and economist Robert Theobald would like to see everyone have "access to relevant information"—who has what, who needs what, etc.—information that could easily be computerized and made available to all people and groups, community districts and regions, and of course to the planetary guidance system which might take the responsibility for collecting this information. Schumacher would like to see "the fullest possible statement of intentions by all people (and groups) wielding substantial economic power, such statements being collected and collated by some central agency. The very inconsistencies of such a composite 'plan' might give valuable pointers." Clement Bezold and William Renfro state (see Bezold, ed.), "Often it is possible to develop 'early warnings' of likely problems and emerging issues by using such methods . . . as trend extrapolation, cross-impact analysis, and simulation models."

Finally, and crucially, a number of New Age-oriented people have emphasized the importance to social design of consciousness change, of ethical growth. Tom Bender gets to the root of the matter when he says, "There is no need to plan or to attempt to control future events if we believe that persons involved in those events will have an ability equal to our own to understand the situation and act rightly. . . . We plan today only because we are incapable of acting rightly and continuing to act rightly with each changing moment." In New Age society, "acting rightly" would mean: acting according to New Age ethics and values. Therefore, a lot of the energy that a socialist society might put into economic planning, a New Age society would put into fostering and refining those ethics and values. Ali Mazrui, an African scholar, has it right (in Mendlovitz, ed.): "The controls we should be aiming for are internalized controls emerging from new human inclinations, rather than external controls applied by organizational mechanisms."

CHAPTER 19

New Age Economic Theory

When many New Agers talk about economic theory, they tend to confine themselves to two main points: small is beautiful, and an environmentally benign economy would mean more jobs. (And even these "truths" are not necessarily true.) For the rest, New Agers tend to assume that they can get all the economic theory they need from the old political "isms's": an assumption that may save us a lot of trouble in the short run, but that will keep us from becoming a political presence in the long run.

I believe that a New Age economic theory is arising that borrows from—but is substantially different from—what can be found in Marx and Kropotkin and Keynes. The reason that this economics is not well known is partly that it's very new (most of the points below are based on material published in 1976 or later) and partly that it tends to be found in writers who are professional and technical rather than "popular." Ironically, while some well-known New Age economists are really only New Left economists with an ecological conscience, there are other relatively unknown economists at Stanford and Harvard and M.I.T. who are coming up with genuinely New Age economic analyses and insights. They are doing so, not because they consider themselves to be standing at the beginnings of a New Age political tradition (probably most of them have never even heard of the term), but simply because they are trying to look at our problems in a fresh and relevant way—in a way that definitely establishes a connection between ethics and economics, that treats people's motives and consciousness as prime.

It has not been easy for these people. Tibor Scitovsky, an economist at Stanford and the author of the book *The Joyless Economy*, could be speaking for many when he writes, "Economists are deeply divided into the Establishment and its radical-left critics, but they were like a harmonious and happy family in their unanimous hostility to my ideas. I was taken aback at first by such an unbroken string of negative reactions . . . and my managing to produce a book in the end I owe largely to my wife's faith in the enterprise and support in times of trouble."

In the pages that follow, I can do no more than briefly mention some of the New Age economic insights that I consider to be especially valuable.

Beyond "Scarce Resources"

Economics is often defined as a study of the "allocation of scarce resources." But economist Eugen Loebl argues (in *Humanomics*) that "the 'allocation of scarce resources' is only one element of many factors economics needs to study." After all, "with the same allocation of scarce resources, the economic results can differ according to the design [of enterprises], the level on which the enterprises operate, macroeconomic decisions, and a multitude of other factors."

The reason economics tends to define itself as the study of scarce resources, says Loebl, is that it is still based on the mechanistic worldview of nineteenth century physics. "The view that the economy is part of the determined world on the same order as [Newtonian] physics tends to narrow down our angle of vision to that which is quantifiable," and scarce resources are quantifiable. "But what really matters —applied science, organization, the intellectual and technical infrastructure, [the moral and motivational infrastructure] and other essential factors . . .—are not at all quantifiable."

What Is Economic Well-Being?

The Gross National Product (GNP) is the standard measure of economic well-being, not only in the United States but in many other places and even (ominously) at the U.N. Basically, the GNP is a measure of the production of all marketable goods and services in the course of a year. Our own GNP is now over 1.2 trillion dollars a year; in 1950 it was around half a trillion.

Obviously, GNP is an extremely misleading measure of economic well-being—are we really twice as well off today as we were in 1950?

Tom Bender states (in *Sharing Smaller Pies*), "The more we must spend for transportation, for education, or for medical services; the farther we must go for oil, wood, and food; the more our GNP grows. And the more it appears that our quality of life is improved. This focus on production has effectively ignored the reality that most production and consumption [90 percent, according to Bender] is actually the COST of replacing and maintaining our stocks of [products] and services rather than a measure of our wealth."

Another problem with GNP is what it leaves out. Economist Scott Burns says, "Virtually all work that is not rewarded with wages is excluded from conventional accounts of the national income. While the household economy is, by far, the largest omission [see below], the volunteer economy and the cooperative economy are also excluded. The common denominator of these forms of economic activity, beyond their failure to use money, is that they are organized around the idea of giving, of mutual need, and of cooperation rather than competition.

. . . Perversely, our system of economic accounts excludes all motives but the competitive desire for money."

Just as important, GNP fails to measure what Gary Snyder (in *East West*, June 1977) calls the "real values," those that are found "within nature, family, mind." He says we should develop a form of national cost accounting that would ask, " 'What is the natural-spiritual price we pay for this particular piece of affluence, comfort, pleasure, or labor saving?' 'Spiritual price' means the time at home, time with your family, time that you can meditate, the difference between what comes to your body and mind by walking a mile as against driving (plus the cost of the gas). There's an accounting that no one has figured out how to do."

True. But it is already possible to devise economic measures that can point us in the right direction. In *Environmental Design Primer*, Tom Bender suggests a number of such measures: "a Gross National Service [index]—measuring amounts of service rendered rather than dollars of products consumed; an Available Satisfactions Index—similar to census information on plumbing, etc., which would measure who or how many people have what available to use; an Unfulfilled Desires Index—which would be a more helpful measure of the success of the productive ability of a society in serving that society. . . ."

Most Americans tend to think of "well-being" and "comfort" as pretty much the same. But according to Tibor Scitovsky, well-being can be met in *two* ways, by seeking comfort or by seeking stimulation; and one of our central problems, here in America, is that we are far too much concerned with comfort, and not enough concerned with stimulation.

Scitovsky cites a number of studies to show that, as our comfort increases beyond a certain point, the pleasure we get from living actually declines. Moreover, he says that for most of us, that point has already been reached; and we are drawn to television, to gossip, to fast cars, to violence—in a phrase, to negative or life-rejecting stimulation —partly at least because we find it so difficult to seek positive or life-oriented stimulation (cf. Chapter 9 above).

We find it difficult for at least three reasons, according to Scitovsky. First, we tend to become addicted to our comforts: "Many comforts . . . soon become routine and taken for granted. Consumer demand for them remains undiminished, but the original motive, the desire for additional satisfaction, is replaced by the new and very different motive of wishing to avoid the pain and frustration of giving up a habit." Second, we tend to feel guilty if we enjoy stimulation too much (for more on this point see Chapter 12). And third, we tend to lack the relevant "consumption skills." We have never been taught to enjoy music, poetry, literature, and history; we have never been taught to make things well or to take good care of our selves.

Scitovsky's distinction between comfort and stimulation paves the way for a political economy that would treat accumulation of things as a function of self-development, rather than the reverse, which is what we have today.

"A native economy is a direct economy," says the Frisco Bay Mussel Group (see Berg, ed.). A direct economy "places value on what is already there. Values are complex; oaks are tree-presence as well as bearers of acorns, tule reeds are both singing spirits and basket material, salmon are annual visitors and smoked winter supplies. They are both personally direct for each person and direct to the place. It is an economy of seasons and migrations rather than accounts. . . .

"Non-natives imposed a transferred economy. Transferred in were foods, materials, and cultural ideas that were familiar to the new occupiers before they came. Transferred out were things from the region that had some value elsewhere. . . . Subsequent waves of regional immigrants have accumulated so much, put up so many buildings, imported so many devices to 'succeed' here, and transferred so much out that the region has been transformed into an enormous junkyard. . . .

"Empty cans for holding Japanese oysters thrown into the Bay spoil nesting beds for native oysters. Housing tracts cover up topsoil that is essential for feeding people. Miles of pavement prevent the natural flow and seepage of water actually causing floods. . . ."

At the end of their pamphlet the Mussel Group urges that we "begin un-doing the damage invader society has done," and it asks: "Considering how much has already been changed . . . how can we become native to what is here now?"

Ethics and Economics

Economics is the study of wealth. But what is wealth? I think John Ruskin, nineteenth century cultural historian and political economist, had it right: "There is no Wealth but Life. Life, including all its powers of love, of joy, and of admiration." In this view, products and services are "wealth" to the extent that they promote life, "illth" (Ruskin's term) to the extent that they do not. And "the real science of political economy . . . is that which teaches nations to desire and labor for the things that lead to life."

But what is "life"? you might well ask; for Ruskin is obviously using the word in a special, ethical sense. New Age economics would say: life in this sense is behavior that is compatible with the four New Age ethics and the six New Age political values. Therefore, products and services are wealth to the extent that they promote these ethics and values, illth to the extent that they do not.

Capitalism is supposed to be built on the principle of "rational self-interest." Ethics and values are supposed to have no place in economics, everyone is supposed to be out for what they can get for themselves, and everything is supposed to be regulated by an "invisible hand" that is somehow capable of turning our amoral behavior into behavior that works for the common good.

Most radical economists like to point to these widely-accepted assumptions to show that the market economies are amoral (or immoral). Economist Fred Hirsch (in *Social Limits to Growth*) doubts that these assumptions are true. Consider, he says, that whenever we find out that a politician—a controller of the market system—has been "out for him- or herself" we are instantly inclined to throw him or her out of office. Consider that a society whose members regularly lied, cheated, stole, and used violence, simply would not work.

The reason that most of us don't resort to such tactics, says Hirsch, even though they may be in our "rational self-interest," is that we are still caught up in vestiges of a genuinely religious morality. "The market system [is], at bottom, more dependent on religious bindings than the feudal system, having abandoned direct social ties maintained by the obligations of custom and status."

Unfortunately for us all, the Prison and its institutions are steadily eroding the vestiges of our old religious morality. And "we may be near the limit of explicit social organization possible without a supporting social morality."

Motivation and Economics

Conventional economics begins by making motivational assumptions about firms and households. Two commonly made assumptions about firms are that they maximize profits and that they tend to be extremely rational economic actors.

A New Age economics would begin—as economist Harvey Leibenstein suggests (in *Beyond Economic Man*)—with the individual person. It would recognize that firms and households do not, strictly speaking, make decisions or have objectives; that all decisions are made by individuals. And so it would ask: on what basis do individuals make decisions in a particular society? What are their values, motives, goals? And how are individuals related to the economic decision units that operate as a group? Only then would it ask, how do the "highly complex groups we call firms and households" behave? (As it is now, we simply assume that groups behave like individuals!)

Economists of all political hues tend to believe in something called "economic man." Economic man is a totally rational creature whose aim in life, says Leibenstein, "is to do as well as he can. Hence he is presumed to maximize profits, or income, or utility, or something like that." Economists tend to make this assumption because the apparent alternative—that people are "irrational"—seems absurd (and also, perhaps, because it would detract from the "predictive value" of economics).

New Age economics would recognize that, as Leibenstein puts it, "there is an important sense in which non-maximizing behavior is not at all irrational." To demonstrate this proposition (which is obvious to many New Agers), Leibenstein develops a series of "dimensions of rationality." One dimension of rationality is "calculatedness," but there are a number of other dimensions as well. For example: our assessment of a situation can range from completely emotional to completely "dispassionate." Or, for example, we can learn nothing from past experience or we can learn an almost infinite amount.

Leibenstein's point is that we tend to find a spot on each of these dimensions (eight in all) that "feels right" to us depending on our personalities and values—that it is, in fact, absurd to assume that we will try to "maximize our behavior" in terms of each dimension or that different people won't give different weight to different dimensions at different times in their lives. "Sensible behavior requires only marginal rationality, not rationality at every point in time. There is no need to assume that people need to stretch themselves along every dimension at each point in time to gain every advantage open to them. It may indeed go against their psychological makeup to do so. They need only do so from time to time when the results seem important."

When mainstream economists criticize the economy, the inefficiencies are all of a kind, what Leibenstein calls "allocational inefficiencies." These are the inefficiencies that arise from how societies organize their production and trade; these are the inefficiencies that are the standard topics of political discussion today. However, Leibenstein summarizes a number of studies that show that "the problem of allocational inefficiency is trivial." The benefits from eliminating monopoly, for example, would raise national income by no more than one-thirteenth of one percent. Eliminating trade restrictions would raise national income by less than one percent.

The reason the "welfare effects of reallocation" are so small is that firms are *shot through* with inefficiencies, and the most important kind of inefficiency has to do with what Leibenstein calls "factor-x inefficiency." It might also be called "motivational inefficiency." As Leibenstein puts it, "Individuals who are members of production (or consumption) groups, and act in part as agents for these groups, have split loyalties (or split motivations)—loyalties to their own ends as well as loyalties to what they see as the group's objectives." To the extent that the members of a firm act on their own personal loyalties or motives (as opposed to those of the firm)—to that extent a firm is "x-inefficient."

One important implication of this view is that "except in extreme cases firms do not minimize costs, maximize profits, or optimize the rate of technological change." These may be the ostensible objectives of the firm; but "the firm" is a collection of individuals, and those individuals will be motivated not only by the firm's objectives but by their own, multiple, and more or less conscious objectives as well. From the owner(s) on down.

Another important implication is that a firm can increase its output without increasing its expenditures by organizing itself around people's motivational needs rather than against or apart from them. It can, for example, reduce its size; reduce the length of the working day; attempt to introduce "synergic principles and practices" (see Chapter 13); and attempt to introduce worker participation in management.

Traditional economists tend to assume that consumption is a function of income. In other words, that the amount of money we spend is dependent on the amount of money we make. But economist George Katona suggests (in *Psychological Economics*) that for most of us, the *opposite* may be closer to the truth. The amount of money we make depends on the amount we feel we need to spend.

Katona suggest that the amount we feel we need is a function of the kind of life-style we feel we want to lead. He says, "Neglecting the constraint supplied by absence of opportunities, there is . . . justification to reverse the traditional equation: Instead of expenditures being a function of income, income becomes a function of consumption."

Three Key Concepts

Social transaction costs. The fastest-growing single cost in monolithic society is the cost of trying to keep the monolith(s) from coming apart. Economist Hazel Henderson calls this cost the "social transaction cost," and she says, "The proportion of Gross National Product that must be spent in mediating conflicts, controlling crime, protecting consumers and the environment, providing ever more comprehensive bureaucratic coordination, and generally trying to maintain 'social homeostasis' [has begun] to grow exponentially. . . . All of those are social costs, *very necessary* social costs that we, as taxpayers, have to incur to clean up and deal with the system that we have created." And she adds, "I would say that the only fraction of the GNP that is growing at this point is the 'social costs' fraction."

Law of the disappearing middle. When technological development takes place outside of a system of ethics and values, or in terms of a system of ethics and values that celebrates growth and size and power, "all ambition and talent *goes to the frontier*," says economist E. F. Schumacher (in *Rain*, Jan. 1977), "the only place considered prestigious and exciting. Development proceeds from Stage 1 to Stage 2, and when it moves on to Stage 3, Stage 2 drops out; when it moves on to Stage 4, Stage 3 drops out, and so on." In this process, "The 'better' is the enemy of the good and makes the good disappear *even if* most people cannot afford the better, for reasons of Money, Market, Management, or whatever it might be. Those who cannot afford to keep pace drop out and are left with nothing but Stage 1 technology."

In Schumacher's example: if you want to farm, and you can't afford a tractor or a combine harvester (Stage 3 technology), you're not going to be able to find efficient animal-drawn equipment anywhere (Stage 2)—and so you're not going to be able to farm. (Stage 1 technology—in this case, the hoe and sickle—does tend to remain available. For the "nostalgia" market.)

Julius Lester puts it well when he says, "We're given two choices only: A shack, or a house that looks like it came in a cereal box. . . . I do not want to retain the shack, but there is something about its spirit which it may be fatal to lose. 'I was made by a person', it says, standing shakily at the edge of a cotton field. . . ."

Material goods, positional goods, and experiential goods. "Material goods" is economist Fred Hirsch's term for products that can be enjoyed no matter how many other people are consuming them. For example, my enjoyment of a meal or a TV set should in no way lessen your enjoyment of a similar meal or TV. "Positional goods" is Hirsch's term for products that cannot be enjoyed if a substantial number of people are also enjoying them. The pleasure that I get from a house in the country is diminished if too many other people have houses in the country. The advantages of a college diploma on the job market would vanish if everybody had diplomas. Hirsch likes to say that having a positional good is like standing tiptoe in a crowd: "If everyone stands on tiptoe, no one sees better."

So long as people are trying to meet their basic physiological and security needs (self-development needs one and two), getting "enough" material goods is their dominant concern. But once people have met their basic material needs, "demands for goods and facilities with a public [social] character"—in other words, demands for positional goods—"become increasingly active."

In this view, our economic problems are a product of our economic *success* and cannot be cured by "priming the economic pump" in the traditional way. Our economic problems come from the fact that most of us have already met our basic material needs and are busily acquiring positional goods, thereby making it harder and harder for us to *enjoy* our positional goods: cottages, diplomas, cars, etc. Our economic problems also come from the fact that none of our political ideologies are able to see this, and so the "solutions" they propose only make things worse. For example, schools are too expensive so we turn to the state to foster equality of educational opportunity, only to see our diplomas lose even more of their value on the job market.

New Age economic theory must recognize two things. First, it must recognize that positional goods are inherently abusive of the New Age political value of "maximization of social and economic well-being," because they tend to require a considerable degree of social and economic inequality for their enjoyment. And, second, it must concede that material goods as defined above are not enough to keep most of us happy—not, at any rate, after we've begun to take our material goods for granted (which has begun to happen in the Soviet Union but not yet in, e.g., China). Therefore, New Age political-economic practice must seek to replace positional with material goods, generally by replacing monolithic with biolithic institutions—shared cabins for private cottages, bicycles and/or mass transit for automobiles, "alternatives to compulsory schooling" for the universal compulsory school, etc.; and seek to replace the desire to acquire positional goods with the desire to acquire "experiential goods." ("Experiential goods" is my term for experiences that can be enjoyed no matter how many other people are having them. Appreciation of the world, psychic research, intellectual or artistic activity, and interpersonal relationships are examples of such experiences.)

Inflation

The left tends to blame inflation primarily on the capitalists; the right, on the unions and their wage demands. New Age economics is not really interested in making debating points along these lines, possibly because it is not interested in winning social classes—as distinct from individuals—over to its way of seeing. New Age economics tends to give more weight to the social and psychocultural factors behind the inflationary spiral, factors that appear to be traceable to all of us, and in about the same proportions.

Social factors. New Age economics sees no point in denying the fact that a large number of people—people whom E. F. Schumacher (in *Rain*, Nov. 1975) refers to as "groups of essential producers," garbage collectors, airline pilots, coal miners, etc.—have recently "discovered that they can successfully insist on much higher incomes than society . . . had hitherto granted them. They can insist because by withholding their goods and services they can bring the whole of society, or essential parts of it, to a standstill." They are, in short, demanding a larger piece of the economic pie—but the rest of us are not prepared to give it to them. The rest of us are determined to defend our own shares "by passing on higher costs and insisting on the maintenance of previously established relativities."

It isn't really a matter of employers gouging workers. Profit levels have—if anything—fallen since the 1940s and after-tax profits range from 3 to 7 percent. It is more a matter of white-collar workers refusing to let their income levels fall below blue-, beginning university instructors refusing to let their levels fall below garbage collectors' levels, and so on. Obviously, says Schumacher, no substantial group can obtain a bigger piece of the pie if the rest refuse to be content with a smaller piece. And so wages (and prices) are pushed up endlessly. . . .

The reason society continues to accede to *all* these groups' demands is that we no longer have a commonly shared system of ethics and values that can tell us what a fair system of income distribution might be. Until we have such a system, each group will feel that it has the right to decide on its own fair share, government will have no basis on which to intervene (without calling down the wrath of the electorate), and inflation will continue. In fact it will continue to get worse, for as society becomes more complexly dependent it becomes more vulnerable to the demands of its "essential producers."

Psychocultural factors. The very fact that we expect inflation to continue, says economist Ezra Mishan, causes us to ask for greater wage benefits and raise prices higher than we ordinarily might. To some extent, inflation is a self-fulfilling prophecy.

The Household Economy

This is one of the most important concepts in New Age economics (and it is a recurring one in American history: John Taylor of Carolina was talking about the household economy in the eighteenth century, Ralph Borsodi in the 1920s). It has recently been explained and interpreted for us by economist Scott Burns in his book *Home, Inc.*

According to Burns, we have not one but three economies: the "market," the "collective," and the "household" economies. The market economy is the sum of all the things and services that are produced in all our privately owned businesses and industries. The collective economy is the sum of all the things and services that are produced in all our publicly owned businesses and industries. And the household economy "is the sum of all the goods and services produced within all [our] households. . . . This includes, among other things, the value of shelter, home-cooked meals . . . weekend-built patios . . . home sewing, laundering, child-care, home repairs, voluntary services to community and to friends, the produce of the home garden, and the transportation services of the private automobile."

The market and the collective economies have long been visible to our conventional economists, "Establishment" and "radical-left" alike. But the household economy has always been invisible to them—to *both* of them. Because they don't consider that it *produces* anything. And they are right in the sense that nearly everything it produces comes without a price tag on it. But if people were paid for working in the household economy, the payments would amount to nearly a third of our Gross National Product—and about half of our disposable consumer income!

Significantly, we saved more money last year by *not* paying for people to wash our dishes, build our patios, grow our vegetables, etc., than was earned after taxes by all the corporations in America. Just as significantly, the household economy is amassing physical wealth faster than the corporate economy. Radical economists are fond of telling us that the one hundred largest industrial corporations control an ever-larger share of corporate assets. But we never hear from them that the corporate share of total national wealth has decreased substantially since 1929, and is continuing to decrease. In fact, by 1976, for the first time since the 1700s, the household economy was expected to contain *as great a percentage* of the U.S. national wealth as the market economy (roughly 41 percent), with the collective economy, at 16 percent, bringing up the rear.

The growth of the household economy implies that people are taking over from the monolithic institutions many of the tasks that they can do more cheaply or more efficiently or more satisfyingly by themselves. Consider, says Burns, that it is now possible to rent almost anything, from medical equipment to cement mixers. Consider that our new small-scale technology is making it possible for us to produce many goods more cheaply by the home than by the marketplace (a $12 tofu maker, for example, can give us an incredibly cheap source of protein). "The most significant aspect of the rise of rented objects and equipment is the fact that the labor usually employed in this equipment has been displaced from the marketplace to the household."

Burns concludes that the household economy is in a "no-lose" situation. If a full employment economy is our social goal, "traditional economic forces will work to push ever more labor out of the market economy and into the household economy, which obviously will continue to grow." On the other hand, if we adopt a guaranteed annual income, "that would allow millions of people to become full-time 'employees' of the household economy."

I am less optimistic than Burns; I think that the major threat to the household economy will come not from the market but from the collective economy. Like the household economy, the collective economy has gained about 5 percent of the national wealth (excluding land) since 1929; and unlike the household economy, the collective economy has many powerful advocates in Congress. The advocates of the collective economy, in their push for full 40-hour-a-week employment for all, are calling for a massive program of public works that would create many "jobs" that would, in effect, be competitive with jobs in the household economy. For example, some environmentalists have recently called for an energy package that would give people jobs putting storm windows on our houses and insulation in our attics.

I don't find it too farfetched to imagine that, in the near future, people will feel a lot of pressure *not* to do much work in the household economy (recycle your own wastes and you'll be doing garbage collectors out of their jobs, etc.). And that would make the concept of biolithic institutions, which allow us to *do for our selves*, about as realizable as the Marxists' "withering away of the state."

Part VII
HEALING SELF AND SOCIETY

CHAPTER 20

Some Guidelines

So far in this book, we've seen that Prison society cripples us in many ways—in so many ways that we tend to become our own best jailers. We have also seen that a genuine alternative to Prison society is at least possible for us now. What we've yet to see is whether we can get from here to there. And, just as important, whether we can do it without becoming like the liberals and Marxists in the process.

One thing is sure, it is important to do *something*. For as we've repeatedly seen, the Prison is growing in depth and strength, and we're becoming ever more dependent on our monolithic institutions (rather than on our selves). Unless this process is reversed, and soon, there will be no escaping from it, and life will become as comfortable, as regimented, and as flat as is life in a real prison. Then there are all the disasters, nuclear and ecological, that are waiting for us if we can't learn to love life more than things (according to Robert Heilbroner, a well-known economist, many of us are already subconsciously thinking, "let the drama proceed to its finale, let mankind suffer the end it deserves").

But what can we do? And where to begin?

Inner Before Outer

Traditionally, political people have believed that we needed to change the outer forms of society before we could—or should—begin to seriously change our selves. And in countries where millions of us are starving, who would disagree?

In the United States today, however, the problem isn't that millions of us are starving (in fact, one symptom of the problem is that millions of us are overeating). The problem is that most of us are trapped by the Prison and its institutions and are therefore *suffocating*—starved for strokes, starved for affection and esteem. Thrown back on our physiological and security needs. Always in need of *things* to ease our boredom (pain).

In the United States today, our problems are different from those of most other countries, and it follows that our strategy must also be different. In the United States our institutions are a fairly accurate reflection of our consciousness. If anything our institutions are better

than we deserve—surveys have consistently shown that our politicians
are *more* knowledgeable, *more* concerned about civil rights and civil
liberties, and *more* concerned about social justice than most of the rest
of us. If we did begin by changing our institutions—if that was our
strategy—then what kinds of changes would we try to bring about?
Inevitably, I think we'd try to make our institutions even more monolithic than they are. I think we'd choose to give up even more of our
power and responsibility to our institutions—including the top-down
state.

If we want to change the United States in a New Age direction, then
we're going to have to begin with our selves: with the Prison, with our
way of looking at the world, with our ethics and values. If we're able
to begin to change these things then our demands on our institutions
will change. Instead of wanting them to do more for us, we'd simply
want them to make it possible for us to do what we need to—for our
selves. We'd change them the better to allow us to lead lives of simple
(and genuine) pleasures such as friendship and creative activity and
service to others.

Werner Erhard and The Hunger Project have drawn our attention to
a very important point. Every attempt to change society takes place in
a particular atmosphere, or context. The context is our way of seeing
the world, and it determines, in large part, the meaning, the quality,
the "content" of what we see and do. In the United States today, I
think it's fair to say that the context—for most of us—is the Prison.
Therefore, when we try to "change the world" we almost inevitably
project the content of the Prison out *onto* the world. For example,
those of us who recognize poverty as a problem inevitably end up
proposing "solutions" that would render us *more* dependent on the
federal bureaucracy and *less* capable of caring for our selves. Those of
us who recognize transportation as a problem end up proposing "solutions" that would speed the tempo of our society up even faster.

Before we can change society deeply—before we can change it on
the third level of analysis—we're going to have to transform the context out of which we see. Specifically, we're going to have to transform
the Prison. And that means transforming our selves (see Chapter 21).

Another reason why it's important to begin with self has to do with
this: personal growth that's undertaken as *part* of a political movement
tends to become something else, something very different from personal growth. People begin to treat themselves as means rather than
ends, try to become "good communists" or "good Findhornians" (or
whatever) rather than who they really are. People begin to subordinate
their personalities and energies to group goals and group standards and
may end up even more out of touch with themselves than when they
started.

If we aren't clear about our own purposes and motives, then those
purposes and motives will return to confound us and corrupt our
political work. In the late 1960s I think that many of us felt too guilty
and/or too beset by urgency to begin with our selves—and it's because

of this that our movements so quickly lost touch with American reality.

"No values are effective," says Rollo May, "in a person or a society, except as there exists in the person the prior capacity to do the valuing, that is, the capacity actively to choose and affirm the values by which [he or she] lives." And, let's face it, that will require a lot of prior personal growth.

Personal growth must be priority number one for racial and ethnic minorities, for ex-felons, for addicts . . . for everyone. John Maher, head of the Delancey Street Foundation and an ex-felon himself, says (see Hampden-Turner), "People have gotta understand that society is all screwed up. We're going to change it. . . . But *before* we do that, we gotta understand that we ain't nice guys either. Social victims are generally pretty dangerous, nasty characters because we're pretty twisted, and we gotta untwist ourselves, so we're human beings. . . ."

And remember: healing one's self leads almost inevitably to a sense of oneness with other beings and to a desire to heal society. But ignoring one's self often leads either to apathy or to a desire to submerge one's self in a movement that gives one a counterfeit sense of identity and power.

J. Krishnamurti says somewhere that, after you become a whole human being, anything you do will be appropriate. However, until you become a whole human being, nothing you do will be quite appropriate.

I love that quote, but I think it's too extreme (product of the non-material worldview). There's no reason for us to wait until we've healed our selves completely (and thanks to our monolithic institutions, how can we—completely?). But there *is* reason to wait until we've at least got some perspective on our selves (that is to say: some humility) and some perspective on the Prison. Until we've at least *begun* to deal with our selves.

Self-awareness and self-development have become the "new panacea," according to a growing number of liberal and radical critics of the consciousness-and-growth movement. They should know: their ideology of "you're not responsible—we'll do it all for you" was certainly the old panacea. But if they mean to imply that the consciousness-and-growth movement makes people self-centered, then they are simply wrong. A number of recent studies have shown that participants in consciousness-and-growth groups are *more* socially responsible and *more* politically sophisticated than most of the rest of us (see, e.g., Donald Stone's work at the Survey Research Center, University of California at Berkeley). As a matter of fact, the real danger in this country—as Rollo May has pointed out—is the tendency to use activism as a substitute for aliveness. "Many people keep busy all the time as a way of covering up anxiety; their activism is a way of running from themselves." If self-awareness is in danger of turning into self-indulgence, then the tendency for social activism to become an acting-out of largely personal problems and grievances is an equally present danger—and a much more "American" one.

The Ballot, the Bullet—or the New Age Strategy?

Some of us believe that elections, all by themselves, can usher us into the New Age. Others of us believe that a violent revolution will be necessary—at least at some point. However, I believe that there's an emerging consensus among New Age people that sees serious flaws in both these solutions, and that calls, instead, for each of us to begin to get in touch with our selves and simplify our life-styles, and begin to work against our monolithic institutions in whatever way seems to flow most naturally from out of our own life situations.

Liberals hope to bring about social change by the ballot—by voting. It is true that many first- and second-level reforms have been voted in, and it's obviously worth our while to continue to vote them in. But we can't change society on the third level of analysis—we can't break out of the Prison—through the electoral process alone.

For one thing, election speeches, door-to-door campaign workers, etc., can rarely if ever change people's underlying ethics and values. (Our attitudes maybe—but the Prison is a matter of our nonconscious ideologies, not of our attitudes.)

For another thing, elections aren't designed to encourage us to make our own decisions or in any way to take responsibility for our lives; instead they're designed to encourage us to give our responsibility away to somebody else who promises to make our decisions for us.

The Marxist solution, on the other hand, and often the anarchist solution, is to call for the bullet—to call for a violent revolution. But if voting helps keep us passive, taking up the gun helps keep us death- and thing-oriented . . . obviously.

According to Richard Falk, the record of history shows that "drastic strategies of change are virtually doomed to produce bloodshed, excess, and a new reign of oppression." Jan Tinbergen reminds us that the resolution of conflict through violence opens the way to nuclear war, "a possibility unknown to the fathers of revolutionary thinking."

Violence could never, in any event, lead to a New Age society, since violence would drive most life-oriented people out of the revolutionary camp. (It always has—which is one reason why violent revolutions turn totalitarian.)

Another problem here, well made by Gene Sharp, is that violence tends to lead to the centralization of power. For one thing, violent revolutionary organizations always seem to require hierarchy and centralization in order to survive police repression; and once begun, this is a process that can never be stopped . . . even "After the Revolution." For another thing, a regime that's born out of violence and centralization will require continued violence and centralization to defend itself against internal and external "enemies." Finally, the violent struggle for power always weakens the independent revolutionary institutions and social groups that grew up before the violence started . . . leaving the new state that much more powerful, that much more of a monolithic institution.

But if the ballot and the bullet are both false options—where then can we turn?

On the second level of analysis, voting and violence do appear to represent all of our options. But on the third level of analysis, we can see that voting and violence are based on the *same false assumptions* about political power. The New Age perspective is based on different assumptions. And so it can lead to a different strategy for change.

On the third level, we can see that both liberals and Marxists assume that political power is ultimately in the hands of an elite—of competing elites or "countervailing powers" (a favorite liberal term) or of a "ruling class." And so both assume that in order to change society, we've got to change elites—by voting in a different elite, or by killing off the ruling class and setting up a "dictatorship of the proletariat," that is, a dictatorship.

Gene Sharp calls this the "monolith theory" of power. He states, "The 'monolith theory' of power assumes that the power of a government is a relatively fixed *quantum* [i.e., 'a discrete unit quantity of energy'], a 'given', a strong, independent, durable (if not indestructible), self-reinforcing and self-perpetuating force. . . . If it were true that political power possesses the durability of a solid stone pyramid, then it would also be true that such power could only be controlled by the voluntary self-restraint of rulers, by changes in the 'ownership' of the monolith (the State)—whether with regular procedures (such as elections) or with irregular ones, or by destructive violence."

The problem with the monolith theory of power is that it is factually not true—"*all* governments are dependent on the society they rule"— and "even a regime which believes itself to be a monolith, and *appears* to be one, can be weakened and shattered . . . when people act upon [a more accurate] theory of power."

Following Sharp (and others), New Age politics has been developing what I like to call the "biolithic theory" of political power. The biolithic theory holds that governments—all governments—depend ultimately on people, and that political power is therefore fragile, very un-stone-pyramid-like, because it depends ultimately on the continuing cooperation of many different groups of people. In this view, as Julius Lester puts it, "Power does not come from the barrel of a gun. Only bullets." Negative sanctions, including violence, may help to maintain a ruler's political power, but even the ability to impose sanctions depends on the obedience and cooperation of at least some of us. And the rest of us would have to fear the sanctions—more than we valued our freedom—for the sanctions to work.

Political power depends, then, ultimately on our consent. And in the United States we give that consent for the most part freely. We give it for many reasons besides fear of sanctions: habit, self-interest, apathy . . . we feel that we should, we identify with our rulers, we know things could be worse, we are lacking in self-confidence . . . our very belief in the monolith theory of power is a tacit way of giving our consent to the powers-that-be. Above all, though, is the fact that the American government is a government of, by, and for the Prison-bound. It is based on, and it fosters, all the Prison values. Is it any wonder that most of us are loyal?

In order to change Prison society, then, we are first going to have to withdraw our consent from the Prison within us. Otherwise we wouldn't *want* to change things on the third level of analysis, and all our elections, all our violence, would only help to produce societies that were more comfortable and more efficient Prisons.

At the same time, though, we can see that changing the Prison within us would not be enough to change Prison society. For the Prison has generated monolithic institutions that are self-perpetuating and that help to perpetuate the Prison within us. Our national government are, themselves, monolithic institutions.

So we are going to have to withdraw our consent from our monolithic institutions—including our national governments (at least to some extent)—as well as from the Prison itself. We are going to have to "withdraw our confidence," as Wendell Berry puts it, "from the league of specialists, officials, and corporation executives who for at least a generation have had almost exclusive charge of the problem and who have enormously enriched and empowered themselves by making it worse."

Withdrawing our consent on these two levels (inner and outer) *is the beginning of New Age politics.*

Political people have tended to disagree—often quite bitterly—over the question of whether it's "better" to work from within the system or outside it. Even some New Age people are at odds on this issue. For example: Donald Keys, of Planetary Citizens, feels there's a real need for "planetary-conscious" people to run for political office, while Stephen Gaskin, of The Farm, urges, "Don't take over the government. Take over the government's function."

There is, however, an emerging consensus among New Age people that suggests that the question is being posed in the wrong way. The point, they say, is first to get in touch with your self, and then to begin to simplify your personal life and life-style in a way that can reflect and deepen your new understandings. From there, each of us "should go where our hearts tell us to go," as David Spangler puts it, "hopefully without prejudgement. . . ."

Some of us will break away from the mainstream of society; others of us will work from within. Still others of us will find some kind of middle ground. If we've begun to transcend the Prison and our dependence on its institutions, if we've begun to see things in terms of New Age ethics and political values, then virtually *anything we did* would contribute to the healing of society. Mike Nickerson goes so far as to say, "An individual deciding to take a walk in the park rather than drive somewhere inclines the culture in a [New Age] direction. . . ."

It's true. There isn't time to wait for 51 percent of us to embark on our own personal journeys. And even if there were time—how could the rest of us wait?

Fortunately, the transition to the New Age doesn't have to wait with baited breath for the formation of a 51 percent majority. A *critical mass* will do the job.

A critical mass is the number of concerned and committed people it would take to move the continent—democratically—in a New Age direction. Estimates of what makes a critical mass range all the way from 2 percent (Transcendental Meditation) to 20 percent (Erich Fromm). The implication is that commitment and concern has a certain political weight of its own and that a minority of concerned people can and *should* affect the democratic process more strongly than a larger number of apathetic people.

If a critical mass is to develop around New Age issues and concerns it would have to be made up of people who are both free (or becoming free) of the Prison and who are willing to act. To Werner Erhard the critical mass would consist of people "who are willing to take responsibility for themselves." To Robert Theobald the critical mass would consist of people who are prepared to act cooperatively around a particular issue.

Some New Age groups have already had impacts way beyond their size. The Clamshell Alliance and the Greenpeace Foundation have demonstrated that life-oriented people united in nonviolent action can generate a lot of sympathetic attention. Citizens on Cycles (listed under Greater Philadelphia Bicycle Coalition) says that if 20 percent decide not to buy or use private automobiles—even for a year—we could have an enormous impact, not only on the automobile industry but on the economy as a whole.

The New Age can be brought about by a concerned and concerted minority acting on behalf of the New Age ethics and political values.

CHAPTER 21

Healing Self

This chapter is about how New Age people are trying to heal themselves. It is about how many of us have begun to break out of the Prison—and it is about further steps that many of us have wanted to take in the spiritual and human potential movements. It is also about a kind of simplified, more life-oriented life-style. Until we have begun to heal our selves, our politics cannot reflect the ethics and values in this book.

Breaking Out of the Prison

In order to *begin* to change our selves deeply, we are going to have to try to break out of at least one side of the Prison. (If we can begin to break out of one side, we can begin to see the rest of the Prison for what it is.)

Many of us who've chosen to focus on our *patriarchal attitudes* have joined men's and women's consciousness-raising groups (which I prefer to call consciousness-changing groups). Many women have found a good brief introduction to consciousness-changing (concept and issues) to be Koedt, Levine and Rapone, eds., *Radical Feminism*, Part IV (first four articles); the whole anthology is an excellent introduction to feminist issues from a "radical feminist" perspective (as distinct from a Marxist feminist perspective). Current issues of interest to feminists are discussed in feminist community newspapers such as *Plexus* (San Francisco) and *Sojourner* (Boston).

The best introduction to consciousness-changing for men that I know of is Part III of Warren Farrell, *The Liberated Man*; he also includes a chapter on joint men's and women's consciousness-changing groups. The most useful introduction to men's issues is Jack Nichols, *Men's Liberation*; he covers such topics as intellect ("the blind man's bluff"), playfulness ("recovering the missing ingredient"), competition ("winning isn't everything"), and dominance ("an impediment to awareness").

If you want to get in touch with a men's or women's group in your home community, you might begin by getting hold of the local contact for the National Organization for Women or the people who put out your local feminist newspaper or magazine.

Those of us who've wanted to break down our *egocentricity* have involved our selves in the spiritual movement. A good brief introduction to the spiritual scene is Theodore Roszak, *Unfinished Animal*. And there are some monthly magazines that can keep us up with issues—and current events—on the spiritual end of things: for example, *Alternatives, East West, New Directions, New Sun*, and *Yoga Journal*.

Nearly every major city now has a number of spiritual groups, and most of them will be kind enough to answer your questions and steer you to the group or groups that are most suited to your temperament and interests.

Those of us who've wanted to break down our *scientific single vision* and get back in touch with the intuitive, emotional, feeling side of our selves have tended to join groups doing "group therapy," or body therapy, or the "new sports" (these activities make up what's often referred to as the "human potential movement"). A good introduction to group therapy is William Schutz, *Joy* (1967); to body therapy, Alexander Lowen, *Bioenergetics* (1975); to the new sports, George Leonard, *The Ultimate Athlete*.

Most cities now have a number of consciousness-and-growth groups. If you can't find one that you like, or if you'd like to work more intensively away from your home, you can write away to any number of growth institutes (e.g., Esalen) or you can take a short-term program or "training" in a major city (from, e.g., Actualizations, Arica, or est).

Some of us who've wanted to get rid of our *bureaucratic mentalities* have been dropping out of the work-world for a year or more, and living cheap and interesting lives on our savings. The Bible for these people has been Ernest Callenbach, *Living Poor With Style*. He covers everything—eating, getting around, dwelling, furnishing, clothing, staying fit, raising children, fun and games. . . .

Others of us have managed to break down our bureaucratic mentalities—and also our *nationalism*—by getting involved in human-scale projects in our local communities. Nearly every community now has (or *should* have!) its own food co-op, parent-run daycare center, co-op radio, alternative school (or simply: alternative educational arrangement), newspaper, bookstore, co-op restaurant . . . and most of these are always on the lookout for volunteer and/or part-time staff. Boston Co-op Handbook Collective's *Food Co-op Handbook* (1976) is a very useful account of the problems that are involved in this kind of activity.

Many of us have gotten over our *big city outlooks* by spending a year or more in the country, or in a communal situation, or in both. Two of the best magazines on country living are *The Mother Earth News* and *New Farm*. Women should also see Sherry Thomas and Jeanne Tetrault, *Country Women: A Handbook for the New Farmer* (1976), a collection of dozens of articles on "how to negotiate a land purchase, dig a well, grow vegetables organically, build a fence and shed, deliver a goat, [etc.], all at the least possible expense and with minimum reliance on outside and professional help."

The best information source on communal living is the bi-monthly

magazine *Communities* which is edited—in part—by the very successful Twin Oaks community.

Breaking Out of Our Programming

Beginning to get free of the Prison is just that—a beginning. For
most of us, breaking through one of the Prison's walls brings us up
against the pain of realizing how badly we have been crippled as
human beings—how difficult it is to be honest or spontaneous or real.
It makes us conscious of old wounds and feelings of inadequacy.

In the long run, though—if we hope really to transform society
rather than get our selves more of the same—it is important for us to
deal with the insights and fears that the Prison has protected us
against. For until we are able to deal with these difficult understandings and fears, we will—most of us—continue to want to cling to the
consolations of the Prison, no matter what our rhetoric might be, and
no matter what our good intentions. (This is why so many political
people can work against sexism, say, or monolithic institutions, and
still be into patriarchal attitudes or the bureaucratic mentality.)

In order to see the kind of programming that we're up against—and
what we can do about it—it helps to understand that, as many New
Age people have recently pointed out, we have not one but three brains-
in-one. National Aeronautics and Space Administration psychologist
William Gevarter calls it the "triune brain" and says that it consists of
the "reptilian," the "old mammal" and the "new mammal" brains.

The reptilian brain, says Gevarter, is associated with "species-
specific" behavior—"basic ways of acting associated with being human"
—and is relatively unmalleable. It is not terribly important for our purposes. The old mammal brain contains our emotional programming—
"the basic value system upon which one acts automatically." The new
mammal brain contains our rational, "mental," "cognitive" programming.

Traditional political people focus thier attention exclusively on the
new brain's programming. What they fail to realize is that all our
responses to a situation are filtered through the old brain's programming as well as the new brain's, and unless we take steps to change the
programming of the old brain—in other words, to change not just our
intellectual selves, but our emotional selves—the old brain will continue to read even the most "revolutionary" new programs in the old
way; to subvert them according to the fears and needs put into us by
our old emotional programming.

According to Gevarter there are basically four ways that we can
change our old brain programming: defusing the emotional programming by removing the emotional "pegs" that hold the programming in
place; adding to the emotional programming "so that the net response
is more favorable"; removing the emotional programming from the
"feedback loop"; and breaking up the normal response patterns to

emotional stimuli. Each of these ways can be effective; each of them appeals to somewhat different life-styles and temperaments.

Defusing the emotional programming. Many of our new group therapies can be of help here. For example, in *Primal therapy* the person tries to go back to the earliest incident that gave rise to a particular program. This incident is relived with full emotional intensity. It is known as the original, or Primal, Pain, because pain is what we feel when we discover, as a child, that being our selves—being real—is unacceptable to our parents. "The real feeling self," said Primal therapist Arthur Janov, "is locked away with the original Pain: that is why [a person] must feel that Pain in order to liberate [him- or herself]; feeling that Pain shatters the unreal self in the same way that denying the Pain created it."

Our emotional programming is also responsible for much of our bodily tension. Therefore, much of the *body therapy* that goes on at human potential centers—rolfing, ta'i chi, acupressure massage and the like—can also serve to defuse our emotional programming (see, e.g., Stanley Keleman, *Your Body Speaks Its Mind*).

Finally, our emotional programming can be defused through *meditation*, which inactivates the new brain and lets our unresolved old brain patterns run themselves out (Lawrence LeShan's book *How to Meditate*, 1974, is a good basic introduction to the various kinds of meditation).

Adding to the programming. We can add to our emotional programming by learning to reprogram our selves with appropriate phrases. Ken Keyes's Living Love Way is based primarily on learning to use such phrases—this one, for example: "I welcome the opportunity (even if painful) that my minute-to-minute experience offers me to become aware of the addictions I must reprogram to be liberated from my robot-like emotional patterns." Instead of kicking the wall, repeat that to your self every time you fail to meet one of your "security, sensation, and power" needs—for example, the next time someone says they'd rather spend their time being somewhere else than being with you. Use those experiences for your consciousness-growth—that's the point. See what it gets you. . . .

The Cornucopia Institute holds workshops in the Living Love Way in major cities all over North America as well as at its center in Kentucky (St. Mary, Ky. 40063). But you can learn to use the Living Love system entirely from Keyes's *Handbook to Higher Consciousness* and from some supplementary materials.

Removing the emotional programming from the feedback loop. Transactional Analysis (TA) is a kind of group therapy that teaches us to distinguish among our three "inner voices": Parent, Adult, and Child. The Parent is said to be stern and judgmental; the Adult, data-processing and prediction-making; and the Child, playful, spontaneous, and creative.

In terms of the "triune brain," it is clear that the Adult is a new brain function and that Parent and Child are old brain functions (i.e., Parent and Child embody our old emotional programming). Therefore, "removing the emotional programming from the feedback loop" would mean learning to use our Adult whenever it seemed appropriate —for example, learning to speak out of our real wants and thoughts rather than out of the ones we're *supposed* to have (Parent). And it would mean learning to hook the other person's Adult whenever they started playing a social or psychological game that we didn't like (see, e.g., Muriel James and Dorothy Jongeward, *Born to Win*, 1971; Claude Steiner, *Scripts People Live*).

Breaking the normal response patterns. We can overload the old brain with emotional stimuli and fatigue so that the normal response pattern is broken up, leaving the old brain much more responsive to new emotional programming. One healing method that makes good use of this technique (among others) is est (formerly known as "Erhard Seminars Training"); see Chapter 27.

Voluntary Simplicity

As we begin to get free of the Prison—as we begin to heal our selves—we will naturally want to change our lives and life-styles from thing-oriented to life-oriented; from status-oriented to personal growth-oriented. A number of New Age people have begun to do this already. They call their new life-style "voluntary simplicity."

"The essence of voluntary simplicity," say Duane Elgin and Arnold Mitchell (in Stanford Research Institute's most popular report ever), "is living in a way that is outwardly simple and inwardly rich. This way of life embraces frugality of consumption, a strong sense of environmental urgency, a desire to return to living and working environments which are of a more human scale, and an intention to realize our higher human potential—both psychological and spiritual—in community with others." In other words: voluntary simplicity is at least potentially an embodiment and expression of the New Age ethics . . . and of many New Age values.

Even the nonviolence ethic is an integral part of voluntary simplicity. Richard Gregg, nonviolent strategist and activist, says, "The concentration of much property in one person's possession creates resentment and envy or a sense of inferiority among others who do not have it. Such feelings, after they have accumulated long enough, become the motives which some day find release in acts of mob violence. Hence, the possession of much property becomes inconsistent with principles of nonviolence."

According to Ernest Callenbach, "Penny-pinching is bad for the spirit," and voluntary simplicity is not a "kind of trim-here and squeeze-there" approach to life. Instead, it "recognizes that buying (with all the cost-consciousness and calculation it involves) is not the central question. The central question is *how to organize your life.* If you decide to organize it by your own standards and desires and needs, you will . . . come to know what your necessities really are. Obviously these will include food and shelter and clothes—possibly on a more modest scale than you tended to think. But they may also include music or flowers or a southern-exposure window; privacy or an open-door policy; lots of heat or lots of fresh air. . . ."

Charles Wagner, a French pastor and educator, is even more insistent on the fact that voluntary simplicity is—above all—an *inner* condition. In his book *The Simple Life*, first published in 1895, he states, "This outward show ["plain dress," "modest dwelling," "slender means," etc.], which may now and then be counterfeited, must not be confounded with its essence and its deep and wholly inward source. *Simplicity is a state of mind*. It dwells in the main intention of our lives. A [person] is simple when [his or her] chief care is the wish to be . . . honestly and naturally human" (emphasis his).

Robert Gilman, a New Age-oriented scientist and builder, feels that the term "voluntary simplicity" is much too narrow. In *CoEvolution Quarterly* (Spring 1978) he writes, "A less catchy but more accurate description would be 'voluntary de-emphasis of the cash economy,' which often leads to a life-style that is more complex, as well as more rewarding, than the one-dimensional existence of the full-time marketplace specialist."

According to Planetary Citizens (in *One Family*, Sept. 1977), voluntary simplicity "is the appropriate stance in the light of the lacks suffered by two-thirds of the human race. . . . Energy, materials, inventiveness, creativity and peoplepower can be freed in large amounts by voluntary simplicity, and can be reoriented toward raising the level of well-being and self-respect of Third World people. . . . At the same time, voluntary simplicity sets a model of creative self-reliance which may assist the 'other worlds' in avoiding an unthinking adoption of the acquisition, competition, complication and consumerism models of Western society."

It is important to understand what voluntary simplicity is *not*. It is not a back-to-the-land movement, though many people and eventually some communities may choose to lead a more agrarian existence. It is not limited to the counterculture; by now probably most "simple livers" would say they were not countercultural. It is not a passing fad—it is rooted too deeply in people's needs and in the emerging new ethics and values for that. Finally, it is the very *opposite* of poverty: poor people tend to *want* the material goods that they can't afford.

As an idea, voluntary simplicity is not new; in Chapter 25, below, we will see that it was practiced and preached by a number of early American advocates of New Age politics. "Historically," say Elgin and Mitchell, "voluntary simplicity has its roots in the legendary frugality and self-reliance of the Puritans" and the Quebecois fur traders and the native North Americans and in "the teachings and social philosophy of a number of spiritual leaders such as Jesus and Gandhi." What gives voluntary simplicity a uniquely modern aspect is the fact that it is no longer merely one way of choosing to live one's life; it is, rather, a rational and altogether *necessary* response (though by no means a sufficient response) to a number of serious social problems. Elgin and Mitchell list them: ". . . the prospects of a chronic energy shortage;

growing demands of the [insufficiently] developed nations for a more
equitable share of the world's resources; the prospect that before we
run out of resources on any absolute basis we may poison ourselves to
death with environmental contaminants; a growing social malaise and
purposelessness. . . ."

Some New Age people have begun to advocate voluntary simplicity
for just that reason: that sooner or later we will almost certainly "have
to" live that way. To which I answer, true enough. But I would rather
point to how much more satisfying a simple life-style might be, than
try to "guilt" or frighten people into exactly the same behavior. The
simplicity must be voluntary, after all, if it is not to become gray and
mean-spirited; and by stressing the positive aspects of voluntary simplicity we may be able to educate people out of the Prison and its
institutions, rather than merely to the fact that the United States is
losing its power in the world.

No one is really sure how many Americans are already living lives
of voluntary simplicity. Elgin and Mitchell estimate that 2½ percent
of the adult population—five million people (!)—are "fully and
wholeheartedly" living in voluntary simplicity with another 7½ percent or so living lives of "partial voluntary simplicity." However,
Michael Phillips (in *CoEvolution Quarterly*, Summer 1977) argues
that these figures are about a hundred times too high. He defines
voluntary simplicity as "the rejection of 'making a lot of money' as a
personal goal," and he says, "almost no one *wants* to earn less next
year than they earned this year. If a public opinion survey asked the
question: 'Would you like to make a lot of money?' you would not find
5,000,000 people saying 'No'." He concludes, "I personally think the
growth of [the] real simple living movement will parallel the spread of
Eastern spiritual practices," and in this I think he is close to the mark:
simple living is implicit in and a result, not of "Eastern spiritual practices" per se, but of all our attempts to break free from the Prison.

Ways to Voluntary Simplicity

You don't have to join a group, lay out money, sign a petition, or
anything else to begin living a life of voluntary simplicity. All you have
to do is decide that you *want* to—and then begin doing some of the
things that are described here. (If you want more information on any
of these topics—or more suggestions!—you should refer back to my
sources: Tom Bender, *Sharing Smaller Pies*; Ernest Callenbach, *Living
Poor With Style*; Center for Science in the Public Interest (CSPI), *99
Ways to a Simple Lifestyle*; Simple Living Collective, *Taking Charge*;
and an excellent newsletter, *Simple Living*.)

First steps. Choosing to live more simply doesn't mean cutting back
on the basics—or "cutting back" at all. What it really means is re-
examining and revising your goals and priorities.

There are a number of ways that this can be done. Lucy Anderson, in *Taking Charge,* suggests one activity that her group—the American Friends Service Committee—has found to be especially helpful. Draw a circle (balloon) in the middle of a piece of paper. Put your name on it. Around this balloon, make a balloon for each of the activities that occupies your waking time each week (for example, job, family, friends, dance, women's group, exploring new ideas, television)—the size of each balloon should represent the amount of time you give to that activity. Then, draw a line from the center balloon to each activity balloon. Make the thickness of the line represent "the strength of your commitment to that activity and the pleasure you receive from it."

What does your balloon chart tell you about your life?

Another good way to begin reassessing your values and priorities is to simply sit down and figure out how you could live on half your present income. One-fourth of your income. Don't say it can't be done, figure out how it *could* be done. Would you have to change your life-style in any way? Would you have to live by different values? Would the differences in life-style and values help you to meet your real priorities? Did you learn anything else from this game? (You might want to try it now, and then try it again after you come to the end of this chapter.)

Finally, it is good to remember that trying to change your values and priorities is like stepping into water. You can always pull back if it gets too uncomfortable. So don't be afraid to try things, even if they seem strange at first. Tom Bender writes, "Any proposal for changes can be met with a thousand reasons why it might not work. Most such questions can only be answered by trying it. One experiment is worth a thousand buts."

Food. Now that you see that voluntary simplicity means living *better,* not "poorer," it is time to get really specific. We'll start with food, because we are always making choices about the foods we eat—and choosing to eat better foods is easy. All it takes is will. And a respect for our bodies (i.e., for our selves).

We can, for example, decide to consume more nutritious foods. Since 1940 per capita consumption of dairy products has declined 19 percent, fresh vegetables, 17 percent, fresh fruits, 44 percent. On the other hand, the pastry and fried snack industries have boomed. And soft drink sales are up by over 100 percent. If you're just plain getting tired of the "usual" foods, chances are good that you're not preparing them in anything like the number of possible ways. You should certainly look into Sigrid Shepard's remarkable *Thursday Night Feast and Good Plain Meals Cookbook* ($12.95 from New Age Printing, Inc., East 9514 Montgomery, Spokane, Wash. 99206)—800 natural food recipes from China, Japan, Indonesia, India, and the Middle East, all using common, easy-to-obtain ingredients.

We can decide to select unprocessed foods. White flour and white rice have been robbed of nutrients and fiber—and good taste! Many food additives are unsafe; nevertheless, since 1955 the number of additives in our food has doubled. And so on. Many cookbooks are now available that rely solely on natural health-giving foods that are free of chemical preservatives, additives, pesticides, and artificial growing conditions; I suppose my favorite is still Sharon Cadwallader and Judi Ohr, *Whole Earth Cook Book* (1972).

We can certainly cut down on our intake of refined sugar. Refined sugar contains neither vitamins, nor minerals, nor protein, and is a chief cause of tooth decay, obesity, and diabetes. Still and all—everyone loves sweets. So check out, e.g., Ruth Laughlin, *Natural Sweets and Treats* (1973).

We can also decide to consume less meat. Most Americans eat more protein than their bodies need; a hangover, perhaps, from the days when most of us were manual laborers. Worse, the amount of vegetable protein used in livestock feed in the United States equals 90 percent of the world's protein deficit! For every pound of meat, we feed a cow from 14 to 21 pounds of protein from sources that could be used directly as food. And things are getting worse: U.S. per capita consumption of beef has *more than doubled since 1940*. But this doesn't have to be. There are many other sources of protein besides meat: dried milk, cheese, fish, eggs, nuts, brown rice, beans, peas. . . . The point is to eat them in their proper combinations, achieving "protein complementarity," a kind of gastronomic synergy! See Ellen Ewald, *Recipes for a Small Planet* (1972).

I am not saying that we should all become vegetarians. But it would make sense for us to eat more vegetables and less meat. If that sounds unpleasant to you, check out Anna Thomas's book *The Vegetarian Epicure* (1972). You will be inspired! You might also investigate tofu (often called bean curd)—an extremely delicious source of nonanimal protein that has always been popular in Japan, and is becoming more and more popular in this country. See William Shurtleff and Akiko Aoyagi, *The Book of Tofu* (1975).

There are many small things we can do that are humanly satisfying and that can give us better, cheaper, simpler food. We can bake our own bread—bake it with lots of honey, which I did one time by mistake and have done ever since. We can bake it in quantity and freeze it. (See Ed Brown's wonderful *Tassajara Bread Book*, 1970.) We can prepare many other food products at home, such as cereals, yogurt, sprouts, party dips, peanut butter, salad dressings, ice cream, and the ubiquitous tofu. We can drink homemade beverages—apple cider, fruit juices, applejack, natural teas, etc. (see Shirley Ross, *Nature's Drinks*, 1974). We can buy foods that are grown close to home, that is, foods that are allowed to ripen on trees and vines, rather than in transit. And we can learn to preserve food—canning, freezing, drying, etc. (see Ruth Hertzberg, et al., *Putting Food By*, rev. ed., 1975).

We can consider growing our own food. If you don't have a yard of your own, you can ask to use a friend's or neighbor's—and volunteer to share some of your produce in return. A fine, New Age-oriented gardening book is Catharine Foster, *The Organic Gardener* (1972).

We can shop more carefully. We can, for example, eat before we shop. If we don't, we'll end up buying more. We can try to avoid buying presliced meats and cheeses. The slicing and packaging can more than double the price. We can avoid buying canned baby food— we can mash up regular people's food for babies. We can plan on shopping for a week at a time (the less often we go into a store, the less we'll spend). We can buy good food in small quantities rather than cheap food in large. A third of a pound of steak, for example, is better than a pound of fatty hamburger. And we can avoid canned vegetables. They're tasteless, and they're far less nutritious than fresh or frozen vegetables.

Finally, we can ask some questions about pet food—and maybe even about our pets themselves. We spend about $2.75 billion a year on commercially-prepared pet food, which is equal to the dollar value of the food needs of nearly 40 percent of the world's poor. All domestic animals can be fed on table scraps supplemented with commercial dry cereals. Pets are, themselves, often the recipients of strokes that we are too shy or selfish or unimaginative to direct to other human beings.

Clothing. The *last* thing we need to do, in order to simplify our clothes habits, is to decide to make "sacrifices" here. That will only induce us to buy more of some other kind of "good" in order to keep our selves from feeling bad. The first thing we need to do is to step back for a moment and get some perspective on our clothes buying.

Susan Lee, in *Taking Charge*, would have us ask, "What is my usual frame of mind when I set out to buy clothes? Do I go clothes shopping because I am not feeling good about myself and therefore need an ego boost? Do I shop when I am bored and need something to do? What else could I do to feel better or active, rather than buying clothes I may not really want?"

Susan Lee goes on to suggest, "Make an inventory of the clothes you own. Consider how many pants, coats, shoes, socks, shirts, and suits you have. Which ones have you worn in the last year? In the last two years? Can you determine how they contribute to your well-being? Might your unused clothing be given, traded, or sold at low cost to others?"

Besides simply buying less (and therefore spending less), there are many options. For one thing, we can make our own clothing. Homemade clothing generally affords a better fit, wears longer, and costs less than factory-made clothing. Besides, sewing and knitting are meaningful activities that allow us to relax and develop a skill . . . and develop our self-reliance. Beyond a certain point they're even fun. For a clear and simple introduction to the simple art of clothes-making, see Sharon Rosenberg and Joan Wiener, *The Illustrated, Hassle-Free, Make Your Own Clothes Book* (1969).

Another thing we can do is to buy more used clothes. Fashion-conscious Americans spend $70 billion on clothes each year. ("This is enough," says Susan Lee, "to drape the Earth.") Most of these clothes are thrown out sooner or later (usually sooner, when styles change), but some of them find their way into thrift stores, secondhand shops, and so on. If you pick out a secondhand store and frequent it occasionally, you should be able to meet your clothing needs for one-fourth or less of what you might otherwise spend.

We can barter for clothing—for example, with friends who don't know how to sew. We can swap clothing—that way we can get a free new wardrobe, and have a lot of fun besides. And we can mend and reuse clothing. And if we don't want to wear mended clothes, we can mend them anyway and barter or swap for something else.

I can't end this section without at least mentioning that, every year in the United States, 12 million animals including beavers, lynx, otters, seals, wolves, foxes, and raccoons are victims of a fur trade that caters to fashion. Many of these animals are caught in the steel-jaw trap, which not only tortures them needlessly but also crushes—"inadvertently"—literally millions of non-fur-bearing animals as well (which trappers refer to as "trash": geese, ducks, song birds, eagles, owls, porcupines, and the like). Spotted cats (including the tiger, leopard, jaguar, cheetah, and ocelot) may soon be extinct because of our need for fashion.

Oh, and we can sleep without pajamas.

Shelter. We don't have to move in order to change our dwelling place—wherever it is—into one that is more economical and more satisfying.

We can insulate properly—heating bills might go down by half. And we can investigate solar heating and cooling systems (see, e.g., Charles Barnaby et al., *Solar for Your Present Home,* 1977, available from California Energy Resources Commission, 1111 Howe Ave., Sacramento, Calif. 95285).

We can decorate our homes more simply and more uniquely. "Home decorations," says CSPI, "are an expression of one's life-style. House plants and simple homemade creations . . . save money, resources, and energy over luxurious decoration."

We can eliminate unnecessary appliances. The average American household has twenty-nine electrical appliances—most of which are not labor-saving devices at all, but are wasteful and inefficient. At the same time, we can share some of our tools and appliances. A city block or a group of friends could arrange to share washers and dryers, power tools, lawn mowers, etc. That could save us hundreds of dollars a year, and provide us with many social opportunities.

It's easy to repair furniture, and even to make furniture (see William Schremp, *Designer Furniture Anyone Can Make,* 1972). Good quality used furniture is better than poor quality new, and can be bought for a fraction of the price at auctions, garage sales, thrift shops, and the like.

We might want to consider asking people to live cooperatively or communally with us.

If you are thinking about building your own home, read and ponder: Ken Kern, *The Owner-Built Home: A How-to-do-it Book,* rev. ed. (1975); Ken Kern et al., *The Owner-Builder and The Code: Politics of Building Your Own Home* (1976, available for $5 from Owner-

Builder Publns., P.O. Box 550, Oakhurst, Calif. 93664); and River, *Dwelling: On Making Your Own* (1974).

Solid waste. Everything around us, it seems, is conspiring to make us add to the planet's garbage. But there are, nevertheless, a number of small but meaningful things that each of us can do to buck the tide.

We can, for example, try to avoid disposable paper products (an insult to trees, a wasteful use of energy). We can try to avoid buying plastic-wrapped items (plastic packaging litters the environment and does not decompose). And we can consciously decide to avoid nonreturnable products—as much as possible, at any rate (there are now 40 *billion* throwaway bottles a year in the United States alone!).

Much can be recycled. Metal cans. Newspapers and magazines. Food scraps, leaves, weeds, grass clippings, wood chips, etc. (this makes a great compost). Most Americans, of course, throw these things out—in green plastic bags!

We can avoid aerosol sprays. They are harmful, expensive, and wasteful, a major source of air pollution, a probable cause of lung cancer, and damaging to the skin.

Finally—last but not least—we can learn to use toilets more wisely. A family of four uses close to 90 gallons of fresh water a day for flushing toilets (at five gallons a flush). If you're squeamish about not flushing, you might want to follow Brad Deam's advice (in *New Age*, Dec. 1978) and try putting a small plastic bleach bottle full of water in the commode tank (would cut down on water used per flush). We might also want to investigate flushless toilets. The flush toilet pollutes whole bodies of water and requires expensive, unreliable, and energy-intensive waste treatment plants. But nonwater toilet systems are available; see, e.g., Sim vander Ryn, *The Toilet Papers* (1978).

Transportation. Most Americans will drive their cars if their destination is more than *two blocks* away. (Several studies have found this to be true.) However, with a little conscious effort, we can free our selves from many of the burdens of the "monolithic mode of transportation."

At the very least, we can begin to share our cars. Every day, 58 million American workers drive their cars to and from work. Of these, 40 million drive alone. If we got together with our friends and neighbors (or with people at work) and set up car pools, we could save hundreds of dollars each in commuting costs (gas, parking, repairs, etc.), do away with "rush-hour traffic," and get a chance to talk with people.

If we live within two miles or so of work, a bicycle—or a good brisk walk—might get us there just as well, and be better exercise and more fun. After we're "grown up" we tend to forget that bicycles are good exercise, convenient, fun, and capable of carrying almost anything. After we've bought our first car, we tend to forget that walking is a pleasure.

We might also begin to use busses and subways and trains more often. When some of us complain about how bad public transportation is in our town, often what we're really saying is that we go stir-crazy if we have to spend time waiting for a bus. We should ask our selves if we could spend this time in a happy or productive way—by thinking about things, by reading a magazine or book, by looking out calmly at the world. I strongly suspect that it is our inability to do this—to enjoy time rather than kill time—that causes us to rush everywhere in cars.

Health. To simplify our lives, we must know how to keep our bodies healthy and how to heal them once they get sick. We must take responsibility for healing our selves medically and view health workers as our assistants rather than our saviors. A number of self-help health books have recently been published; three that I consider essential are Mike Samuels and Hal Bennett, *The Well Body Book* (1973), which tells us how to treat the causes rather than the effects of our diseases; Naboru Muramoto, *Healing Ourselves* (1973), a good basic introduction to Eastern healing concepts; and Boston Women's Health Book Collective, *Our Bodies, Ourselves,* 2nd ed. (1976), subtitled "A Book By and For Women." For an introduction to the whole concept of medical self-care (and an overview of the burgeoning field of self-care), see Berkeley Holistic Health Center, *The Holistic Health Handbook* (1978).

I don't mean to imply that we need to "do it all our selves." Even now, some communities have community-based health clinics that encourage us to take a lot more interest in our health. Often these "alternative" health clinics operate on shoestring budgets. But they tend to make good use of volunteer and paraprofessional staff; they tend to be very honest about what they can and cannot do; they tend to tell you exactly what is wrong with you and why—to treat you like an adult rather than a dependent; they are often controlled by the people who use and work in them; and they can save you a lot of money.

I should also mention dental care here. Most of us treat our teeth badly. By age fifteen, the average American has had eleven decayed teeth. Read Thomas McGuire's wonderful book *The Tooth Trip* (1972). Follow it like the wilderness guide that it is.

Some things we can do with no reading, no investigation, no preparation at all. For example, we can decide not to abuse drugs. Overall we spend $10 billion a year on drugs, mostly pills, whose purpose is to calm us down, stimulate us, put us to sleep. . . . In many cases these drugs are just substitutes (and poor ones at that) for getting in touch with our selves and learning to rest and relax.

We can stop smoking cigarettes. A person who smokes half a pack a day surrenders, on the average, 5½ years of life. (Nevertheless, the number of smokers is on the rise again.) The person I dedicated this book to, an inveterate smoker, died of lung cancer at the age of fifty-three. She used to laugh at this section in its earlier drafts.

We can try not to drink too much. Most of us drink alcohol to loosen up, to get rid of our inhibitions, to get free, for a fleeting time, of the Prison. We spent about $32 billion on alcohol in 1978, or about $150 for every man, woman, and child.

And we can try to watch weight. Over half of the American population weighs at least 10 percent more than the norm for their particular age, sex, and height! Nearly 30 percent of us weigh 20 percent more than the recommended weight. Most of these people are suffering from no more than overeating and lack of exercise. The best type of exercise —walking and jogging—requires no fuel energy, capital, maintenance, expense, or rigorous training.

Fun and fulfillment. Most of the things we do in order to enjoy ourselves are neither very enjoyable nor very fulfilling.

Take television, our real national pastime. Jerry Mander, in *Four Arguments for the Elimination of Television* (1978), says, "People [are] seeing television images of Borneo forests, European ballets, varieties of family life, distant police actions, current events, or recreations of historical crises, and they [are] believing themselves to be experiencing these places, people and events. Yet the television image of the Borneo forest or the news or historical event [is] surely not the experience of them. . . . It [is] only the experience of sitting in a darkened room, often alone, with the body totally stilled, even the eyes unmoving . . . passively staring at flickering light."

The average adult, in America today, watches TV for almost four hours a day, according to Mander. (The average *set* is on for over *six* hours a day.) That's roughly half of the adult nonsleeping, nonworking time.

Or look at our travel habits. "People travel for many reasons," say the editors of *Rain* (April 1976), "yet very few of those reasons can best be satisfied by travel. Entertainment, rest, and 'getting away' can all take place in our own home communities. Wise travel requires that we first minimize unnecessary travel by improving the places where we live and our relationship with the people with whom we live."

If we do begin to spend less time watching TV, and if we do begin to travel less, than we might find that there's more to do than we ever thought possible.

We can begin, perhaps, by deciding to treat our best friends well. We might engage them in honest conversations; we might try to express our affection for them. We might also be open to new friendships and to many different kinds of relationships.

We can get to know our communities better. Most communities have at least a couple of beautiful parks; tennis courts, baseball fields, etc., are often available; hanging out in different neighborhoods is fascinating and educational. And it's remarkable how many things go on in our communities that we could attend free, or for a very low cost. Check out the newspapers, especially the weekend newspapers, which often have listings of museums, special exhibitions, political meetings, lectures, free or low admission concerts, dances, court sessions, city council meetings; check out community and "alternative" newspapers; check out bulletin boards, especially the ones in libraries and around universities and colleges (where most events, including movies and plays, are reasonably priced).

We can begin to think about expressing our selves, rather than buying in to the world that we see on the screen and from the so-called freeway. For example, we can try to give creative gifts, rather than store-bought ones. "Most of us," say Lucy Anderson and Susan Lee (in *Taking Charge*), "usually head for a store when we want to get a gift. . . . But how often do these purchased gifts make a statement that is genuinely personal, showing thoughtful consideration of the recipient's personality and interests, as well as being truly expressive of values we want to uphold? . . . Creative simplicity can inspire us to find or make meaningful gifts for those we care about"—gifts such as a jar of homemade preserves, a dragonfly wing, a poem, a song, a day of house-cleaning by friends.

Or we can try to create our own celebrations. Certainly, rituals and celebrations don't need to be bought ready-made from the dominant culture. For example, on Easter day we could make a point of traveling to a beautiful spot with our friends, and read to each other—words of rebirth; or, for example, we could declare a day in early July "Interdependence Day," a day to celebrate planetary consciousness (Planetary Citizens actually did this one year). Write away for the *Alternate Celebrations Catalogue,* 5th ed., 1978 ($5 from Alternatives, 1924 E. 3rd St., Bloomington, Ind. 47401).

We certainly don't need to be "professionals" to enjoy expressing our selves artistically. The arts can, and should, be practiced for their own sake—and for your own sake! With little money, we can practice —and often become quite good at—dancing and ballet, choral arts and singing, painting and sculpting, photography and drama, piano and guitar. . . . We can practice weaving, embroidering, batiking, appliqué-ing, knitting, quilting. We can make puppets, prints, collages, ceramics, toys. . . .

We can use our local library, which offers us free books, magazines, films, talks, and presentations.

We can learn to camp and backpack. And we don't need to take along every home comfort—see Colin Fletcher's wonderful book *The Complete Walker* (1974).

And we can learn to enjoy participatory and inexpensive sports— sports that cost little or nothing in either equipment, travel to site, or fuel energy: tennis, outdoor swimming, basketball, soccer, baseball, fishing, skating, jogging, judo, gymnastics. . . . And see New Games Foundation, *The New Games Book* (1976), an illustrated compendium of games such as Tweezli-Whop, Catch the Dragon's Tail, Ooh-Ahh, and Slaughter.

Work. Many of us feel trapped by our jobs. And many others of us are afraid to dwell on our jobs too much, for fear that we will feel trapped. We must, however, pluck up our courage, if we want to live more simply, and look our jobs full in the face. We should try to reevaluate them, and what we want from them.

Lucy Anderson suggests, "Make a list of what you would like to do in your lifetime or write up your own *Who's Who* entry as if it were written about you at age 70. Be imaginative and complimentary. What do you really want to do? Please dream! . . . Having described what you want to do, examine what skills, abilities, and experiences you have or need to carry out your vision. . . . Assess each new skill according to the time and effort it involves. Research and discover the most resourceful ways to acquire the needed skills." Ask yourself what relation your present job has to your real hopes for your self. To the skills and experiences you'll need to actualize those hopes.

You might want to ask whether you do, in fact, need a full-time job. Look over the ways to simple living, above, and ask your self: Am I spending too much on food? Are my clothing needs exaggerated? Could I do without my car? Could I fill my leisure time with inexpensive and rewarding things to do? If so, wouldn't I *rather* have time than money? And so on.

Tom Bender asks, "Is what you produce a luxury or does it fulfill a real need? Will what you do be affordable when we are less wealthy?" He advises, "Move toward more useful and secure kinds of work."

Certainly you should try to get out of debt. The average American—man, woman, and child—is over $500 in debt. There's nothing like "credit" buying to keep a person working at a useless, boring, and degrading job.

You can also try to create or invent your own job. Many communities need child-care centers, legal aid services, honest car repair services, tutors. . . .

If you have decided that you don't need a full-time job (and the salary from same), you might want to consider job sharing. In job sharing, jobs that would ordinarily be filled by one person are divided and shared by two or more people. In his important article "Job Sharing Is Good" (*CoEvolution Quarterly*, Summer 1978), Robert Gilman states, "It is a remarkably flexible concept in terms of the time cycle of the sharing, the number of people per full time position, and the types of occupations to which it is applicable. . . . It is hard to imagine an occupation that would not be amenable to some form of job-sharing *as long as the cycle period was properly chosen*" (emphasis his).

Mark Zwick, a psychiatric social worker, says (in *Taking Charge*), "Working half-time allows me as a husband to have more energy to plan and do things with my wife and children. . . . I can now think about community involvement with my wife, writing, and being involved in my children's education." And Susan Steinberg, who is sharing a teaching job with a friend, says (in *Simple Living*, Winter 1977), "It's remarkable how much more space I feel in my life. . . . The difference, I think, is that my job is no longer my whole life. I can become absorbed in the people in my life and so my life has many more dimensions. . . . Of course, I do have less money and that has taken adjusting to. I've especially had to cut back on the money I spent to entertain myself and to ease the pain: less movies, less eating out, less buying new clothes to counteract my depression. But I also need all those things less."

You might even want to consider income sharing. "Income sharing means equal distribution (or distribution according to need) of earnings within a family, an extended family, or an intentional community" (*Taking Charge*). In fact, income sharing could be practiced among *any* group of friends. Instead of *everyone* working *all* the time, everyone could take turns working—and pool the income. Everyone who wasn't working would be free to spend their time as they liked (New Agers would spend the bulk of their time in healing self and healing society). The point is to have something useful and compelling to do.

CHAPTER 22
Healing Society

This chapter is about how New Age people are trying to heal or transform (at this point the words are synonymous) society.

A number of New Age people have argued that the process of social transformation should take place in three fairly distinct stages: cultural change, "group work," and political and institutional change. There is, however, an emerging consensus among many New Age people that would avoid all talk of stages and, more generally, all advice to others about what they "should" do next.

In this view, the assumption that there can be one "correct" scheme for healing society is an assumption that leads almost inevitably to authoritarian political parties—and authoritarian societies. Moreover, the United States is now so interconnected and interdependent that just about *anything* we do that is in tune with the New Age ethics and political values would help bring New Age society about.

If enough of us, a "critical mass," share in the New Age ethics and political values and are active in the areas that are most accessible to us or that "feel right" to us when we've begun to meet our needs for love and esteem and self-actualization and self-transcendence—then society will begin to move in a New Age direction. More rapidly than we might imagine.

People tend to "burn out" (to get bored or depressed by working for social transformation) for either or both of these reasons: they have not bothered to begin healing self; they are engaging in the social transformation activities that they think they *should* be doing rather than the ones that come most naturally to them. However, it is rare that a person who begins to get in touch with him- or herself doesn't come to feel a deep inner need to help transform society in at least one of the ways in this chapter. And each of them can help to move society in a New Age direction.

In the pages that follow, I survey four basic, and complementary, strategies for social transformation: group work, intentional communities, nonviolent action, and electoral politics. All of the groups mentioned in this chapter are described more fully in Chapter 27 (unless their address is in parentheses).

Group Work

One of the ways that New Age people have been trying to heal or transform society has been by working in small or small-ish groups.

Most New Age political thinkers feel that this is an essential part of the process of transforming society. Herb Kohl, educator and activist, says, "No one can struggle alone with as much energy as is required to sustain something of value in this culture. . . . This is not a time for prophets but a time for action initiated and sustained by small groups of people."

New Age caucuses are all those groups that are trying to work for New Age-oriented change-and-transformation from within our already established social, cultural, economic, and professional organizations and institutions. The typical New Age caucus consists of a number of factory workers or office workers or professionals who know and trust each other and spend part of their time trying to encourage fellow factory workers, etc., to think of themselves less as economic people, and more as self-developing persons.

Caucus members do this by trying to bring New Age perspectives to bear on immediate workplace issues and by trying to change office rules, union demands, professional standards, etc., in line with these perspectives. For example: a New Age factory caucus might emphasize such New Age "basics" as: worker participation in management; bringing "synergic principles" to bear on the workplace; the right to choose a 20- or 30-hour work week (leaving people free to work 40 hours if they wished); and a narrowing of the income gap among all those connected with the enterprise.

Caucus members usually do not expect their concerns to be adopted, or even taken very seriously—at first; but they often find that standing up for them can provide an "opening wedge" for New Age ideas and energies.

One very active New Age caucus is the Social Change Network of the Association for Humanistic Psychology, a concrete outcome of the Social Action Theme Group that met each morning at the 1978 AHP Annual Meeting. The stated purpose of the Network is "to raise the consciousness of AHP members about the working of government and other powerful organizations."

Planetary Citizens suggests that we join existing insititutions (which might include unions or professional organizations) *as a planetary citizen.* "You should convey the idea that you are there to carry out your planetary citizenship responsibility by helping them, and you hope that your participation will also serve to strengthen the awareness of how their particular part of the picture fits into the whole." They also suggest that we encourage unions, professional organizations, and the like to set up "study commissions" that will consider their "global responsibilities."

New Age business and professional organizations are becoming more visible.

The Association of Humanistic Psychology and the Transpersonal Association (P.O. Box 3049, Stanford, Calif. 94305) are New Age-oriented alternatives to the American Psychological Association. The Briarpatch Network is a regional—San Francisco Bay area—alternative to the traditional merchants' association. The Association for

Humanistic Gerontology (1711 Solano Ave., Berkeley, Calif. 94707) is "open to anyone interested in facilitating positive and creative images of the aging and services for the aged." The Holistic Health Organizing Committee is a New Age version of the A.M.A (in other words: it is very, very different from the A.M.A.).

The Soycrafters Association of North America (P.O. Box 76, Bodega, Calif. 94922), founded in 1978, "is a nonprofit organization of individuals, groups, and businesses engaged in the production and popularization of fine natural foods made from soybeans." One of its purposes is to establish its own health and quality standards, and to aid member shops in meeting those standards. The Association for World Education (P.O. Box 589, Huntington, N.Y. 11743) is an association of teachers "who [feel] the need to be in touch with each other as they [seek] to introduce broader images of the world and its problems into the educational process."

Alternative institutions now include food co-ops, co-op stores, community radio and television stations, community and alternative newspapers, alternative schools, neighborhood repair groups, health care clinics, print shops, credit unions, craft collectives. . . . In their structure and goals they are often quite different from one another, but the important thing—what makes them "alternative" institutions—is that they are based on most or all of the New Age ethics and political values.

Most alternative institutions are community-based, but some are regional, national, or even planetary in scope. The Centre for Studies in Food Self-Sufficiency (90 Main St., Burlington, Vt. 05401) is "working toward a plan for increasing Vermont's self-sufficiency" (and has openings for "research interns"). The Institute for Alternative Futures is exploring "the concept of a college in Washington functioning as a shadow government, raising alternative policies." Planetary Citizens hopes to convene—annually or periodically—the "Planetary Elders," "the people who have the insight into the human race, about where it is going, about what needs to be done. . . . When they speak on the nature of [our] dilemma, . . . the world will listen and statesmen will pay heed."

New Age discussion groups are springing up across the country: the Political Science Committee of the Institute for the New Age . . . New Age Feminism . . . Frisco Bay Mussel Group (P.O. Box 31251, San Francisco, Calif. 94131). The Mussel Group is a study group and "committee of correspondence" that meets to discuss Bay Area "regional identity and watershed consciousness." It is currently developing information about: "native inhabitants, small self-sufficient early homesteaders, new settlers"; "the extent of the watershed"; "priorities for restoring natural systems and removing exploitation threats"; the extent of the "renewable soil, energy and materials within the region" (basis for an environmentally sound and regionally self-sufficient industry and agriculture); and "the spirit of multi-species relationships within the region."

New Age-oriented research groups cover a remarkable variety of topics and concerns. The Farallones and New Alchemy Institutes are investigating "appropriate" technologies, especially in agriculture, housing, and energy. The New-Age Foods Study Center is researching "creative solutions to the present world food/protein crisis," and the Organic Gardening and Farming Research Center (33 E. Minor St., Emmaus, Pa. 18049) is "embracing established scientific methods in organic research" in order to make "significant contributions to the areas of self-sustaining home food production and commercial organic farming."

The Union of Concerned Scientists is researching the whole issue of nuclear power and nuclear safety—and even its critics concede that it makes an excellent case for the defense, i.e., against nukes. The Institute for Alternative Futures is investigating the New Age concept of "anticipatory democracy," and the Synergy Power Institute, the New Age concept of "synergic power." The Princeton Center for Alternative Futures (58 Hoge Road, Princeton, N.J. 08450)—Carter and Hazel Henderson—likes to describe itself as a "mom and pop think tank," and it is doing path-breaking work in the field of political economy.

The Institute for the Study of Conscious Evolution is investigating the revelance of "transpersonal consciousness and conscience" for the "survival and evolution of the species and the planet." The Cross-Cultural Studies Program is studying American Indians, Buddhist monks, and yogis in order to find "human visions/values that transcend personal and cultural diversities." And the Institute of Noetic Sciences is engaged in research on—among other things—the possibility of a "Universal, spiritually-based value system" and the "outer limits of educability." Its explicit goal is to use research to "reduce the wide gulf between what Creation allows us to be and what we usually are."

New Age education groups (or group projects) try to propagate what I have called the New Age ethics and values—in an almost infinite number of ways.

The California Institute of Asian Studies, the Humanistic Psychology Institute, the Synthesis Graduate School, the Naropa Institute, and many other New Age-oriented schools, are trying to combine what was best about the "free universities" with what is best about the more traditional universities.

Mangrove, a men's performance collective, seeks to help us move beyond our conditioning as men, and make us aware of the "richness and vitality of human experience." Planet/Drum Foundation's "Re-inhabitary Theater" seeks to "declare the reinstatement of human co-existence with other species." And Barbara Ann Teer's National Black Theater (9 E. 125th St., Harlem, N.Y. 10035) is trying to go beyond the narrow definition of Western theater to create a "Communication Station, Temple of Liberation, Centre of Re-Education, and a Theatre for a Black Nation." "Politics just reflects the culture," says Teer. "We went to religion first, and discovered a creative process that can drastically change the total thrust of Western culture. Then we translated it into an art form that's in line with the spiritual age."

The Hunger Project is trying to create the psychocultural "context" for an end to hunger and starvation on the planet. According to The Hunger Project, creating the "content" is relatively easy—"there are at least four carefully thought-out and tested solutions" to the problem of starvation. But creating the context—"creating the end of hunger as an idea whose time has come"—is going to be more difficult . . . and is no less necessary.

Planetary Citizens has launched a "Planetary Citizens Campaign" whose purpose is to educate people to their "planetary responsibilities," first of all by registering them as "planetary citizens" and urging them to carry—and use!—the Planetary Passport on their travels.

Movement for a New Society's political study groups ("Macro-Analysis Seminars") investigate ecology, foreign affairs, domestic affairs, "visions of alternative orderings of society," and strategies for change. The seminars last about twenty weeks, operate best with 10–12 participants, have a democratic group process, and provide a structure which helps groups develop their own creative social change programs."

Creative Initiative Foundation (222 High St., Palo Alto, Calif. 94301) offers courses and seminars designed to open us up to a "new level of consciousness" of self and others and reality—to a new level of evolutionary awareness.

New Age-oriented special-interest groups can be as tough-minded, as persuasive, and—even now—occasionally as powerful, as thing-oriented and life-rejecting special-interest groups. Most of them have small budgets (especially when compared with what they should have and could use), but what they lack in "green power" they often make up for in "people power"—volunteers. Some of them have full- or part-time lobbyists in Washington and/or in selected state capitals. Any roll call of competent special-interest groups would have to include the following:

• Environment: Environmental Action, Friends of the Earth, Sierra Club;

• Human Population: Zero Population Growth;

• Nonhuman Population: Friends of Animals, Greenpeace Foundation, Jonah Project (whales and dolphins; P.O. Box 476, Bolinas, Calif. 94924);

• Consumer Affairs: Public Citizen (Ralph Nader's group; P.O. Box 19404, Washington, D.C. 20036);

• Agriculture: National Land for People, Rural America;

• Human Rights: Amnesty International, International League for Human Rights;

• World Order: Institute for World Order, New Directions, World Citizens Assembly (P.O. Box 2063, San Francisco, Calif. 94126);

• The Future: Princeton Center for Alternative Futures, World Future Society.

Local chapters of various New Age-oriented special interest groups —usually combining education and action—offer us many excellent opportunities to involve our selves in community problems and national issues.

A number of volunteers and staff people at Friends of the Earth, an environmental-action group, have recently reported on "A Day in the Life" of FOE (*Not Man Apart*, July 1977), and it looks something like this:

Bunny Gabel, a staff person for New York FOE, writes, "Since 1974 I've been FOE representative on the coalition against Westway [an interstate highway], studying the issues, talking to politicians, making calls, preparing testimony, speaking at meetings, ringing doorbells and baking cakes to raise money for the lawsuit against the interstate, passing out literature at street corners and block parties, and maintaining liaison with other groups fighting the interstate."

Ann Roosevelt, a staff person for New England FOE, says, "[A number of people here] volunteer for at least one full day a week. . . . Nancy Shelmerdine works on wildlife issues, helps organize volunteers, and is trying to raise funds so we can set up an environmental intern program. . . . Bob Elgin, a physicist and life member of FOE, . . . has testified on clean air and is working now on analysis of Carter's energy program and various energy bills. Kerry Mackin is a professional photographer who teaches at night and often works during the day for FOE." Carolyn Nelson, District of Columbia FOE: "The afternoon is quieter, usually—a time to catch up on the chores you didn't get to in the morning. I leave at five because two children are waiting, but there are always people working on until who-knows-when."

Some New Age special-interest groups have an already impressive number of local chapters. Friends of the Earth has sixty. The Sierra Club has fifty-three chapters and 268 "local groups." Movement for a New Society has about thirty local groups and affiliated groups ("Friends of MNS").

Zero Population Growth has more than forty chapters and state federations. Chapter efforts are said to be "crucial in mobilizing a consensus" (behind zero population growth), and chapter members try to dramatize—in whatever ways they feel are appropriate—the relationships between population growth and the energy, housing, and jobs shortages, as well as effects on environmental decay.

World Future Society has seventy-five chapters in the United States alone. Society chapters and local activities offer speakers, educational courses, seminars, discussion groups, and other opportunities for people to exchange ideas.

Amnesty International–U.S.A. has 146 "adoption groups" and nine "action groups." Each adoption group, which consists of about fifteen to twenty-five people, is assigned up to three "prisoners of conscience" from countries of different political systems. "Members write to the appropriate government, embassy, and prison officials to secure freedom for the prisoners. Members often write to the prisoners themselves and to their relatives to offer encouragement." Action group members "work on emergency cases requiring immediate attention, where torture or the threat of execution is involved."

Community and regional development groups have an important role to play in the New Age.

The Institute for Local Self-Reliance believes that communities can —and should—be much more self-reliant than they are now. In their book *Neighborhood Power*, Institute members David Morris and Karl Hess suggest that community activists might want to, for example:

● Make an inventory of community resources. Partly to show how much wealth there is in the community—how much money, how many skills, etc.—and partly to show that more money is flowing out of the community (in taxes and fees) than is coming back in (in services and public welfare);

● Begin to build up alternative institutions;

● Begin to develop community- and household-based food and energy sources;

● Begin to develop community industry (begin small, they say, perhaps by contracting with the city or district to provide such services as police protection, fire protection, sewer maintenance, and waste collection . . . and then by using the savings to establish small manufacturing facilities);

● Create community credit unions and development banks.

The Institute for Community Economics is "engaged in the initiation and implementation of economic alternatives for decentralized community development." Among other things, it is setting up a Community Land Trust (see National Community Land Trust Center) and it is setting up a Community Investment Fund so that New Age-oriented investors can commit a portion of their investment portfolios to New Age-oriented enterprises.

The Center for Community Economic Development (639 Massachusetts Ave., Ste. 316, Cambridge, Mass. 02139) is an important advocate of what has come to be called Community Development Corporations (CDC's). The Center states, "A CDC is essentially a cooperative, set up in a neighborhood to run economic and social service programs for the community. Its main activity at the moment is operating business or profit-making-ventures for the community. . . . The CDC can be set up by civic groups and churches, by a [government agency], or by any group of individual residents of that community. It really merits the title of CDC, however, if any community member may join.

"Once it is established by law, it has the legal rights of any corporation, including the right of limited liability."

A number of people in and around the Center have begun to develop what Charles Hampden-Turner calls "the strategy of social marketing." Essentially, the strategy is to create a supplier-consumer alliance; in terms of this book, the alliance would be between those who were organized into CDC's and other community enterprises, and those who had begun to break free of the Prison, those who had begun to live by the New Age ethics and political values. CDC's and similar suppliers would invite such consumers "to make socially, politically and ethically motivated purchases, based on accurate knowledge of what a CDC stood for and the social purposes which it was accomplishing."

As more of us begin to break out of the Prison, the market for such products might grow quite large. In fact, if 5 percent of American consumers is eventually willing and able to meet some of its needs through CDC's—then literally billions of dollars might pour in to businesses and industries that were run by and/or for our communities. CDC's wouldn't even have to begin by manufacturing goods, they could begin more simply (and cheaply) by using the "social marketing" strategy to retail, wholesale, and mail-order supplies manufactured by others.

Reach-out groups (or branches of groups) are meant to serve other people with a minimum of red tape, simply and directly; "just people helping people" is how reach-out workers like to put it.

One outstanding example of a reach-out group is PLENTY, founded on The Farm in 1974 because "after three years The Farm was taking care of itself and was strong enough to reach out to help some other folks who were in worse shape." (Farm members were making well under $1,000 per person per year at the time, but they had already learned to be self-reliant and cooperative.) PLENTY went down to Guatemala when the earthquake struck in February 1976, but unlike most of the rest of the relief crews from around the world, PLENTY stayed on after the emergency work was done.

Matthew writes (in *New Directions*, no. 23), "We fell in love with the Indians who had been up against it before the earthquake. We began to understand that we were in a position to help them learn some of the beneficial aspects of a [human-scale] technology that we were using with good results in America. . . . Since then we've sent down thirty-seven more folks, two trucks, a school bus, . . . and tons of food, clothes, tools, medical supplies, and CB radios. We've helped rebuild a town in which 1,200 of 1,400 houses were destroyed and we've put up twelve schools in twelve different villages. . . .

"After we built the schools and the houses, CIDA [Canadian International Development Agency] told us there would be funds for more projects, and if we came up with some designs, they would see about supplying us with the materials for those projects. . . .

"One of the best things we've been able to do is work out a deal with the U.S. Immigration Service that allows some native Guatemalan Indians to come up here to The Farm and live with us for a while and . . . learn a skill or a trade that will be of benefit to him or her 'back home'. . . .

"When we go to CIDA or to anybody about helping us with our projects in Guatemala, it's with this thought in mind: we are with the Indian people. We understand their needs, and we will stay on the scene and help them connect. . . . It's no longer like we're swooping in like a silver eagle and dropping our gifts on an unknown land with a mysterious population: it's more like helping our cousins."

New Age-oriented political groups are beginning to spring up here and there across the country—harbingers of things to come.

Land, Equality and Freedom (LEAF; 454 Mission Valley Center W., San Diego, Calif. 92108) is based on the ideas of one of the early

American forefathers of New Age politics, Henry George (see Chapter 25 below). It is working to remove all taxes from homes, buildings, property improvements, crops, and factories—and to "concentrate the property tax onto community-created land values." In the process, it is calling for many related tax and social reforms—and it is trying to build a grass roots social movement to carry them out.

Proutist Universal is working toward a synthesis of the personal, the political, and the spiritual. It is teaching classes in "Prout theory" and doing some political organizing (much more of both in the future). It states, "Social institutions must facilitate the all-around growth of individuals; and the abilities of individuals should primarily serve the . . . welfare [of everyone]."

Self-Determination: A Personal/Political Network was founded in early 1975 by California State Assemblyperson John Vasconcellos and others. It is not engaged in lobbying, nor does it focus on any particular issue; rather, "the Network has been organized to promote *positive processes* of interaction among persons, and between persons and institutions. . . . It exists to help persons effect personal and community change in areas of their own choosing."

In the summer of 1977, a number of spiritually and politically aware young people came together to form the California New Age Caucus. Daniel Maziarz, a spokesperson for the group, says, "I think we have two unique contributions. One: we are advocating a comprehensive lifestyle. Two: we are organizing grass roots support for governmental policies that promote this life-style.

"New Age people have learned how to improve their lives by living in a way that is ecological, spiritual, personal, and at the same time economically sound. We like to call it 'simple living and high thinking'. Because this whole idea has worked so well for us, we feel it is the answer to other people's problems too."

William Duryea, another spokesperson for the group, adds, "Our strategy is grass roots—down home, person-to-person communication. . . . We're going to go door to door and tell people about this, and pass out literature [initially an excellent brief newsletter, *The New Age Harmonist*], and organize a statewide network of people. . . ."

The Caucus has already worked out a tentative platform; see Chapter 24 below.

At the end of 1978, a number of New Age-oriented neo-Marxist groups came together to form The Organization for the American Revolution. The Organization laments, "We Americans used to pride ourselves on being more creative, more self-reliant, more self-governing and freer than any people on [E]arth. . . ." It hopes to develop "the new ideas needed to build a new America" and to organize chapters from coast to coast.

Also in 1978, for the first time, a number of New Age-oriented people began to speak openly about the need for a New Age-oriented political party. For example: Jim Benson, founder of the Institute for Ecological Policies, wrote (in *Environmental Action*, April 22, 1978),

"Huge corporations, governments and centralized technologies are really only products of our way of thinking. We need a *new* way of thinking if our societies are to be free, healthy and sustainable. . . . To make this vision a reality, we need a political party. . . . But it needs to be a movement rather than just another political party. Its structure and platform must reflect the [new] values which the participants themselves must possess. . . ." Benson wants interested people to write him in care of the Institute.

Last but not least, in the spring of 1979 I began to try to facilitate the formation of a new political organization that could bring together many of the insights and energies of the people and groups that I've mentioned in this book. In a letter to most of the groups and periodicals in the back of this book, I said, in part: "The organization that I have in mind would be more than a network but less than a political party that was run from the top down. It would be committed to articulating and implementing what many people see as an emerging new alternative to monopoly capitalism and state socialism—an alternative that sees *scale* and *consciousness* as primary political problems— . . . an alternative that is humble enough to borrow what it needs from each of the old political "ism's," but bold enough to transcend them." Interested persons should write me in care of the Institute of Noetic Sciences, 600 Stockton St., 6th flr., San Francisco, Calif. 94108.

Support groups are for those of us who are most committed to New Age values and who are most eager to propagate and live by them. They tend to arise—as Susanne Gowan et al. point out—"from already existing friendships, workplace ties, religious affiliations, etc., and range in size from about three to twelve individuals. They grow as cells grow, by division, and can proliferate rapidly when conditions are ripe."

Support group members tend to live together (in communes, ashrams, and the like), partly so they can "act the New Age out in the present" by living simply, and partly so they can devote the bulk of their energies to the task of speeding up New Age evolution. But living together isn't really a defining aspect of support groups. The important point is that support group members are actively involved in helping to heal each other . . . and helping to heal society.

Some support groups are made up of people who spend the bulk of their time and energy in New Age caucuses, alternative institutions, special-interest groups, and so forth; other support groups have their own special projects. The Philadelphia Life Community—branch of the Movement for a New Society—consists of fifteen "autonomous household units" of 6–10 people each "with diverse interests and collective commitments," and thirteen collectives working on a variety of concerns (feminist, nonviolence training, "global justice," etc.). "Each collective, while in constant communication with other work groups . . . is responsible for its own life and concerns." The household units and the work collectives each appear to function as support groups (MNS prefers the term "teams"). Gowan et al. note, "The often criticized tendency in mass movements for a kind of mob hysteria to sweep people away is not likely in a movement made of teams. On the other hand, the positive movement feelings of joy and celebration of community can be captured by teams."

Training communities are being set up to help New Age-oriented activists learn how to translate their insights and understandings into effective political action.

The School of Living (P.O. Box 3233, York, Pa. 17402) offers "workshops, seminars, apprenticeships and long term living opportunities" at various centers relating to such topics as "New Age consciousness," decentralism, cooperation, "intimate relationships," and nonviolence.

Movement for a New Society sponsors a nine-month training program that "seeks to provide participants with the knowledge, skills, confidence and sensitivity necessary for effective change agents." Through workshops, seminars, participation in community (communal) living, and involvement in the "field," people are helped to explore what MNS considers to be "essential elements" of self-and-social transformation, including: personal growth, spiritual growth, interpersonal skills; analysis, vision, strategy; consciousness-changing (how-to); subsistence living (how-to); group dynamics; "organizing and technical skills"; nonviolent action; and the new culture.

Planetary Citizens hopes to have summer workshops that "will deal both with the outer preparation—concerning knowledge, practical use of skills and efficiency in problem areas, and also with the process of inner awareness and development of consciousness appropriate to becoming a fully functioning human (and planetary) being."

Networking, says *Cascade Magazine* (Sept. 1977), is "the process of bringing people together to cooperatively change their communities, their environment, or their self-perceptions." New Age networking is the process of bringing people together on behalf of some or all of the New Age ethics and political values.

Magazines like *The Mother Earth News*, catalogues like the *Rainbook*, special-interest newsletters like *Growing Without Schooling*, and regional newsletters like *Cascade*, for a "paper network" that helps put people and groups and ideas in touch with each other. Network: Quodlibeda (c/o Bob Welke, Box 5367, A.P.O. New York, N.Y. 09633) is an attempt to let New Age-oriented people report on whatever they themselves find interesting and important in the New Age movement. The hundreds of "correspondents" include a number of people from the magazines and groups in Chapter 27 below. Western Europe is covered as thoroughly as North America.

Steve Johnson (in *Rainbook*) reports that "Conferences, meetings and workshops have created networks . . . of people with common ground, or reasons to know each other." Three well-known examples have been the Toward Tomorrow Faire (1976, Amherst, Mass.) and Habitat Forum and the World Symposium on Humanity (both 1976, both Vancouver, B.C.).

Many of the groups that have been mentioned in this chapter and in Chapter 27, below, have begun to share their views through newsletter exchanges and visitations.

A number of groups exist partly or primarily to bring people and groups together . . . to help us "network" with each other. Among these groups are: National Center for Appropriate Technology; World Future Society; Community Service, Inc., and Federation of Egalitarian Communities (for intentional communities); International Cooperation Council and Rainbow Family Tribal Council (for New Age-oriented people in all fields); and Turning Point (for New Age intellectuals and activists in England).

A "linkage system" has recently been developed by Robert Theobald and Jeanne Scott. People who share in the New Age outlook on things (defined more specifically by Theobald and Scott) are invited to fill in an 8½ by 11″ sheet "which will convey as clearly as possible your interests, concerns and visions"; these sheets are then duplicated (by Theobald) and sent out periodically to everyone in the linkage system.

Theobald stresses that the linkage system is *not* a network. "The linkage system can be seen as a finding technique for networks which operate for particular purposes: it is understood that all the members of the linkage system would not benefit from meeting everybody else." A number of people from Chapter 27 are part of this system. For more information write: Linkage, P.O. Box 2240, Wickenburg, Ariz. 85358.

Intentional Communities

Some of us have chosen to leave our cities and towns and come together in "intentional communities" that are more expressive of the New Age ethics and values. Sometimes these people are accused of "copping out," of leaving the really important social change to others. But there a number of reasons why intentional communities are an important and even an essential part of the New Age strategy for social transformation.

For one thing, their existence suggests—to those who might never join such communities themselves—that *there are other ways of doing things*. As Theodore Roszak puts it, "Nothing—no amount of argument or research—will take the place of such living proof."

Some intentional communities are able to demonstrate the viability of new kinds of *structural* arrangements. For example: Simple Optimum Living ("SOL"; P.O. Box 6018, San Diego, Calif. 92106) intends to establish an "experimental New Age community" for about 4,000 residents in southern California, and it will be carefully designed to promote or encourage: use of solar energy; production of organic foods within a controlled greenhouse environment; small, nonpolluting industries; community-wide solid waste recycling systems; democratic citizen participation; etc. Other intentional communities are able to demonstrate the viability of new kinds of *social-emotional* arrangements. And to David Spangler, the Findhorn community, in particular, has been able to demonstrate the viability of New Age *consciousness,* the viability of what I would call the trans-material worldview—the fact that it is potentially more useful and potentially more productive of fulfillment and joy than the old materialist worldview.

Intentional communities are a kind of *laboratory for New Age activists* as well as a kind of display-window for the rest of us. Rosabeth Moss Kanter, sociologist and communard, points out that the intentional community is a great place for learning about "the possibilities for new forms of social organization and the practical limitations of these new forms." Intentional communities confront almost "every known problem of social organization . . . and almost every social-psychological issue." They are a way of trying aspects of the New Age out in the present . . . trying them on for size.

To Stephen Gaskin, intentional communities provide a space—the necessary ground—where New Age people can begin working out a different life-style. In The Farm's brochure he states, "We're trying to settle on a standard of living that would be fair if everybody in the world lived that way—not grim, but graceful and fun and full of love and friendship and being happy living together—a level that everybody in the world could make it on with the existing resources."

Finally, many New Age people would say that intentional communities are useful because of their effect on the people involved. Vince, of the Twin Oaks community, feels that the presence of many of what I've been calling the New Age ethics and values is a factor "leading to healthy, responsive people." Ananda Cooperative Village believes that intentional communities are particularly well suited to helping us in our spiritual growth. And according to David Spangler, "Findhorn allows us as individuals to bring the different levels of our being into a meaningful whole"—to meet and merge our material, emotional, mental, and spiritual needs.

There are over 750 known intentional communities in the United States today, and many of them are looking for new members (see the *Directory of Intentional Communities,* published annually by *Communities* magazine). Nine or ten of the best-known are listed in Chapter 27 below.

Nonviolent Action

Some New Age people have begun to use nonviolent action as a tool that can help in bringing the New Age about—a tool that can help us in our work against our monolithic institutions and also, at the same time, help us learn to be more self-reliant and cooperative. Refusing to cooperate with draft boards, blocking the entrances to nuclear power plants, boycotting South African wines or neighborhood Safeways—all can be what Jim Douglass calls "symbols of invitations" to people, "living statements" that invite people "to realize their own power, if they would only do likewise and act in concert."

Nonviolence has often been presented as a turn-the-other-cheek, we-can-endure-longer-than-you-can-hate kind of philosophy. But as Julius Lester points out, "The opposite of violence is not its absence—nonviolence. The very word commands one *not* to do something. But it does not say what one should do."

To Gandhi, nonviolence was an aspect of *satyagraha* which he defined as "the Force which is born of Truth and Love" and which is often translated, more simply, as "soul-force." Following Gandhi's lead, most nonviolent activists have defined nonviolent action in positive terms: as action that seeks to actualize Truth and Love (however that might be defined). Most New Age political people would say that Truth and Love are embodied by what I have called the New Age ethics and political values; therefore, most New Age political people would say that nonviolent action is action that attempts to actualize the New Age ethics and political values—nonviolently.

Some New Age people believe that nonviolent action is never coercive. But most believe that nonviolence can and *should* sometimes contain an element of coercion—noncooperation, boycott, strike. The difference, as Joan Bondurant points out, is that in violent coercion "deliberate injury is inflicted upon the opponent," whereas in nonviolent coercion injury indirectly results—"withholding of services or profits [or rent] may cause a very real discomfiture to the opponent, . . . but compared with physical destruction . . . the contrast is significant."

Some New Age people would include the concept of "armed self-defense" under the category of nonviolent coercion. The rationale is as follows: nonviolence means doing no harm to others *or to self*, and failure to defend one's self from physical violence—by any means necessary—is a kind of self-abuse. Julius Lester says sometimes physical violence "is one's only defense, . . . the only way in which one can insure [one's] physical survival and that of others. In that instance, and, only in that instance, is physical violence permissible." However, it is possible to argue that the willingness to use physical violence almost always leads to more suffering, overall, than the refusal to use physical violence; see, e.g., Sharp. The question of whether or not "armed self-defense" is consistent with the New Age ethics and political values, and an effective defense strategy, may turn out to be an extremely important one for New Age activists.

In many ways, nonviolent action is an almost ideal tool for New Age activists. Richard Gregg, Gene Sharp, and many other nonviolent strategists and activists have emphasized that nonviolent action is a way of healing *self*. It encourages us to end our submissiveness by getting us to stand up to people and groups that may have seemed "superior" before (Gregg feels that this may be the single most important contribution that nonviolent action can make). It is, or should be, motivated by love—and it tends to encourage a vulnerability that can only be sustained by love for others (Gregg). It increases our sense of self-respect (Sharp) and it gives us esteem in the eyes of significant others (Gregg). It breaks the psychological link between masculinity and violence by establishing new group standards in which the willingness to suffer, and despite or even because of this suffering to *become and remain whole*, is the highest expression of so-called manly courage (psychologist Jerome Frank, in Sharp). And it increases—through the power of example—our willingness to defy authority, our ability to break out of what Milgram called our "agentic state of mind."

Erik Erikson, Harvard psychologist, compares nonviolent action to psychotherapy and finds many interesting parallels; for instance, that in both movements the practitioners learn to be nonviolent to themselves as well as to others. Chogyam Trungpa, Tibetan Buddhist, draws a distinction between aggressive and truthful action. He says that Christ chasing the money lenders out of the temple is an example of truthful action, "because he saw the precision of the situation without watching himself or trying to be heroic." And he adds: "We need action like that."

Unlike some political activity, nonviolent action does not try to make other people feel guilty or evil or that they have nothing to contribute to the solution of the problem at hand. It does try to point out to others that they're on the wrong course—in some cases it even tries to prevent others from carrying out their wrongdoing—but as Erikson says, it simply couldn't work if its practitioners lost all respect for their opponents.

Nonviolent action is, in fact, an almost perfectly *synergic* form of conflict resolution. Leroy Pelton, who is a social psychologist as well as a nonviolence strategist, says, "Nonviolent action does not aim for victory over the adversary. Conflict is not taken as a game in which there is a winner and a loser and in which we attempt to 'beat' the other party. On the contrary, the nonviolent activist strives to avoid this game mentality. What is sought is a resolution of the conflict at a higher level of understanding and satisfaction [for both parties] than perhaps either party possessed before the conflict resolution. The resolution that emerges is ideally a new Gestalt, or structure, in which both parties are somewhat transformed."

New Age political people are less interested in obtaining behavior change alone than in attitude or value change—change on the third level of analysis. All too often, as Gregg points out, behavior change alone rests on the "suppression or repression of the energy of the wishes or will of the defeated party, and this is certain to result in waste, friction and trouble sooner or later." In order to obtain attitude and value change along with behavior change, one should, as Pelton notes, "apply the minimum pressure necessary. . . . Nonviolence perhaps represents the minimum pressure necessary." Even nonviolent coercion is capable of producing attitude and value change if the nonviolent activist "seeks to offset the psychological resistance engendered by noncooperation with simultaneous friendly, sympathetic, trusting, and helping gestures. . . . [These] may generate attractions to offset the resistance."

The larger point, in any case, is that an enduring peace cannot rest upon behavior change alone: cannot rest upon grudgingly given concessions or upon violent force. Gregg concludes, "Peace imposed by violence is not psychological peace but a suppressed conflict. . . . The outer condition is not a true reflection of the inner condition. But in peace secured by true nonviolent resistance there is no longer any inner conflict; a new channel is found, in which both the formerly conflicting energies are at work in the same direction and in harmony." And he adds, "The nonviolent [activist], by using longer psychological leverages, may have to move more slowly sometimes, but the work is more effectively done and tends to be more permanent."

For a New Age activist, nonviolent action is more effective in another way too: if violence centralizes, *nonviolence decentralizes*. For one thing, nonviolent groups wouldn't have to be dependent on a central committee for weapons or money. Their tactics would require few or no weapons, little or no money, and lots of sensitivity to local nuances and needs. For another thing, a successful violent revolution tends to vest great powers of violence in the top-down state . . . as we've seen; and that tends to make us feel helpless against it forever after. But nonviolent action is different—as Sharp suggests, the more that we engage in it, the most potent a tactic it becomes in our hands . . . and the more willing and able we are to use it when it suits us.

In what is probably the single most influential book among radicals, *The Wretched of the Earth*, Algerian psychiatrist Frantz Fanon argues that revolutionary violence is necessary and desirable because it serves a therapeutic function for the oppressed. In the United States, however, where most of us are "oppressed" above all because of the Prison and its institutions, it would seem more therapeutic for us to assert our strength in a way that was not Prison-bound—in a way that was oriented to life rather than death. Nonviolent action would depend on our doing just that.

A number of nonviolent groups are oriented to New Age ideas and energies: Fellowship of Reconciliation, Greenpeace Foundation, Peacemakers. . . . The Clamshell Alliance is a loose coalition of antinuclear/pro-solar energy organization from the New England area. It has become a model for New Age activists not only because the media like to cover its activities, but also—and primarily—because it has begun to devise some important and effective "new" approaches to nonviolent action.

For one thing, Clamshell is trying to go "beyond protest"—is trying to demonstrate a life-giving *way of life*, not just a particular stand on nuclear power. Susan Hoak, a Clamshell Alliance activist, writes, "The Seabrook statement was not simply and exclusively 'No Nukes'. This time the 'protestors' were demonstrating alternative directions in *everything they did*—from the very way they said what they said and organized what they did, down to the renewable energy sources they proposed to replace nuclear power."

For another thing, Clamshell is trying very hard to make sure that women are a substantial part of the nonviolent action. Hoak writes, "The contributions women made were extremely crucial, and what to a large extent made this action different from demonstrations in the '60s.

. . . Women dealt with the media, they were medics, marshals, they facilitated huge, tense meetings, organized support functions . . . handled legal proceedings. . . ."

Clamshell insists that "participatory decentralization" be practiced *on the spot*—it is not to be postponed until "after the revolution" or transformation or whatever. Hoak writes, "The Seabrook occupation was a mass action organized in such a way that individuals did not get lost in the crowd. Everyone who occupied went through a nonviolence preparation session beforehand and then joined an 'affinity group' of eight to fifteen people. The affinity group members stayed together throughout the action. . . . When decisions had to be made during the action, the [affinity group's spokesperson] would relay the consensus of the affinity group to a representative group of all the affinities. . . ."

Clamshell wants its nonviolent activists to manifest community— and what I've referred to as "synergic power" vis-à-vis its opponents. Hoak writes, "Some baffled journalists attempted to describe what they saw as 'military efficiency' and 'discipline'. . . . But what they did not understand they were seeing was the force of . . . a group of people committed—not only to a cause—but to each other, to communication with 'opponents,' and to a sense of community evolving out of conflict. . . . [A] sense of community created not only through common experience, but through shared feelings, needs, humor—the caring for each other that makes us open to both appreciating our strengths and giving support through our weaknesses. . . ."

Finally, Clamshell is insisting that its activists do some political work in their *own* communities—away from the "center stage" of demonstrations. Sharon Tracy, another Clamshell organizer, explains (in *New Age*, Feb. 1978), "We have to build a movement that's based upon more than occupations. By having people go door-to-door, talking about nuclear power, alternative energy, and why they are occupying *before* the action, they will have a clear understanding of what they are about to do, and so will the fellow citizens they talk to."

Electoral Politics

In Chapter 20 I argued that electoral politics is not *the* way to New Age social transformation. But it can be *a* way—it can get us *part* of the way there. John Saloma, a former William Scranton speechwriter who is now an advocate of New Age politics, says (in *Parties*, 1972), "There are all kinds of action opportunities for enterprising citizens who want to invest . . . time, attention, skills and financial support [in party politics]. With relatively minimal efforts it is possible for citizens with a strategy to reach and influence any party or government official. . . . A dedicated group of party activists can reshape a state party organization. . . ."

Electoral politics can be a way to New Age social transformation when it involves working for candidates or reforms that are based on at least some of the New Age ethics and political values, and involve an extension of popular and local control, as distinct from bureau-cratic and/or centralized control. In other words: New Age-type elec-toral activity should be conducted on behalf of candidates and pro-posals that can advance us toward New Age society. It should *not* be conducted on behalf of candidates or proposals that might serve to reinforce the Prison or to strengthen monolithic institutions.

Often this will cause New Age political people to disagree sharply with traditional "left-wing" candidates and proposals. For example: compulsory government-run automobile insurance, a favorite left-wing proposal, does tend to save drivers money. But for that very reason, it tends to reinforce our reliance on the private automobile. Wherever it's been tried it's tended to *increase* the number of two-car families; *increase* the "need" for highways and wider streets; *perpetuate* our love affair with speed; and *discourage* our thinking about alternatives to the private automobile. There are many other similar instances in which short-term economic savings involve long-term social losses, and New Age people must have the courage of their convictions and point this out to people.

In Chapter 24, I propose a mock "New Age political platform" that contains some 200 political proposals that at least some New Age-oriented people are working for *right now*. Possibly one of these 200 proposals will be right for you.

CHAPTER 23

Celebration of Wholeness: Beyond Hope and Despair

In the last three chapters I tried to suggest a way out of Prison society—a way that would be democratic and evolutionary and based on New Age ethics and values. But if it isn't possible for there to be an evolutionary transformation of society until a significant number of us have at least begun to heal self and society—then what hope does it have, really? And therefore what hope do *we* have? What is there that can keep us from despair?

Psychologists tell us that we're born with hope, and when we lose it we become corrupt and harden our hearts. The only apparent alternative to hope is despair, and I believe it is to ward off this despair that liberals continue to fool themselves about the nature of Prison society, and Marxists continue to dream of violent revolution in the United States, and academic intellectuals like L. S. Stavrianos continue to believe that the Third World will show us the way. Those of us who have begun to heal our selves should know that we need to get to a point that is beyond hope and despair . . . that transcends both, and by doing so, allows us to see things clearly enough to be able to survive as ethical and compassionate and vulnerable persons.

In order to survive with integrity we must begin with the fact that we are Prisoners. But we must never allow our selves to believe that we are only Prisoners—a mistake that the trans-material worldview can help us avoid. In order to survive with integrity in a world that seems bent on self-destruction and in which we seem to be our own best jailers, we have got to learn an important lesson from Eastern philosophy (and from our Puritan and transcendental heritage): we have got to learn to be *in* the world, but not *of* it. We have got to learn to do things for our own reasons, to measure our selves by our own standards, to live by the ethics and values that emerge effortlessly from the process of healing our selves.

One of the consolations of the liberal and Marxist philosophies is that their practitioners sometimes get to "act like heroes." New Age politics sees that the descent of the Prison is not an event but a part of daily life, and in these kinds of circumstances the old kind of heroism is dead—as dead as Patty Hearst's friends. Storming the Pentagon or shooting some corporation executive will not help to end the culture of things and of death. New Age politics sees that we need to develop a new concept of heroism—one that recognizes that in the United States the struggle to evolve in a New Age direction, as individuals and as a culture, may be more valuable than trying to inspire Prison-bound people to fight for more *things*.

Robert Lifton sees heroism in the person who "out of courage, refuses violence." Robert Theobald sees heroism in the act of taking personal responsibility for one's life and one's immediate situation. Kate Millett sees heroism in doing to make our selves personally vulnerable. And Jane Roberts sees heroism in daring to "fully be"—and daring to allow "doing" to emerge as a "natural characteristic" from fully being, wherever that might lead.

A number of leading academics and activists have decided that trying to heal our selves at this late date can only be seen as narcissism or self-indulgence. (Curiously, trying to get psychiatrists to do the healing *for* us is still considered legitimate.) What these people tend to forget is that social action that is not based on a firm sense of self can only be based on guilt or rage—and guilt or rage does not allow us to see clearly; renders us, in fact, extremely susceptible to manipulation by demagogues.

Moreover, by refusing to work for a traditional revolution we would not be "giving up the struggle." As we saw in the previous three chapters, we *would* be struggling—nonviolently—against the Prison and its institutions, which are more responsible for the sterility of our lives (and our society) than "human nature" or "capitalism." But even if we can't do any more than embark on the stage of self-healing, even if we can't get a strong group together, or if all our group efforts fail to heal society, we would still be learning to preserve our worth as human beings. And that is an essential part of the political process today. For without life-oriented people—without people who have reached self-development stages six or seven, or are definitely on their way there—there can be no New Age evolution. And only New Age evolution can take us off of the production-consumption continuum and out of the Prison.

Prison society celebrates material growth, speed, power, revenge; New Age evolution celebrates wholeness.

To David Spangler, wholeness means nourishing one's self fully—physically, emotionally, psychologically, and spiritually.

To Herb Kohl, wholeness "means being conscious of the different components of one's existence; means keeping social and historical awareness present along with personal and psychological need and insight; means attempting to bind together the internal and external, physical and spiritual, conscious and unconscious, cultural and personal, communal and individual aspects of one's life no matter what pain or conflict is involved. This last means breaking away from the dichotomized life that is one characteristic of [our current] way of living. Wholeness also means utilizing what one knows about the self and the world instead of filing away whatever knowledge might lead to conflict and change."

In terms of this book, wholeness means meeting one's needs on all seven stages (or levels) of self-development. And it means learning to be at home in all four states of consciousness—learning to use the trans-material worldview rather than the materialist or the non-material worldviews. And it means learning to live by the ethics and political values that emerge effortlessly from out of the trans-material worldview (among other sources).

Along with wholeness, New Age evolution celebrates life-as-a-learning-experience. E. F. Schumacher tells us that our social problems can usefully be seen as "a strain-and-stretch apparatus to develop the Whole [Person]." Jonas Salk tells us that "the development of wisdom, or acting as if [we] were sagacious, could become a game through which [we] could reach fulfillment." ("Such a challenge . . . could give purpose to all interested in playing the game of life for what can be given to it and received from it, [as distinct from] how much can be taken and how little can be given.") And Ken Keyes advises us to use "every uncomfortable emotion" as an opportunity for consciousness growth. He says, "Everything and everyone around you is your teacher. If your washing machine won't work, [imagine that] you are being checked out on your ability to peacefully accept the unacceptable. . . . If someone does something that 'hurts your ego,' you will grow fastest if you consciously regard him or her as your teacher who is enabling you to discover which addictions you will have to reprogram." He concludes, "Your moment-to-moment stream of consciousness becomes interesting and real when you experience everything as a step in your growth toward higher consciousness."

Experiencing life as a learning situation is very *different* from coming to see society as one big schoolhouse—the approach that is being taken in, e.g., China and Cuba. John Holt says that the schoolhouse society would be a place "in which one group of people did things to another group of people, without their consent, because still another group thought this would be good for them. . . . A global schoolhouse would be a world, which we seem to be moving toward, in which one group of people would have the right through our entire lives to subject the rest of us to various sorts of tests, and if we did not measure up, to require us to submit to various kinds of treatment, i.e., education, therapy, etc., until we did." He adds, "A worse nightmare is hard to imagine."

New Age politics is based on the assumption that, as E. F. Schumacher puts it, "Nothing is worth having in this sphere unless it comes from the *inside* of you." Schumacher draws an essential political point from this assumption: "I believe that it is everyone's personal task to try and demonstrate in some way, by word or deed, what [he or she] considers to be true, adequate, right, etc., and not look over [his or her] shoulder whether people follow [his or her] example or believe what [he or she] says." If people then start ridiculing you, or criticizing you, "you say, 'Yes, thank you very much. I hear what you say.' You just carry on."

Schumacher adds, "It is not so easy to maintain this sturdy attitude. In India they call it 'karma yoga': you just do what you consider right, and you don't bother your head with whether you are successful or not, because if you don't do what you consider is right, you're wasting your life!"

Bill McLarney, of the New Alchemy Institute, puts it this way: "Well, I don't suppose any of us is fool enough to think that we can save the world. But if each of us were to look at some of the directions we'd like to see the world go in—and then to put our own little bit of force behind one of them—and to have a hell of a good time while we're doing it, well then, that's what we should do."

Beyond hope and despair, then, there is something absolutely essential to do, and that is to live. To live with simplicity and intensity, gentleness and generosity, so that the idea of a freely self-developing humanity does not die, no matter how comfortable or "happy" or obedient the mass of the people may become.

Part VIII

A NEW AGE "POLITICAL PLATFORM"

CHAPTER 24

A New Age
"Political Platform"
Offered as a
Discussion Document

Laws cannot substitute for the transformation of the minds, hearts, and self-perceptions of the American people. In fact, as we have seen (Chapter 4), "good" laws might have the effect of reinforcing our old attitudes and patterns of behavior by filling us with resentment and by causing us to feel alienated from our society. So this Part is not meant to suggest that we can create a good society without at least beginning to heal our selves. But it is meant to ask: what are some of the *specific* measures that we might want to support, after we have begun to get free of the Prison? What are some of the measures that might contribute to the healing of this *society*?

I want to emphasize that this is not a political platform, except maybe in name. Any real political platform is an embodiment of the efforts and energies of the whole spectrum of people that it purports to represent, and this document represents neither more nor less than my notion of what a New Age-oriented political platform might look like. Then again, any real platform tries to be comprehensive, and mine just tries to be representative and suggestive. Finally, any real platform would explain the why's and wherefore's of its planks, and these planks contain little or no explanation. That is because they are all recommendations based on what has been said so far in this book. In fact, I consider this Part to be a kind of policy-oriented summing up of the arguments, and Argument, contained in this book.

I would like it to serve as a discussion document for a New Age-oriented political party . . . if and when. And I would like it to serve as a standard for comparison with the other political platforms, such as those of the Democratic and Republican parties. More immediately, I would like it to help us in focusing out political discussions and debates. In choosing these 200 "planks," I was more interested in raising the relevant questions and issues than I was in being "right."

A number of people have told me that the platform is contradictory —that some of the planks are "right-wing" and others are "left-wing." My answer is that the planks are only contradictory when seen from the sterile "Who does it?" perspective of the traditional political left-and-right. The more relevant criteria—the ones used here—are: does this measure foster individual self-reliance, community self-reliance, planetary responsibility? Is this measure something that a life-loving, self-reliant, and generous person (or society) might find helpful and useful? Is this measure in keeping with the New Age ethics and political values?

The state in my "discussion document" is neither the government-that-governs-best-governs-least type state of Jeffersonian philosophy, nor is it the centralizing state of Hamiltonian (and liberal and Marxist) philosophy. It is a state that has achieved a clear-eyed recognition that a good society will require some constraints, some assistance, and some prodding; but that sees these things as alternatives to coercion rather than as pallid and ultimately unsatisfactory versions of same. It is the state of John and John Quincy Adams, rather than Jefferson or Hamilton; of Herbert Agar and Arthur Morgan, rather than FDR or Robert Taft (see Chapter 25 below). It is neither centralist nor libertarian, but responsibly ethical . . . with room for communities and regions to create their own alternatives to the planks below.

My most useful single source was Friends of the Earth, ed., *Progress As If Survival Mattered* ("FOE" in the text), which is the closest thing we have so far to a political platform from the environmental wing of the New Age movement (its original subtitle was *A New-Era Testament for America*). And I was able to use three actual platforms: the New Zealand Values Party platform ("V" in the text), the original California New Age Caucus platform ("N"), and the U.S. Libertarian Party platform ("L"). None of these three was entirely satisfactory, however. The Values and Caucus platforms seemed to me to rely much too much on government initiative; whereas the Libertarian Party platform not only managed to redress that imbalance, but to do so with a vengeance. (However, in May 1978, the California New Age Caucus had its first state convention, and the overemphasis on government initiative was corrected. Many references to government initiative in the platform were deleted—"leaving it open to how it'll happen," as one Caucus spokesperson put it.)

I would like to acknowledge the assistance or advice that I have received from people from: Clamshell Alliance, Delta Books, Global Education Associates, Institute for Alternative Futures, Institute for Ecological Policies, Institute for Liberty and Community, Institute for PsychoEnergetics, National Land for People, California New Age Caucus, Planetary Citizens, Proutist Universal, *Sojourner* newspaper, and Wesleyan University (College of Science in Society), Middletown, Conn. This is *not* to say that these people or groups would want to associate themselves with this platform, or—even—that they would like the way that I've made use of their assistance or advice.

So—to begin:

A NEW-AGE ORIENTED NATIONAL GOVERNMENT MIGHT:

National Affairs

A. Ethics

(1) Attempt to define an "absolute good" according to which we might live and work (Wendell Berry, in *The Unsettling of America*,

defines this absolute good as "health—not in the merely hygienic sense of personal health, but the health, the wholeness, finally the holiness of Creation, of which our personal health is only a share") ;

(2) Attempt to articulate a series of ethical and political values that embody and reflect this good (cf., on a planetary scale, the Institute for World Order; and see Chapter 12 above; and *note*: all groups and references in these parentheses are listed more fully in Chapter 27 below) ;

(3) Gradually adjust our laws and regulations to be consistent with these ethical and political values.

B. Income and Welfare

(1) Encourage voluntary simplicity—as an ethic and as a life-style (Duane Elgin and Arnold Mitchell, in *CoEvolution Quarterly*, Summer 1977) ;

(2) Establish both minimum and maximum income levels. Income above the maximum would be completely taken away. While the maximum income would initially be a high one, a New Age government would, over time, seek to bring the maximum down to about ten times the minimum. (This would require us to finally decide who should get how much more than another—thereby putting an end to the wage-price spiral, an important source of inflation.) (Herman Daly, in Daly, ed., *Toward a Steady-State Economy*; and cf. Rajni Kothari, in Saul Mendlovitz, ed., *On the Creation of a Just World Order*) ;

(3) Apply a "negative income tax" to all income levels below the agreed-upon national minimum. In other words, everyone gets a guaranteed subsistence income. It should be a *subsistence* income, one that would require us to live simply if we wanted to live well. (But it would force employers to pay adequate wages for unpleasant jobs. And it would free millions of people from the "job economy," opening jobs up to those of us who wanted them and allowing the rest of us to channel our energies into self and social healing.) (Robert Theobald, *Beyond Despair*) ;

(4) Use the guaranteed subsistence income to replace welfare benefits, and to substitute for most unemployment and Social Security benefits;

(5) Recruit 100,000 people who would agree to work on the guaranteed subsistence income for two years, organizing self-help projects in the following areas (among others): health, education, housing, solar energy, voluntary simplicity, rural living. Require periodic reports from these workers—nothing more. Provide a modest budget for expenses—nothing more.

C. Finance and Money

(1) Between the minimum and maximum income levels, enforce a standard and uniform individual income tax rate with no loopholes and few exemptions;

(2) Phase out the sales tax and other regressive taxation on basic

consumer goods (all food, all housing, some clothing and medical care);

(3) Phase out all tariffs and import quotas. (This would save billions of dollars a year for consumers and would introduce competition into some previously concentrated markets.) (L; *Nader Report on Antitrust Enforcement*) At the same time, permit some community and regional governments to set their own tariffs and import quotas (see sect. V below);

(4) Prohibit deficit budgets (L), except in certain exceptional circumstances;

(5) Limit spending to a fixed percentage of the net national income;

(6) Strive to eliminate the national debt by the year 2000, partly by declaring one year a "National Turnaround Year" with vastly reduced government-sponsored social services, correspondingly increased volunteer social services, and a vastly reduced military budget. America is ripe for this proposal;

(7) Calculate the ratio of the total amount of energy flowing in the economy to the total amount of money (include all energies, natural, fuel, and artificial). As the amount of energy increases or decreases, increase or decrease the amount of money, to keep the ratio the same. (Money would be worth a set amount of energy—this would help control inflation.) (Howard and Elisabeth Odum, *Energy Basis for Man and Nature*; and cf. Ralph Borsodi's plan for a commodity-backed currency. The Odums's plan is more practical);

(8) Do not increase property taxes on buildings because of restoration and energy improvements (Institute for Ecological Policies; Land, Equality and Freedom).

D. Business and Industry

(1) Immediately increase the funds available for small business loans (N; V). These loans should be made available at favorable interest rates and with a minimum of red tape;

(2) Ensure that all forms of government aid to business are "readily available to community development corporations, cooperatives, and the like. At present this is not the case" (Barry Stein, "Small Business," in de Moll and Coe, eds., *Stepping Stones*);

(3) Establish federal guidelines for loans to worker- and worker-community groups for the purchase and operation of industrial plants that are facing planned shutdowns (Joseph Blasi, social science writer for *Communities* magazine);

(4) Consolidate the antitrust functions of the Federal Trade Commission (an "independent" agency) and the Antitrust Division of the Justice Department into a "unified new administrative agency—the Competition Protection Agency"—with power to enforce planks 5–7 below (*Nader Report on Antitrust Enforcement*);

(5) Order divestiture (deconcentration) of all firms with more than $250 million in annual sales in all industries whose four-firm concentration ratio exceeds 50 percent of annual sales or whose eight-firm

ratio exceeds 70 percent. "Less concentrated industries would still be open to prosecution upon direct proof of oligopolistic behavior" (*ibid.*);

(6) "In antitrust proceedings resulting in divestiture orders, the units to be divested should be functionally complete, and able to operate as firms in the market. Preference for purchase should be given to independent groups; those preparing to distribute control broadly within communities, or among workers or relatively disfavored persons, should have access to financial assistance" (Barry Stein, *op. cit.*);

(7) Prohibit interlocking mergers between two or more competing corporations. Prohibit interlocking directorates between corporations and banks, customers, or suppliers that are not competitors. Ban all joint ventures between or among corporations in all cases where one of the corporations could have entered the market independently (*Nader Report on Antitrust*);

(8) Abolish the corporate income tax (it encourages expansion for expansion's sake, since "shareholders are generally better off if corporations plow back their earnings into expansion"; and it is a regressive tax, since corporations can and do merely pass their taxes on to consumers in the form of higher prices). Instead, tax each shareholder on the basis of his or her full share of the corporation's earnings, "regardless of what portion of those earnings was actually paid in dividends" (*ibid.*);

(9) Require corporations whose gross assets (including those of subsidiaries) exceed $100,000 to obtain a federal license, or "charter," to engage in interstate business. This charter should be very specific about corporate governance (duties of outside board of directors—how nominated and elected); corporate disclosure (tax returns, toxic substances in the workplace, multinational "job exportation," etc.); employees' rights (privacy, freedom of expression, nondiscrimination on account of race, religion, creed, sex); and corporate concentration (as in 5 above) (Nader et al., *Taming the Giant Corporation*);

(10) Alternatively to 5–7 above, require any corporation whose assets exceed $250 million, or any corporation which ranks among the top eight producers in an industry where the eight-firm concentration ratio is 70 percent or higher, to obtain another kind of federal charter. This charter would prohibit firms from: acquiring the stock, assets, or property of another company; granting or receiving any discrimination in price, service, or allowances; engaging in any tie-in arrangements or exclusive dealerships; and participating in any scheme of interlocking control over any other corporation. At the same time, the charter would require firms to: serve all customers on reasonable and nondiscriminatory terms, and license patents and know-how to other firms on a reasonable royalty basis (This may be a more "New Age" proposal than 6–9 above, depending on how concerned a government is about bigness per se. Unlike 5–7, it would not limit the growth of giant firms on the basis of "superior efficiency, technological innovation, or market success." It would only limit growth artificially induced via merger,

restrictive practices, etc. Or more philosophically, it would not seek to organize society, merely to regulate it.). (Walter Adams, "The Antitrust Alternative," in Nader and Green, eds., *Corporate Power in America.*).

E. Population

(1) Strive to bring the American population down to about 175 million—the 1958 population (currently we are at about 220 million officially, 235 million unofficially);

(2) Repeal all tax code provisions that discriminate in favor of parenthood, and gradually reverse them to discriminate in favor of childlessness and small families (FOE; L);

(3) Promote the teaching of population problems and sex education at all educational levels and in all kinds of educational institutions (FOE; Zero Population Growth);

(4) Increase support of contraceptive research and development—contraceptives for both women and men (FOE; Zero Population Growth);

(5) Ensure that abortions are available to (and affordable by) all women who want them, regardless of age and regardless of consent of spouse or parent. "Without safe abortion available on demand to all women, we face . . . thousands of . . . women dead of illegal abortion or suicide, [thousands of] children beaten to death by unwilling parents, [thousands of] children abandoned and growing up to become next generation's criminals" (FOE);

(6) Pass and enforce the Equal Rights Amendment. This would encourage women to define themselves as more than just bearers of children; also, "as both sexes enter each other's domains, less feeling is repressed" (Sharona Ben-Tov; New Age Feminism);

(7) Set annual quotas for immigration, based on emigration figures from the U.S., so that the base of the population is not increased through immigration (V; Zero Population Growth). At the same time, grant immediate immigrant status to up to 100,000 social or political refugees each year—regardless of country of origin ("social or political refugees" may be defined as all those who are unable or unwilling to return to the country of their habitual residence because of persecution or well-founded fear of persecution on account of race, religion, nationality, membership of a particular social group, or political opinion) (cf. Amnesty International–U.S.A.);

(8) Take all necessary steps to end illegal immigration. At the same time, take all necessary steps to end hunger, universalize social security, and improve living conditions—all over the planet (see sect. W below) (Garrett Hardin, in *Ecologist*, Aug./Sept. 1977; Zero Population Growth).

F. Labor

(1) Upon passage of the guaranteed subsistence income (B–3 above), repeal all laws which impede the ability of any person to find employment—including minimum wage laws, "protective" labor legis-

lation for women and children, and restrictions on the establishment of private day-care centers (L);

(2) Repeal all licensing requirements (L). Professional organizations might continue to license "qualified" practitioners, but practitioners would not be required to have a license in order to practice (Ivan Illich, *Tools for Conviviality*);

(3) Encourage job sharing, to the point of requiring businesses and industries of a certain size—and trade unions—to permit job sharing (see Robert Gilman, in *CoEvolution Quarterly,* Spring 1978);

(4) Encourage 16-, 20-, 24-, 32-hour (etc.) work weeks, to the point of requiring businesses and industries of a certain size—and trade unions—to permit shorter work weeks (*Simple Living,* Winter 1977);

(5) Encourage job rotation, to the point of requiring businesses and industries of a certain size—and trade unions—to permit job rotation wherever feasible (*ibid.*);

(6) Encourage the participation of wage and salary workers in decision-making at all levels of industry (Jaroslav Vanek, *The Participatory Economy*; and cf. New School for Democratic Management);

(7) Provide incentives, such as differential tax rates, for businesses and industries that are community- or worker-controlled (V);

(8) Take advantage of the union press to spread information on safety and health regulations, and encourage Labor Department compliance officers to concentrate their efforts on the protection of employee rights in nonunion plants. Encourage employees, especially union employees, to "accept the responsibility for initiating solutions to their own occupational health and safety problems." Admonish unions to "stop complaining about the Labor Department's shortage of inspectors long enough to do something about the small size of their own safety and health staffs" (*Nader Report on Disease and Injury on the Job*).

G. Agriculture

(1) Encourage the small or "family" farm, to the point that a minimum of 20 percent of U.S. citizens are members of farm families, nuclear or "extended" (today that figure is more like 4 percent. But it was 20 percent as recently as the 1940s) (cf. Wendell Berry, *op. cit.*, and Michael Marien, in *Futures*, Oct. 1977);

(2) Enact a progressive property tax that would allow small and modest-sized land holdings to be taxed at lower rates than large farms (Brian Livingston, in *Cascade*, Feb./March 1978; Wendell Berry, *op. cit.*);

(3) Prohibit land holdings in excess of a fixed number of acres, maximum to be determined on a bioregional basis by number of frost-free days per year and by soil type (M.S.). Alternatively, "levy a graduated tax on agricultural marketings by one producer in excess of the amount that can reasonably be produced on the optimal family sized farm" (this would encourage the breakup of larger-than-family-

sized farms—and especially the breakup of large-scale mechanized farms) (Institute for Liberty and Community);

(4) Eliminate depreciation and investment credits which subsidize investment in new and high-priced machinery (the machinery itself demands larger tracts of land) (*ibid.*);

(5) Limit the total amount of government payments any farmer can receive (would greatly reduce the incentive to invest in more land) (*ibid.*);

(6) Prohibit investment in farmland by nonfarmers, absentee investors, and nonfamily corporations (their investment in farmland drives farm prices artificially high) (Livingston, *op. cit.*);

(7) Require that the owners of farm land live within fifteen miles of their land (National Land for People; Rural America);

(8) Encourage and initiate programs to help urban people make the transition to farming (Howard and Elisabeth Odum, *op. cit.*);

(9) Make low-interest loans available to all those wishing to buy family-sized farms—especially low-income people and young people (National Land for People; N);

(10) "Create a National Land Trust for the purpose of acquiring arable units, subdividing them into family-farm sized units, and selling them to individual farm families"—not necessarily nuclear families— on easy terms. Trust would retain development rights and so assure that the farmland remains in farm use—or that the development "benefits" are shared by all (Institute for Liberty and Community; cf. National Community Land Trust Center);

(11) Encourage the formation of cooperative farm equipment organizations or pools among farm families (V; Institute for Liberty and Community);

(12) Reduce as much as possible the use of highly toxic insecticides and herbicides, and convert U.S. agriculture "as rapidly as possible to more natural and sustainable methods of insect, disease, and weed control" (FOE). Promote "natural" and organic farming methods (see, e.g., *Organic Gardening and Farming*, passim; Tom Putnam, "Natural Agriculture in Missouri," *East West*, March 1978);

(13) Encourage communities and states to promote urban farm markets, roadside stands, and growers' and consumers' co-ops (would encourage local self-sufficiency in food consumption and marketing) (FOE; Berry, *op. cit.*);

(14) Resolve Indian and Chicano land claims with land, not money (National Land for People).

H. Environment

(1) Encourage the recycling and reuse of domestic, organic, and inorganic wastes (V). Set an example by using recycled materials in government as much as possible (FOE);

(2) Support recycling research and, through tax incentives and other inducements, help recycling industries get started (FOE; V);

(3) Rapidly phase out production and use of all nonreturnable

containers—especially those made of metal, glass, or plastic compounds (FOE; V);

(4) Require manufacturers of durable goods "to design them for easy maintenance and repair, and ultimately, for easy recycling" (FOE);

(5) Encourage communities to base their waste collection system on the principle that all waste products will be sorted by the users (V). Require every community "to operate an organic-waste depot where sewage, garbage, waste paper, and the like would be composted and given or sold at cost to farmers" (Wendell Berry, *op. cit.*);

(6) Encourage communities to permit the use of septic tanks, rather than flush toilets (V);

(7) Develop an objective system for defining individual property rights to our air and water, and modify the laws of nuisance and negligence to cover damage done by air and water pollution (L; Ezra Mishan, *The Costs of Economic Growth*);

(8) Set noise-pollution standards and strictly enforce them (FOE);

(9) Promote the preservation and restoration of older buildings (not just "historic sites") (V). Provide tax credits to home owners wishing to restore their older dwellings;

(10) Fashion a rule that allows "environmental issues to be litigated before federal agencies or federal courts in the name of the inanimate object about to be despoiled, defaced, or invaded by roads and bull-dozers and where injury is the subject of public outrage. Contemporary public concern for protecting nature's ecological equilibrium should lead to the *conferral of* [*legal*] *standing* upon environmental objects to sue for their own preservation" through lawyers (if corporations, estates, and infants can do it, why not trees and valleys?) (Supreme Court Justice William O. Douglas, in FOE—emphasis added; and see Christopher Stone, *Should Trees Have Standing?*, 1975).

I. Energy

(1) Explicitly adopt a "soft technology energy strategy" involving rapid development of renewable energy sources, use of transitional fossil fuel technologies, use of thriftier technologies ("technical fixes"), and a much greater commitment to the pleasures of simple living (Amory Lovins, *Soft Energy Paths*);

(2) Remove the subsidies now given to the conventional fuel and power industries via tax loopholes, depletion allowances, foreign tax credits, promotional rate structures, etc. (James Benson et al., "The Wolfcreek Statement," *Ecologist*, Aug./Sept. 1977; Lovins);

(3) Vigorously enforce the antitrust laws in the fuel and power industries (Lovins);

(4) Place a "severance royalty" on all nonrenewable energy resources. In other words, increase the price of all nonrenewable fuels at the point of severance—wellhead or mine. Gradually increase this "royalty" until the cost of nonrenewable energy is equal to or higher than the cost of renewable energy ("Wolfcreek"); or until it makes

energy prices "consistent with *what it will cost in the long run* to replace our dwindling stocks of cheap fuels." "It would, in effect, be a depletion allowance backwards. Its effects would work through the economy and be reflected automatically in the price of goods and services in proportion to their direct and indirect energy content" (Lovins, emphasis added);

(5) Adopt minimum energy-efficiency standards for products such as automobiles, air conditioners, and appliances—and mandatory energy labeling to "provide market advantages to responsible manufacturers" ("Wolfcreek");

(6) Require all utilities to apply flat, even inverted utility rate structures (use less, pay less) rather than discounts for large users (Lovins);

(7) Provide each dwelling unit with up to $1,000 for installed energy conservation measures (thermal insulation, heat pumps, more efficient furnaces, etc.) (Institute for Ecological Policies, "Conservation/Tax Cut Bill," draft discussion paper, Dec. 1978);

(8) Alternatively to 7 above, mandate loans from utilities to householders for fuel-saving investments. The utilities "should loan the money at the same rate at which they would loan themselves money to buy a new power station" (*result*: hard and soft energy technologies would enjoy equal access to capital). "Borrowers should repay the loan (through their utility bills) at or below the rate at which the fuel-saving investment is expected to save them money" (*result*: loan repayments would *not increase* our utility bills). "The utility would only loan the money. It should neither execute nor control the project, either directly or indirectly" (*result*: we would not have to install the utility company's—or the government's—"approved" equipment) (Amory Lovins, "Free Enterprise Can Finance Our Energy Future," *Politicks*, April 11, 1978);

(9) Massively and decisively support a program of research, development, and deployment of clean energy sources such as solar, wind, geothermal, and generation of methane from organic wastes (New Directions, Worldwatch Institute, etc.);

(10) Encourage the development of energy-efficient intentional communities—for demonstration purposes (see, e.g., Cerro Gordo community, and the work of Simple Optimum Living). Remodel the White House and the Capitol Building to be stringently energy conserving and passive-solar oriented—again, for demonstration purposes, and to give clear expression to our nation's new commitment;

(11) Phase out all nuclear power programs—for safety's sake, because electricity can be generated more efficiently by small decentralized plants, and because nuclear technology absorbs talents and resources that can be better spent on solar (FOE). Alternatively, encourage the states to demand—as a condition for further nuclear construction—a demonstration of presently operating permanent disposal techniques for long-lived nuclear waste (a modest demand—but there are no such techniques) (Clamshell Alliance);

(12) Establish a national task force to plan for an orderly transition to a state of lower energy consumption—lower inflows of energy,

lower outflows of energy—with the eventual goal of reaching a low-level "steady state" (Herman Daly, *op. cit.*; and Howard and Elisabeth Odum, *op. cit.*).

J. Science and Technology

(1) Support research into—and development of—various kinds of "appropriate" technologies (FOE; National Center for Appropriate Technology). At the same time, *reduce* research into—and *cease* development of—most kinds of monolithic technology;

(2) Establish research review boards from a diverse constituency to review all state-supported scientific projects, projected or current. Boards would pass judgment on the use-value of these projects, monitor them on a continuing basis, and issue periodic reports (Dennis Pirages and Paul Ehrlich, *Ark II*).

K. The Future

(1) Establish a Commission on the Future whose task is to know as much as possible about what's really happening and to chart the various paths that are open to us. The time frame should range from "as soon as possible" to fifty years or more. In identifying the range of alternative futures facing the nation, the Commission should be very careful to include those paths that are seen as capable of taking us to a biolithic, decentralized society ("New Age society");

(2) Develop ongoing participatory planning mechanisms that would allow citizens to invent *their own* alternative futures and to develop their preferences for policies and spending priorities (this should also be done by regions, states, cities, and neighborhoods) (Institute for Alternative Futures);

(3) Investigate alternative uses for our "great" urban centers, interstate highways, skyscrapers, power plants, etc. (Howard and Elisabeth Odum, *op. cit.*; and see, e.g., Clement Bezold, "Lucas Aerospace," in *ibid.*, ed., *Anticipatory Democracy*);

(4) Ensure that legislators and congressional committees "make explicit the assumptions about the future underlying or motivating proposed legislation." Ensure that the congressional committee report accompanying each bill sent to the floor of the House or Senate include an outline of the bill's foreseeable middle- to long-term effects and possible secondary or side effects—and not just with regard to federal law and the budget. Committee reports on legislation should include plans to cope with unwelcome side effects (Institute for Alternative Futures);

(5) Encourage citizen and corporate groups to identify the side effects of the positions they advocate. "This could work to overcome the 'blindness' of legislative policy-making to side effects which the rise of single-issue politics from both citizen and corporate groups has contributed to" (*ibid.*).

L. Human Rights, Animal Rights, and Civil Liberties

(1) Enforce the equal rights of all citizens, regardless of sex, race,

religion, national origin, sexual preference, or social or economic creed. Enforce these rights with the proviso that representatives of the various sexes, races, religions, etc., do have the right to operate certain private establishments by and for themselves; and with the additional proviso that representatives of the various sexes, races, religions, etc., do have the right to set up autonomous and semiautonomous community districts to run as they see fit (see sect. V below);

(2) Refrain from reviewing all correspondence, bank and other financial transactions and records, doctors' and lawyers' communications, employment records, etc., without the consent of all parties involved. Ensure that all records kept on an individual by any organization, including the various levels and branches of government, be available on demand to that person or his or her legal representative for perusal and correction (L);

(3) Abolish the House Internal Security Committee and the Senate Subcommittee on Internal Security, and oversee the destruction of all their files on individuals and groups (L);

(4) Repeal all laws proscribing sexual practices in private between or among consenting adults;

(5) Support the concept that all animals, domestic, and non-, are citizens of the state, deserving equal protection from unnecessary harm (Friends of Animals). Dwell on the fact that, being lower on the food chain, the extinction of a plant takes more life forms with it than the extinction of most animals. There is a human bias in favor of animals over plants (Institute for Ecological Policies; and see sect. H, no. 11 above).

M. Crime and Punishment

(1) Repeal all federal, state, and local laws creating "crimes" without victims. In particular, repeal all laws prohibiting the production, sale, possession, or use of drugs; all laws regarding prostitution and solicitation; and all laws regulating or prohibiting gambling (L). At the same time, since engaging in these activities does result in social costs that are borne by us all, there must be intensive education in the dangers of abuse (cf. Proutist Universal);

(2) Phase out imprisonment for most crimes against property, and replace it with community service (V; and see Calvert Dodge, ed., *A Nation Without Prisons*);

(3) Phase out most prisons, and replace some of them with small community "hostels" (*ibid.*);

(4) Begin to "move back to the older model of the jury in which the individual is tried by a group of his or her peers—people who know the accused's situation and what behavior is likely in the future" (Robert Theobald, *op. cit.*);

(5) Increase the importance of small-claims courts which, with their simplified procedures, allow us to argue our own cases in hearings that take no more than minutes. Allow such courts to be used to press any claim that can be measured in monetary terms up to $10,000 (the

upper limit in the U.S. is currently $3,500, in Georgia; the upper limit in forty-six states is currently $1,000 or under) (Jethro Lieberman, in Nader and Green, eds., *Verdicts on Lawyers*);

(6) Allow two or more parties to agree to submit their present or future disputes to private arbitrators rather than lawyers or judges (*ibid.*). Allow some legal functions to be taken over by religious bodies or by other institutional codes, mutually agreed upon (Howard and Elisabeth Odum, *op. cit.*);

(7) Encourage community and state police to plan for fewer cars and computers (*ibid.*);

(8) Encourage the "regular" police to train and support unarmed (?) squads of "citizen" or "neighborhood" police (in Dayton, Ohio, neighborhood police have been responsible for a majority of the arrests for minor crimes in the neighborhoods) (David Morris, "Independent Cities," in de Moll and Coe, eds., *Stepping Stones*).

N. Youth, Age, and the Family

(1) Encourage a thorough sharing of family roles, as in Sweden (*New Age Feminism*; James Robertson, *The Sane Alternative*);

(2) See that the rights, privileges, duties, and responsibilities of adult citizens are made available to any young person, of whatever age, who wants to make use of them. These might include: the right to the full and equal protection of the law; the right to vote; the right to work for money; the right to own, buy, and sell property; the right to control and direct one's own learning—to decide what they want to learn and how and when they want to learn it; the right to travel; the right to live away from home without parents' permission; the right to receive the guaranteed subsistence income; the right to choose legal guardians other than one's parents; the right to choose to live as a fully legally responsible citizen (John Holt, *Escape from Childhood*). Minimum age levels might have to be set for most of these rights and responsibilities;

(3) "Repeal all laws establishing any category of crimes applicable to minors for which adults would not be similarly answerable." Put real pressure on the states to end the practice of jailing children accused of no crime (L);

(4) Actively investigate "ways to provide young people with challenges that will enable them to test their minds and their bodies without disrupting society" (Robert Theobald, *op. cit.*; and see, e.g., Earth Camp One, and the "war games" passages in Ernest Callenbach, *Ecotopia*);

(5) Encourage families to take in their relatives—especially their elderly relatives; and to share their space with legally unrelated persons. In other words, encourage the extended family, in its many sizes and guises (Robert Thamm, *Beyond Marriage and the Nuclear Family*);

(6) Ensure that day-care and overnight facilities are available to all (V);

(7) Define the rape of a spouse or child as a criminal act, punishable by law. We must change the tendency of older laws to treat women and children as property.

O. Consumer

(1) Provide tax subsidies for many natural and organic products;

(2) Reduce "filth tolerance" levels in processed foods (N). Phase out within five years all artificial colors, flavors, and other nonessential chemical additives to food (FOE);

(3) "Restrict food advertising to products that are food conserving and contribute to the public health. Such products would include, but not be limited to, fresh fruits and vegetables, legumes, and unrefined grains and flours (or products made from such flours)" (FOE);

(4) Provide a tax incentive for firms to make products with longer lives (V);

(5) Strengthen and enforce all laws against fraud and misrepresentation (L);

(6) Limit the number of times an advertisement can be shown on TV each week (V);

(7) Levy a 100 percent tax on all advertising expenditures of monopolies and oligopolies (as defined in D–5 above), and disburse the tax funds among consumer organizations to finance "counter-advertisements" (*Nader Report on Antitrust Enforcement*);

(8) Refuse to impose or promote the metric system—we do not need that degree of standardization in language or in measures (L; and see John Mitchell, "A Defense of Sacred Measures," *CoEvolution Quarterly,* Spring 1978);

(9) Gradually remove all standardized federal highway signs, and leave it to the communities and states to put up their own signs (there are some easy and obvious ways to promote bioregional consciousness).

P. Transportation

(1) "Withdraw all direct and indirect subsidies to energy- and resource-intensive modes of transportation such as airplanes, automobiles, and long-haul trucks" (FOE);

(2) Ban supersonic transport planes from all U.S. airspace (threatens the ozone layer, represents the mindlessness of technological "advance" for its own sake) (FOE);

(3) Introduce rigid emission control standards to control the polluting effects of all vehicles (V);

(4) Tax automobiles according to weight (Pirages and Ehrlich, *op. cit.*);

(5) Prohibit automobile companies from manufacturing automobiles that average less than 20 miles per gallon over a standard test run (cf. Pirages and Ehrlich, *op. cit.*);

(6) Encourage municipal initiatives to limit the use of private automobiles in high-density urban areas, and to create "car-free zones" (FOE);

(7) Set a speed limit of 50 mph on automobile travel between cities. This would save energy and lives—and help get the pace of life back under control (cf. Ivan Illich, "Energy and Equity," in *ibid., Toward a History of Needs*);

(8) Subsidize the development of the self-charging solar automobile (see the work done by, e.g., Friends of the Sun). Investigate the development of an automobile fuel from plant sources (see Lewis Fork, in *New Age*, Oct. 1978);

(9) Subsidize the passenger train, to the point where train travel costs the same cross-country as bus travel. At the same time, end all featherbedding on Amtrak, Conrail, etc.;

(10) Encourage walking and bicycling—encourage us to *prefer* to get places "under [our] own power" (FOE);

(11) Encourage community and state governments to promote the development of a complete, interrelated network of safe and efficient bicycle paths—especially in our cities (Greater Philadelphia Bicycle Coalition; Citizens on Cycles);

(12) Legalize hitchhiking (cf. Denny Wiseman, "Legal Thumbing," *New Age*, Sept. 1978);

(13) Encourage the establishment of an effective and affordable telecommunications system. This would eliminate the need for travel in some cases (Barbara Ward, *The Home of Man*).

Q. Health

(1) Establish the right of individuals to contract freely with health practitioners of their choice, whether licensed or not, for all health services (L). Amend the Constitution, if necessary, to allow for freedom of choice in cancer and other therapies (Peter Barry Chowka, in *New Age*, Sept. 1978);

(2) Encourage each health discipline to develop its own certification system (Holistic Health Organizing Committee)—for information purposes only;

(3) Encourage the teaching of medical self-care in elementary and high schools (Tom Ferguson, editor of *Medical Self-Care*)—and in many other places as well, such as churches, hospitals, community centers, etc.;

(4) Ensure the training of a substantial number of lay paramedics (Ferguson). These paramedics should work out of community-based clinics, or make inexpensive house calls the way "general practitioners" used to;

(5) Foster and encourage various "natural" and Eastern medical practices in addition to traditional Western medicine (see, e.g., Naboru Muramoto, *Healing Ourselves*);

(6) Encourage training programs for midwives. Permit midwives to manage and care for women and their infants during the stages of normal childbirth (Suzanne Arms, in *New Age*, Oct. 1977). Encourage all programs that attempt to prepare women and couples in the techniques of natural childbirth and in the techniques of home birth (e.g., Homebirth, Inc.);

(7) Encourage humanistically-oriented gerontology services—programs that can help the later years be a time for "health, vitality, expanded awareness, and the realization of self that comes from having lived a long and full life" (Association for Humanistic Gerontology; Sage Project);

(8) Add "the right to choose to die" to the Bill of Rights (Robert Theobald, *op. cit.*);

(9) Encourage people to adopt the dietary goals recommended by the Senate Select Committee on Nutrition in 1977, including: increased consumption of fruits, vegetables, and whole grains; decreased consumption of red meat, increased consumption of poultry and fish; decreased consumption of butterfat, eggs, and other high cholesterol products; decreased consumption of sugar and salt (*East West*, Nov. 1977);

(10) Enact a system of National Health Insurance without viewing it as a cure for the ills of our present health care system—in fact, enactment of NHI may induce some people to avoid the really fundamental questions about the adequacy of the present medical system and its technological orientation. And any system of NHI carries built-in dangers of rising costs and expanding bureaucracies. Therefore, place substantial limits on total expenditures for NHI, relating these to the total overall budget; and set a standard fee for each type of medical service (cf. George Armelagos and Phillip Katz, in *Ecologist*, Aug./Sept. 1977);

(11) As an integral part of NHI, launch a program of *preventative* health care involving: control of the environment (of noise pollution, of the automobile, rampant industrialization, etc.), improved health education, and—especially—"an emphasis upon life-style as a vital component in determining health" (*ibid.*).

R. Education

(1) Repeal all compulsory education laws (L; Illich, *Deschooling Society*);

(2) Insist that no one be denied an available job solely on the basis of school credentials. Ensure that whenever a credential is needed for a job, there be a way of getting that credential without going to school (apprenticeship training, equivalency exams, etc.) (John Holt, *Instead of Education*);

(3) Support the development of less formal educational agencies—learning exchanges, "alternative" schools, and "schools without walls" —such as the Vermont Institute of Community Involvement (90 Main St., Burlington, Vt. 05401) which meets in church basements, public buildings, and homes (Illich, *op. cit.*; Holt, *op. cit.*);

(4) Encourage schools to be maximally self-maintaining and self-sufficient, with materials recycling, maintenance instruction, agricultural instruction and production, etc. (FOE);

(5) Encourage schools to rely more on student-teacher rapport, and less on capital equipment such as teaching machines, elaborate textbooks, and videos (FOE);

(6) Encourage the use of "humanistic" and "transpersonal" methods of teaching—methods that can develop our emotions, our imaginations and intuitions, our wills, and our higher selves, as well as our intellects (Institute for Wholistic Education). Encourage the teaching of "new games" rather than competitive sports—games that require a minimum of equipment and are designed to encourage creativity, spontaneity, and participation by young and old, "skilled" and "unskilled" . . . (New Games Foundation, P.O. Box 7901, San Francisco, Calif. 94120). Encourage the teaching of yoga and other Eastern physical cultures as a means of maintaining optimum physical health. Encourage the teaching of some forms of meditation and concentration as a means of maintaining mental discipline and advancing mental development (N; and cf. the work of the Meditation Group for the New Age). Encourage the development of courses promoting individual self-reliance such as carpentry, handicrafts, organic gardening, "wilderness experience," small business accounting, and elementary mechanics (FOE);

(7) Urge communities and states to eliminate all sex bias from teaching materials and school books. "Ensure that all trainee teachers receive instruction in how to perceive and counteract sex stereotyping of their pupils." Encourage school systems to attach preschools to secondary schools. (This would enable students of both sexes to be involved in child care.) Encourage men to be more involved in elementary and secondary education (all V).

S. Housing

(1) Induce local authorities to abolish most or all restrictions on self-built private dwellings: where and how they can be built; kinds of materials used; size and shape of rooms . . . (cf. River, *Dwelling*; Ken Kern et al., *The Owner-Builder and The Code*);

(2) Induce communities and states to permit community labor to engage in construction work on community projects (see Colin Kowal, in *Seriatum*, Spring 1977);

(3) Make finance more easily available to people wishing to buy or maintain older homes than to people wishing to buy or build new homes;

(4) Require the installation of stringent energy conservation and passive solar technologies on all new government buildings ("Wolfcreek," *op. cit.*). Require that all new homes be stringently energy conserving and passive solar-oriented in order to be eligible for federal mortgage loans and other federal programs (Institute for Ecological Policies' "Conservation/Tax Cut Bill," draft discussion paper, Dec. 1978).

T. Media

(1) Encourage the media to provide access to groups and individuals who have made positive contributions to society (N);

(2) Enforce the Fairness Doctrine, which requires that broadcasters allot a portion of their broadcast time to reporting and discussing

significant issues in a way that fairly reflects divergent viewpoints on those issues (FOE);

(3) Rule that all television commercials be shown at random (Pirages and Ehrlich, *op. cit.*);

(4) Eliminate all television advertising aimed at children (*ibid.*);

(5) Encourage the establishment of viewer-sponsored television stations, including pay TV;

(6) Prohibit cross-ownership of broadcast and print media in the same city. Prohibit nonmedia ownership of media, and vice versa (FOE).

U. Government Reform

(1) Oppose federal funding of election campaigns. At the same time, set stringent campaign-spending ceilings for all presidential, congressional, state, and local candidates (Pirages and Ehrlich, *op. cit.*);

(2) Ensure that the names and affiliations of all major campaign contributions are regularly reported during the course of each campaign. A "major" contribution might be defined as: $1,000 for presidential races, $500 for congressional, $100 for state and local (combination of N; Institute for Ecological Policies; Pirages and Ehrlich; Proutist Universal);

(3) Encourage the development of a multiparty system that would give a broader spectrum of representation in politics (Pirages and Ehrlich). To begin with, insist that all broadcast media give "equal time" to all parties and candidates that managed to receive a minimum of 5 percent of the vote in pursuit of the same office in the previous election, if a local election; 2 percent if a national election.

V. Localization and Regionalization

(1) Build incentives to decentralize (and *dis*-incentives to centralize) into the tax structure (FOE);

(2) Assist in the funding of community-run and community-oriented "alternative" institutions such as day-care centers and neighborhood clinics. Assist in the development of community- and household-based food sources. Assist in the development of community credit unions and development banks (cf. David Morris and Karl Hess, *Neighborhood Power*; and the work of the Institute for Local Self-Reliance);

(3) Permit local authorities to charter those corporations, or branches of corporations, doing business or intending to do business in their localities (Richard Barnet and Robert Muller, *Global Reach*);

(4) Permit all community districts (cities or counties or contiguous counties) to opt for full sovereignty by majority vote—also all regions (states or contiguous states or states-and-contiguous-counties);

(5) Permit all community districts and regions to opt for partial sovereignty ("sovereignty-association") by majority vote every twenty years. Sovereignty-association would allow community districts and regions to decide on such things as: social services, housing and em-

ployment policies, income distribution, foreign policy, defense policy, kind of economy. It would, however, require community districts and regions to continue to pay some federal taxes, and to continue to adhere to the nationally chosen ethics and values; and it would allow citizens to continue to vote in national elections, to serve in the national army and militia, to own extraregional land, and to carry an American passport.

Planetary Affairs

W. Planet Earth

(1) Attempt to educate the American public about the appalling dimensions of planetary poverty and misery (V; The Hunger Project);

(2) Seek to develop with other nations a "planetary guidance system" whose long-range goal would be to regulate planetary society according to the New Age ethics and political values (cf. Ervin Laszlo, *Goals for Mankind*; Saul Mendlovitz, ed., *On the Creation of a Just World Order*), and whose immediate goal would be to try to provide a degree of collective security. (As it is now, "national security" interests and fears are causing nations to compete against one another for arms, for scarce resources, and for favorable balances of payments.) (Global Education Associates; Gerald and Patricia Mische, *Toward a Human World Order*);

(3) Explicitly align ourselves with the "Fourth World"—with native peoples and with all those peoples who choose and prefer to live simply and well (Planet/Drum Foundation; Gary Snyder, *The Old Ways*);

(4) Commit not less than 1 percent of our Gross National Product (GNP) each year to international aid programs (today that figure is more like 0.3 percent) (Jan Tinbergen, coord., *RIO: Reshaping the International Order*; Club of Rome). In addition, commit an increasing proportion of our GNP to international aid programs—say an additional 0.1 percent a year—until the percentage of our material wealth begins to approximate the percentage of our population (today we have 5 percent of the planet's population—and 30 percent of its material wealth);

(5) Refuse to give aid to regimes that are resisting important reforms (except in emergencies, for humanitarian purposes). All other things being equal, give more aid to countries that adhere to the New Age ethics and political values than to those that oppose them;

(6) Design aid programs to promote the economic and political self-sufficiency of the IDC's (insufficiently developed countries). Especially, help other countries make the transition to food self-sufficiency —and provide food aid as *supplementary support* for that purpose (FOE);

(7) Put economic and diplomatic pressure on the IDC's to carry out thoroughgoing programs of agrarian reform (Tinbergen);

(8) Encourage programs to universalize social security abroad (fear

of poverty, especially in old age, is the main reason why people in the IDC's tend to have so many children) (FOE);

(9) Encourage nations to join together to work out a "planetary industrial strategy" that could help them in formulating their own self-chosen industrial policies within the limits of planetary ecological energy and resource capacities (cf. Tinbergen);

(10) Support the establishment of a system of planetary taxation on resource use (*ibid.*);

(11) Phase out support for others' nuclear power programs. "Insist that the International Atomic Energy Agency cease promoting nuclear power and devote itself instead to curbing nuclear proliferation." Authorize economic sanctions against nations that are actively developing nuclear technologies (FOE);

(12) Support the planetwide deployment of solar and other environmentally-sound energy systems "at least as actively as we have hitherto promoted nuclear power" (FOE);

(13) Call for an end to the use of torture as an instrument of interrogation (Amnesty International; International League for Human Rights). Authorize economic sanctions against nations that continue to use torture;

(14) Call for intellectual, cultural, and spiritual freedom for all peoples, everywhere. Authorize economic sanctions against nations that continue to abuse these freedoms *and* that refuse to allow people to emigrate;

(15) Proclaim that both the sea and the seabed are the common heritage of planet Earth and that all nations have the right to benefit from them . . . first of all according to ecological criteria, and then according to population and economic need;

(16) Urge all nations to declare a ten-year moratorium on whaling "during which experts would determine the conditions [if any] under which whaling might safely be resumed." Authorize economic sanctions against nations that reject such a moratorium (FOE);

(17) Vastly increase the size of the Peace Corps. Make its number one task the introduction of "appropriate technologies" into the IDC's (see the work of the Intermediate Technology Development Group). At the same time, increase financial aid to selfless-service-type private organizations such as the PLENTY Project (see Chapter 27).

X. Multinational Corporations

(1) Limit profits "repatriated" by corporations from abroad to the level of domestic profits. This would limit the incentive to invest abroad in search of quick profits (Pirages and Ehrlich, *op. cit.*);

(2) Require at least 51 percent ownership of corporate facilities abroad by the countries in which those facilities are located. Everybody's long-run interest is served when each country controls, or can control, foreign investment (*ibid.*).

Y. Defense

(1) Gradually but firmly, cut the defense budget by 40 percent.

This would entail no loss in effective defense capacity (see Philip Morrison and Paul Walker, "A New Strategy for Military Spending," *Scientific American*, Oct. 1978);

(2) Declare that our nuclear weapons are only to be used to protect our selves (and our allies) from nuclear attack. Encourage all nuclear-weapons states to accept a pledge never to use nuclear weapons first (Institute for World Order). Encourage all nuclear-weapons states to accept a pledge never to use nuclear weapons against non-nuclear weapons countries (*ibid.*);

(3) Reject use of the neutron bomb under any circumstances (a nuclear weapon that has no value whatsoever unless used first). Seek an agreement with all other countries to prohibit the use of all incendiary weapons, such as napalm, and to prohibit the research, development, manufacture, and stockpiling of all chemical and biological weapons (Institute for World Order);

(4) Seek an agreement with the other "superpowers" to reduce the number of strategic arms (missiles and bombers) by 20 percent a year for ten years. At the same time, seek an agreement with all other nations to reduce military expenditures by a given percentage each year. "At the point where annual expenditures would pass below the amount needed for simple maintenance of existing weapons, [arms] would be effectively reduced because of obsolescence and decay." (Budget cuts are more effective than limited arms control agreements. "Arms control" tends to restrict some types of weapons while allowing and in fact encouraging new deployments of other weapons) (*ibid*);

(5) Gradually reorganize the armed forces into a multipurpose civilian-defense-and-social-service organization that would train us in the arts of nonviolent and "territorial"—nonviolent plus guerrilla—defense (cf. Adam Roberts, *Nations in Arms*; Gene Sharp, *The Politics of Nonviolent Action*);

(6) Reestablish the civilian draft. Without a citizen army the powerful life-rejecting people in this country may never peacefully relinquish their power; and without a citizenry professionally trained in the arts of nonviolent and territorial defense, we may never dare to put an end to the arms race;

(7) Extend the draft to women, students, paraplegics, everyone— no exceptions whatsoever; and have it apply to everyone for a minimum of one year beginning the Monday after their eighteenth birthday;

(8) Use draftees for peaceful purposes, especially for helping to start self-care organizations and movements and also for jobs that society deems especially unattractive;

(9) Create a "citizens' militia." Have communities elect or appoint people to organize for nonviolent and/or territorial defense on a block-by-block basis;

(10) Provide limited amounts of overt nonmilitary support to New Age-oriented and third force-radical movements abroad; especially diplomatic support (e.g., to prevent unjust confinement) (cf. Fellowship of Reconciliation);

(11) Help to create a permanent transnational police force, "indi-

vidually recruited and responsible to a global authority" (Institute for World Order), whose tasks would be limited to preventing outside military intervention—any kind, anywhere.

Z. Interdependence Day

(1) Declare July 5th our annual "Interdependence Day" (Planetary Citizens). This would be a day to acknowledge that, in an important sense, we are all One.

Part IX

THE NEW AGE PERSPECTIVE

This Part contains two essays that have been milestones in my understanding of what a New Age politics is and can be. (Following sect. O–8 in the Platform above, I speak of milestones and not kilometer-stones.)

The first essay, "Hooker to Frank to You," shows that aspects of "New Age politics" have always been with us here in America. The idea is that New Age politics is an indigenous, even a mainstream, American political philosophy.

As a New Age political person, I have always found it easier to identify with blacks and women in American history than I have with white men. I wrote the first essay in answer to the question, "Have there been white men in American history who were New Age-oriented?" I think the results speak for themselves.

Another essay in this Part has yet to be written. Charlotte Bunch, Mary Daly, Susan Griffin, Bonnie Kreps, Patricia Mische, Robin Morgan, Carlagaye Olson, Allison Platt, Christina Rawley, Adrienne Rich, and many other feminists, known and unknown, have been articulating what I would call a New Age feminism; and in the next edition of this book, I would like to include a guest chapter by a woman who is thinking, living, and acting along New Age feminist lines.

I would also like to include separate essays on black and Chicano contributions to New Age politics. (As early as the 1910s, Waldo Frank was writing that the "Hispanic-American" contribution would be crucial.)

Feminist philosophy has been important to me for a number of reasons, not least of which is that for a few crucial years (1968–1975?) feminists were just about the only radicals around who were strong enough and self-confident enough to articulate a non-Marxist radicalism. The second essay in this Part, "Clearing the Ground," will tell you why I think that's so important. It is a New Age critique of Marxism and, by extension, of much of what passes for "radicalism" in this country today.

CHAPTER 25

Hooker to Frank to You: Some Early American Advocates of "New Age Politics"

> Our hope lies in the fact that we once had a
> political tradition which could give an answer . . .
> to this false [capitalist-or-socialist] dilemma.
> —Herbert Agar, *Land of the Free*, 1935

Important aspects of the New Age impulse are not new in American life. Historians have tended to see American politics as a battleground between Hamiltonians and Jeffersonians, the one centralizing, conservative, elitist, and finance-capitalist, the other decentralizing, "radical," "democratic," and more or less agrarian; but there has always been a separate, third strain in American politics, easy to see if you lose your vested political or emotional interest in the positions mentioned above.

Twenty of these "third strain" or New Age Americans are introduced—all too briefly—in this chapter. Keep in mind that I have not included people the bulk of whose work comes after 1945, which is why Aldo Leopold is missing, and Maslow and Mumford. . . .

Thomas Hooker (1586–1647), *clergyman*. Hooker was one of the founders of the state of Connecticut. He came from a plain, yeoman family, and no matter how high he rose in the colonial hierarchy, he always held fast and without any self-consciousness to the principles of voluntary simplicity (his friends were shocked when he died and the small size of his estate was finally revealed).

Hooker was more balanced in his radicalism than his arch-rival, Roger Williams, more sensitive to nuance, more deeply aware of the second- and third-order consequences of his radicalism. On the one hand, he vigorously defended the new gospel of free judgment in religious matters against the likes of John Cotton; on the other, he insisted, against Williams, that the government has the right and the power and, indeed, a moral obligation to enforce social values. He said that without a coherent and socially observed set of ethics or values (loose or strict, as communities wished) society would drift into chaos or authoritarianism.

John Wise (1652–1725), *clergyman*. Wise was the son of an indentured servant. He led a tax resistance movement in the 1680s and was a vigorous opponent of the witchcraft trials. He is known as one of our first "true democrats," but he should really be known as one of our first "New Age democrats." For he argued, against the Mathers and the Presbyterians and virtually everyone else of authority in New England at the time, that you can't have a spiritual and moral people for long without a political democracy. He argued that access to the spiritual and religious states of consciousness, with the ethics and values that those states imply, leads inevitably to the desire for democracy—for freedom of choice in all matters and not just in the "religious."

Wise combined his democracy with a hard-won knowledge of people with their vanity and fears, their selfishness and pride. And so he insisted that individuals and the state be prepared to shoulder a lot more personal and collective responsibility than we might like; individual *and* collective responsibility, and not just more of either.

John Woolman (1720–1772), *Quaker*. Woolman was one of our first spiritual radicals (as distinct from religious radicals). He was a simple man, with no schooling to speak of and a modest tailor's trade; but by and by he began to experience what later generations would flatten out with terms like "mystical yearnings" and "spiritual insights." Two hundred years before George Leonard, and without any access to the works of the East, he began to sense that the Earth was pulsing with a kind of energy, which he attributed to a divine and universal love and which he called "love's motion." And he began to experience a tender and choiceless sympathy with all humankind and all natural things, indeed all things.

Woolman left his tailor's shop to become a minister, and he embarked on a series of journeys that lasted, on again, off again, for thirty years and took him the entire walkable part of this land (for he walked wherever he went)—year in and year out, speaking against slavery and speaking of God; speaking against Indian conversion and speaking of God; speaking against taxation for military supplies and all the time speaking of the God of love.

Richard Henry Lee (1732–1794), *statesman*. Lee was a Revolutionary statesman from Virginia who opposed, and eventually led the opposition to, the proposed new Constitution of the United States. He felt that the Articles of Confederation was a much more genuinely decentralist document. He also felt that the Constitution represented "a transfer of power from the many to the few," indeed almost a coup d'etat, since the convention in Philadelphia had been called specifically to revise the Articles and not to replace them.

At the height of the debate he wrote *Letters from the Federalist Farmer*, which became a kind of textbook for the opposition to the Constitution. It is just as relevant to democratic theory as the Constitutionalists' better-known *Federalist Papers*. In it Lee traces the "present agitation" to "two unprincipled parties," those who "avariciously grasp at all power and property" and those "who want no law" (Hamiltonians and Jeffersonians again, industrial and agrarian militants again, them-against-us-against-them again). Both dislike free government, said Lee; both are more interested in being right than in being free; both would rather be winners *or losers* than be reconciled to a less than *monolithic* America. But the "vast majority of small farmers" will be completely wiped out by that kind of reasoning, said Lee. . . .

John Adams (1735–1826), *President of the United States.* Adams was our second President. He argued against both agrarianism and finance-capitalism, thinking the one impractical and quixotic and the other aggressively exploitative. He urged us to work out a kind of economy that was genuinely ours (those others reflected *past* realities, said Adams), that borrowed from both but transcended them also; that left most of us on the land, for instance, but also made it possible for us to manufacture our own goods here in America, and to regulate the production of those goods. And mark my words, said Adams: if push comes to shove and we really do have to choose between an unregulated capitalism and a single-vision agrarianism, then an unregulated capitalism is what we'll get.

Adams was right, of course; but he offended both sides by his talk of a new way in economics, and because he insisted on providing checks and balances, checks and balances when the gung-ho "radicals" and manufacturers of our early history were both still trying to be unchecked and unbalanced.

John Quincy Adams (1767–1848), *President of the United States.* John Quincy Adams was John Adams's eldest son, the sixth President of the United States and "the one great man since Washington whom America had no cause to fear" (Theodore Parker). John Quincy's commitment to a politics of healing and reconciliation was so great that on his election to the Massachusetts State Senate he proposed that two or three of the governor's council be "of opposite politics to our own." Not surprisingly, he was mistrusted by all political parties after that—not least of all his own.

John Quincy Adams is responsible for the closest thing we have in early American history to a New Age *theory* of politics. He took Tom Paine's central argument, that a people can do anything it chooses to do, and asked: but what about the fact that we are "endowed by our Creator with certain inalienable rights"? If a popular majority is "bound by no law human or divine, . . . what possible security can any citizen of the nation have for the protection of [his or her] inalienable rights?" We can forgive him if he failed to give a sufficiently concrete answer to the obvious next question: but where do our "inalienable rights" come from? (New Age politics would say that it is an essential task of the various communities and regions to define these rights *for themselves*, provided only that their definitions of these rights are consistent with the New Age ethics and political values; see Chapter 12.)

William Ellery Channing (1780–1842), *minister.* Despite an over-serious and painfully self-conscious boyhood, Channing was able to become the most highly respected minister of his day. He took the punishment- and guilt-oriented God of New England Christianity, and almost singlehandedly turned that God into a God of love and justice.

Channing's sermons were talked about in the same way that we talk about good books and movies today. They were dense, beautifully proportioned, and they made people think. He regularly preached against violence, against slavery, against the annexation of Texas, and against all coercive centralizing power. He defined religion as "the adoration of goodness." And 130 years before Planetary Citizens would begin to speak of an emerging "planetary consciousness," he said, "In looking at our age I am struck immediately by one commanding characteristic, and that is, the tendency in all its movements to expansion, to diffusion, to universality. . . . This tendency is directly opposed to the spirit of exclusiveness, restriction, narrowness, monopoly, which has prevailed in past ages. . . . The privileged, petted individual is becoming less, and the human race is becoming more. . . ."

Theodore Parker (1810–1860), *minister*. Parker was one of eleven farm children—and painfully sensitive, like Channing. And he too went on to become one of the most influential Americans of his day. His was a voice, not of power, but of undeniable *authority*.

Parker is still fairly well-known as a New England abolitionist and transcendentalist. He is less well known than Ralph Waldo Emerson, but he is, in truth, much less the cold Yankee than Emerson, less prissy, less "serene," less abstract. From his pulpit he called for a democracy that would base itself on an ethical system rather than an economic one, a democracy that would attempt to "enact God's justice into human laws." From his pulpit he regularly attacked the materialism and greed of America in general and Boston in particular, and not just "Boston" but particular people in Boston—he named names; and not just names but particular deeds, particular incidents. And yet he was always careful to direct his criticisms at *particular* individuals and at particular social *values*, and not at social and economic *classes* per se.

John Humphrey Noyes (1811–1886), *social reformer*. Noyes was the leading advocate of "perfectionism," which, like transcendentalism, was a fascinating synthesis of social, political, economic, and religious radicalisms. Noyes has been called a "spiritual anarchist," but he was actually caught in a constant running battle between the right wing of his movement, which he felt was overly moralistic, and the "anti-legalist" left wing, which he felt was irresponsible and childish.

Noyes was careful to keep from defining perfectionism in too "utopian" a way. By a "perfected person" he meant, not what we might mean, but one who had discovered the reality of what New Age-oriented psychologists like Assagioli would come to call the "higher self"; one who might be characterized by a "loving heart," a "renewed mind," and an insatiable desire for personal, social, and spiritual evolution. Noyes felt that the good society would be one that tried to propagate such "perfect" people, not by doing away with government but by carefully substituting education and moral pressure for the force of law. And he founded the Oneida Community in upstate New York to give clear and powerful expression to his beliefs, which it did, becoming the most conspicuously successful of all the community experiments of the nineteenth century.

Alexander H. Stephens (1812–1883), *Vice President of the Southern Confederacy.* Stephens was brought up in severe poverty, self-taught, sickly (never weighing as much as one hundred pounds), and never quite trusted by the planter aristocracy. Still, they had to trust him to some extent, because he managed to make himself into the ablest defender of the doctrine of secession that this country ever had—and, some say, our ablest Constitutional scholar.

In his 1,500-page masterpiece, *A Constitutional View of the War between the States*, Stephens demonstrates convincingly that state sovereignty existed *prior* to the union; that it was carefully *guarded* at the Constitutional Convention; and that states therefore have the right to become sovereign *again*. This is a view that has never been adequately refuted, except on the battlefield. And it would appear to give states a mandate to ask or bargain for *partial* sovereignty ("sovereignty-association") as well.

Henry George (1839–1897), *political economist.* George dropped out of school at fourteen and went to sea. He ended up in dreadful poverty in California, which he wrote his way out of, first as a newspaperman and then as the author of one of the most penetrating books on economics ever written (and among plain people possibly the most popular), *Progress and Poverty*.

Progress and Poverty was a deliberate attempt to work out an economics that would be appropriate to the United States, as distinct from what he called a more "collectivistic" country. Its thesis is that the primary source of economic injustice is neither the "capitalism" of the Marxists nor the "human nature" of the liberals but rather the fact that *land* is not taxed properly (briefly: the property tax should be removed from homes, buildings, crops, factories, and improvements, and concentrated onto land values which are created by the efforts of the community as a whole). Along the way, George argued that each of us has a *natural right* to "the use of so much of the free gifts of nature as may be necessary to supply all the wants of [our] existence." His passages on the exploitation of labor and on the evils of monopoly are in my opinion superior, both in depth of insight and in the palpable sense of caring, to similar passages in Marx and Engels. He was very much a decentralist, and very aware of the *political* importance of the spirit; and there is an uncanny anticipation of Maslow's theory of the stages of self-development.

In 1886, Henry George ran for the office of mayor of New York City. He may have won, too, but he was "counted out."

John Muir (1838–1914), *environmentalist*. Muir grew up on a homestead near Portage, Wisconsin, where at thirteen he was splitting rails, mowing with the scythe, and reading every book he could get his hands on. By the time he dropped out of the University of Wisconsin he was a first-rate botanist and geologist, and he traveled the length and breadth of this country for years keeping a minutely detailed journal that he drew on for the rest of his life. At the same time, he began to develop a nature philosophy that borrowed from the transcendentalists but went beyond them, was more rooted in the minute, the palpable, the observable particulars (he also began to feel that anyone who lives close to the mountains for long becomes psychically attuned and aware).

Muir came down from the mountains in 1875 resolved to make all the wilderness better known and loved, for its own sake and also because of its healing powers. He said that we must be made conscious of our origins as children of nature. He felt that if we could somehow learn to bring our selves into right relationship with nature we would see that we were not primarily separate entities whose task it is to subdue nature, but primarily parts of the whole, whose task it is to evolve *within* and *through* nature. He became one of our first "environmental activists" and he co-founded and ran the Sierra Club for many, many years.

Frederick Jackson Turner (1861–1932), *historian*. Turner just missed John Muir at Portage, Wisconsin, but he was there early enough so that memories of explorers and fur traders, memories of an America of promise and mystery, lurked behind every lined face and pine tree.

Turner grew up to be a history professor who loved being a professor of history . . . and he was very good at it. He is still well known for his paper "The Significance of the Frontier in American History," written and delivered when he was in his twenties; but what is not well known is that his paper was meant to be merely the first step in the construction of an entirely new *theory* of American history. The new theory was to be embodied in a book called *The Significance of Sections in American History*. Its argument was to be that the history of this country could most usefully be seen as a struggle among sections —not just North and South, but *all kinds* of "natural [i.e., bioregional], economic, and social" sections depending on the issue at hand.

Turner failed to finish his book or to finally establish his theory (the book by that name is a posthumous series of essays and a pale reflection of Turner's guiding vision). His failure came partly because he did love being a professor, and partly because in 1910 he accepted a professorship at Harvard where virtually none of his colleagues were interested in or even particularly respectful of his desire to find a uniquely American explanation for the dynamics of American history, let alone one that leant sympathy to regionalism.

John Jay Chapman (1862–1933), *social critic.* Chapman was a lawyer but, disgusted by the law, soon went into politics. He attempted to build our first "non-socialist-radical" urban political organization, in 1895–1900 in New York City; his main argument being that by denouncing corporations and trusts the socialists merely struck at the symbol: "What they really hate is the irresponsible rapacity which these things typify, and which nothing but moral forces will correct." He gave speeches from a cart-tail and bought his hecklers drinks.

Chapman gave up his political activism when he began to feel that what we needed first was an "extension of the sense of life" which might possibly give us a *motive* for being other than greed-oriented. He wrote: "I have seen death in the heart of this people. . . . Whatsoever life itself is, that thing must be replenished in us." He became a cultural critic of politics and a political critic of culture at a time when politics and culture were supposed to be separate and definitely unequal activities (see, e.g., his "biography" of William Lloyd Garrison, in Barzun, ed.). He called on us to read and act, act and read, because the "experienced knowledge of books" was one way we had of extending our sense of life.

Hutchins Hapgood (1869–1944), *social critic.* Hapgood grew up in a small town in the Midwest. He hated it there, and left it as soon as he could; but he developed out of that experience a burning desire to create a "revitalized America." Eventually he became a central figure in the early (read: real) Greenwich Village.

Hapgood's major contribution to our social and political literature is a now forgotten book called *The Spirit of the Ghetto.* This was an answer to Jacob Riis and some other early "muckrakers," who went into the Jewish ghetto at the turn of the century and found only dirt, poverty, vice, ignorance, immorality. Hapgood went into the very same ghetto and found, as well, qualities that America could lose only at its peril, qualities such as intellectual vitality, energy, hope, humor, compassion, community, a *perspective* on "respectability," and a kind of spiritual unity.

If we are simply to level our ghettos and then forget about them, said Hapgood; if we fail to realize that our encounter with ghetto culture is giving us exactly the opportunity we need in order to grow; if we fail to realize that we need to *get* as much from the ghetto as we have to *give*—then America will become a vast wasteland, where people will be even less happy, even less whole than they are now. (For America is being "leeched of its wholeness in the headlong industrial thrust.") But that was altogether too modest a perspective for the reformers of Hapgood's day, who were much more intent on proving how badly the country needed them than on engaging in any kind of give and take with our various cultural communities; and who were anyway deeply suspicious and resentful of our ethnic cultures—the "radicals" because they seemed to get in the way of labor unity and the liberals because they seemed to get in the way of national unity.

Ralph Borsodi (1888–1977), *political economist*. Borsodi co-founded the School of Living and the magazine *Free America*. He spent much of his life trying to *live* his philosophy on homesteads and in various intentional communities. His masterpiece, *This Ugly Civilization*, is a kind of decentralist *Das Kapital*, the most comprehensive and satisfying argument for what I have called the "household" or "homestead" economy that I have ever read.

Borsodi was an advocate of "appropriate technology" long before Schumacher. He was one of the first Americans to realize that the problem with our institutions is not, ultimately, that they are capitalist or state-socialist, but that they are monolithic; and he anticipated Fromm's and Maccoby's concept of psychocultural class analysis, speaking not of life-, thing-, and death-oriented classes, but of quality-, herd-, and quantity-minded "types." As early as the 1920s he zeroed in on the impulse to "efficiency" as the real motive force behind rampant industrialism, which led to a biting critique of socialist economic remedies ("Socialization [of production] cannot solve the problem of industrial 'civilization' because it contains no balm for efficiency-scourged [humankind]").

Richard Gregg (1885–   ), *political economist*. Gregg was a fairly conventional labor lawyer and industrial relations expert before going to India and discovering the importance—for us—of Gandhian political theory. For the next fifty years he tried to show us that nonviolent action is potentially the most *effective* form of opposition to injustice as well as the most humane.

But for Gregg, the passionate commitment to nonviolent action was only one part of what he felt we needed to learn from Gandhi. Like Gandhi, he never tired of telling us that voluntary simplicity is important because it allows us to lead richer lives and *not* because it makes us all "equal." He said that money should be, not replaced, but weakened in the New Age, weakened by intergroup service and barter and payment in kind (wealth, he said, isn't really a "fixed quantity to be struggled for" but "a continual flow of energy in various forms"—an argument that has recently been made available to economists in Howard and Elisabeth Odum's *Energy Basis for Man and Nature*). He pointed out the value of human-scale, community-based technology and the advantages of decentralized, community-based democracy. He said that society "needs a profound religion" in order to understand correctly "the true nature of the self" and of nature. And long before Willis Harman and Lawrence LeShan, Philip Slater and Charles Tart, he was saying that "recent" discoveries in physics indicate that the world is trans-material.

Arthur Morgan (1878–1975), *social thinker*. Morgan spent twenty years as president of his own engineering company building dams all over North America and another couple of years as administrative head of the Tennessee Valley Authority. In 1927 he said that he had no respect for those who were so caught up in "transcendental" ways of thinking that they had no stomach or enthusiasm for vast new social planning projects or for the further mastery of human nature through science and technology.

At some point, though, Morgan began to listen to his own intuitive promptings, to his own "human nature"; and when he left the TVA he said, "If personal character is on a low level, then there comes a time when no refinement of social planning and no expenditure of public wealth, however great, will create a good social order. . . . In my opinion [personal character] in America is approaching that point . . . [and] for perhaps the next half century or more the burden of our attentions and of our loyalties, and the full drive of our aspirations, should be given to bringing about a revolution in the personal character of the American people" (*The Long Road*).

Morgan then asked, how are our characters formed in America? And he answered, by the community. And he devoted the rest of his life to working out a strategy for communities, so that they might be able to foster such "primary" and "elemental" values as "good will, neighborliness, fair play, courage, tolerance, open-minded inquiry, patience." He decided first of all that these communities needed to be relatively small, relatively self-sufficient, relatively autonomous (later he added a spiritual, yes, a "transcendent" dimension to his notion of community). And in his book *The Small Community*, and in his organization, Community Service, Inc., he worked out a scenario for a nation of diverse communities and regions cooperating around common general values for common general ends. America *likes* to use different kinds of social organization, he said.

Herbert Agar (1897–   ), *social critic*. Agar was a brilliant student at Princeton, a top-notch editor at the *Louisville Courier-Journal*, and a leading American "distributist" (everyone should have access to a *sufficient* amount of property). He co-edited the magazine *Free America* (with Borsodi) and the book *Who Owns America?* which was our first decentralist anthology with a national focus. It argued against even "rationally administered" socialism, and for a "human-scale" capitalism; and it called for a devolution of federal *and state* power, taking New Age politics beyond Alexander Stephens and states' rights (ultimate power would be held in fact by community districts).

In his own books, Agar pleaded with us to finally stop imitating Europe in our politics; urged us to "build the sort of world where religion might revive"; and asserted that the American people "would still prefer to have their small store or farm or workshop than to have greater [material] wealth, more goods for consumption." He took pains to remind us that "the evil in human nature belongs to all [humankind]" and that "our enemies are always partly good"; and he declared that "if the world is out of joint we must all have played our part in the dislocation" ("Abraham Lincoln took that view of the American civil war; but the members of his cabinet did not . . .").

Agar's unread masterpiece, *Land of the Free*, is a remarkable real-life demonstration of the healing power of the New Age concept of patriotism, as distinct from the Prison-bound concept of nationalism (see Chapter 13). If any book can make you believe in the potential of this country, it is Herbert Agar's *Land of the Free*.

Waldo Frank (1889–1967), *social critic*. Frank was an intellectual who read a thousand books before he even went to college. *And* who was able to see, in 1919, that the richness of the "buried cultures" of the Indian and Spaniard, with their rejection of materialism and their nature- and spiritual-mindedness, provided a dimension (or three) that was missing and badly needed in America. He liked to call himself a "naturalistic mystic," meaning one who is as dedicated to living—passionately—in the material world, as he or she is dedicated to "cosmic understanding."

Frank wanted to revive for us what he called "The Great Tradition," which was our tradition of spiritual and ethical unity as it was contained or reflected in the Judeo-Christian tradition (and in all the other great religions); a tradition that was seriously weakened in the West (he said, before Mumford) not only by the machine but by modern science, and by rationalism itself. Even communism he came to see as one of "The Desperate Remedies" which Europe was trying out in place of "The Great Tradition."

But Frank did not fall into the trap of counseling a full-scale return to "The Great Tradition." Instead, he called for a "new synthesis" based partly on insights from the Indian and Hispanic cultures and partly on renewed respect for the richness of everyday life. He said, "The revolution that I desire must begin with the transformation of [people]"; and he said, "We must begin to generate within ourselves the energy which is love of life."

CHAPTER 26

Clearing the Ground: A New Age Critique of Marxism

In the United States, the old liberal system is on the verge of collapse. Good-bye, says Garry Wills at the end of his bittersweet swan song, *Nixon Agonistes*, to all our old beliefs: that the system rewards us fairly; that there is a "free enterprise" system; that our problems are traceable to "bad men"; and so on. (Maybe these beliefs were never really believable, says sociologist Robert Bellah, but now they're not even useful as myths.) And just as important, the liberals have begun to admit that they're—well, not wrong—but at their wit's end. For example, the respected liberal columnist, Anthony Lewis, recently conceded in the *New York Times* that no social or economic program "known to us now" can solve the problems of crime and violence in New York City.

You would think that the collapse of the liberal mythology would clear the ground for a new awakening: for vigorous new analyses to be made, goals proposed, strategies debated. But, no. With the exception of the work done by the people I've referred to in this book (and their like), there are no new analyses, goals, or strategies afoot in the United States today. Instead, most of those who are searching for so-called radical solutions to our social problems have been charging bravely into the nineteenth century and coming up with one or another variety of Marxism.

This chapter is an attempt to present a New Age critique of Marxism. The first part concentrates on Marxism in practice and is necessarily pretty subjective. There are some Marxists who cannot be criticized on these grounds, but in my opinion that is because they are strong enough to *resist* certain tendencies in the Marxist *weltanschauung*. The second and third parts concentrate on Marxism in theory.

Before I begin, though, I would like to make something clear: there is a big difference between criticizing Marxism and saying that there's nothing of value in Marxism, that we have nothing to learn from Marxism. New Age politics is not afraid to borrow from Marxism. And it is not afraid to borrow from many other political (and social and spiritual) movements and traditions.

Marxism in Practice

In the United States today, I believe that Marxism's appeal is not so much intellectual as it is psychocultural, even (fraudulently) religious.

After all, liberalism *is* collapsing, the times *are* desperate—and Marxism is the only coherent alternative to liberalism, at the present time. (The only *coherent* alternative: that's an important point. A lot of intellectuals seem to need a political philosophy that might or might not speak to their experience of the world, but is *above all* intellectually coherent and "complete.")

And consider this: we have lost our cultural bearings, our morality, our ethics, our values. In this context, it's very difficult to say, all right, we're going to have to create another culture, another value system. Many of us are going to be tempted to "escape from freedom," as Erich Fromm put it (somewhat self-righteously) many years ago, and lay our ethics, our values. In this context, it's ver ydifficult to say, all right,

Let me speak from my own experience. In high school Marxism was forbidden fruit, like sex; and when we learned, usually on our own or at a good university, that Marx had things to say that weren't dreamed of in liberal philosophy—well, was it all that surprising that some of us chose to go all the way with him? Marxism's very lack of respectability among the "bourgeoisie" only serves to *increase* its respectability in "radical" circles.

And there's another thing. Marxism is the only academically "respectable" alternative to liberalism. It is difficult to master, impressive to espouse, and has a 140-year-old intellectual tradition behind it. Radical-liberal professors tend to present it as the only "serious" alternative to liberalism . . . and as the only *possible* alternative to liberalism.

Then there's the "fighting philosophy" aspect of Marxism. In a society that's overwhelmingly smug and self-satisfied, what could be more engaging than a philosophy that promises us combat, struggle, dedication, zeal, self-sacrifice—ultimately, the barricades—and inevitably, sweet, sweet Victory? To a people that feels only half alive, what could be more satisfying than that?

As a philosophy that purports to speak for the poor, Marxism contains a powerful appeal to our underlying sense of guilt—for not being poor, or for not being poor enough. I've observed that we can be "guilted" into just about anything by Marxists, once we've begun to accept their premises.

Finally, Marxism seems to me and to many other observers to be a kind of substitute religion. Consider the use of religious language in Marxism (e.g., Marx and Engels first considered calling the *Communist Manifesto* the *Communist Catechism*). Consider the use of the works of Marx and Engels to settle arguments and justify policies— just like some devout people use the Bible or the Koran. Henry Mayo says that Marxism "may be regarded as a revelation, a gospel of deliverance to the poor"—and that the proletariat may be regarded as "a kind of Chosen people, who alone will possess the New Jerusalem." After the revolution will come the Great Judgment—the dictatorship of the proletariat—to separate the proletarian sheep from the bourgeois goats. Beyond the struggle lies—the millennium. Eden before the Fall bears a striking resemblance to—the stage of primitive communism. In both monolithic religion and Marxism, there is the same belief in inevitability, the same belief in ultimate victory—guaranteed by the "eternal laws" of history and the universe. And there is the same claim to universally valid truths.

In Chapter 7 I spoke of monolithic *institutions*. Perhaps I should have also spoken of monolithic *ideologies*.

Some of the arguments that some Marxists use to justify their claims are highly illegitimate. In criticizing them, I am also asking us to beware of using similar arguments on behalf of New Age ideas and insights.

Often Marxists will imply that only socialism is "political," that is, politically serious, politically worthy of consideration. They'll say that a book or a person is "very political," "quite political," or "political," depending on how close he or she or it comes to their brand of Marxism. If an idea is nonliberal but non-Marxist, it's often called, not "wrong"—that would be to take it too seriously—but "nonpolitical" (or, worse, "poetry"). This virtual identification of "socialist" with "political" has been a powerful factor in discouraging many of us from working out a new political philosophy.

Marxists often imply that socialism is, and has been, the only true carrier of such ideals as fraternity, cooperation, and equality. However, as Soviet dissident Igor Shafarovich points out (in Solzhenitsyn, ed.), fraternity, cooperation, equality, etc., go all the way back to Plato (who was an idealist—the very opposite of a Marxian materialist); were first propagated in schools of philosophy and narrow *mystical* circles; later penetrated to the Gnostic sects; were introduced into various heretical religious movements in the Middle Ages; and began to adopt the trappings of the western European enlightenment only in the eighteenth century. Fraternity, cooperation, equality, etc., are essentially the ideals of dissident *spiritual* groupings.

Marxism stresses the importance of economic as distinct from psychocultural factors; so much so that psychocultural factors are said to be ultimately a reflection of the economic. It isn't surprising then that individual Marxists tend to put the bulk of their time and energies into the "social struggle"—saving the so-called personal stuff until "after the revolution."

In Russia, for example, Wilhelm Reich tells us that after the revolution young Marxists threw themselves so passionately into their organizing activities that they spent virtually no time working out their lives together in their communal quarters, let alone enjoying themselves. People's self-understanding and sense of themselves actually *withered* in the early stages of the revolution, and that, according to Reich, was one reason why it was able to turn so repressive.

Our Marxists haven't learned much. Theodore Roszak recently observed that there's no more shelter for the person in Marxist movements than in the societies they're meant to overthrow; an observation that's only reinforced by the accusations such as "narcissistic" and "self-indulgent" and (lately) "psychobabble" that Marxists like to hurl at all aspects of the consciousness-and-growth movement. Jerry Rubin recalls that the 1960s "vision of the model human being was a totally committed person fighting against oppression, willing to sacrifice his life and freedom for the people." But if the 1960s taught us anything, he says, it's that "people out of touch with their bodies and souls cannot make positive change."

As human beings, Marxists are neither better nor worse than the rest of us (in fact, as we've seen, they are probebly more religiously motivated than most). But I believe that Marxist theory induces and even requires us to act in ways that are arrogant and self-righteous. Let us make sure that New Age politics never proclaims itself to be the one "correct" way to world development; proclaims itself to represent the one true "science" of society; preaches a doctrine of "us-against-them" and "they're doing it to us" as a way of stirring up tensions and hatreds; has as its goal the setting up of a dictatorship; and is willing to use violence to attain that goal (or any goal).

Historically these traits have led to the fact of the Soviet "labor" camps—tens of millions of victims, according to Solzhenitsyn; to the fact that between five and ten million Chinese have been slaughtered *since* the revolution of 1949 (Peter Berger, *Pyramids of Sacrifice*); to the fact that up to 1.4 million Cambodians were executed by the first revolutionary Cambodian government, which felt it had the right to create what it called the "new man," initially by eliminating all those whose class backgrounds might have stood in their way (Jean Lacouture, *New York Review of Books*, March 31 and May 26, 1977).

Closer to home, Marxist arrogance and self-righteousness can be seen—can be previewed—in their pet phrase, "If you're not part of the solution you're part of the problem"; in the emphasis Marxist groups place on doctrinal purity (an emphasis that's led to the flourishing of literally dozens of Marxists sects—and an incredible amount of bitterness among them); and in the brusque and humorless manner with which the Marxist "heavies" deliver their explanations, try to "enlighten" us on all points, drag our their favorite quotations from Father Karl or Father Leon as if to settle the issue. (Platt remembers how one young revolutionary, bothered by all her questions, "stopped and regarded me with an unbelieving and suspicious look, and then said: 'I thought you were *with* us'.")

Perhaps most disturbing of all, Marxist arrogance and self-righteousness can be seen in the bland insistence that the camps, the dictatorships, the unfreedoms, and the killings that have taken place as a result of all the other Marxist revolutions, wouldn't happen *this* time around. There's an almost congenital inability to hold Marxian socialism accountable—even in part—for its failures (as distinct of course from its successes). Marxian socialism is defined as what is ideal, and then when a socialist project or government turns out to be less than ideal the Marxists turn around and say; but that's not socialism! For example, Leszek Kolakowski, the Polish Marxist, once wrote an article whose first part, "What Socialism Is Not," is a virtual history of socialism everywhere. The next and last part is titled "What Socialism Is" and it consists of one sentence: "Socialism is a good thing." Similarly, Samir Amin, a much more tough-minded Marxist, states categorically (in *Accumulation on a World Scale*, 1974) that socialism "cannot exist unless it is superior to capitalism in every way."

Marxism in Theory

The following ideas are, in my opinion, basic to Marxism. If they change, Marxism becomes that much less Marxist.

Capitalism is the enemy. Capitalism, say the Marxists, is the root of our problems, and being radical means: going to the root. Therefore . . .

Throughout this book I argue that capitalism (as we know it today) and also socialism (as we know it today) can more usefully be seen as *symptoms* of our problems: of the Prison and its institutions. I argue that if we are able to break out of the Prison (i.e., begin to change our consciousness) and convert our monolithic institutions to biolithic ones, then capitalism would or at least could be humane. (Same with socialism.)

Economic determinism. The economic structure of society is said to be the "real foundation" of society and is responsible for the political "superstructure" and also for people's consciousness. Some Marxists try to trace everything back to the "powers of production" but more sophisticated Marxists tend to argue that the economic structure is determining only "ultimately" or "on the whole" or "in the final analysis"—whatever that means.

I believe that the whole material-conditions-versus-social-consciousness debate is a chicken-and-egg problem—strictly speaking, there can be no "ultimate" answer. And short of "ultimately," society is determined by everything in it and by everything people think about it. (Twentieth-century physics as well as Eastern philosophy bear me out in this: as Fritjof Capra, the physicist, summarizes them, "everything in the universe is connected to everything else and no part of it is fundamental.")

Still a political activist will want to take a clear-cut stand with regard to "ultimately" because of the political (strategic) importance of the issue. If material conditions are said to be "ultimately" determining, then there is a strong inducement for people to define themselves primarily as *victims*. It was important to get people to think of themselves as victims in the nineteenth century because many if not most of them felt that they were (and/or God was) totally responsible for their lives and that nothing could or should be done to ease their pain. However, today the situation is very different. In the United States today people have given up much too much of their power and responsibility to their monolithic institutions, including the top-down state; nearly everyone feels victimized and nearly everyone wants their institutions to "give" them more. A pair of black Marxists said it: in the United States today, the Marxist assumption that we're *not* ultimately responsible leads to dependency and parasitism, not to social change (see James and Grace Lee Boggs, *Revolution and Evolution in the Twentieth Century*, 1974).

For me (and for New Age politics as I understand it), the lesson is clear. Before society can change at its core, we are going to have to be willing to assume a lot more personal responsibility for our selves, our communities, and the planet as a whole. If consciousness (rather than material conditions) is said to be "ultimately" determining, then there is a strong inducement for people to define themselves primarily as responsible creatures rather than primarily as victims (not *totally* responsible—the emerging new trans-material worldview would see to that; see Chapter 11).

Throughout this book, I have argued that consciousness is "ultimately" determining. That is my perspective. It is not "right" or "wrong"—there is no "ultimate" answer. But it's a valid answer, as valid as the Marxists', and it's a lot more useful to us in the United States today.

Materialist worldview. The metaphysical basis for Marxism *and* liberalism *and* anarchism. . . . It is criticized at length in Chapter 11 along with its symbiotic opposite, the non-material worldview; and a more relevant and sophisticated worldview, the trans-material worldview, is proposed.

Dialectical analysis. According to Marxists, the dialectic is a "true description" of nature, and also of history; and it expresses the "iron laws" of nature and history, as follows: (1) the gradual accumulation of small changes leads, over time, to a sudden qualitative change (revolution!); (2) every thing or event is a unity ("thesis"); then contradictions appear which negate the thesis, and these accumulate to become the "antithesis"; (3) the contradictions continue to accumulate until there's a transition—a sudden leap—to a new equilibrium, a new unity. And then the process begins again.

We can see why the Marxists would want to treat the dialectic as an "iron law": it appears to prove that revolution is inevitable. But apart from the fact that it appears to give a kind of scientific (actually—blush —metaphysical) validity to the Marxists' belief that the end of capitalism is at hand, it is difficult for me to see why anyone should take the dialectic to be more than what it really is: a special case of logic, useful in describing some historical events and processes, less useful in others, and useless or misleading in most.

Then again, it's not so difficult. Remembering my own early infatuation with the dialectic, I can report that it was my need to believe in the ultimate rightness and goodness of what I was doing that caused me to think of the dialectic as an "iron law" rather than as a special case.

In some cases the dialectic can be positively harmful. It should always be used with extreme caution, since it's so clearly an expression of the dualistic consciousness that is fostered by the Prison (if we want to think dialectically we have to forever be dividing things up and polarizing them). Very often, in fact, one or both sides of the dialectic are distorted in order to make them fit the dialectical pattern of thesis/antithesis. For example, at Robert Bly's Third Annual Conference on the Great Mother and the New Father, some participants objected to the thesis/antithesis of anima/animus. Mary Fell said, "I feel . . . as though an image were being projected on women" (see Shepherd Bliss, in *East West*, Feb. 1978). Similarly, some black social scientists say that the thesis/antithesis of bourgeois/proletariat strips the black experience of much of its complexity—much of its meaning (see Ladner, ed.).

Consider too that the dialectic can be used to "prove" almost anything. Lysenko used it to "prove" his now discredited theory of genetics. Engels used it to "disprove" immortality, and I can use it to "prove" immortality: life is the thesis, death the antithesis, and immortality the synthesis. Dennis Forsythe, a black sociologist, tells us (in Ladner, ed.) that Marx welcomed the British conquest of India, feeling that it was Britain's "historic" mission to carry out—in Marx's words—"the annihilation of old Asiatic society and the laying of the material foundations of Western society in Asia." Similarly, Engels regarded the conquest of Algeria by the French as a working out of the dialectic—as (in Engels's words) "an important and fortunate act for the progress of civilization."

My point—to repeat—is not that the dialectic is always wrong, but that it is a special case in logic, applicable to some ideas and events and processes, but more often not. "Neither in ideas nor in nature is it true that opposites always generate a synthesis," says Mayo. "In the realm of ideas, sometimes a number of conflicting theories may be discarded as wholly false." Boulding says that the dialectical pattern "is too simple; history always refuses to fit into intellectual strait jackets. Its cyclical movements are never particularly neat; systems are not usually succeeded by their opposites; change is sometimes regular and slow, sometimes cyclical and violent; chance plays an important part at critical moments; history sometimes does and sometimes does not repeat itself; and so on." Mumford reminds us that "there are many modes of change, other than dialectic opposition: maturation, mimesis, mutual aid are all as effective as the struggle between opposing classes."

New Age people have been making use of a number of alternative ways of thinking about things—alternatives that can be used in place of or along with dialectics:

● Tri-level analysis. See Chapter 5.

● Intuition and imagination. Robert Pirsig's alternative to dialectics, in *Zen and the Art of Motorcycle Maintenance*.

● Meditation. "Meditate deeply," says Swami Kriyananda, "and when you feel very peaceful, very calm, pose alternatives and see which feels harmonious in the heart and which doesn't."

● Integral Thinking. A refusal to make polarizing distinctions—an insistence on remaining open to the opposites without and within. "If either side is preferred at the expense of the other, the result is death," says Andre Carpenter of the Human Dancing Company (in *Communities*, no. 17).

Mad Bear Anderson, a medicine man from the Tuscarora tribe, Iroquois Nation, tells us (see Boyd) that it is "a mistake to think of any group or person as an opponent, because when you do, that's what the group or person will become. It's more useful to think of every other person as another *you*. . . . If you have a sense of opposition— that is, if you have contempt for others—you're in a perfect position to receive their contempt. . . ." There are many opposites within us, says Jungian analyst June Singer, they've been there all along, and they'd "coexist in harmony if only we did not drive a wedge between them" and project one opposite out onto the "other," the "enemy."

● Reconciliation of opposites. E. F. Schumacher points out that a thing can be true and its opposite true at the same time. "A pair of opposites—like freedom and order—are opposites at the level of ordinary life, but they cease to be opposites at the higher level, the really *human* level," where they are, instead, reconciled and transcended.

How are they reconciled and transcended? By mobilizing such "higher faculties and forces" as love and empathy, understanding and compassion. For example, a New Age-oriented school system would probably not stress freedom at the expense of discipline—or vice versa; but it could only reconcile and transcend these opposites if teachers, pupils, and administrators were all operating at the "higher level"—at the level of self-actualization and self-transcendence—at the level of love and empathy, understanding and compassion.

● The cosmic dance. According the Fritjof Capra, twentieth-century physics asserts that the world can no longer be seen as completely causal and determinate (as in nineteenth-century science). Rather, twentieth-century physics shows that the world is engaged in endless activity—is engaged in "a continual cosmic dance of energy"—and that the cosmic dance is almost infinitely varied and complex. There are no "iron laws" that can be attached to it, and if we want to understand it we have to make use of a number of different analytic frameworks.

Economic theory of class. Marxists claim that it is useful for us to think of people in terms of their "relationship to the means of production" and/or in terms of economic "class" generally (bourgeois, proletariat). In Chapter 10 I argue that, in the United States today, economic class analysis tends to be misleading, and I make a case for the usefulness of psychocultural class analysis (life-oriented, thing-oriented, and life-denying classes).

Class struggle. According to this theory, all of history is the history of class struggles. Moreover, class struggle is how the dialectic chooses to work itself out in history; therefore, class struggle is inevitable, and also inevitably "progressive" and good.

But as social philosopher Jacques Ellul points out at some length (in *Autopsy*), most social conflict and most major "turning points" in history can only be inadequately understood in terms of the class struggle theory ("turning points" are emphasized by neo-Marxists).

The Spartacus rebellion, yes; the American revolution, very partially; the conquests of Alexander or the struggle of Papacy versus Empire, no. Mumford points out that the voluntary renunciation of their feudal rights by the French aristocracy did more to transform French society than the most vicious "struggles" of the French revolution—his point being that class understanding and class cooperation have *also* played a constructive role in history and that without them society might be "thrown back into barbarism" (certainly it could never be healed).

It is difficult to explain the events in postwar America according to the doctrine of the economic class struggle. It is fairly clear, at least to me, that the current struggles are over worldviews and values (see Part IV of this book). Ellul makes the case that value conflict has been at least as much of a factor in history as class conflict; he also points out that, "The loss of values suddenly renders intolerable a social or economic situation that was otherwise bearable. The social and economic factors are the pretext and not the basis; they are the cause only in so far as there is no longer any reason to go on living and what made life bearable has disappeared."

As for the notion that the class struggle is inevitable—once the dialectic is assigned a more limited role, the class struggle is no longer theoretically inevitable (since class struggle is how the dialectic is said to work itself out in history). Eugen Loebl, once one of Dubcek's top economists and now a refugee in this country, adds that in practice the notion of class struggle is a *self-fulfilling prophecy*, that with it we create ("we are induced to create") the conflict that we say we see. About the Soviet Union and Czechoslovakia he says, "The believers in this concept, of whom I was one, actually fostered the most militant, ruthless, and inhumane class struggle known in history. We even turned peasants and small shopkeepers into a 'class enemy' by persecuting them and their children." Let his conclusion stand as a warning: "The way we categorize influences the way we act."

False consciousness. People who disagree with Marxists do not just "think differently" and they are not just "wrong." They are said to be suffering from "false consciousness." Their understanding of reality is *deficient* and needs to be remedied—by persuasion if possible, by coercion if necessary (as in Vietnam and China).

I find the notion of false consciousness to be morally offensive and politically extremely dangerous. It implies what sociologist Peter Berger calls "the hierarchical view of consciousness. There is something medieval about this . . .—the mind of God is at one end, that of the dumb animals on the other, and in between are we humans, carefully stratified in terms of proximity to either pole." For a Marxist, only "revolutionary" consciousness can raise the proletariat to the level of humanity. And revolutionary consciousness has to be brought by someone else, someone who is, by definition, more human already.

With the concept of false consciousness, says Berger, "the intellectual identified with the 'vanguard' lays claim to a cognitively privileged status: [He or she] and only [he or she] has reality by the shortest possible hair. This cognitive superiority, which allows [him or her] to designate other people's consciousness as false, is (by that very fact) a human superiority: the cognitively superior individual is, by virtue of [his or her] consciousness, at a higher level of freedom, and thus of humanity."

Clearly, this is the assumption that gives Marxist parties the notion that they have the right to herd literally millions of people, i.e. "the" people, whom they claim to respect so much, into "reeducation" camps for unlimited time periods.

Berger's conclusion: "Put simply, no one is 'more conscious' than anyone else; different people are conscious of different things. . . . No one is in a position to 'raise' anyone else. . . . All of us are moving around on the same level, trying to make sense of the universe and doing our best to cope with the necessities of living."

Most political activists would agree that people should have the right to participate in the decisions that are made about their lives. New Age people go further and say that people should have the right to participate in the *theories* that are made and that define-describe the reality within which the decisions are made. All known political ism's are loathe to relinquish this right. Still, as Berger says, "It is a very limited notion of participation to let an elite define a situation in complete disregard of the ways in which this situation is *already defined* by those who live in it—and then to allow the latter a voice in the decisions made on the basis of the preordained definition. A more meaningful notion of participation will include a voice in the definitions of the situation that underlie this or that decision-making option."

Dictatorship of the proletariat. According to Marx and Engels (and to "humanist" Marxists generally), the dictatorship of the proletariat, the dictatorship of the popular majority over the "bourgeois" minority, would last only a short time—only until the bourgeoisie was stripped of its power and of its ability to make a counterrevolution. And *within* the dictatorship, among the "proletariat," there would be a great deal of genuine democracy.

Marx and Engels prided themselves on their tough-mindedness, but the assumptions they made about the dictatorship of the proletariat can only be regarded as wishful thinking.

• "Any dictatorship must have its hierarchy" (Loebl). Therefore the leadership of the proletariat, that is, the Marxist party, tends to become the source of authoritarian rule.

• Any dictatorship needs to stifle all genuine democracy as a matter of sheer survival.

• Inevitably—since dictatorships are loathe to give up their power —they have tended to claim that the bourgeoisie has managed to maintain *or even increase* its power after the revolution (vide Stalin and Mao). They've also redefined "bourgeois" to mean: anyone who disagrees with the existence of the dictatorship. This does two things: it provides justification for the continuation of the dictatorship, and it provides justification for the strengthening of the dictatorship.

• To a large extent, defining the bourgeoisie as the enemy is a self-fulfilling prophecy.

• It is only a short step from the position that a proletarian dictatorship is necessary "to the argument that a government on behalf of the proletariat, serving their 'real' interests, can hardly be called a dictatorship at all" (Mayo).

Counterproductive as the idea of a "dictatorship of the proletariat" may be, the problem that the Marxists are speaking to is very real. Though they lack the political honesty to put it in these terms, it is: how can we change society deeply if we don't have a 51 percent majority?

In the United States, I believe that any committed person pulls more weight politically than the weight of sheer numbers. If a "critical mass" of 10–20 percent of us were actively engaged in self-and-social healing (on the basis of the New Age ethics and political values), then society would definitely change in a New Age direction (see Chapter 20).

Economic theory of imperialism. Imperialism "refers to any relationship of effective domination or control, political or economic, direct or indirect, of one nation over another" (Benjamin Cohen, political scientist, in *The Question of Imperialism*). According to Marxism, economics is the "taproot" of imperialism, and imperialism is a "final stage" or at least a necessary part of capitalism (not, however, of socialism).

A number of writers have pointed out that there are three likely sources of imperialism: (1) our values, perceived needs, wants and prejudices, selfishness and aggressiveness; (2) political factors ("national security," national prestige, the nation-state system itself); (3) economic factors. New Age politics believes that imperialism owes its existence primarily to (1), and that (2) is generally more causative than (3).

In Part I of this book I argue that imperialism, like racism, environmental degradation, and the like, is primarily rooted in (1) above —in a complex of cultural attitudes that I call the Six-Sided Prison and that can be traced back hundreds or even thousands of years before capitalism.

Many New Age writers have emphasized that the state has been the determining factor, has had the final say, with regard to imperialism (as compared to the corporations). Cohen argues that "traders and investors" have more often been used as the instruments of diplomacy than the reverse. His conclusion: "Imperialistic behavior is a perfectly rational strategy of foreign policy . . . [a] response to the uncertainty surrounding the survival of the nation." In this view, it's the nation-state system itself that's largely at cause—a view shared by Boulding, who sees imperialism as an "essential part of the dynamic of national defense—wherever a 'defense vacuum' exists in the world, some armed power may be expected to occupy it."

Richard Barnet, political economist, argues that the state continues to be primarily responsible for imperialism in the era of the multinational corporation: "The [MNC] has certain crucial advantages. . . . Yet the nation still holds the strongest cards." Seymour Melman, political economist, argues that many of our biggest corporations have become overly dependent on state subsidies, contracts, tax favors, etc., and have thus become more or less docile servants of the state—at home and abroad.

What of the contributing argument, that imperialism is a final stage or, at least, a necessary part of capitalism? Boulding reminds us that "imperialism is a much older institution than capitalism, and states with all kinds of economic systems have been imperialistic, both states with planned economies [ancient Egypt, modern Russia] and states with capitalistic ones." Barnet tells us that "a society dedicated to growth will make the same demands on resources whether it is capitalist or socialist. . . . If the price for ending imperialist policies is to cut wasteful consumption, then the solution must be more radical than socialism as it has been preached." Barrington Moore looks at each of the leading primarily economic explanations for capitalist imperialism (need for raw materials, need for extra profits, need for new outlets for investment) and finds each of them wanting. He notes that, for example, most noncapitalist governments have been more than willing to trade with us; and that there is no evidence to show that individual corporations have had difficulty finding profitable ways to reinvest. He also says that Marxism has never been able to prove that economic institutions are unchangeable under capitalism, a point made also by Barnet, Cohen, and Melman. What each of these writers emphasizes is, in Moore's words, "the absence of a demand for change—not the impossibility of change." Which brings us back to point (1). . . .

Labor theory of value. This theory—the central one in Marxist economics—does not quite go so far as to say that the price or value of goods is determined by the labor that goes into those goods. What it does say is that every good that is produced in society, as well as the output of society as a whole, can be regarded as the outcome of what Boulding calls "a series of acts of labor." Everything else, capital, technical knowledge, etc., can be regarded as "raw material" that depends on labor to give it substance and shape. Therefore—and this is the point of the theory—the "proletariat" is obviously being deprived of a share of its rightful income.

The problem with this theory can be seen if, as Boulding suggests, we stand it on its head. Suppose labor is seen as a raw material like iron or coal that doesn't and can't produce anything of value until it's been organized by a clever entrepreneur. Then we get an "entrepreneurial theory of value" that holds that the organizer of labor is responsible for the production of all the goods of a society (but isn't allowed to enjoy the fruits of his or her entrepreneurship because of all those *unions*).

My point is not that the entrepreneurial theory is the correct one (though logically speaking it's no less correct than the labor theory). My point is that neither labor nor entrepreneurship, acting alone, is sufficient to produce commodities. (Economist Walter Weisskopf has suggested that Marx may have exaggerated the value of labor in general, and of industrial labor in particular, because labor represented and still represents the *male principle* to the Prison-bound consciousness; service and leisure, the female principle.)

Then there is the fact that the kind and the quality of the *institutions* in a society—legal, social, spiritual—definitely affects the course of economic development, and so is part of the productive process too. And then there are the *values and attitudes* that are prominent in society; for as economist Harvey Leibenstein points out, it is not really labor time that's crucial for production, it is the amount of directed effort. And directed effort involves motives and choices on the part of those directing their efforts (and motives and choices are intimately bound up with values and attitudes).

Because of all this, I would like to propose, as the New Age alternative to the labor theory of value, the *synergic theory of value*. It says that the goods that are produced in a society as well as the output of the society as a whole, can be regarded as the outcome of a complex and synergic (see Chapter 15) mixture of such factors as labor time, entrepreneurial skills, organizational efficiencies, institutional elements, and values and attitudes.

Exploitation—or negative symbiosis? Exploitation is a technical term in Marxist economics, but Marxists often use it more generally to mean that people are being taken advantage of, that people are being hurt. As a descriptive term exploitation has some merit, but I balk at the implication that the harm is all being done *to* us by a "them." Therefore, I would like to steal a term from ecology and propose that we are living in a state of *negative symbiosis* with our society.

In a symbiotic relationship, both parties come to need each other. If they come to need each other's strengths, the relationship is often called positively symbiotic. If, however, they come to feed off (and reinforce) each other's weaknesses, the relationship is often called negatively symbiotic.

Parts I–III of this book are about how and why our needs and those of the society have become negatively symbiotic. They argue that we are, by nature, self-defining and self-developing, but that the descent of the Prison within us has made us much more interested in self-aggrandizement than in self-development. And so we have created monolithic institutions that make it almost impossible for us to meet our needs for love and esteem and self-actualization and self-transcendence, but that *do* make it possible for us to meet the needs that are generated by our Prison-bound personalities—for romance, for power, and most of all, for a seemingly endless supply of products and services (literally, ten times as many products and services as we need to meet our physiological and security needs).

Inevitably, as time went on we became more and more dependent on our monolithic institutions, until our Prison-bound personalities and our monolithic institutions began to reinforce and perpetuate each other in a classic case of negative symbiosis.

Where does this leave us? Liberals who think of themselves as part of a "social contract" are able to feel warm and secure . . . and justified in their use and abuse of others. Marxists who think of themselves as "exploited" are able to feel self-righteous and vengeful . . . and have a cover for their envy (of precisely what they claim to want to destroy). But those of us who understand that we're living in a state of negative symbiosis with our society can take no comfort in the fact. We can only take comfort in our efforts to change our monolithic institutions —and to change our selves.

"Alienation"

Many of us are initially drawn to Marxism because of the concept of alienation. In this section I want to show that the concept of alienation goes back long before Marx; that what he meant by aliena- tion is far too narrow to explain our predicament; and that he misled us badly by blaming alienation on capitalism. Then I am going to describe three crucial dimensions of alienation that Marxism under- states or misses: political, self, and spiritual alienation.

To the Romans "alienation" meant separation from the body in the mystery rites (and they heartily disapproved!). To the early Christians it meant the separation of people from God. Grotius introduced the term into political philosophy in the seventeenth century—he took it to mean the transference of authority over one's self to another person or to government. Beginning in the early nineteenth century, Kierkegaard and other philosophers analyzed the various forms of alienation that we suffer from as individuals. Marx *narrowed* the meaning of the term; and he traced its cause to the world of work.

Marx identified four kinds of alienation, as follows: alienation of the worker from the process of his or her work; alienation of the worker from the product of his or her work; alienation of the worker from his or her fellows; and alienation of the worker from him or her self. Also, Marx traced the root of alienation to capitalism—to the fact that the worker does not control his or her workplace and/or own the things that he or she produces.

It is important that in all four instances Marx was speaking of the alienation of the *worker*. As David Herlihy puts it (in Frank Johnson, ed., *Alienation*, 1973). "Marx was not concerned with individual alienation, self-alienation (individuals who believed themselves isolated from their society), but rather with social alienation." Indeed, Marxists tend to regard individual, self-alienation as a sign of "bourgeois indi- vidualism" and/or as a sign of "social decadence."

Marx was right about one thing: boring, meaningless work over which the worker has no control, *does* alienate the worker in the ways he described. But Marx was wrong to limit his use of the concept in the way that he did. By doing so he managed to keep many political activists—not just Marxists—from taking seriously some of the other key aspects of alienation: the political aspects (Grotius), the self aspects (Kierkegaard), and the spiritual aspects (early Christians).

And to the extent that it diverts us from consideration of these other types of alienation Marx's concept itself serves to "alienate" us from a true understanding of our selves and our society.

Marx was also wrong to trace the source of alienation, even worker alienation, to capitalism. Worker alienation does not appear to vary significantly according to whether a company is publicly, privately, or worker-owned, or according to whether a country calls itself socialist or capitalist. Roderic Gorney, the psychiatrist, reports on one extensive study, done in Yugoslavia, that demonstrates conclusively that "membership in workers' councils made no significant difference in the degree of alienation or job satisfaction"—this in a socialist country! To find out what the true reasons are for worker alienation—for alienation as Marx defined it—we need to look, not to orthodox Marxists, but (ironically) to the kinds of people whose work makes up the emerging New Age politics.

Among these people, David Dickson, an appropriate technologist, suggests that worker alienation is primarily a result of the kinds of machines and technologies that are used by a society; and especially whether these are human scale, and easily or fully understood by the workers who use them. Charles Hampden-Turner, political economist and psychologist, suggests that the key question is whether or not the workers' product has a social purpose that the workers can understand and identify with. Frederick Thayer, a political scientist, suggests that worker alienation is a function of hierarchy at the workplace: the more hierarchy, the more alienation . . . period. And Gorney suggests that we'll always be alienated from work "so long as [we are] forced to work by scarcity and the necessity to make a living" (another good reason for granting us access to the guaranteed subsistence income that I advocate in Chapter 24).

In the United States, in the latter part of the twentieth century, the kinds of alienation that Marx consciously downplayed or ignored in his formulations—political, self, and spiritual alienation—run at least as deep as worker alienation . . . and point the way to the kinds of political changes that are needed.

Political alienation. By this I mean two things. First, the fact that we have allowed our selves to become more and more dependent on the top-down state (on exactly the kind of centralized state that was envisaged in Marxist philosophy). Second, the fact that we have abdicated far too much of our personal responsibility to our other monolithic institutions (see Chapter 7).

In order to end our political alienation, as defined above, we need to stop defining our selves primarily as producers and consumers of goods —as "economic people." Because with this self-definition we might very well continue to prefer a comfortable, "plastic" unfreedom to the challenges and responsibilities of true, decentralized democracy. But before we can begin to redefine our selves we need to get in touch with our selves at a very deep place. And that brings us up against the other two alienations that are searing us today.

Self-alienation. On the one hand, we experience a natural desire, a hunger for closeness and affection; on the other hand, we find it almost impossible to achieve this closeness, get this affection (except in tantalizing bits and flashes). Because we have never been taught to cultivate our selves. Because we have been taught that to do so is "self-indulgent navel gazing"—in men, even a little "queer." But as Anaïs Nin puts it, "If we did not spend some time in creating our selves in depth and power, with what were we going to relate to others? . . . How could we love, how could we give, how could we trust, how could we share what we didn't have to give?"

Carl Rogers, a therapist, has focused on our tendency to alienate our selves from our experience of our selves. The fact that our needs for closeness, affection, esteem, etc., are frustrated, makes us feel less than worthy as human beings; and in response (and out of self-protection) we learn to "perceive our experience selectively," that is, to make sure that negative experiences are either "perceived . . . distortedly as if in accord with the conditions of worth" or are "in part or whole, denied to awareness." According to Rogers, this is a *natural* tendency that may begin as early as infancy; and if it is ignored—if it is not consciously dealt with—it will remain "the basic estrangement" in people.

Abraham Maslow, a psychologist, points out that we are cut off from our "primary thought patterns": from our original and creative and playful thoughts. At home and at school especially, we are taught that "revery, poetry, and play" need to be suppressed because "reality" is harsh and demands "a purposeful and pragmatic striving." (In other words: we're systematically cut off from the "mythic state of consciousness.")

Spiritual alienation. Marxist theory may pretty much ignore political and self-alienation (as defined above), but it is positively joyous about the existence of spiritual alienation, about the fact of our estrangement from what we shyly call "life's mysteries." Bourgeois twaddle, the opiate of the people, say the Marxists, all in unison.

Nikolai Berdyaev, the Russian "personalist" philosopher who fled after the revolution, had a different position. The bourgeois, he said, *is the person who's banished all mystery from life.* And Theodore Roszak is even clearer. "The spiritual void in our lives," he says, ". . . is the prime political fact of our time. It is the secret of our discontent."

What is this "spiritual void"? Lawrence Blair puts it well when he says, "We are aware of only a fraction of the spectrum of nature in which we have our being. . . . It is generations now since we were close to the immediate symbolism of poetry, the cyclical pulse of birth and death. . . . We cannot see the seasonal movement of the lichen across the continent, as did the Red Indians. . . . We of the cities scarcely gaze up at the night sky any more, and when we do, what we see is flat, pinpricked like a board—not coiling with suns through deep dimensions of time. . . ."

The spiritual void cannot be filled unless and until we learn to get in touch with the non-material states of consciousness (see Chapter 11). Until we do the void will continue to be felt—and we will continue to search for a "fix" on the material plane: continue to indulge our selves in overconsumption; continue to live vicariously through the television tube and the lives of our "stars"; continue to engage our selves in mindless mass movements and in dreams of violent revolution, dreams of revenge for what it is we've lost.

Part X
RESOURCES

CHAPTER 27

The New Age Speaks

I. 250 New Age Books

This doesn't pretend to be a list of the 250 "best" or "most important" New Age books (who could choose?), but it is a list of the 250 books and articles that I relied on most while writing *New Age Politics*. More than three-fifths of them have been published since 1974, more than half of them since 1975. More of the entries in this bibliography were published in 1976 *alone* than in all the years before 1971. Interestingly, the years 1967–71 range from 2–10 entries each; the years 1972–78, from 21–42 entries each.

Nancy Adair and Casey Adair, *Word Is Out: Stories of Some of Our Lives* (New Glide/Delta, 1978). Demonstrates that compulsive heterosexuality is a monolithic institution—and that conscious homosexuality is a viable biolithic option.

Maya Angelou, *I Know Why the Caged Bird Sings* (Bantam, 1970). A New Age response to oppression.

Roberto Assagioli, *Psychosynthesis: A Manual of Principles and Techniques* (Viking, trans. 1965). Personal growth and spiritual development, and their interconnections. See also *ibid.*, *The Act of Will* (1971).

Elizabeth Bardwell, *More Is Less: The Case Study of a City that May Be Growing Too Big for its Citizens' Good*, 2nd ed. (1974; available for $2.50 from the publisher, The Capital Community Citizens, 114 No. Carroll St., Madison, Wisc.). Argues against big cities on economic, political, and sociocultural grounds.

Richard Barnet, *Roots of War: The Men and Institutions Behind U.S. Foreign Policy* (Penguin, 1972). "The corporations continue to exercise the dominant *influence* . . . but the *power* keeps passing to the state."

Richard Barnet and Ronald Muller, *Global Reach: The Power of the Multinational Corporations* (Simon and Schuster, 1974). Critique of the MNC's from an "antigrowth, anticonsumption, antihierarchy" perspective.

Ellen Bass, *Of Separateness and Merging* (Autumn Press, 1977). Poems that convey—with real authority—what it's like to live and feel, work and love in the "New Age" way.

Gregory Bateson, *Steps to an Ecology of Mind* (Ballantine, 1972).

"The unit of survival is organism plus environment . . . is a flexible organism-in-its-environment." See esp. Parts V and VI.

Robert Bellah, *The Broken Covenant: American Civil Religion in Time of Trial* (Seabury, 1975). Sociologist calls for a "reawakening" of the religious state of consciousness.

Daryl Bem, *Beliefs, Attitudes, and Human Affairs* (Brooks/Cole, 1970). Tri-level analysis of consciousness. Also, advertising is less persuasive than we think.

Tom Bender, *Environmental Design Primer: A Book of Meditations on Ecological Consciousness* (Schocken, 1973). In my opinion, this is still the most inspired—and inspiring—book that the *Rain* magazine people have put out.

————, *Sharing Smaller Pies*, paper (1975; available for $2 from the publisher, *Rain* magazine, III below). New Age values; appropriate technology; what is to be done.

James Benson, *Energy and Reality: Three Perceptions*, pamphlet (1977; available for $1.25 from the publisher, Institute for Ecological Policies). Distinguishes among the liberal, socialist, and New Age perceptions of the energy problem.

Nikolai Berdyaev, *Slavery and Freedom* (Scribner's, 1944). Argues against Marxism and liberalism from an explicitly trans-material perspective.

Peter Berg, ed., *Reinhabiting a Separate Country: A Bioregional Anthology of Northern California* (1978; available for $6 from the publisher, Planet/Drum Foundation, IV below). Persuasive arguments for "regional reinhabitation"/self-sufficiency/autonomy (or semi-autonomy)—specifically with regard to the "state of Shasta," but the argument applies to all our bioregions. See also Michael Zwerin, *A Case for the Balkanization of Practically Everyone* (1976)—a sympathetic account of some of the movements for regional autonomy in western Europe today.

Peter Berger, Brigitte Berger, and Hansfried Kellner, *The Homeless Mind: Modernization and Consciousness* (Vintage, 1973). The materialist worldview is the "modernizing ideology" that the Marxists and liberals share.

Peter Berger, *Pyramids of Sacrifice: Political Ethics and Social Change* (Anchor, 1975). Questions Marxist and liberal "development" strategies; questions concept of false consciousness.

Wendell Berry, *A Continuous Harmony: Essays Cultural and Agricultural* (Harvest, 1972). Good introduction to the range of Berry's passions and concerns (from poetry to community to the need for a reawakening of personal responsibility).

————, *The Unsettling of America: Culture and Agriculture* (Avon, 1977). "Modern" agriculture as a monolithic institution. Berry's alternative: what I call the "homestead economy."

Clement Bezold, ed., *Anticipatory Democracy: People in the Politics of the Future* (Vintage, 1978). Useful introduction to "anticipatory democracy," part of the New Age alternative to top-down government planning. See esp. the essay by James Dator, which identifies A/D as part of the "third force" in American politics.

Black Elk (as told through John Neihardt), *Black Elk Speaks: Being the Life Story of a Holy Man of the Oglala Sioux* (Pocket, 1972). Trans-material worldview in action.

Lawrence Blair, *Rhythms of Vision: The Changing Patterns of Belief* (Warner, 1976). Spiritual and mythic states of consciousness—an anatomy.

James and Grace Lee Boggs and Freddy and Lyman Paine, *Conversations in Maine: Exploring Our Nation's Future* (1978; available for $4.80 plus postage from the publisher, South End Press, P.O. Box 68, Astor Station, Boston, Mass. 02123). Arrives at many New Age or quasi-New Age ideas by questioning and extending, and in part transcending, the authors' Marxist belief system. A very stimulating book. See also: "Beyond Usual Politics" (10¢); "But What About the Workers?" (75¢); "Change Yourself to Change the World" (50¢)—all from the Boggs's new political grouping, The Organization for the American Revolution, IV below.

Joan Bondurant, *Conquest of Violence: The Gandhian Philosophy of Conflict*, rev. ed. (Univ. of California Press, 1965). Good, "tough-minded" introduction that spells out some of the implications for our time and place.

Kenneth Boulding, *The Organizational Revolution: A Study in the Ethics of Economic Organization*, 2nd ed. (Quadrangle, 1968). Searching critique of bureaucracy and the bureaucratic mentality.

Doug Boyd, *Rolling Thunder* (Delta, 1974). About an American Indian medicine man; about a practical, down-to-earth spirituality.

Fernand Braudel, *The Mediterranean and the Mediterranean World in the Age of Philip II*, 2 vols., rev. ed. (Harper & Row, trans. 1974). Outstanding example of tri-level analysis. See also J. H. Hexter, "Fernand Braudel and the *Monde Braudellien* . . . ," *Journal of Modern History*, vol. 44 (Dec. 1972), pp. 447–539.

Lester Brown, *The Twenty-Ninth Day: Accommodating Human Needs and Numbers to the Earth's Resources* (Norton, 1978). Argues that our demands on the Earth's resources may *already* exceed the Earth's "long-term carrying capacity." Calls for "a new social ethic of accommodation."

Scott Burns, *Home, Inc.*, paperback as *The Household Economy: Its Shape, Origins, and Future* (Beacon, 1975). Best introduction to the "household economy"—and how and why it's overtaking the market economy.

Helen Caldicott with Nancy Herrington, *Nuclear Madness* (Autumn, 1978). Devastating and accessible critique of nuclear power—nuclear technology—nuclear proliferation. See also Sandi MacDonald, "Helen Caldicott, Earth Healer," *New Age* (Nov. 1978).

Ernest Callenbach, *Ecotopia* (Bantam, 1975). Novel about Washington, Oregon, and Northern California after they've separated from the U.S. and evolved a society based on appropriate technology and ecological consciousness.

————, *Living Poor with Style* (Bantam, 1972). All you ever wanted to know about simple living. Goes too far for some folks.

Fritjof Capra, *The Tao of Physics: An Exploration of the Parallels Between Modern Physics and Eastern Mysticism* (Bantam, 1977). Shows that the material state of consciousness needs to be redefined, expanded.

Carlos Castaneda, *Journey to Ixtlan: The Lessons of Don Juan* (Pocket, 1972). Vivid description of the non-material states of consciousness and of a positive "master"-student relationship.

Center for Science in the Public Interest, *99 Ways to a Simple Lifestyle* (Anchor, 1976). Very basic book on simple living. Meant to appeal to the thing-oriented.

Benjamin Cohen, *The Question of Imperialism: The Political Economy of Dominance and Dependence* (Basic, 1973). Argues—convincingly—that the state's role is dominant and the corporations' role secondary. Suggests that people's values is the really determining factor.

Edward Cornish et al., *The Study of the Future: An Introduction to the Art and Science of Understanding and Shaping Tomorrow's World* (1977; available for $9.50 from the publisher, World Future Society, IV below). Useful introduction to the field of "futurology." (Many futurologists are New Age-oriented.)

Ted Cox, *Through the Black Hole: A Prophetic Chronicle of Mankind's Emerging New Age* (Albuquerque N.M.: Sun Books, 1978; available for $5.50 from the author, P.O. Box 4151, Palm Springs, Calif. 92262). An unpretentious and utterly disarming short novel about New Age society in the year 1999—same year as Callenbach's *Ecotopia* which it complements and extends in many ways. Written from the point of view of a man in his seventies.

James and Marguerite Craig, *Synergic Power: Beyond Domination and Permissiveness* (ProActive Press, 1974; available for $3.95 from Synergy Power Institute, IV below). New Age approach to power.

Harold Cruse, *The Crisis of the Negro Intellectual* (Morrow, 1967). Advocates an alternative to Marxism based on ethnic-group consciousness and psychocultural analysis.

Herman Daly, ed., *Toward a Steady-State Economy* (W. H. Freeman, 1972). New Age economics. See esp. Daly (all), Johnson ("The Guaranteed Income as an Environmental Measure"), and Weisskopf ("Economic Growth Versus Existential Balance").

Mary Daly, *Beyond God the Father: Toward a Philosophy of Women's Liberation* (Beacon, 1973). One woman's approach to feminist spirituality. Very good on its social and political implications.

Elizabeth Gould Davis, *The First Sex* (Penguin, 1971). History of women's experience from the matriarchies to the present.

Sebastian de Grazia, *Of Time, Work, and Leisure* (Anchor, 1962). Makes the case for a "leisure economy."

Vine Deloria, Jr., *God Is Red* (Delta, 1973). We have more to learn from North American Indian spirituality than we do from Christianity.

Lane de Moll and Gigi Coe, eds., *Stepping Stones: Appropriate Technology and Beyond* (Schocken, 1978). If *New Age Politics* came with three books of readings, this would be one of them (for the others, see Friends of the Earth and Lindisfarne below). See also its "companion volume," editors of *Rain, Rainbook* (1977), which lists and describes literally thousands of New Age and New Left publications and organizations.

David Dickson, *The Politics of Alternative Technology* (Universe, 1974). Good introduction to biolithic technology and its implications —plus a good critique of monolithic technology.

Calvert Dodge, ed., *A Nation Without Prisons: Alternatives to Incarceration* (Lexington, Mass.: Lexington Books, D.C. Heath, 1975). See esp. Chapters 2 ("Toward a New Criminology") and 5 ("Community Alternatives to Incarceration").

James Douglass, *Resistance and Contemplation: The Way of Liberation; The Yin and Yang of the Non-Violent Life* (Doubleday, 1972). Spiritual growth and nonviolent activism, and their interconnections.

Constantinos Doxiadis, *Anthropopolis: City for Human Development* (Norton, 1974). Devastating critique of the modern city. Presents an alternative whose purpose would be to foster personal growth.

Rene Dubos, *A God Within* (Scribner's 1972). A very wise book on subjects like "perceptual and conceptual" environments and "conservation" vs. "stewardship."

Andrea Dworkin, *Woman Hating* (Dutton, 1974). Radical feminism, pagan spirituality, androgyny. Dworkin represents the anarchist wing of the New Age movement.

Richard Easterlin, "Does Money Buy Happiness?" *The Public Interest*, no. 30 (Winter 1973). Beyond the hard-core poverty level, the answer is no.

Editors of *The Ecologist, Blueprint for Survival* (Signet, 1972). One of the first book-length arguments for a politics based primarily on the insights of the science of ecology. Cf. "The Future of America," special issue of *The Ecologist*, now *The New Ecologist* (Aug./Sept. 1977).

Anne Ehrlich and Paul Ehrlich, *Population, Resources, Environment: Issues in Human Ecology*, 2nd ed. (W. H. Freeman, 1972). Good basic introduction.

Duane Elgin and Robert Bushnell, "The Limits to Complexity: Are Bureaucracies Becoming Unmanageable?" *The Futurist* (Dec. 1977). New Age-oriented critique of large-scale public bureaucracies.

Duane Elgin and Arnold Mitchell, "Voluntary Simplicity," *Co-Evolution Quarterly*, no. 14 (Summer 1977). Who, what, when, where, why. Stanford Research Institute's most popular report ever. See also Robert Gilman, "Job Sharing Is Good," *ibid.* (Spring 1978).

Jacques Ellul, *Autopsy of Revolution* (Knopf, trans. 1971). "We have no legacy to fall back on; everything must be initiated."

———, *The Political Illusion* (Vintage, trans. 1967). There's more to politics than—conventional politics. Values must be transformed; technique dethroned; the state decentralized.

Joe Falk, *Cooperative Community Development: A Blueprint for Our Future* (1975; available for $2.95 from the publisher, The Future Associates, P.O. Box 912, Shawnee Mission, Kans. 66201). An approach to community organizing that stresses healing rather than polarizing one's constituency.

Richard Falk, *A Study of Future Worlds* (Free Press, 1975). Argues for a planetary guidance system based on four of the six New Age political values.

Marc Fasteau, *The Male Machine* (Delta, 1974). A good basic introduction to men's liberation and its implications. See also Warren Farrell, *The Liberated Man* (1974).

Hassan Fathy, *Architecture for the Poor* (Univ. of Chicago Press, 1973). Critique of monolithic housing policy. Presents a biolithic alternative that was actually tried (in Egypt). See also "Eco-Architecture" issue, *New Age* (April 1978).

Shulamith Firestone, *The Dialectic of Sex: The Case for Feminist Revolution* (Bantam, 1970). Patriarchal attitudes came before capitalism, racism.

Jerry Fletcher, "Human Potential Education and Public Schooling," paper (1978; available from the author at: Education Division, Department of Health, Education and Welfare, 200 Independence Ave., Ste. 317H, Washington, D.C. 20201).

———, "The Outer Limits of Human Educability: A Proposed Research Program," paper (1978; available from *ibid.*).

———, "The Outer Limits of Human Educability: A Rationale," *OD Practitioner*, vol. 10 (Spring 1978). Very good on how to get the human potential message across to the majority . . . especially when they're young.

Edgar Friedenberg, *The Disposal of Liberty and Other Industrial Wastes* (Anchor, 1975). Critique of monolithic institutions. Cultural conflict now underlies class conflict.

John Friedmann, *Retracking America: A Theory of Transactive Planning* (Anchor, 1973). Task-oriented working groups; working group assemblies; networks of assemblies.

Friends of the Earth (Hugh Nash, ed.), *Progress As If Survival Mattered: A Handbook for a Conserver Society* (San Francisco: Friends of the Earth, 1977).

Erich Fromm, *The Anatomy of Human Destructiveness* (Fawcett, 1973). Provides the intellectual-theoretical basis for my life-oriented, thing-oriented, and life-rejecting psychocultural classes.

———, *To Have or To Be?* (Harper & Row, 1976). Along with life-death, the basic distinction between Prison and New Age society. Makes use of many untranslated German New Agers' writings.

Buckminster Fuller, *Utopia or Oblivion: The Prospects for Human-*

ity (Bantam, 1969). Good general introduction to his thought. See also Alden Hatch, *Buckminster Fuller* (1974).

Stephen Gaskin, *Volume One: Sunday Morning Services on the Farm* (1977; available for $3.95 from the publisher, The Book Publishing Co., Summertown, Tenn. 38483). Lectures by the founder and spiritual teacher of The Farm (IV below).

William Gevarter, "The Human Brain and Its Programming," in *Loving*, no. 1 (1976; available for $1 from the publisher, Cornucopia Institute, St. Mary, Ky. 40063). The "triune" brain—and how it can be reprogrammed by the consciousness-and-growth movement.

Robert Ghelardi, *Economics, Society, and Culture: God, Money and the New Capitalism* (Delta, 1976). Essays—literally, steps—toward a new analysis that would link the far left and far right. A pathbreaking book . . . and an intellectual roller coaster. Cf. Garry Wills, "The Future of Liberalism," Part V of *Nixon Agonistes* (1970).

Allen Ginsberg, *The Fall of America; poems of these states, 1966–1971* (City Lights, 1972). Successful integration of the political, spiritual, Hebraic, and poetic consciousnesses (i.e., of all four states of consciousness).

Erving Goffman, *The Presentation of Self in Everyday Life* (Anchor, 1959). The social role as a monolithic institution.

Roderic Gorney, *The Human Agenda* (Bantam, 1972). Thorough reexamination of evolution, love, work, play, values, racism, by a New Age-oriented psychiatrist.

Susanne Gowan, George Lakey, William Moyer, and Richard Taylor, *Moving Toward a New Society* (1976; available for $5 from the publisher, Movement for a New Society, IV below). Analysis, goals, and strategy of Movement for a New Society.

Richard Gregg, *The Power of Nonviolence*, rev. ed. (Schocken, 1959). The New Age approach to nonviolent action. If you have time, the longer original edition is well worth while (II below).

Charles Hampden-Turner, *From Poverty to Dignity: A Strategy for Poor Americans* (Anchor, 1974). Chapters 4–8 are very good on the promise of Community Development Corporations.

———, *Sane Asylum* (San Francisco Book Co., 1976). John Maher and the Delancey Street Foundation (IV below).

Willis Harman, *An Incomplete Guide to the Future* (San Francisco Book Co., 1976). Probably the best single "scholarly" introduction to New Age politics.

———, "Knowledge and the World of the Future," lecture (1978; available for $1 from Institute for Noetic Sciences, IV below).

———, "The Societal Implications of Consciousness and Psychic Research," lecture (1975; available for $1 from *ibid.*).

———, "Dr. Willis Harman: A *New Realities* Interview," by James Bolen, *New Realities* (June 1978).

Paul Hawken, *The Magic of Findhorn* (Bantam, 1975). An inspiring account of the Findhorn community (IV below). See also Shoshana Tembeck, ed., *The Findhorn Garden* (1975).

Carlton Hayes, *Nationalism: A Religion* (Macmillan, 1960). Thorough critique of nationalism and the nation-state. Cf. Herbert Agar, *Nationality versus Nationalism*, pamphlet (1954).

Hazel Henderson, *Creating Alternative Futures: The End of Economics* (Berkley, 1978). A stimulating grab-bag of New Age and New Left ideas and energies.

Karl Hess, *Dear America* (Morrow, 1975). Goldwater's former speechwriter describes his journey from "right-wing populism . . . to militant left-wing advocacy" to a kind of left-libertarianism that overlaps significantly with New Age politics.

Fred Hirsch, *Social Limits to Growth* (Harvard Univ. Press, 1976). Material goods vs. "positional goods" (see Chapter 19, sect. V).

Shere Hite, "Toward a New Female Sexuality," in *ibid., The Hite Report: A Nationwide Study of Female Sexuality* (Dell, 1976). New Age sexuality. Alternatives to the "stroke economy."

Lex Hixon, *Coming Home: The Experience of Enlightenment in Sacred Traditions* (Anchor, 1978). "From Enlightenment radiate the insight, compassion, and power needed to resolve individual and collective human problems."

John Holt, *Escape from Childhood: The Needs and Rights of Children* (Ballantine, 1974). Young people should be able to make use of the rights and responsibilities of adult citizens . . . if they want to.

————, *Instead of Education: Ways to Help People Do Things Better* (Delta, 1976). Excellent critique of monolithic education— many biolithic alternatives suggested. Cf. "A Lifetime of Learning" issue, *New Age* (Feb. 1978).

Marjorie Hope and James Young, "The Third Way: Thich Nhat Hanh and Cao Ngoc Phuong," Chapter 6 of *ibid., The Struggle for Humanity: Agents of Nonviolent Change in a Violent World* (Maryknoll, N.Y.: Orbis, 1977). The "third force" in Vietnam was easily the largest, but was opposed equally by Father Ho and by the Americans.

Jean Houston, "Reseeding America: The American Psyche as a Garden of Delights," *Journal of Humanistic Psychology*, vol. 18 (Winter 1978). Argues for a new politics based on: "Global interdependence," a greatly expanded sense of human potential, a "new blending" of the male and female principles, and "a vivid sense of Godfulness as a creative loving force working through evolution."

William Howton, *Functionaries* (Quadrangle, 1969). New Age-oriented critique of bureaucracies and the bureaucratic mentality.

The Hunger Project, "An Idea Whose Time Has Come: The End of Starvation Within 20 Years," booklet (1978; available for $1.50 from the publisher, The Hunger Project, IV below). A consciousness-and-growth approach.

Ivan Illich, *Tools for Conviviality* (Perennial, 1973). General critique of monolithic institutions ("radical monopolies"); biolithic institutions envisioned; evolutionary political strategy proposed.

————, *Toward a History of Needs* (Pantheon, 1978). Four essays on monolithic institutions, including one on the "job economy," and a critique of monolithic development strategies. Includes his best piece of writing, "Energy and Equity" (on monolithic/biolithic transport). See also *Deschooling Society* (1973), which is actually superseded by an essay in this volume; and see *Medical Nemesis* (1976).

Arthur Janov, *The Primal Scream; Primal Therapy: The Cure for Neurosis* (Delta, 1970). Good introduction to the subject—and to the origins of the stroke economy.

George Katona, *Psychological Economics* (Elsevier, 1975). Interesting attempt to combine the disciplines of psychology and economics.

Stanley Keleman, *Your Body Speaks Its Mind: The Bio-Energetic Way to Greater Emotional and Sexual Satisfaction* (Pocket, 1975). "You are your body." Personal, social, and spiritual implications.

Ken Keyes, Jr., *Handbook to Higher Consciousness: The Science of Happiness*, 5th ed. (1976; available for $2.95 from the publisher, Cornucopia Institute, St. Mary, Ky. 40063). The "Living Love Way" to happiness and higher consciousness. A contemporary, practical condensation of thousands of years of spiritual wisdom.

Donald Keys, *The United Nations and Planetary Consciousness* (1977; available for $2 from the publisher, Planetary Citizens, IV below). Planetary consciousness and the real world.

Anne Koedt, Ellen Levine, and Anita Rapone, eds., *Radical Feminism* (Quadrangle, 1973). Basic, "radical" feminism (as distinct from Marxist feminism). Includes Joreen, "Tyranny of Structurelessness"; Koedt, "Politics of the Ego"; Bonnie Kreps, "Radical Feminism 1."

Herbert Kohl, *Half the House* (Bantam, 1974). On personal survival, personal growth, and working for social change in small groups.

Lawrence Kohlberg, "Development of Moral Character and Moral Ideology," in Martin Hoffman and Lois Hoffman, eds., *Review of Child Development Research*, vol. I (Russell Sage, 1964). The stages of moral development. Cf. Thomas Roberts, "Developing Thoughts on Developmental Psychology and Moral Development," in *ibid.*, ed., *Four Psychologies Applied to Education* (1975).

Leopold Kohr, *Development without Aid: The Translucent Society* (Llandybie, Wales: Christopher Davies, 1973). Takes the argument for "self-sufficient localism" to an unnecessary, and not altogether unconvincing extreme.

————, *The Overdeveloped Nations: The Diseconomies of Scale* (Schocken, 1977; orig. continental Europe in the 1950s). Many of our problems "can be attributed to a single cause: the excessive size of nations." See also *The Breakdown of Nations* (1957). Kohr was the spiritual/intellectual godfather of Schumacher and Illich.

Joel Kovel, *White Racism: A Psychohistory* (Vintage, 1970). Racism is ultimately traceable to psychocultural factors (the Prison).

Joel Kramer, *The Passionate Mind: A Manual for Living Creatively with One's Self* (1974; available for $3.95 from the publisher, Celestial

Arts, 231 Adrian Rd., Milbrae, Calif. 94030). Critique of the mono-lithic mind; instruction in how to develop the biolithic mind. See also Joseph Goldstein, *The Experience of Insight* (1976).

Bonnie Kreps, "Compulsive Heterosexuals," *Homemaker's* (March 1978).

————, "Mother-Daughter," *Miss Chatelaine* (May 1977).

————, "Roll Over, Play Dead: Just How 'Dead' Is the Women's Movement?" *Homemaker's* (Sept. 1977).

J. Krishnamurti, *The First and Last Freedom* (Harper & Row, 1954). Good introduction to the range and radical nature of his thought.

Swami Kriyananda, *Crises in Modern Thought, Vol. I: The Crisis of Reason* (1972; available for $5 from the publisher, Ananda Publica-tions, 900 Alleghany Star Route, Nevada City, Calif. 95959). Includes a critique of monolithic institutions, a reinterpretation of evolution, and a discussion of New Age values.

Elisabeth Kubler-Ross, "Death Does Not Exist," *CoEvolution Quar-terly*, no. 14 (Summer 1977).

————, "Out of the Body: A New Age Interview with Elisabeth Kubler-Ross," by Peggy Taylor and Rick Ingrasci, *New Age* (Nov. 1977).

————, Elizabeth Kemf, "E. Kubler-Ross: 'There Is No Death'," *East West* (March 1978). A trans-material approach to death, and to all the "little deaths" of life's transitions.

Joyce Ladner, ed., *The Death of White Sociology* (Vintage, 1973). Black sociologists indict liberal and—often enough—Marxist social science. See esp. essays by Forsythe and Scott.

Ervin Laszlo, *A Strategy for the Future: The Systems Approach to World Order* (Braziller, 1974). Advocates a planetary guidance system (based largely on synergic power) rather than a nation-state writ large.

Ervin Laszlo et al., *Goals for Mankind: A Report to the Club of Rome on the New Horizons of Global Community*, rev. ed. (Signet, 1978). Summarizes the ostensible goals of the various nations, pro-poses a series of "global goals" that are consistent with the New Age ethics and political values, and looks for support for those goals in the ideas and ideals of: the great religions, liberalism and Marxism, and the emerging New Age movement.

Harvey Leibenstein, *Beyond Economic Man: A New Foundation for Microeconomics* (Harvard Univ. Press, 1976). Begins with "de-cision-making individuals" (their motives) rather than with the firm.

E. E. LeMasters, *Blue-Collar Aristocrats: Life-Styles at a Working-Class Tavern* (Univ. of Wisconsin Press, 1975). Deceptively simple study of blue-collar trade unionists by a sociologist who has no ideo-logical ax to grind.

George Leonard, *The Transformation: A Guide to the Inevitable Changes in Humankind* (Delta, 1972). Well-written overview of New Age insights and understandings from a human potential perspective.

————, *The Ultimate Athlete: Re-visioning Sports, Physical Educa-*

tion, and the Body (Avon, 1975). Sports as a path to personal enlightenment and transformation.

Lawrence LeShan, *Alternate Realities: The Search for the Full Human Being* (Ballantine, 1976). Four "alternate realities" that are, essentially, my four "states of consciousness."

Doris Lessing, *The Golden Notebook* (Ballantine, 1962). Novel; shows that a life based on love, friendship, creative activity, and political awareness can be rich and rewarding.

Julius Lester, *All Is Well* (Morrow, 1976). Autobiography; covers the black movement in the 1960s and Lester's own growth through Marxism to a spiritually aware, "third-level" politics.

Simon Leys, *Chinese Shadows* (Penguin, trans. 1977, orig. 1974). What the Marxists won't tell us about China.

Robert Jay Lifton, *Home From the War; Vietnam Veterans: Neither Victims nor Executioners* (Simon and Schuster, 1973). Presents the New Age alternative to "thought reform" (brainwashing): confrontation of self; reordering of personal and social priorities; renewal of self and society.

John Lilly, *The Center of the Cyclone: An Autobiography of Inner Space* (Bantam, 1971). "This is the story of my personal search of some fifty-six years for meaning in life as we know it." Includes a conceptualization of the system taught by Oscar Ichazo of the Arica Institute (IV below).

Lindisfarne Association (Michael Katz et al., eds.), *Earth's Answer: Explorations of Planetary Culture at the Lindisfarne Conferences* (Lindisfarne/Harper & Row, 1977).

Jack Litewka, "The Socialized Penis," (*Liberation*, March 1974).

George Lodge, *The New American Ideology* (Knopf, 1975). Capitalism is not the enemy; therefore, American values need to be reinterpreted from a New Age perspective—not changed. Includes an important New Age critique of Galbraith.

Eugen Loebl, *Humanomics: How We Can Make the Economy Serve Us—Not Destroy Us* (Random House, 1976). Ideas for a non-liberal, non-Marxist economics. By one of Dubcek's top economists (once). . . .

Amory Lovins, *Soft Energy Paths: Toward a Durable Peace* (Friends of the Earth/Ballinger, 1977). Chapter 2 is an excellent nontechnical introduction to the "soft" energy path—and an excellent brief critique of the "hard." Chapter 11 urges us to get "out of the nuclear business" altogether.

Ferdinand Lundberg, *The Rich and the Super-Rich: A Study in the Power of Money Today* (Bantam, 1968). The kind of behavior that makes people rich in the United States today, including the fact that most of us envy and even imitate this behavior, in our smaller ways.

Eleanor Maccoby and Carol Jacklin, *The Psychology of Sex Differences* (Stanford Univ. Press, 1975). Survey of studies of sex differences. Finds that women are not "naturally" passive, irrational, etc.

Michael Maccoby, "Emotional Attitudes and Political Choices,"

Politics and Society, vol. 2 (Winter 1972). "Quantitative" approach to Fromm's life- and death-orientations. Questionnaire, data, interpretation.

Joan McIntyre, ed. (for Project Jonah), *Mind in the Waters: A Book to Celebrate the Consciousness of Whales and Dolphins* (Scribner's/Sierra Club, 1974). A moving introduction to the subject.

Mark Markley, "Human Consciousness in Transformation," Chapter 11 of Erich Jantsch and Conrad Waddington, eds., *Evolution and Consciousness: Human Systems in Transition* (Addison-Wesley, 1976). "History as a series of episodic paradigms, eras, or epochs . . . rather than as a continuing series of incremental adjustments and adaptations to emerging conditions." See also James Baines, "The Peace Paradigm," *New Age* (Oct. 1978).

Abraham Maslow, *The Farther Reaches of Human Nature* (Viking, 1971). Posthumous essays. Pioneering concern with self-transcendence, spiritual development. See also *ibid.*, "Politics 3," *Journal of Humanistic Psychology*, vol. 17 (Fall 1977).

———, *Motivation and Personality*, 2nd ed. (Harper & Row, 1970). Systematic presentation of his stages of self-development.

Rollo May, *Man's Search for Himself* (Delta, 1953). Remarkable early anticipation of New Age psychology (need for a sense of self, of wholeness, before one can act "authentically"; need for a series of ethics and values that come out of the experience of one's own authentic self).

Henry Mayo, *Introduction to Marxist Theory* (Oxford Univ. Press, 1960). Devastating critique of Marxism from a liberal perspective that doesn't often get in the way.

John Mbiti, *An Introduction to African Religion* (London: Heinemann, 1975). The trans-material worldview on the African continent.

Margaret Mead, *World Enough: Rethinking the Future* (Little, Brown, 1975). Seminal New Age insights, viz.: sense of social justice isn't enough; it's counterproductive to identify indiscriminately with the oppressed; we tend to see life as literally man-made. . . .

Seymour Melman, *The Permanent War Economy: American Capitalism in Decline* (Touchstone, 1974). "The new state-controlled economy, whose unique features include maximization of costs and [maximization] of government subsidies."

Saul Mendlovitz, ed., *On the Creation of a Just World Order: Preferred Worlds for the 1990s* (Free Press, 1975). Visions ("relevant utopias") and strategies by scholars from five continents. See esp. essays by Mazrui (on the emerging planetary culture); Lagos (on the "revolution of being"); Galtung (who envisions "nonterritorial organizations crosscutting self-sufficient territorial units"); and Kothari (who speaks of the need for "autonomous choices and diverse perspectives").

Richard Merrill and Thomas Gage, eds., *Energy Primer: Solar, Water, Wind, and Biofuels*, rev. ed. (Delta, 1978). Every person's guide to alternative energy. See also Wilson Clark, *Energy for Survival* (1975).

Mihajlo Mesarovic and Eduard Pestel, *Mankind at the Turning*

Point: The Second Report to the Club of Rome (Signet, 1974). More sophisticated computer projections than the earlier "Limits to Growth" study—same general conclusions.

Donald Michael, *On Learning to Plan—and Planning to Learn: The Social Psychology of Changing Toward Future-Responsive Societal Learning* (Jossey-Bass, 1973). Argues that social planning can be "a means for societal learning rather than . . . a means for social engineering."

Stanley Milgram, *Obedience to Authority: An Experimental View* (Harper & Row, 1974). Description and interpretation of the famous Yale experiments. His main conclusions: we need to assume more personal responsibility and we need more nonauthoritarian social settings.

Jean Miller, *Toward a New Psychology of Women* (Beacon, 1976). Surveys women's psychological strengths; treats self-development, "affiliation," and personal power as "mutually reinforcing attributes"; redefines power.

Kate Millett, *Sexual Politics* (Avon, 1970). Chapter 2 is still an outstanding treatment of patriarchal structures and attitudes. See *Flying* (1974), autobiographical, for her alternatives to patriarchal attitudes.

Marcia Millman and Rosabeth Kanter, eds., *Another Voice: Feminist Perspectives on Social Life and Social Science* (Anchor, 1975). Many alternatives to orthodox liberal and Marxist approaches. See esp. essays by Hochschild and McCormack.

Gerald and Patricia Mische, *Toward a Human World Order: Beyond the National Security Straitjacket* (Paulist Press, 1977). The nation-state as a monolithic institution (nations must inevitably compete against one another for favorable balances of trade, for scarce resources, and for superiority of weapons). Proposes a "world order" system that would strip the nation-state of some of its power.

Patricia Mische, "Women, Power and Alternative Futures," *The Whole Earth Papers*, Vol. 1, no. 8 (1978). "What evolutionary role does the ascent of women in this country have in the . . . forging of a new age in human history?"

Ezra Mishan, *The Costs of Economic Growth* (Praeger, 1967). Growth generates "bads" as well as goods; so we need to start taking social costs into account.

Edgar Mitchell (and John White, ed.), *Psychic Exploration: A Challenge for Science* (Capricorn, 1974). Covers the whole spectrum of psychic research and its political and philosophical implications.

Stephen Monsma, *The Unravelling of America* (Downers Grove, Ill.: InterVarsity Press, 1974). Critique of all ism's "from the point of view of 'evangelical Christianity'."

Barrington Moore, Jr., *Reflections on the Causes of Human Misery and upon Certain Proposals to Eliminate Them* (Beacon, 1972). Critique—by a "radical"—of much of what passes for radicalism today. Argues that future movements must seek to combine the achievements of "liberalism" and "revolutionary radicalism."

Arthur Morgan, *The Community of the Future and the Future of Community* (1957; available for $2.20 from the publisher, Community Service, Inc., IV below). Still a good introduction to our need for community (especially small communities)—and still a good argument for community self-sufficiency.

Robin Morgan, "Metaphysical Feminism," in *Going Too Far: The Personal Chronicle of a Feminist* (Vintage, 1977). Feminism's "third possibility"—blending "passion and thought, feeling and ratiocination."

David Morris and Karl Hess, *Neighborhood Power: The New Localism* (Beacon, 1975). A "left"-ish but effective argument for local self-reliance.

Philip Morrison and Paul Walker, "A New Strategy for Military Spending," *Scientific American*, vol. 239 (Oct. 1978). Argues that our military needs could be adequately met by a military budget 40 percent smaller than the current one. For New Age politics, this is the *first step* on the way to a system of nonviolent and/or guerrilla defense.

Lewis Mumford, *The City in History: Its Origins, Its Transformations, and Its Prospects* (Harbinger, 1961). The overlarge city has often been with us.

———, *The Condition of Man* (Harvest, 1944). Attempts to work out a kind of American personalism that builds on Whitman's *Democratic Vistas,* Ruskin's economics, and the concept of "social synergy."

———, *The Myth of the Machine*:
Vol. I, Technics and Human Development (Harvest, 1967);
Vol. II, The Pentagon of Power (Harvest, 1970).
Covers the origin and development of the Prison and its institutions. Also covers Prison-free attitudes and "biotechnic" institutions.

Gunnar Myrdal, *The Challenge of World Poverty: A World Anti-Poverty Program in Outline* (Vintage, 1970). Much more important that our aid to the IDC's "are the needed social and economic reforms within these countries themselves."

Ralph Nader et al.:
(A) Walter Adams, "The Antitrust Alternative," Chapter VIII of Ralph Nader and Mark Green, eds., *Corporate Power in America* (Penguin, 1973);
(B) Mark Green with Beverly Moore and Bruce Wasserstein, *The Closed Enterprise System: Ralph Nader's Study Group Report on Antitrust Enforcement* (Grossman, 1972);
(C) Jethro Lieberman, "How to Avoid Lawyers," in Ralph Nader and Mark Green, eds., *Verdicts on Lawyers* (Crowell, 1976). The legal profession as a monolithic institution;
(D) Ralph Nader, Mark Green, and Joel Seligman, *Taming the Giant Corporation* (Norton, 1976);
(E) Joseph Page and Mary-Win O'Brien, *Bitter Wages: Ralph Nader's Study Group Report on Disease and Injury on the Job* (Grossman, 1973).

Ruben Nelson, *The Illusions of Urban Man*, pamphlet (Macmillan of Canada, 1975; available free from the Distribution Unit/ICOM, Ministry of State for Urban Affairs, 373 Sussex Dr., Ottawa, Ont., Canada K1A-OP6). Our society and our lives "are not convincing"— and our problems are deeper than we imagine.

Jack Nichols, *Men's Liberation: A New Definition of Masculinity* (Penguin, 1975). Good introduction—from a resoundingly New Age perspective.

Mike Nickerson: *BAKAVI: Change the World I Want to Stay On* (Ottawa, Ont.: All About Us, 1977; available for $3.95 from The Bakavi Foundation, P.O. Box 2011, Station D, Ottawa, Ont., Canada). Presents a strategy for "cultural evolution" based on the principles of ecology, voluntary simplicity, and appropriate technology.

Anaïs Nin, *The Diary of Anaïs Nin, Vol. Two, 1934–1939* (Harvest, 1967). A foray into the world of friendship, creative activity, self-development, and political awareness.

Robert Nisbet, *Twilight of Authority* (Oxford Univ. Press, 1975). Critique of the monolithic state by a nominally conservative New Age thinker. Calls for the rise of the biolithic state (not necessarily small, but one with many "intermediate groupings").

Will Noffke and Michael Toms (interviewers), "Politics and Consciousness," four-hour cassette tape (1975; available for $15.50 from New Directions Foundation, IV below). John Vasconcellos, Ron Dellums, Eugene McCarthy, Michael Rossman, Jerry Rubin, others. See also Ken Dychtwald (interviewer), "Humanizing Politics: An Interview with John Vasconcellos," *New Age* (Oct. 1978).

Michael Novak, *The Experience of Nothingness* (Colophon, 1970). Behind our frenetic activity is the collapse of our values—and a fear of the nothingness we think we see.

Howard Odum and Elisabeth Odum, *Energy Basis for Man and Nature* (McGraw-Hill, 1976). A New Age approach to economics-and-ecology. "Everything that happens is an expression of the flow of energy in one of its forms."

Howard Odum and Harry Moore, *American Regionalism: A Cultural-Historical Approach to National Integration* (Holt, 1938). Pioneering arguments on behalf of "American regionalism," which "represents the philosophy and technique of self-help, self-development, and initiative" (and implies industrial and political decentralization). See also Kevin Phillips, "The Balkanization of America," *Harper's* (May 1978)—hostile but informative.

James Ogilvy, *Many Dimensional Man: Decentralizing Self, Society, and the Sacred* (Oxford Univ. Press, 1977). Argues that our notions of self, society, and the sacred are all deeply interconnected—that the decentralization of one implies or even requires the decentralization of the others.

William Ophuls, *Ecology and the Politics of Scarcity: Prologue to a Political Theory of the Steady State* (W. H. Freeman, 1977). Brilliant introduction to the "sudden emergence of ecological scarcity" and its social, economic, political, and metaphysical implications.

Robert Ornstein, *The Psychology of Consciousness* (Penguin, 1972). Left and right sides of the brain: differences; implications; need to integrate.

Joseph Pearce, *The Magical Child: Rediscovering Nature's Plan for Our Children* (Dutton, 1975). New Age developmental psychology.

Leroy Pelton, *The Psychology of Nonviolence* (Pergamon, 1974). Psychocultural arguments for nonviolence—and for "reconciliation" rather than "victory."

Michael Phillips (with Salli Rasberry et al.), *The Seven Laws of Money* (Random House, 1974). New Age business—principles, practices, and practical benefits for self and society.

Marge Piercy, *Small Changes* (Fawcett, 1974). Feminist novel. Personal awareness and growth ("small changes") as a source of political change . . . and as a *precondition* for political change.

Dennis Pirages and Paul Ehrlich, *Ark II: Social Response to Environmental Imperatives* (Viking, 1974). Aware that our old "institutions, values and behavior" cannot carry us through—and very concerned with mapping out concrete and immediate programs for change.

Robert Pirsig, *Zen and the Art of Motorcycle Maintenance: An Inquiry into Values* (Bantam, 1974). A philosophical adventure story. It introduces the concept of "Quality" and argues against dialectical analysis, arguing instead for "intuition and imagination."

Political Science Committee of the Institute for the New Age, *Looking In, Speaking Out: Six Essays on New Age Politics*, pamphlet (1978; available for $1.50 from the publisher, Political Science Committee, IV below). Asks us to look at our political opinions as manifestations of our personal needs, desires, and—especially—prejudices and fears. The results (e.g., why do some of us *really* want to see a violent revolution in South Africa today?) are startling, and lay the groundwork for a New Age politics.

Ram Dass (with Stephen Levine), *Grist for the Mill* (1976; available for $3.95 from the publisher, Unity Press, 113 New St., Santa Cruz, Calif.). Book of spiritual teachings. "Every experience you have is grist for the mill of awakening."

Charles Reich, *The Sorcerer of Bolinas Reef* (Bantam, 1975). Autobiography by a man who, many lifetimes ago, wrote *The Greening of America*, and is now a gay activist and advocate of New Age politics.

Luke Rhinehart, *The Book of* est (Holt, Rinehart and Winston, 1976). Fictional account of *est* (IV below)—and of the monolithic mind transformed.

Adrienne Rich, *Of Women Born: Motherhood as Experience and Institution* (Bantam, 1976). Demonstrates that the patriarchy is rooted in men's fear of women—not in economics. Introduces the concept of "transformative power." Says we must begin to "think through the body."

Tom Robbins, *Even Cowgirls Get the Blues* (Bantam, 1976). New Age novel. Sex, politics, feminism, spirituality, love of the Earth and love of life. See also Robbins, *Another Roadside Attraction* (1971).

Adam Roberts, *Nations in Arms: The Theory and Practice of Territorial Defense* (London: Chatto & Windus, 1976). One New Age alternative to nuclear *and* nonviolent defense.

Jane Roberts, *The Nature of Personal Reality: A Seth Book* (Prentice-Hall, 1974). "You choose your own experiences" (including your sex, parents, etc.)—a starting point for viewing reality.

James Robertson, *The Sane Alternative: Signposts to a Self-fulfilling Future* (1978; available for $4 from the author at Turning Point, IV below). An outstanding brief introduction to New Age politics by a British political scientist. Could easily be mass-marketed in this country.

Carl Rogers, *On Becoming a Person: A Therapist's View of Psycho-Therapy* (Houghton Mifflin, 1961). Path-breaking book for the human potential movement. Traces the path "from fixity to changingness, from rigid structure to flow."

Michael Rossman, *On Learning and Social Change* (Vintage, 1972). Critique of industrial society by a radical Taoist.

Theodore Roszak, *Person/Planet: The Creative Disintegration of Industrial Society* (Anchor, 1978). A manifesto for the person (as distinct from the possessive individual *and* the collective individual). See also *ibid., Unfinished Animal* (1975), a good broad overview of the spiritual and human potential movements.

———, *Where the Wasteland Ends: Politics and Transcendence in Postindustrial Society* (Anchor, 1972). Critique of urban-industrial society—and urban-industrial consciousness—from a neopersonalist perspective. (*Person/Planet*, above, is our first *explicitly* personalist book since Mumford's *Condition of Man*, above.)

Jerry Rubin, *Growing (Up) at 37* (Warner, 1976). Why he's no longer a New Left radical. His experiences in the consciousness-and-growth movement. "Revolution as an evolutionary process."

Dane Rudhyar, *Occult Preparations for a New Age* (Wheaton, Ill.: Theosophical Publishing House, 1975). Western evolutionary philosopher argues for—and points to—the "repotentialization" and "planetization" of our consciousness. Cf. Alice Bailey, *The Destiny of the Nations* (1949), a stimulating attempt to explain the political in terms of the spiritual.

Rosemary Ruether, *Liberation Theology: Human Hope Confronts Christian History and American Power* (Paulist Press, 1972). In my opinion, this is a much more intellectually courageous book that her better known—and more conventionally socialist—*New Woman/New Earth* (1975). See esp. Chap. 8, "Mother Earth and the Megamachine."

John Ruskin, *"Unto This Last": Four Essays on the First Principles of Political Economy* (London: Smith, Elder and Co., 1862). An early New Age economist. "There is no wealth but life," etc.

Jonas Salk, *The Survival of the Wisest* (Harper & Row, 1973). New Age approach to human evolution. Why a "transvaluation of values" is at hand.

Mark Satin, *Big Plans*, published as *Confessions of a Young Exile* (Toronto: Gage, 1976). Desperately honest novel about "the 1960s."

Leonard Schein, "An Introduction to Male Psychology, Consciousness," paper (1975; free from the Non-Sexist Psychology Association, 2211 Parker St., Vancouver, B.C., Canada V5L-2L8).

E. F. Schumacher, *Small Is Beautiful: A Study of Economics as if People Mattered* (Perennial, 1973). Still the best single book from the environmental/appropriate technology wing of the New Age movement. Calls for an economics appropriate to a society of appropriate technology plus voluntary simplicity . . . and calls for a return to the "traditional wisdom." For more on the latter, see *ibid., A Guide for the Perplexed* (1977) which outlines a metaphysical/philosophical basis for a New Age politics.

E. F. Schumacher:

(A) "Changing Knowledge to Wisdom: An Interview with E. F. Schumacher," by Sherman Goldman and Bill Tara, *East West* (Nov. 1976).

(B) "On Inflation," *Rain* (Nov. 1975).

(C) "Technology and Political Change," *Rain* (Dec. 1976 and Jan. 1977).

Franz Schurmann, "Arcana of Empire," Part I of *The Logic of World Power* (Pantheon, 1974). Government has become more powerful than business, "ideology" more powerful than corporate-bureaucratic "interests."

Bob Schwartz (interviewed by Sam Keen), "American Business Needs You!" *New Age* (March 1976). Introducing—the New Age entrepreneur. Schwartz is director of The School for Entrepreneurs (IV below).

Tibor Scitovsky, *The Joyless Economy: An Inquiry into Human Satisfaction and Consumer Dissatisfaction* (Oxford Univ. Press, 1976). "We get and pay for more comfort than is necessary for the good life, and some of our comforts crowd out some of the enjoyments of life."

Gene Sharp, *The Politics of Nonviolent Action* (Porter Sargent, 1973). Thousand-page study of nonviolent action: history, theory, practice. Presents nonviolence as the most *effective* military strategy.

William Shurtleff and Akiko Aoyagi, *The Book of Tofu: Food for Mankind* (Autumn, 1975). Every genuine political movement has a cookbook; this one is ours.

The Simple Living Collective—American Friends Service Committee, *Taking Charge: Achieving Personal and Political Change Through Simple Living* (Bantam, 1977). Some useful essays.

June Singer, *Androgyny: Toward a New Theory of Sexuality* (Anchor, 1976). "Androgyny as [a] guiding principle of the new age."

Philip Slater, *Earthwalk* (Anchor, 1974). Very good analysis of our egocentricity—our fear of community—our "mechanical-mindedness."

———, *The Wayward Gate: Science and the Supernatural* (Beacon, 1977). A very persuasive argument for the trans-material worldview. He almost says, paraphrasing Che, "It is not my fault that reality is trans-material."

Hedrick Smith, *The Russians* (Bantam, 1976). What the Marxists won't tell us about Russia.

Huston Smith, *Forgotten Truth: The Primordial Tradition* (Colophon, 1976). Another independently worked-out version of the trans-material worldview.

Gary Snyder, *The Old Ways: Six Essays* (City Lights, 1977). Critique of "what occidental and industrial technological civilization is doing to the earth." See also *ibid.*, *Turtle Island* (1975), New Age poetry. And see Peter Chowka (interviewer), "The Original Mind of Gary Snyder," *East West* (June through Sept. 1977).

Paolo Soleri, *The Bridge Between Matter and Spirit Is Matter Becoming Spirit: The Arcology of Paolo Soleri* (Anchor, 1973). Evolutionary theory behind Soleri's "cities in the image of [people]."

Alexander Solzhenitsyn and Igor Shafarevich, eds., *From Under the Rubble* (Bantam, 1975). Political statement of the spiritual wing of the Soviet dissident movement.

David Spangler, *Revelation: The Birth of a New Age,* 2nd ed. (San Francisco: The Rainbow Bridge, 1976; available for $6 from The Findhorn Foundation, IV below). Many people's favorite introduction to New Age spirituality.

———, "Economics as a Way of the Spirit," cassette tape (1976; available for $7 from The Findhorn Foundation, IV below).

———, "From Strategy to Wholeness . . . The Meaning of Community," *Yoga Journal* (March/April 1977).

———, "Identity in Action: The Power of Knowing Who You Are," *New Age* (Feb. 1975).

L. S. Stavrianos, *The Promise of the Coming Dark Age* (W. H. Freeman, 1976). Kind of a left-wing version of *New Age Politics.* Something's missing. And see Walter Laqueur's critique in *Commentary* (Feb. 1977).

Claude Steiner, *Scripts People Live* (Bantam, 1974). Transactional analysis ("TA") explained and extended. Introduces the concept of the "stroke economy." For more on TA, see Muriel James and Dorothy Jongeward, *Born to Win* (1971).

John Stoltenberg on men's liberation: *WIN* Magazine (July 12, 1974); *WIN* (March 29, 1974).

Merlin Stone, *When God Was a Woman* (Dial, 1976). On the matriarchies, and on matriarchal attitudes.

Grace Stuart, *Narcissus: A Psychological Study of Self-Love* (Macmillan, 1955). Critique of egocentricity (reflects not self-love but self-hate).

Patricia Sun, "Sounds of the Sun," series of audio cassette tapes

(1977; available for $6 and up per tape from New Dimensions Foundation, IV below). "I . . . [create] an opportunity for people to experience who they are, really to experience their own power. . . ."

Elaine Sundancer, *Celery Wine: The Story of a Country Commune* (1973; available for $2.50 plus postage from the publisher, Community Service, Inc., IV below). One person's account—honest and insightful—of the first two years of her own rural commune. The most satisfying introduction I know of to the problems and promise of communal living. For a more "sociological" approach, try Rosabeth Kanter, ed., *Communes* (1973).

Charles Tart, "Science, States of Consciousness, and Spiritual Experiences: The Need for State-Specific Sciences," in *ibid.*, ed., *Transpersonal Psychologies* (Colophon, 1975). Our first "multiple-vision" science.

Charles Tart, *States of Consciousness* (Dutton, 1975). Lays out a theoretical basis for the trans-material worldview.

Robert Thamm, "Toward a Family of the Future," Part One of *ibid.*, *Beyond Marriage and the Nuclear Family* (Canfield, 1975). Summarizes the communitarian critique of monogamy, marriage, and the nuclear family. Presents many biolithic alternatives.

Frederick Thayer, *An End to Hierarchy! An End to Competition!: Organizing the Politics and Economics of Survival* (New Viewpoints, 1973). Hierarchy and competition—not capitalism—is the problem. Nonhierarchical, synergic, face-to-face decision-making groups are the solution.

Robert Theobald, *Beyond Despair: Directions for America's Third Century* (New Republic, 1976). Need for value change, networking, "win-win" model, etc. Important critique of the job economy.

———, *Habit and Habitat* (Prentice-Hall, 1972). New Age political economy. "Sapiential authority," "systemic thinking," more. See also *Teg's 1994* (1972), "communications-era" novel by Theobald and Jeanne Scott.

Third World Communications, *Time to Greez! Incantations from the Third World* (New Glide, 1975). Prose and poetry by yellow, black, red, and brown Americans. Demonstrates a considerable overlap between Third World and New Age sensibilities.

William Irwin Thompson, *Darkness and Scattered Light: Four Talks on the Future* (Anchor, 1978). Exuberant and insightful arguments against civilization as we know it, and in favor of "the contemporary planetary cultural transformation." See also *Evil and World Order* (1976).

———, *Passages About Earth: An Exploration of the New Planetary Culture* (Perennial, 1974). Portraits of some New Age thinkers, assessments of some New Age-oriented ideas. See also *At the Edge of History* (1971).

Jan Tinbergen, coord., *Reshaping the International Order: A Report to the Club of Rome* (Dutton, 1976). Devastating factual summary of planetary inequities; "post-ideological" solutions proposed.

Nancy Todd, ed., *The Book of the New Alchemists* (Dutton, 1977). Their "experiences in attempting to create a wholistic technology for small communities" (see IV below). See esp. John Todd, "A Modest Proposal," and Nancy Todd, "Ecology and Feminism."

Alvin Toffler, *The Eco-Spasm Report* (Bantam, 1975). Argues for a "service economy" and for "anticipatory democracy."

Chogyam Trungpa, *Cutting Through Spiritual Materialism* (Shambhala, 1973). Tibetan Buddhist approach to personal and spiritual growth.

Peter van Dresser, *Development on a Human Scale: Potentials for Ecologically Guided Growth in Northern New Mexico* (Praeger, 1973). Good introduction to "watershed politics" (bioregional rehabitation). See also Watersheds issue, *CoEvolution Quarterly* (Spring 1977).

Jaroslav Vanek, *The Participatory Economy: An Evolutionary Hypothesis and a Strategy for Development* (Cornell Univ. Press, 1971). Workers' self-management as the basis for a "new major economic system."

Mitch Walker, "Visionary Love: The Magickal Gay Spirit-Power," *Gay Sunshine,* no. 31 (Winter 1977).

———, "Becoming Gay Shamanism: More Visionary Love," paper (San Francisco, 1977).

———, "Love and Gay Consciousness," Chapter 8 of *Men Loving Men: A Gay Sex Guide and Consciousness Book* (1977; available for $6.95 from the publisher, Gay Sunshine Press, P.O. Box 40397, San Francisco, Calif. 94140). Introduction to gay men's spirituality. Argues that gay consciousness has an important contribution to make to the New Age, and vice versa.

Barbara Ward, *The Home of Man* (Norton, 1976). Critique of monolithic housing policies. Says we need human-scale communities, an ecology ethic, and a "new economic order." Full of practical suggestions.

Frank Waters (with Oswald White Bear Fredericks), *Book of the Hopi* (Ballantine, 1963). Spiritual and ecological consciousness. Hopi as practitioners of the New Age ethics and values.

Alan Watts, *Beyond Theology* (Vintage, 1964). What the Judeo-Christian tradition can learn from Eastern philosophy and from the "ecological view of [people]."

Walter Weisskopf, *The Psychology of Economics* (Univ. of Chicago Press, 1955). A psychocultural history of economic theory.

H. B. Wilson, *Democracy and the Work Place* (Montreal: Black Rose, 1974). Workers' self-management—an evolutionary perspective.

Langdon Winner, *Autonomous Technology: Technics-out-of-Control as a Theme in Political Thought* (MIT Press, 1977). Fascinating attempt "to reevaluate the circumstances of our involvement with technology."

II. 20 Interesting Books by Some Early
American Advocates of "New Age Politics"

This is a bibliography for Chapter 25 above.

John and John Quincy Adams, *The Selected Writings of John and John Quincy Adams,* ed. Adrienne Koch and William Peden (Knopf, 1946).

Herbert Agar, *Land of the Free* (Houghton Mifflin, 1935).

Herbert Agar and Allen Tate, eds., *Who Owns America? A New Declaration of Independence* (Houghton Mifflin, 1936).

Ralph Borsodi, *This Ugly Civilization* (Simon and Schuster, 1929).

William Ellery Channing, *The Works of William E. Channing,* new ed. (Boston: American Unitarian Assn., 1891).

John Jay Chapman: *The Selected Writings of John Jay Chapman,* ed. Jacques Barzun (Farrar, Straus, 1957).

Waldo Frank, *The Death and Birth of David Markand: An American Story* (Scribner's, 1934).

————, *The Re-Discovery of America: An Introduction to a Philosophy of American Life* (Scribner's, 1929).

Henry George, *Progress and Poverty* (New York: Robert Schalkenbach Foundation, 1958, orig. 1879).

Richard Gregg, two pamphlets: "Gandhiism versus Socialism" (New York: John Day, 1932); "The Value of Voluntary Simplicity" (Wallingford, Pa.: Pendle Hill, 1936).

————, *The Power of Nonviolence,* 1st ed. (Lippincott, 1934).

Hutchins Hapgood, *The Spirit of the Ghetto: Studies of the Jewish Quarter in New York,* ed. Moses Rischin (The Belknap Press of Harvard Univ. Press, 1967; orig. rev. ed. 1909).

Arthur Morgan, *The Long Road* (Washington, D.C.: National Home Library Foundation, 1936).

————, *The Small Community: Foundation of Democratic Life* (Harper & Brothers, 1942).

John Muir: *The Wilderness World of John Muir,* ed. Edwin Teale (Houghton Mifflin, 1976).

John Humphrey Noyes, *The Berean: A Manual For the Help of Those Who Seek the Faith of the Primitive Church* (Putney, Vt.: Office of *Spiritual Magazine,* 1847).

Theodore Parker: *Theodore Parker, American Transcendentalist,* ed. Robert Collins (Metuchen, N.J.: Scarecrow Press, 1973).

Alexander H. Stephens, *A Constitutional View of the Late War between the States,* 2 vols. (Philadelphia: National Publishing Co., 1868, 1870).

Frederick Jackson Turner, *The Significance of Sections in American History* (Holt, 1932).

John Woolman: *The Journal of John Woolman and "A Plea for the Poor,"* ed. Frederick Tolles (Citadel, 1961).

III. 50 New Age Periodicals

This is not meant to be a "complete" list, but it is meant to be representative and suggestive, and I'd like to think that I've managed to include most of our "best" periodicals. I would certainly urge any New Age-oriented bookstore—and any competent library—to carry most or all of them. (On the other hand, the Widener Library at Harvard carries only about 20 percent of them. It doesn't even subscribe to *CoEvolution Quarterly* or *New Age,* though it subscribes to their left-wing equivalents, *Socialist Review* and *Mother Jones.*)

Some after-the-fact statistics: of the fifty-six periodicals that are actually listed here, sixteen have their editorial offices in California, thirteen in New York-Pennsylvania-New Jersey, six in New England, six in D.C., and five in Canada or Great Britain; thirteen are primarily environmental/appropriate technology, eleven are consciousness-and-growth, six are self-help, six are simple living/rural living, two are feminist, two are world order, and the rest are hopelessly mixed; about 60 percent of them have female editors or co-editors.

Akwesasne Notes (occasional; Mohawk Nation via Rooseveltown, N.Y. 13683; subscriptions by donation or request; $1 an issue).

Covers native people's events from a number of different perspectives—from the conventionally "radical" to the New Age as I've described it in this book. Areas of special interest include: political movements and spirituality (and their interconnections), ecology, alternative technology, self-sufficiency.

Alternative Sources of Energy (bi-monthly; Route 2, Box 90-A, Milaca, Minn. 56353; $10 a year, $1.75 an issue).

Covers "the development of alternative [mostly energy] technologies with emphasis on small scale and community sized technologies"; tries to "provide a communications network" for those of us who share these goals.

Alternatives (monthly; P.O. Box 330139, Miami, Fla. 33133; $12 a year, $1.50 an issue).

"We emphasize balanced personal growth and responsibility through self-help articles on consciousness and healing." Monthly features explore the arts, humor, books and records, New Age gatherings, tools for holistic living, natural foods, games, and interviews.

Brain-Mind Bulletin (bi-weekly; P.O. Box 42211, Los Angeles, Calif. 90042; $15 a year, 75¢ an issue; "send stamped, self-addressed envelope for sample copy").

Well-written newsletter in the field of brain-mind research. Covers new discoveries, new theories, and the practical applications of same;

covers conferences and workshops, books and journals, and the New Age political implications of brain-mind research (editor Marilyn Ferguson is the author of the book *The Aquarian Conspiracy: Personal and Social Transformation in the 1980s,* J. P. Tarcher, 1979).

Briarpatch Review (occasional; 330 Ellis St., San Francisco, Calif. 94102; $5 for four issues, $1.25 an issue).

Articles, thoughts, etc., on New Age-oriented businesses (problems, practices, experiences in). Also articles, thoughts, etc., on the philosophy of "right livelihood and simple living." Written and published by the Briarpatch Network (IV below). Issues through 1977 are available as *The Briarpatch Book* (New Glide/Reed, 1978).

Bulletin of the Atomic Scientists (monthly; 1020 E. 58th St., Chicago, Ill. 60636; $19.50 a year, $2 an issue).

All kinds of scientists (not just physicists) wrestle with some of the thorny specific issues that are raised by the New Age ethics and political values. How best to express our obligation to the international human rights movement? What limits to impose on the application of science and technology to human affairs?

Cascade: Journal of the Northwest (bi-monthly; P.O. Box 1492, Eugene, Ore. 97440; free or donation to Pacific Northwest groups that are "involved in community change activities," $10 for ten issues to everyone else; $1 an issue).

A model New Age networking magazine. Regular contents include: developments in groups and community organizations around the Northwest, organized under twenty topics including ethnic cultures, economics, food, spirit, and women/men; good ideas in periodicals and publications from around the region; and readers' comments on subjects of regional and national interest.

Christopher Street (monthly; 250 W. 57th St., Ste. 417, New York, N.Y. 10019; $18 a year, $2 an issue).

Informative and joyful look at the new gay men's sensibility (which has some points in common with the New Age sensibility). Some recent articles: the "new masculinity" of gay men; should gays in high school come out? "We're happy to be a vital part of the growth of a gay nation-within-a-nation."

CoEvolution Quarterly (P.O. Box 428, Sausalito, Calif. 94965; $12 a year, $3.50 an issue).

An intellectual journal for the New Age. Excellent in-depth features on appropriate technology, voluntary simplicity, "watershed politics," space colonies, Gregory Bateson, etc., plus *Whole Earth Catalog*-type book reviews and Robert Crumb cartoons. *Too California hip for some tastes, but don't let that fool you.*

Commentary (monthly; 165 E. 56th St., New York, N.Y. 10022; $24 a year, $2.50 an issue);

In These Times (weekly; 1509 N. Milwaukee Ave., Chicago, Ill. 60622; $17.50 a year, 50¢ an issue);

Inquiry (semimonthly; P.O. Box 19270, Washington, D.C. 20036; editorial offices in San Francisco; $12.50 a year, $1.25 an issue);

Mother Jones (monthly; P.O. Box 2482, Boulder, Colo. 80321; editorial offices in San Francisco; $8.88 a year, $1.50 an issue);

Time (weekly).

There are no New Age newsmagazines—yet. But we can read newsmagazines from a number of different political perspectives, keeping always in mind that each of them expresses a part of the truth (not necessarily an equal part). *In These Times* is neo-Marxist, *Mother Jones* is neo-New Left, *Inquiry* is libertarian left, *Time* is your standard liberal weekly, and *Commentary* is neoliberal (or "neoconservative").

Communities (bi-monthly; P.O. Box 426N, Louisa, Va. 23093; $7.50 a year, $1.50 an issue).

"Journal of Cooperative Living." Especially for people involved in communal living or in cooperative ventures of some sort. Most issues have a major theme (government, sex, planning, spirituality); regular features include Reach ("places, events, and people to connect with"), Grapevine ("new projects beginning, notes from all over"), and Resources (how to get connected).

Critical Mass Journal (monthly; P.O. Box 1538, Washington, D.C. 20013; $7.50 a year, $37.50 for business institutions, government; 65¢ an issue).

Offers consistently good coverage of antinuclear/pro-solar movements and issues. Crisply written articles, effective newspaper format, minimum of rhetoric. Published by the Critical Mass Energy Project of Public Citizen, one of the Ralph Nader groups. CMEP works with over 175 local citizen groups on a variety of energy issues.

East West Journal (monthly; P.O. Box 505, Whitinsville, Mass. 01588; editorial offices near Boston; $12 a year, $1.50 an issue).

"We explore the dynamic equilibrium that unifies apparently opposite values: Oriental and Occidental, traditional and modern, religious and technological. We investigate the play of balance in all fields— from ecology, agriculture, and nutrition to economics, politics, and spirituality." Areas of special interest include organic and macrobiotic alternatives.

Environmental Action (monthly; 1346 Connecticut Ave., N.W., Ste. 731, Washington, D.C. 20036; $15 a year).

Good detailed coverage of the environmental movement and (where it overlaps) the antinuclear movement. "Some of our best received articles during 1978: a piece about how Coca-Cola is squeezing out the small bottling companies—and returnable bottles along with them . . . [and our] 'Declaration of Solar Independence'."

Fellowship (monthly; P.O. Box 271, Nyack, N.Y. 10960; $6 a year, 75¢ an issue).

The only peace magazine I know of that is closer in spirit to New Age politics than to New Left politics. Informative and reflective—planetary in scope—underlying spiritual/religious sensibility. Favors "a broad-based movement with openings toward the middle." Published by Fellowship of Reconciliation (IV below).

Free America (monthly, then quarterly; 19 E. 97th St., New York City; $1 a year, 10¢ a copy; ten volumes published, 1937–1947; R.I.P.).

"Stands for individual independence and believes that freedom can exist only in societies in which the great majority are the effective owners of tangible and productive goods and in which group action is democratic. . . . [Therefore, believes that] ownership, production, population, and government must be decentralized." Editors included Herbert Agar and Ralph Borsodi (see Chapter 25).

The Futurist (bi-monthly; 4916 St. Elmo Ave., Washington, D.C. 20014; $15 a year, $2.50 an issue).

Reports the forecasts made by scientists, academics, and others. Explores the consequences of these forecasted developments on self and society and discusses what we can do to further or to stop them. Most shades of political opinion are represented, including New Age politics. Published by World Future Society (IV below).

Green Revolution (monthly; P.O. Box 3233, York, Pa. 17402; $8 a year, $1 an issue).

"A Voice for Decentralization." Grounded in the homestead- and simplicity-oriented philosophy of Ralph Borsodi (one of the progenitors of New Age politics; see Chapter 25). Areas of special concern include land trusts, personal relationships, and the cooperative movement. Published by School of Living (IV below).

Growing Without Schooling (bi-monthly; 308 Boylston St., Boston, Mass. 02116; $10 for six issues, $18 for 12 issues; subscriptions begin with issue #1; #1–6 were in print as of Dec. 1978).

Editor John Holt writes, "This . . . newsletter [is] about ways in which people, young or old, can learn and do things, acquire skills, and find interesting and useful work, without having to go through the process of schooling. . . . Much of what is in it [comes] from its readers. . . ."

Holistic Health Review (quarterly; P.O. Box 166, Berkeley, Calif. 94701; $4–10 a year, "the most you feel you can afford"; $1.50 an issue).

Holistic health practitioners, etc., seek to speak *for* and *to* the holistic health movement. Each issue includes: an article on the philosophical, social, and public-policy aspects of holistic health; an article on a holistic health center; an interview with a notable holistic health provider; and more. Sponsored by the Holistic Health Organizing Committee (IV below).

In Business (bi-monthly; P.O. Box 323, Emmaus, Pa. 18049; $14 a year).

Addresses ways of starting and managing new small businesses based on many of the values and alternatives in this book. Some articles: "New Age Business," "New England's Tofu Factory," "A.T. for Women." Plus practical advice from professionals in financing, marketing, systems and management. Plus "Your hotline to people, ideas, and places for information exchange."

Journal of Humanistic Psychology (quarterly; 325 9th St., San Francisco 94103; $10 a year, $14 for institutions; $3.50 an issue).

Articles by people in many fields who are working for New Age-oriented changes in their lives and in society. Theoretical papers, "experiential reports," research studies, personal essays, applications of humanistic psychology, analyses of contemporary culture. Journal of the Association for Humanistic Psychology (IV below).

Journal of Transpersonal Psychology (twice yearly; P.O. Box 4437, Stanford, Calif. 94305; $10 a year, $7.50 for students; $5 an issue).

Articles on transpersonal values, theories and practice of meditation, "unitive consciousness," spiritual paths, peak experiences, "sacralization of everyday life," etc. A little "farther out" than the JHP (above) in subject matter, but no less serious or solid. Published by the "Transpersonal Institute."

Manas (weekly; P.O. Box 32112, El Sereno Stn., Los Angeles, Calif. 90032; $10 a year, $7.50 if poor; sample copies free).

Every genuine political movement has a journal of philosophy and practical psychology; this one is ours. It is an excellent review of New Age literature and ideas in many fields, and it is written "in as direct and simple a manner as its editors and contributors can write."

Medical Self-Care Magazine: Access to Medical Tools (quarterly; P.O. Box 717, Inverness, Calif. 94937; $10 for four issues, $2.50 an issue, brochure free).

Edited by a recent graduate of Yale Medical School who is also Medical Editor of *CoEvolution Quarterly*. Carries articles on: basic paramedical skills, how your life-style affects your health, psychological self-care, how to use the medical literature, how to establish self-care classes and study groups. Exudes warmth and competence.

The Mother Earth News (bi-monthly; P.O. Box 70, Hendersonville, N.C. 28739; $12 a year, $2.50 an issue).

Small-scale farming and natural living. Concern is with the practical, with self-sufficiency and independence. Some of my favorite regular features: "The Plowboy Interview" (long and searching) and "Positions and Situations" which is "designed to help would-be back-to-the-landers get in touch with folks already out there."

New Age (monthly; 32 Station St., Brookline, Mass. 02146; $12 a year, $1.50 an issue).

Covers the consciousness, holistic health, education, and environmental movements and the effects that these movements are having on self and society. Issues are thematic and include: natural foods, sex, aging, work/money, personal activism, and global politics. Each issue is aimed at empowering the individual and nurturing a humanistic evolution. *Written in too relentlessly bright and positive a style for some people, but don't confuse that with superficiality.*

New Dimensions Audio Journal (90-minute audio cassette tape quarterly; 267 States St., San Francisco, Calif. 94114; $35 a year).

Compiled and produced from programs presented on New Dimensions radio (IV below) with some new material. "The experience of actually *listening* to someone is wholly unique and different than *reading* their words. . . . The first year will bring you in touch with space colonies, inner space travel, right livelihood, money as energy. . . ."

New Directions (occasional; 2173 W. 4th Ave., Vancouver, B.C., Canada V6K-1N7; $10 for 12 issues, $1 an issue).

Excellent coverage of spiritual and spiritually oriented people and ideas and events. Main concerns: "ecology, energy, consciousness, community, healing, and sacred arts." Says, "*New Directions* exists to serve [the] 'new age' movement. We are part of the movement ourselves—members of an urban [spiritual] collective" and organizers of the World Symposium(s) on Humanity.

New Ecologist (bi-monthly; 73 Molesworth St., Wadebridge, Cornwall, U.K. PL27-7DS; $9 a year, $1.50 an issue; "specimen copy sent on request").

"Journal of the Post-Industrial Age." One of the most substantial—and interesting—of the ecology and environmental-issues magazines. Articles also deal (harshly) with various monolithic institutions and with social theory, and there is a regular section on environmental politics ("Ecopolitics").

New Farm (bi-monthly; 33 E. Minor St., Emmaus, Pa. 18049; $10 a year, $2 an issue);
Organic Gardening (monthly; same address; $9 a year, $1 an issue).

OG is full of practical information, news and reviews, tips, resources. *NF* describes itself as "the thoughtful farmer's magazine" and tries to promote "a gentler, healthier, more efficient way of farming . . . guided by an insightful understanding of Nature and a committed partnership with her." Both published by Rodale Press, Inc.

New Humanity (bi-monthly; 51a York Mansions, Prince of Wales Drive, London, U.K. SW11; $7 for eight issues, $1 an issue).

Dedicated to achieving "a synthesis of politics and higher spiritual ethics" (subtitle: "The World's First Politico-Spiritual Journal"). Also states, "The New Age represents a power that begs political representation." Some recent articles: "The Third Way," "Where Marx Went Wrong," "Guidelines for Politico-Spiritual Action."

New Realities (bi-monthly; P.O. Box 26289, San Francisco, Calif. 94126; $9 a year, $1.50 an issue).

At last—an explicitly New Age magazine whose purpose is to speak to the majority of Americans. And it just might: interesting articles, accessible style, attractive design. Covers the whole range of New Age subjects, from psychic research to electoral politics, and has already featured a number of people from sect. I above.

New Sun (monthly; 282 Cabrini Blvd., #3-B, New York, N.Y. 10040; $11 a year, $1 an issue).

"The *New Sun* is about how we experience and relate to ourselves, and to others, in the city and on this planet, . . . in the light of the new and heightened awareness of our interconnectedness; and of the revised revolutionary self-concept of *who we are* and *what we are capable of*."

Not Man Apart ("fortnightly"; 124 Spear St., San Francisco, Calif. 94105; $10 a year).

Likes to call itself—not unjustly—the *New York Times* of the environmental movement. "*NMA*'s obvious bias in favor of a livable planet frees it to present material that manages to escape many other papers." Published by Friends of the Earth (IV below) and written by staff, members, and sister organizations of FOE.

People & Energy (occasional; 1413 K St., N.W., 8th flr., Washington, D.C., 20005; $12 for 12 issues).

Focuses on energy developments and issues of national importance . . . particularly to alternative energy/antinuclear activists and community organizers. Features and news items provide names and addresses for references, contact people. Regular features include "Solar Update" and "Keeping an Eye on the Feds." Published by Institute for Ecological Policies (IV below).

Planet Earth (quarterly; 777 United Nations Plaza, 10th flr., New York, N.Y. 10017; $15 a year).

Analyses of planetary issues and problems from a more or less explicitly New Age point of view. Envisions not a "nation-state writ large" but a much greater degree of planetary cooperation and sharing. Precondition: "planetary consciousness." Published by Planetary Citizens (IV below).

Rain (monthly; 2270 N.W. Irving St., Portland, Ore. 97210; $15 a year, $7.50 if "living lightly"; $1.50 an issue).

One of the most interesting and informative magazines on environmental and appropriate-technology issues, concerns, politics. Substantial feature articles; current information on projects, people, groups, events; many brief book and pamphlet reviews.

Resurgence (bi-monthly; Pentre Ifan, Felindre Farchug, Crymych, Dryfed, Wales; $10 a year).

"*Resurgence* is a voice of new civilization, it is a journal of new politics, concerned with small nations, small communities, decentralism, and ethnic cultures. It is a philosophical, ecological, and spiritual forum" that publishes the New Age-oriented followers of people like Ivan Illich, E. F. Schumacher, and Leopold Kohr.

Self Determination (quarterly; 2431 Forest Avenue, San Jose, Calif. 95128; $25 "membership donation" a year, less—up to you—if "low income").

Goal: "to provide a forum for exploring positive avenues of personal growth and political change" and their interconnections. "Each issue has a specific major focus (holistic health, cooperative organizations, etc.), and articles explore options for creating alternatives." Published by the Self Determination network (IV below).

Self-Reliance (bi-monthly; 1717 18th St., N.W., Washington, D.C. 20009; $8 a year, $15 for institutions; $1 an issue).

"[Our] primary purpose is to report on the efforts and successes of community-based groups around the country that are working toward the devolution of power and control to the local level." Also covers community issues. Tough-minded, intelligent. Published by Institute for Local Self-Reliance (IV below).

Seriatim (quarterly; 122 Carmel St., El Cerrito, Calif. 94530; $9 a year, $2.50 an issue).

A journal about "Ecotopia" where "an environmentally-attuned, stable-state society is emerging. *Seriatim* aims to document and foster the growth of that society. . . ." Regular sections now include: shelters, transport, agriculture, forestry, A.T.; recent topics have included holistic health, electric vehicles, new experiments in community living, wind power, urban farming, and "survival in our time."

Sierra (bi-monthly; 530 Bush St., San Francisco, Calif. 94108; $8 a year, $1.50 an issue).

An excellent magazine on environmental issues and concerns. Especially good on conservation issues and on what's happening in Washington, but the articles cover a broad range of other topics, e.g.—in one issue—"Biomass Energy," "Toward a Coalition for the Urban Environment," "Willa Cather's Pastoral Vision," and more. Published by Sierra Club (IV below).

Simple Living (occasional; 514 Bryant St., Palo Alto, Calif. 94302; subscriptions $3 or whatever you can afford; subscriptions last for an indefinite time period).

Well-written, well-thought-out newsletter that focuses on different aspects of simple living (recent issues: barter, bicycle transport, human scale, roots, needs, nonviolence). Articles tend to combine intellectual analysis with personal insight and personal experience. Published by the American Friends Service Committee—the Quakers.

Sojourner (monthly; 143 Albany St., Cambridge, Mass. 02139; $5 a year, 50¢ an issue).

New Age feminist newspaper. Even the design tends to suggest a certain dignity and sufficiency. Special issue format (e.g., politics, spirituality, children, money); regular features include interviews, "viewpoints," and two pages of poetry. "*Sojourner* welcomes submissions from feminists everywhere."

Solar Age (monthly; P.O. Box 4934, Manchester, N.H. 03108; $20 a year, $1.95 an issue).

Excellent coverage of new developments in solar technology—also very good on public-policy developments with regard to solar. Intended to be "essential reading for the solar professional." Perspective: "most [solar energy] systems would make good economic sense if they weren't such underdogs to the competition: subsidized conventional fuels."

Tract (quarterly; The Gryphon Press, 38 Prince Edwards Road, Lewes, Sussex, U.K.; $8 a year, $2.25 an issue).

New Age-oriented intellectual journal. Some recent articles: Henryk Skolimowski, "Ecological Humanism" (I above); Mumford, two-part interview; George Grant, "Can We Think Outside Technology?"; nature of "theocratic humanism"; critique of empiricism (with call for an "adequate philosophy of ethics"); rediscoveries ("re-appraisals") of a number of neglected New Age thinkers. *Should be better known, but as editor Peter Abbs puts it, "The 'intellectual' life of the metropolis demands its own orthodoxies."*

Tranet (quarterly; P.O. Box 567, Rangeley, Me. 04970; $15 a year).

Describes itself as "a newsletter-directory *of, by*, and *for* those . . . who are actively developing appropriate-alternative technologies." Features include an ongoing "directory of A.T. centers" and a review of A.T. news and publications.

Whole Earth Papers (quarterly; 552 Park Ave., East Orange, N.J. 07017; $10 a year, $2.50 an issue).

Hard-hitting "realpolitik" type analyses of planetary problems from a New Age point of view (systemic change and spiritual/moral growth both seen as essential). Published by Global Education Associates (IV below).

WomanSpirit (quarterly; P.O. Box 263, Wolf Creek, Ore. 97497; $7 a year, $2.50 an issue).

Feminist spirituality—eclectic, frequently pagan (not Eastern). One of the writers says, "For us, [feminist spirituality] is a *radical* search for a NEW way to live together on this planet." Sixty-four pages an issue, illustrated, publishing since 1974.

Yoga Journal (bi-monthly; 2054 University Ave., Berkeley, Calif. 94704; $7.50 a year, $1.50 an issue).

Focuses on yoga practices "in a modern Western context." Has instructional articles on asanas, meditation, and body work techniques; also has articles on spiritual teachers, nutrition, holistic healing, and the environment. Each issue contains interviews, book excerpts, and book reviews "reflecting current developments in the field of yoga."

IV. 100 New Age Groups

Again, this is not meant to be a complete list, but I think it's fairly representative. It is *not* meant to suggest that est is "better" than the Cornucopia Institute (which I haven't listed), Greenpeace more effective than the Jonah Project, and so on . . . and on and on. And by the way: none of these groups asked to be listed here. (Same with the periodicals above.)

In order to inspire some of you to read this list from beginning to end, I have started it with a birth project, and ended it with a death-and-dying project. The quotes I use are all from the literature that the groups send out to people. I've taken the liberty of merging and condensing some passages when it felt right—my purpose was to get down some of the different tones, some of the different styles of the various New Age groups. (Diversity *is* our highest social value—in practice.) I wanted every reader to feel, after he or she had finished this book, that somewhere out there is a New Age group that might be right for him or her.

Homebirth, Inc. (Boston Univ. Station, P.O. Box 355, Boston, Mass. 02215).

Group of parents "interested in reclaiming control over the birth experience of their children at home or in the hospital. . . . We [do] feel that, in the absence of medical contraindications, home birth is a safe alternative to hospital birth for the well-prepared woman or couple. Indeed, in many cases it may be the medically and psychologically sounder choice. Our goal is to provide parents with the resources, educational materials, and instruction necessary to prepare physically, mentally, emotionally, and spiritually for childbirth and parenting." Offers a series of classes in "responsible birthing"; "Homebirth Leader Training"; reprints; and a quarterly *Newsletter*.

Actualizations (3632 Sacramento St., San Francisco, Calif. 94118).

"Creates a 'greenhouse' environment for individuals in search of more joyful lives. . . . Actualizations Workshop participants make use of sharing, interaction, guided experiences, and information over a concentrated 3½ day period. In addition, Actualizations offers a graduate program that continues to support and maintain growth initiated in the Workshop." According to Steward Emery and Carol Augustus, co-founders of Actualizations: "We get an education to be competent at all things in life except how to relate. . . . The world would work if everybody who was with someone at this moment were relating to one another passionately, freely, with a sense of having touched each other's essence. . . ."

Amnesty International (U.S.A. national section: 2112 Broadway, New York, N.Y. 10023);
International League for Human Rights (236 E. 46th St., New York, N.Y. 10017).

Two groups dedicated to the protection and promotion of human rights. Each has been careful to document abuses of human rights on both the left and right, though Amnesty gives priority to political prisoners and torture and the League is concerned more broadly with the whole spectrum of freedoms and liberties, including freedom of speech and of the press, the right to return to a country, and family reunification (and, e.g., it was the League that helped organize the appeal to the present government of Vietnam; see sect. II–E). Amnesty is more of a mass membership-type organization than the League, with over one hundred "adoption groups" in the U.S. alone; see Chapter 22.

Ananda Cooperative Village (125 members; 900 Alleghany Star Route, Nevada City, Calif. 95959; "visitors welcome—advance arrangements preferred, but not required");
The Farm (1,100 members; 156 Drakes Lane, Summertown, Tenn. 38483; "visitors welcome").

Pair of spiritually-oriented intentional communities. The Farm—founded by Stephen Gaskin (sect. I)—says, "We're complete vegetarians, growing most of the food we eat. We're also delivering our babies at home—more than 1,000 deliveries with better statistics than hospitals. We have our own school, bank, motor pool, construction company . . . utilities, medical clinic, and ambulance service. . . . We hold all property in common and share what we have according to need." Publications; see also PLENTY Project below.

Ananda—founded by Swami Kriyananda (sect. I)—"lays great emphasis on yoga techniques of meditation, and on the practical application in the everyday world of the insights gained through meditation. Individuals and families have their own homes and work in various community industries. Some Ananda businesses are privately owned, others belong to the community as a whole."

Another Place (Route 123, Greenville, N.H. 03048).

"A conference and networking center, and an extended community of people working to develop viable, healthy models for a peacefilled world. . . ." About thirty-five conferences occur each year at Another Place. Some conference subjects: Education, Right Livelihood Business, Women and Spirituality, Men and Brothers, Dance and Music, Healing Arts, Social Healing. "[The] conferences are designed to encourage and catalyze the evolution occurring in all of our lives. We all gather together to connect—to share resources, information, and support—and to celebrate the work and all creation."

Arcosanti (Cosanti Foundation, 6433 Doubletree Rd., Scottsdale, Ariz. 85253).

City being built under the direction of architect Paolo Soleri (sect. I) in the middle of the Arizona desert. Goal is to provide a "functioning example" of Soleri's "arcology"—architecture plus ecology. City will eventually have 5,000 residents and twenty-five stories "facing south for sun orientation." Directly below will be a four-acre greenhouse "that will grow food for the community and supply heat energy to the Arcology." Since construction began, over 2,000 students and professionals have attended the workshops, building the city (Soleri stresses that a participant in the workshops comes "as a builder first and a student second").

Arica Institute (235 Park Ave. So., New York, N.Y. 10003).

Publishes and presents "training programs, short courses, and self-study materials to assist people interested in the development of their life potential to the fullest." "The goal of mysticism is to see reality," says Susan Lydon, formerly of *Ramparts* and now the editor of Arica's newspaper. "Arica is a school of scientific mysticism, a school that develops objectivity and reason. . . . One learns to use the components of reasoning to build a bridge of empathy to whatever problem, person, or situation one addresses. This is real consciousness-raising. . . . In the Arica system reasoning is the ultimate tool by which one achieves enlightenment, unity." Founded by Oscar Ichazo (sect. I, under Lilly).

Association for Humanistic Psychology (325 9th St., San Francisco, Calif. 94103).

Humanistic psychology (as distinct from Freudian or behaviorist psychology) tends to emphasize such New Age topics and concerns as self-realization, spontaneity, choosing, creativity, valuing, responsibility, authenticity, transcendence, and joy. The AHP "exists to link people who have a humanistic vision of the person; to encourage others to share this vision; and to show how this vision can be realized in the life and work of all. Membership is open to anyone who shares these values and wishes to support these efforts." Local chapters and groups; "Social Change Network" (see below); monthly *Newsletter* and quarterly *Journal* (sect. III).

Autumn Press (25 Dwight St., Brookline, Mass. 02146);
New Glide Publications (330 Ellis St., San Francisco, Calif. 94102).

Two publishing houses that are New Age-oriented and that are competent and assertive about their publications. Autumn has published—among other titles—Ellen Bass' *Of Separateness and Merging*, Helen Caldicott's *Nuclear Madness*, and William Shurtleff and Akiko Aoyagi's *The Book of Tofu*. It describes its interests as "planetary consciousness; nutrition/holistic health; philosophy/religion; esoteric knowledge/occult history; psychology/growth; environment;" and is on the lookout for promising manuscripts by unknown New Age authors. New Glide has published—among other titles—Nancy and Casey Adair's *Word Is Out, Time to Greez!* compiled by Third World Communications, and *The Briarpatch Book*.

Bear Tribe Medicine Society (P.O. Box 9167, Spokane, Wash. 99209).

A group of native and non-native people "striving daily to relearn their proper relationship with the Earth Mother, the Great Spirit, and all of their relations in the mineral, plant, animal, and human kingdoms. . . . Our tribe is located on sixty acres of land outside of Spokane. . . . We have many visitors who come to learn what they can of Native American philosophy and country living skills. . . . At our Self-Reliance Center we give four-day intensive courses in the Native way and [in] self-reliance skills." Literature list, "medicine wheels," crafts, tipis; *Bear Tribe's Self-Reliance Book* ($3.95); quarterly magazine, *Many Smokes* ($2 a year).

Briarpatch Network (330 Ellis St., San Francisco, Calif. 94102).

Network of hundreds of New Age-oriented businesspeople around the Bay Area. "[We] have three values in common: we are in business because we love it; we find our reward in serving people rather than in amassing large sums of money; and we share our resources with each other as much as we can, especially our knowledge of business. We share management and marketing information, legal and technical knowhow, names of suppliers. . . . We are committed to keeping our books and financial records open. . . . If you share these values, then you, too, are a Briar." Publishes *Briarpatch Review* (sect. III); and see Chapter 18.

Burklyn (administrative offices: 1700 Montgomery St., San Francisco, Calif. 94111).

A New Age workshop and conference center in northern Vermont. Mansion, 736 acres, view. "Even if you come here just to be—even if you do not partake in any of the sports, recreational or fitness activities, or participate in the groups . . . —even if you come here to write, or to be with nature, or with yourself, Burklyn will renew you." Some recent workshops that I'd have liked to attend: Marilyn Ferguson and Charles Tart, "Potentials of the Human Mind"; Judith Skutch and Willis Harman, "Transformation of Self and Society"; Ira Einhorn and Christopher Bird, "Where Do We Go From Here And Now?"

Burklyn Humanistic Business School (1700 Montgomery St., Ste. 230, San Francisco, Calif. 94111);
School for Entrepreneurs (Tarrytown House, E. Sunnyside Lane, Tarrytown, N.Y. 10591).

The School for Entrepreneurs, directed by Bob Schwartz, offers an intensive two-weekend course for the New Age entrepreneur; see Chapter 18. The Burklyn Humanistic Business School, directed by Marshall Thurber, "is an experiment in combining instruction in fundamental business skills with 'new age consciousness' techniques. The school offers an intensive residential six-week program designed primarily for those who desire to manage their own business and who are also committed to contributing to the well-being of humankind. The purpose of the program is 'to transform the experience of business into the celebration of life'."

California Institute of Asian Studies (3494 21st St., San Francisco, Calif. 94110).

Founded in 1968 by Haridas Chaudhuri, an East Indian scholar, the Institute is "engaged in exploring the bridges where East and West meet," and it offers interdisciplinary courses and programs which "concentrate on concepts of human development presented in Eastern and Western cultures. . . . The primary aim of the Institute is to foster the actualization of total self-integration through the education process." Offers M.A. and Ph.D. programs in six departments including "East/West Psychology" and "South Asian Studies." Courses include "The Good Person and the Good Society" and "Images of the Future: Toward an Integral World View."

Cerro Gordo Community (Dorena Lake, Box 569, Cottage Grove, Ore. 97424);
Cooperative College Community (P.O. Box 299, Cambridge, Mass. 02138).

CCC writes, "We are a group of persons including academics and artists that is attempting to create a community in which art, ecological balance, self-reliance, health, and education are valued more highly than personal wealth and professional advancement. We envision seventy-five adult members . . . in a rural Northeast setting."
Cerro Gordo residents are planning a "car-free" village of 2,500 people. "Our first home was begun in August 1977. . . . Future residents will plan and finance their own neighborhoods and houses. . . . We wish our town to be as diverse as possible within our ecological guidelines and cooperative community orientation."
Newsletters are available from both communities.

Clamshell Alliance (62 Congress St., Portsmouth, N.H. 03801).

Loose coalition of antinuclear/pro-renewable energy groups from the New England area. Hopes to change people's consciousness about nuclear power through nonviolent direct action. Recent actions have focused on the nuclear construction site at Seabrook, N.H.—over 1,400 people were arrested there in 1977, and tens of thousands demonstrated legally there in 1978. In the process, and just as importantly, Clamshell has evolved or rediscovered some effective new nonviolent-action practices and techniques; see Chapter 22. Organizes education and outreach programs; circulates articles, brochures, and a newspaper. Has inspired at least thirty other regional alliances all over the United States.

College Courses in New Age Politics.

Very recently, a number of college courses have been developed that cover the same ground that this book does, and from about the same perspective. Five representative courses are:

Leonard Duhl, "Deliberate Social Change for Health Professionals," School of Public Health, Univ. of California, Berkeley, Calif. 94720. *Will answer inquiries, send outline of course on request. Prof. Duhl is in the College of Environmental Design, Dept. of City and Regional Planning.*

Ira Rohter, "New Age Politics," Dept. of Political Science, Univ. of Hawaii, Porteus 640, 2424 Maile Way, Honolulu, Haw. 96822. *Will answer inquiries, send course outline. Prof. Rohter also teaches a course subtitled "The Politics of Everyday Life."*

Mark Roseland, "Social Ecology," College of Science in Society, Wesleyan Univ., Middletown, Conn. 06457. *Course outline available for $1 from the College—not from Prof. Roseland.*

Phillip Warren, "Transcendence and Transformation," Dept. of Psychology, Douglas College, P.O. Box 2503, New Westminster, B.C., Canada V3L–5B2. *Will answer inquiries, send course outline.*

Stephen Woolpert, "Politics and Humanism: Eupsychian Society," Dept. of Government and Politics, Univ. of Maryland, College Park, Md. 20742. *Syllabus available from World Order Studies Program, Dept. of Government and Politics—not from Prof. Woolpert.*

Community Service, Inc. (P.O. Box 243, Yellow Springs, Ohio 45387).

"A center where ideas and practices concerning community are appraised, developed, and circulated. Central to our work is the conviction that the small community in its many forms [including the intentional community—M.S.] is basic to social survival and social evolution." Sponsors conferences; publishes a bi-monthly *Newsletter* ("which reports on our work and interprets the research of others"); has an excellent booklist including many publications by CS staffers on the social and economic problems of small communities and of society. Founded by Arthur Morgan, one of the progenitors of New Age politics (see Chapter 25).

Cornerstones, Inc. (54 Cumberland St., Brunswick, Me. 04011).

School for owner-builders. "We believe in people taking an active role in designing and building their own homes. We offer three-week courses that provide the information [you'll need] to design a personal and economical house; support and guidance through the design and construction stages; [and] hands-on experience through working in the school's experimental building program. . . . Why the plural form of Cornerstones? It is our belief that you will find here not only the beginning of your new/renewed home, but also the cornerstone for a more rewarding lifestyle." Sells building books, facilitates cooperative wholesale buying of materials.

Cross-Cultural Studies Program (P.O. Box 4234, Topeka, Kans. 66604).

"Research and communications" program founded by Doug Boyd (sect. I); goal is to promote "intercultural and transcultural understanding" ["part of the general human potential"]. Research objectives: to make cross-cultural comparisons of traditional views of humankind and nature; to search for common key points in the ideas and practices of various cultures; to find human visions/values that transcend personal and cultural diversities. Will report research findings to educators, other researchers, etc., and will communicate "cross-cultural 'common denominators'" to the general public. Current projects include studies of American Indians, Buddhist monks, and yogis. Publishes a newsletter.

Delancey Street Foundation (360 residents; 2563 Divisadero St., San Francisco, Calif. 94115; "drop in any time for coffee").

"A live-in, therapeutic, [self-governing] community of former addicts and ex-convicts, living independently of government funding and relying, for the most part, on our own resources. . . . Considers a two-year commitment essential to its goals . . . men's heads shorn of hair, women's faces wiped clean of makeup . . . participation three nights a week in Delancey Street's version of the group encounter sessions [three-hour 'confrontations,' 12-hour 'containment games' and weekend 'dissipations'] . . . operates six businesses which not only generate working capital but provide on-the-job training . . . [operates] a federally-chartered Credit Union . . . strong emphasis is placed on education." See sect. I, under Hampden-Turner.

Earth Camp One (Winter Camp: P.O. Box 2421, Truckee-Tahoe, Calif. 95734; Summer Camp: Montgomery Creek, Calif. 96065).

"An entirely unique concept in camps. 'An Educational Community for Children of the New Age,' in pristine wilderness, where children and teenagers can discover and explore their natural heritage. . . . A place where people take time for the things that really count in life: like getting to know the special meaning of friendship . . . living in total self-sufficiency on a wilderness backpack trip . . . confronting the future as you peer through a telescope into the immensity of a distant galaxy. . . . Each group [of campers] shares in the responsibility for planning their own program, setting their own rules, and finding their own direction." *Has received the highest accreditation score ever awarded by the American Camping Association.*

Environmental Action (1346 Connecticut Ave., N.W., Washington, D.C. 20036).

National environmental lobbying organization. "We coordinated Earth Day in 1970. Since then we have been busy helping local ecology-minded groups and campaigning against our Dirty Dozen (you've probably heard of our work to unseat Congressmen who vote continually against the environment). . . . With the help of our supporters we've been able to win important legislative battles. For example, we won the fight to . . . stop the supersonic transport (SST) project and [the fight to] change the Highway Trust Fund to include funding for mass transit. . . . Now our energies are devoted to making solar energy a reality."

Environmental Education Project (Far West Laboratory, 1855 Folsom St., San Francisco, Calif. 94103).

"The central problems of our environment—and their possible solutions—have continued to be obscured by . . . narrow and partisan [interests]." In response to this understanding, EE is preparing a series of teacher training materials that can help teachers and others get a perspective on the environment that is: "holistic and integrated," "interdisciplinary and transdisciplinary," and "problem-focused and decision-making oriented." Our teachers should then be able to help: analyze environmental problems; predict short- and long-term side effects of environmental programs; and make "long-term life-style decisions which are compatible with the requirements" of the environment.

Esalen Institute (Big Sur, Calif. 93920).

The original—and still the best known—"growth center." Conducts workshops in personal and spiritual growth, body awareness, gestalt, "conscious childbirth," psychosynthesis, massage, self-healing, etc. Describes itself as "a center to explore those trends in education, religion, philosophy, and the behavioral sciences which emphasize the potentialities and values of human existence. Our activities consist of seminars and workshops, residential programs, consulting, research. . . . We ask that persons come to our programs out of an educational interest. We ask that no one come whose interest is 'cure'." Work-study programs; scholarship programs (funded by friends of Esalen); quarterly *Catalog*.

est (765 California St., San Francisco, Calif. 94108).

est—Latin for "it is"—"is a practically-oriented philosophical educational experience, created out of Werner Erhard's personal experience into a four-day (sixty hours) 'Standard Training.' The *est* training is concerned with transformation: to transform is to alter fundamentally the context in which experience is held. *est* is not about content. The purpose of the training is to allow you to see that the circumstances of your life, and your attitudes about them, are held in a particular system of knowing—an epistemology, a context—and that it is possible to transform that context. . . . It's possible for you to choose the context for the content of your life."

Farallones Institute (Rural Center, 15290 Coleman Valley Rd., Occidental, Calif. 95645; Integral Urban House, 1516 Fifth St., Berkeley, Calif. 94710).

"A Community of scientists, engineers, designers, biologists, and craftspeople dedicated to evolving a society more in balance with natural systems. To implement this vision . . . the Institute operates two Centers for research, education, and demonstration of energy-conserving technologies appropriate to urban and rural settings. . . . Educational programs range from one- and two-day practicums and discussions of appropriate technologies; to residential skills training workshops in solar systems, composting toilets, building construction, organic gardening, and animal husbandry; to year-long resident apprenticeships. . . . The focus is on 'hands-on' learning in practical skills and the application of appropriate technology to daily living." Reports, newsletters.

Federation of Egalitarian Communities (Box NAP78, Tecumseh, Mo. 65760).

"We are a Federation of Communities located throughout North America. We range in size and emphasis from small, homestead-oriented groups to village-like Communities similar to the Israeli Kibbutz. We represent over 200 people, own over 2,000 acres of land, and do over a million dollars of business a year. We are trying to synthesize the advantages of rural and urban living. . . . Our common ideological base, which includes a central belief in cooperation, equality, ecology, and nonviolence, has brought us together in an effort to offer more people a real alternative to a competitive and consumption-oriented society."

Fellowship of Reconciliation (P.O. Box 271, Nyack, N.Y. 10960).

Composed of people who "recognize the essential unity of all humanity" and who wish to confront human differences with the power of truth and the power of "nonviolent, compassionate, and reconciling love." Members pledge to: "identify with those of every nation, race, and religion who are the victims of injustice and exploitation, and seek to develop resources of active nonviolent intervention with which to help [them]"; refuse to participate in war or to give sanction to "physical, moral, or psychological preparation for war"; "endeavor to show reverence for personality"; etc. "Commitment cards," monthly magazine.

Findhorn Community (265 members; The Park, Forres, Scotland IV36-OTZ; visitors write in advance).

"[We are] pioneering a new consciousness through planetary service. . . . With the establishment of Cluny Hill College we have expanded into a new age center of education and culture with an ongoing program of workshops and conferences. . . . We see our basic purpose as demonstrating a consciousness of wholeness, where spiritual ideals are manifested in daily life. . . . [And we are] primarily a working community. The exploration of spiritual principles is directly related to work programs. . . . All who come add their time and energy to tasks that need to be done." Publications, tapes, newsletter, journal (*Onearth*).

Foundation for Inner Peace (P.O. Box 635, Tiburon, Calif. 94920).

Publishes and teaches "The Course in Miracles," a "spiritual how-to book" and a New Age thought system designed to "remove the blocks to our awareness of love's presence . . . through showing us just how to forgive. . . . Through forgiving others we forgive ourselves, and so we gradually become aware of the one Self that we all share." Judith Skutch, president of the Foundation, puts it well when she says, "The central conflict is always between fear and love. A universal theology is impossible but . . . a universal experience is imperative."

Friends of Animals (11 W. 60th St., New York, N.Y. 10023).

A "humane conservation organization" that's out to "reduce and eliminate the suffering which humans inflict upon their fellow creatures," and ultimately hopes to "achieve a national humane ethic with the non-humans of this Earth. . . . [Our] policy is to identify areas of human exploitation of animals, expose them to public view, [and] initiate action programs to reduce or eliminate them." Counts 60,000 members whose energy—green and other—is "our principal source of support. . . . Among these [members] are more than 1,000 activists, who promote [FOA's] objectives via grass roots communications, hunt sabotage, picketing and the like." Publishes some grisly pamphlets.

Friends of the Earth (124 Spear St., San Francisco, Calif. 94105).

A prominent environmental-action group. "We join and intend to speed a major effort to bring about the transition that must be made if the Earth and its living passengers, including us, are to flourish." Lobbies "substantially" in Congress; staff people in various cities are "arrangers and casting directors for FOE activities on state issues"; sixty branches across the U.S. "stress local issues, help focus local support for state and national action, and conduct a variety of local activities, ranging from nature hikes for underprivileged children, to recycling, to testifying before state and local authorities." Many publications, excellent "newsmagazine."

Futures Network (2325 Porter St., Washington, D.C. 20008).

"Dedicated to bringing the options for a *positive* future into the public arena." Activities include: The Theater for the Future, a computerized multimedia presentation of "the 15-billion-year drama of our evolutionary history" (from earth to life to humanity to universal humanity; from synthesis of elements to photosynthesis to culture to conscious evolution); Act III, "a two-day educational experience that serves as a participatory follow-up to the Theater . . . with a particular focus on the pragmatic actions that can be undertaken now"; and publication of *The Evolutionary Journal*, an inspirational quarterly. Guiding geniuses: Barbara Marx Hubbard, John J. Whiteside.

Global Education Associates (552 Park Ave., East Orange, N.J. 07017).

Nonprofit educational organization that "promotes the efforts of concerned persons to achieve a more human and just world order" and hopes to develop a "broadly-based, multi-issue constituency" of world-order activists and planetary citizens. "Underlying GEA's program is an analysis of the 'straitjacket' of national security mobilization which prevents all nations from meeting the basic human needs of their peoples." Conducts lectures, workshops, seminars, institutes (on five continents); offers consulting services for groups and individuals; operates a resource center; publishes *The Whole Earth Papers* (sect. III).

Greater Philadelphia Bicycle Coalition (P.O. Box 8194, Philadelphia, Pa. 19101);
Le Monde à Bicyclette/Citizens on Cycles (5550, Ave. du Parc, Montréal, Québec H2V-4H2).

Philadelphia says: "We see the bicycle as a healthful, inexpensive, and immediate vehicle for urban renewal." Montréal goes further: "The bicycle will free people from economic and psychological dependence on cars—[and] this new sense of freedom will not be limited to transport." Both groups are advocating political measures to aid bicyclists and their kind, e.g., "establishment of bike routes in central Philadelphia," "establishment of incentives to encourage bicycle commuting." Both groups sponsor mass bicycle festivals and tours; both publish newsletters; and together they publish an impressive calendar, "Cycle and Recycle" (e.g., for 1979 *and* 1990 and 2001).

Greenpeace Foundation (240 Fort Mason, San Francisco, Calif. 94107).

Takes a nonviolent-action approach to nuclear weapons testing, proliferation of nuclear reactors, and the destruction of whales and seals. Has sailed ships into nuclear test zone areas, and more recently Greenpeace members have been positioning themselves between whales and seals and those who would kill them—saving thousands of animals in all—and at least as importantly, focusing world attention on what we are capable of doing to other living beings. Focusing world attention on our Prison-bound behavior. "Our ultimate goal . . . is to help bring about that basic change in thinking known as 'planetary consciousness'." Publishes newsletters, newspapers.

Hanuman Foundation Dying Project (P.O. Box 624, Santa Cruz, Calif. 95061).

Ram Dass writes: "We recognize that life is primarily a vehicle for spiritual awakening, and thus dying, being a part of living, must also fulfill that function. . . . However, it is necessary that an individual be prepared in the sense of purification, philosophical understanding, and meditation. And it is most helpful if the individual is surrounded at the time of leaving the body by a supportive environment for this liberating effort that is no effort. . . . Succinctly, then, we might say that this project is concerned with awakening through dying." Sponsors five-day, meditation-oriented, "conscious living/dying" retreats; publishes a newsletter.

Holistic Health Organizing Committee (P.O. Box 166, Berkeley, Calif. 94701).

"Community-based service organization" whose purposes are: "to promote health care which acknowledges the interdependence of the physical, mental, emotional, and spiritual dimensions" of people; to create a "support base" for holistic health practitioners and encourage them to "responsibly define their roles"; "to support the right of individuals to seek the health practitioner of their choice"; "to facilitate a developing sense of harmony between self, community, and environment." "Educates political/health policy makers"; encourages and supports relevant health care legislation; is active in consumer advocacy; conducts weekend country retreats and urban seminars. Sponsors *Holistic Health Review* (sect. III).

Humanistic Psychology Institute (325 Ninth St., San Francisco, Calif. 94103);
Synthesis Graduate School for the Study of Man (3352 Sacramento St., San Francisco, Calif. 94118).

Two New Age-oriented, interdisciplinary centers of graduate study and scholarship. HPI was founded by the Association for Humanistic Psychology in 1970; it offers an M.A. in Psychology and a Ph.D. in Philosophy and in "Humanistic Sciences." The Synthesis Graduate School's "foundations . . . lie in an integrative approach to learning which is designed to bridge the everyday life of the human being with the world of meaning and purpose. . . . The combination of theory and understanding with practice and direct experience is a fundamental aspect of the educational philosophy of S.G.S." It offers M.A. and Ph.D. degrees in "Clinical/Counseling Psychology," "Medical Synthesis," and "Psychology with Special Emphasis" (e.g., Psychology of Management, of Politics, of Physics).

The Hunger Project (P.O. Box 789, San Francisco, Calif. 94101).

Hopes to help "create the context" for an end to hunger and starvation on the planet, not by collecting money to send food to the hungry, but by educating us to the fact that the way we *see* things causes us to accept hunger as "a part of the condition in which we live our lives." And by encouraging us to take responsibility for healing our selves, which is *how to transform* the way we see. "When we experience the context of the end of hunger [instead of the context of the 'inevitability' of hunger] . . . the action that is generated is aligned with that context."

Institute for Alternative Futures (1624 Crescent Pl., N.W., Washington, D.C. 20009).

Established in 1977 "to act as a center for encouraging the development of Anticipatory Democracy (A/D) processes." What is A/D? According to Clement Bezold, director of the Institute, it is "the blending of future consciousness and genuine popular participation. . . . Only through more conscious awareness of the range of alternative futures and their implications can citizens make better-informed decisions, and only through more effective citizen involvement is the future likely to provide social and economic justice." Organizes "foresight seminars and workshops" for Congress and state legislatures; networks with state, local, and regional A/D groups; prepares and distributes publications and reports.

Institute for Community Economics (639 Massachusetts Avenue, Cambridge, Mass. 02139).

"Engaged in the initiation and implementation of economic alternatives for decentralized community development." Supports the community land trust movement through the National Community Land Trust Center (see below); is establishing a Community Investment Fund, "a vehicle enabling concerned investors to commit a portion of their investment portfolios to socially beneficial, environmentally responsible, and community conscious enterprises"; "sponsors seminars on questions of land tenure, monetary systems, and appropriate economics"; "publishes materials relating to these areas of activity."

Institute for Ecological Policies (9208 Christopher St., Fairfax, Va. 22031).

(A) Setting up a decentralized, national alternative political network. Using local and national issues to organize around. Presently recruiting volunteers. (B) Evaluating "new and existing" policy alternatives in energy, environment, education, economics, etc. Seeking to articulate new alternatives "which fit together in a holistic manner." ("The new set of values and goals [underlying these alternatives] must be internally consistent and self-reinforcing. Criteria by which to judge the new [alternatives] include whether they lead to: full employment, greater liberty and equality, elimination of nuclear weapons, sustainable society, less crime. . . .") Publications (e.g., sect. I, under

Benson), journal (sect. III). Memberships include an occasional newsletter reviewing Institute activities.

Institute for Liberty and Community (Concord, Vt. 05824).

Nonprofit public policy research and educational organization with principal interests in: preservation of individual liberty; restoration of small-scale communities; "changing distributions of wealth, income, and land ownership"; "restoring and strengthening genuine private property ownership" (as distinct from monopolistic or exploitative private property ownership); decentralization of concentrations of economic, social, and political power; individual and community self-help techniques. Publishes a "decentralist bibliography" which includes works of authors occupying widely divergent positions on the conventional political spectrum. Institute President John McClaughry expects to publish a "Decentralist Reader" by 1980. He characterizes the Institute, and himself, as "Jeffersonian, decentralist, distributist."

Institute for Local Self-Reliance (1717 18th St., N.W., Washington, D.C. 20009).

Goal is to encourage local self-reliance—"local production from local resources for local consumption. . . . We pursue this goal because we believe that human scale is a prerequisite of any equitable and democratic [system]. . . . We provide technical assistance to community groups and municipalities; we conduct research; we do demonstration projects of new and viable energy, waste, and food production technologies; and we provide input into federal policy in an effort to convince the government to encourage self-reliant development at the local level." Develops educational materials; distributes literature; publishes *Self-Reliance* (sect. III).

Institute for the New Age (45 E. 78th St., New York, N.Y. 10021).

"A nonprofit educational organization devoted to the development of people's creative selves and the unification of their various aspects: body, mind, spirit, and emotions. Central to the Institute's work is a process of revealing and transforming misconceptions in the personality in order to reach the core or higher self of an individual. This work is done on an ongoing basis by Institute members and has been integrated with many fields: therapy, business, vocations, political science, education, health, science, and the arts. The Institute offers lectures, workshops, courses, conferences, and publications."

Institute for PsychoEnergetics (126 Harvard St., Brookline, Mass. 02146).

"Meditation [is] largely aimed at opening up to the superconscious. Hypnosis [is] involved with directing the subconscious. Putting them together [you have] a more complete approach which is made even more effective by the latest . . . developments in biofeedback training.

The system is called BioMeditation. . . . BioMeditation is one part of [our] integral program in self-development. Other aspects include work with the body and the emotions incorporating bioenergetics, therapeutic massage, yoga, and free movement. . . ." Also engaged in research on orgone energy, solar and planetary energies, life energies, auras, and psychokinesis. Offers books, tapes, biofeedback instruments (affordable!), and psychic training devices.

Institute for the Study of Conscious Evolution (73 Hillside Ave., Mill Valley, Calif. 94941).

"Humanity can no longer assume that the species and its institutions will evolve spontaneously and unconsciously. We are apparently entering an age wherein new cooperative participation and responsibility is required. To foster such involvement . . . the Institute is exploring the relationship of human and planetary consciousness. [And it is asking:] In what ways is it possible for humanity to intentionally and consciously participate in the survival and evolution of the species and the planet? . . . Activities include research, socially beneficial projects, courses of instruction . . . conferences and publications. Inquiry is interdisciplinary, in such areas as evolutionary psychology, parapsychology, religion, ecology, education, and human values."

Institute for Wholistic Education (P.O. Box 575, Amherst, Mass. 01002).

"We believe that [the teacher's] task is to draw out—educate—the expression of each student's unique and essential life purpose." To this end, the Institute conducts workshops in humanistic and transpersonal psychology; functions as a "clearinghouse for the dissemination of ideas, people, consultants, books, conferences, projects, and developments in the field of consciousness and education"; and sponsors an M.A. degree in "wholistic, humanistic, and transpersonal education." The M.A. program "has been an exciting learning experience for all involved. . . . The students may live in the Amherst area or remain where they are. . . . [The program includes] a final project which allows each student to make an original contribution to wholistic education." Publishes a newsletter ($6 a year).

Institute for World Order (1140 Ave. of the Americas, New York, N.Y. 10036).

"Seeks to inform, educate, and stimulate a worldwide social movement dedicated to the transformation of the present international system of competing sovereign states to a just world order which has the capacity to provide peace, social justice, economic well-being, and ecological balance throughout the globe. Sees the transformation as occurring in three overlapping phases: research and education, mobilization, and implementation. Now in second phase—making specific policy recommendations and attempting to catalyze a social movement dedicated to their realization. Academic and public education programs, World Order Model Project, WOMP book series, *Alternatives: A Journal of World Policy*, ongoing series of *Working Papers*." More "*radical-liberal*" *than "New Age" in basic political orientation, but its work is definitely helping to bring the New Age about.*

Institute of Noetic Sciences (600 Stockton St., San Francisco, Calif. 94108).

Noetic science is centrally concerned with subjective experience (rather than "objective" experience), and IONS is helping to create a body of scientific knowledge about subjective experience—about who and what we really are. It is also helping to articulate the "basic principles" of this new science ("It is the esoteric core of all the world's religions, East and West, ancient and modern, becoming exoteric, 'going public'"). And it says, "The influence of these principles can be brought to bear on social and business decision-making right now." Edgar Mitchell, the astronaut, is chairman of IONS, and Willis Harman—dean of New Age political theorists—is president (see sect. I for both men). Publications, *Newsletter.*

Interface (63 Chapel St., Newton, Mass. 02158).

Goal: to "empower individuals to develop their innate capacities for self-healing and self-evolution." In pursuit of this goal, Interface schedules a calendar-full of lectures, classes, workshops, and special events "that will help you find a greater sense of balance in your life"; and it encourages members to attend the monthly Circle of Truth, "an evening when we meet, share with each other, and deepen our common bonds." Some recent offerings: a workshop, "Transmuting Fear into Love"; another workshop, "From Atom to Cosmos" (an analysis of levels of consciousness); and a conference, "Healing the Earth."

Intermediate Technology Development Group (9 King St., London, U.K. WC2E-8HN).

"Founded in 1965 by E. F. Schumacher to provide advice and assistance on the application of appropriate, intermediate technologies, both for [overdeveloped and insufficiently developed] countries. The group is concerned with the dissemination of Schumacher's concepts . . . of creating a balance between urban and rural life, and providing meaningful work for the world's population." Consultancies, field projects, publications; "nearly 300 panel members provide voluntary advice and assistance"; "undertakes the development and testing of intermediate technologies"; "gives support to the growing number of [A.T.] centers in Latin America, Africa, and Asia."

International Cooperation Council (8570 Wilshire Blvd., Beverly Hills, Calif. 90211).

Coordinating association of more than 200 organizations that "foster the emergence of a new universal person and civilization based on unity in diversity among all peoples. . . . The Council is constantly taking steps to contact individuals and groups which share [this goal]. Activities are aimed at making the work and ideas of these new age people and organizations better known and at facilitating the exchange of information and ideas among the groups themselves in order to bring about greater cooperation in areas of common concern." Sponsors "area councils" and a "World Festival" (yearly, in L.A.); newsletter, magazine.

Lindisfarne Association (closed in 1978; description included for historical reasons, and to commemorate a good idea).

Lindisfarne—founded by William Irwin Thompson—is "a *group of people* committed to the realization of a planetary culture" and dedicated to the proposition that "a relatively small group of people may sometimes act as a catalyst for cultural change." It is a *place* (in fact, a magnificent old church and rectory in the middle of New York City) where people can come together. And it is "a *residential community* in which . . . daily life is shaped by a program of spiritual practice, scholarship, and communal labor." There are lectures and classes for the general public and special small seminars for residents and members. There is a notable Annual Conference and an output of tapes, papers, and books.

Lorian Associates (229 Mead's Mountain Rd., Woodstock, N.Y. 12498).

Founded by David Spangler and other ex-residents of Findhorn (above). "We use spiritual and educational strategies such as the lecture, the written word, music and the performing arts, workshops and conferences, networking and meditation, and subjective spiritual inner action. Out of these strategies we seek to create a community of consciousness which can be a foundation for cooperative, informed, and inspired action. . . . We recognize the existence of a 'groupless group' in which all who are awakening to the needs of humanity are participating, and we seek to emphasize the reality of this invisible community." Conferences, records, tapes, publications; "we have a mailing list which you can join."

Mangrove (499 Alabama St., #120, San Francisco, Calif. 94110).

A dance collective of five men. "Our process is an outgrowth of [our roots in 'contact improvisation'], focusing on immediacy of action and response, yielding to flow in motion and true economy of energy. . . . In our work we struggle to share our vulnerabilities as well as our strengths, moving past the limitations of our conditioning as men and rejoicing in the spiritual ties of male experience. . . . Through contact improvisation our primary focus becomes communication, both among ourselves and between us and those for whom we dance." Gives classes in contact improvisation, theater, voice, etc.; travels extensively.

Meditation Group for the New Age (P.O. Box 566, Ojai, Calif. 93023).

"The usual [notion] of meditation on the one hand and of action on the other is misleading. ['Meditation' and 'action' are really] two successive phases of conscious, purposeful action. . . . We distribute free of charge a bi-monthly meditation course dealing with the psychology of meditation and meditation as a service to humanity. . . . [We] have a considerable membership throughout North America and a large international network." Participants are considered to be members of a "subjective community . . . helping to create the planetary milieu that will assist the emerging of a new planetary consciousness."

Movement for a New Society (c/o Network Service Collective, 4722 Baltimore Ave., Philadelphia, Pa. 19143).

"Widespread network of small groups working nonviolently for fundamental social change." Also working to develop an original overall analysis of society, vision of the future, and strategy for change. Most MNS analyses hold "capitalism" partly but not entirely to blame for our troubles; some MNS visions avoid words like "socialism," feeling we need something more (or different) than that. In other words: some MNS people feel quite close to the ideas in this book; others, much less so. Offers "orientation weekends," political study groups ("macro-analysis seminars"), two-week training programs, and nine-month residential training programs; "re-evaluation counselling" (people counsel each other) gives the personal its due. Many publications.

Naropa Institute (1111 Pearl St., Boulder, Colo. 80302).

Founded in 1974 by Chogyam Trungpa, a Tibetan Buddhist scholar and meditation master, Naropa "brings together intellectual and artistic study with the practice of awareness (meditation, body awareness, and movement). . . . Courses are designed to spark the wisdom we inherently possess." B.A. degrees in Buddhist Psychology and in Buddhist Studies; M.A. degrees in Buddhist and Western Psychology and in Buddhist Studies; certificates in Dance, Poetics, and Theater. Summer sessions have attracted over 1,500 students a year; see Rick Fields, ed., *Loka I* and *Loka II* (Anchor, 1976 and 1977). Teachers have included five people in sect. I above.

National Center for Appropriate Technology (P.O. Box 3838, Butte, Mont. 59701).

Hopes to develop A.T. solutions to energy- and energy-related problems experienced by low-income communities; to promote social, economic, and technical self-reliance and self-determination on the part of low-income communities; and to expand A.T. solutions "which address all aspects of the ecosystem and the political economy." Even hopes to establish regional centers "which undertake work tailored to the unique characteristics of each biological region." But it may be a victim (and/or too much a part) of the Washington bureaucracies.

National Community Land Trust Center (639 Massachusetts Ave., Cambridge, Mass. 02139).

A Community Land Trust "is a legal entity that acquires land . . . ; retains those interests in the land [that are socially relevant, e.g., mineral and 'development' rights]; and conveys the remaining interests to others," typically to those who are committed to living on the land. The CLT Center not only serves the CLT movement as a clearinghouse and a research/resource center but also conducts an "aggressive outreach program." The outreach program provides: training materials and seminars for CLT organizers; slide shows and tapes; model by-laws and lease agreements; a speakers bureau; and access to expert advice.

National Land for People (2348 No. Cornelia, Fresno, Calif. 93711).

"Research, public education, and litigation farmers' group dedicated to democratic rural land control" and the promotion of small farms ("our office is on a small family farm"). "We are involved in trying to put people on the land that our public resources have made productive for the advantage of big farms. That's the first step. . . . We are also doing a low-energy, natural reversal of a formerly chemically worked vegetable farm, to show how long the change-over will take." Lobbies hard in Washington (their "Reclamation Lands Opportunity Act" was introduced in Congress); encourages alternative food distribution systems ("land control . . . is not enough"); publishes a newspaper.

National Organization for an American Revolution (c/o Advocators, P.O. Box 07249, Gratiot Stn., Detroit, Mich. 48207).

This is the first, well, New Age Marxist organization—co-founded in 1978 by James and Grace Lee Boggs (sect. I) and others. A brochure states: "We are at the beginning of a new era in human history. . . . Our challenges are no longer technological and economic. Our challenges are now ethical and political. . . . Our organization has accepted responsibility for: challenging Americans to begin pursuing the happiness which comes from taking responsibility for our selves, for our communities, and for our country; changing our selves so that we will be living examples of the 'New Woman' and 'New Man'. . . ."

New Age Caucus (11771 Santa Monica Blvd., Los Angeles, Calif. 90025).

"Our main purpose is to unite New Age people and groups into a political force. To that end, we've brought together many groups in the fields of ecology, health, and technology, and we've built a state network of several thousand people from activists to interested parties. . . . [Recently] we've assisted in the creation of two new groups, Golden State Land Trust and Earth Day, both of which we feel express our vision of a New Age society. Also, we've started letter-writing campaigns and organized picket lines. And we've maintained personal contact with [the Governor's office]. . . ." Holds state conventions; distributes literature; publishes a quarterly newspaper, *New Age Harmonist*.

New Age Feminism (c/o Anne Ironside, 1144 Robson St., Ste. 1, Vancouver, B.C., Canada).

"An exploration of feminism and its relationship to New Age consciousness." Seminars and discussion groups.

New-Age Foods Study Center (P.O. Box 234, Lafayette, Calif. 94549).

Founded in 1975 by the authors of *The Book of Tofu*, William Shurtleff and Akiko Aoyagi. Some of its goals and activities are: "to work toward creative, low-cost solutions to the present world food/protein crisis; to introduce soy protein foods (tofu, soymilk, tempeh, soy flour, miso, etc.) to people throughout the world and to encourage their production on a community or commercial scale by providing technical manuals, advice, and equipment; to encourage the adoption of balanced meatless diets; to offer lecture/demonstrations and cooking classes; to provide a catalog of publications and materials; and to work actively to promote . . . food self-sufficiency and simpler . . . lifestyles."

The New Alchemy Institute (P.O. Box 47, Woods Hole, Mass. 02543).

"A small, international organization dedicated to research and education on behalf of humanity and the planet. . . . Our major task is the development of ecologically derived forms of energy, agriculture, aquaculture, housing, and landscapes that will encourage a repopulation and revitalization of the countryside." The Institute offers free workshops and tours each Saturday from May through October, weather permitting: "Among the topics covered are agriculture, wind and solar energy, bioshelters, aquaculture, and the social implications embodied in [our] work." Publishes an annual *Journal*; also see (sect. I,) under Todd. Calendars, posters, and a quarterly *Newsletter* are published for the membership.

New Dimensions Foundation (267 States St., San Francisco, Calif. 94114).

"A positive alternative to the consistently negative thrust of the media is required. Providing this alternative has been a continuing concern of New Dimensions." ND has presented literally hundreds of New Age-oriented people through its radio program series (at least thirty-three people from sect. I), and "radio stations from Newfoundland to Santa Cruz are now broadcasting our program material." Most of these programs are distributed as audio tapes "to individuals and groups throughout the world" (write for a catalogue). ND also sponsors public programs and events; "communications and marketing seminars for nonprofit groups"; and an *Audio Journal*.

New Directions (305 Massachusetts Ave., N.E., Washington, D.C. 20002).

Nationwide membership and lobbying organization "concerned with U.S. policy on the solution of interlocking world problems such as arms, energy, hunger, population pressures, and human rights. . . . A staff of highly committed and experienced lobbyists in Washington works with the Executive Branch, members of Congress and their staffs on issues of concern to New Directions members. . . . Our members organize local activities to build public support and understanding of our concerns." Some "action priorities": "reducing arms sales abroad"; "increasing U.S. support of multilateral and bilateral aid programs which help the poor"; "encouraging development of renewable energy sources."

New School for Democratic Management (589 Howard St., San Francisco, Calif. 94105).

"The only business school that provides practical business and management training based on principles of democracy in the workplace." (Some stated objectives: to encourage the growth of "democratic, cooperative, and collective" economic enterprise, and to design "a practical business curriculum of the highest caliber" specifically for such enterprise.) Offers courses in sessions of different lengths—from weekend seminars to ten-week semesters—and is willing to conduct its briefer courses "anywhere it is guaranteed one hundred or more participants." Is also developing special programs for unions and for new directions in public sector work relations and management.

Peacemakers (P.O. Box 627, Garbervile, Calif. 95440).

"A movement dedicated to the transformation of society through the transformation of the individuals therein. . . . There is no statement to sign, no membership fee, no national office. . . . Peacemakers are those who accept the principles of the philosophy we state." Main points of the philosophy: commitment to nonviolence; commitment to "nonviolent social and economic revolution"; withdrawal from war work; nonpayment of war taxes; noncompliance with conscription; simplicity and sharing. "Although the movement is widely scattered, individuals within it try to keep in touch with one another for mutual support and occasional unitive action." Sponsors "several get-togethers each year"; publishes a newsletter.

Planet/Drum Foundation (P.O. Box 31251, San Francisco, Calif. 94131).

"A growing circle of members and correspondents . . . [who know] that human beings live here mutually as one species among others . . . [and who are] evolving shared knowledge about the emergent concerns of bioregional priorities, [regional] reinhabitation, and watershed integrity. We are in the midst of discovering that [regionally] adaptive and diverse human cultures offer us as a species the richest possibilities for wholeness and survival." Distributes books, a newsletter, and "seasonal 'bundles' of ideas and visions generated by people who are exploring cultural and economic forms appropriate to the places where they live—an ongoing discussion of 'nativeness'."

Planetary Citizens (777 United Nations Plaza, New York, N.Y. 10017).

"The next big step for humanity is an identity with a planetary awareness," says Donald Keys of Planetary Citizens, "rather than a lesser or more partial awareness. . . . [So] we are trying to help people make a basic commitment which kind of galvanizes awareness in them. For instance, when they sign the pledge of Planetary Citizenship they make a commitment. . . ." Planetary Citizens also offers "Planetary Passports"; designs educational programs and resource sheets; sponsors workshops and symposia (e.g., "A Workshop for World Warriors"; see Chapter 22); and gives advice and support to all world-servers. Newsletter, journal. *Fifteen of the authors in sect. I above are on the Board of Directors or Advisory Council of Planetary Citizens.*

PLENTY Project (156 Drakes Lane, Summertown, Tenn. 38438).

Charitable wing of The Farm. "PLENTY workers are drawn from the pool of voluntary peasants who are members of The Farm, and who receive no salary. Projects include continuing work in Guatemala [see Chapter 22] . . . and 'Integrated Development' projects—soybeans, soy dairy, water systems, emergency radio nets connecting the highland villages, [etc.] and training the local people in all these technologies. One of [our] central principles—To help the native peoples of the world in their efforts to retain their identity and their integrity. . . ." Other programs are underway in Bangladesh, southern Africa, the South Bronx, Chicago, St. Louis, and Miami.

Political Science Committee of the Institute for the New Age (45 E. 78th St., New York, N.Y. 10021).

Developing "positive nonpartisan alternatives to current political practices. Our work is based on the belief that we can and do create our political realities with our attitudes, thoughts, and actions. . . . The process we have developed integrates personal and political reality. . . .

Much of our work is experiential [role playing, group interaction, simulation, etc.]. . . . In working on an environmental issue, for example, we might begin by expressing our attitudes toward our own inner environments. We would also explore the underlying negative feelings as they are expressed by the parties involved." Meets frequently; "shares its process" through workshops, lectures, and individual and group consultations.

Prison-Ashram Project (P.O. Box 39, Nederland, Colo. 80466).

Provides "encouragement and support for inmates who wish to use their 'time' for deepening their spiritual awareness." Among other things: distributing thousands of books and tapes free of charge to inmates, staff, and prison libraries; "developing our own series of books," called *Inside-Out: A Spiritual Manual for Prison Life*; "voluminous personal correspondence"; workshops and classes in prisons throughout the country; "training seminars for people who work or plan to work in corrections"; "helping other [groups] to develop their own prison projects." "We're presently in touch with thousands of people in and out of over 500 institutions worldwide."

Proutist Universal (413 Malden Ave. E., Seattle, Wash. 98112).

One of the few groups that is trying to work out an explicit and coherent alternative to Marxism and liberalism. ("Prout" stands for "Progressive Utilization Theory" which is a fascinating synthesis of tantra, socialism, transpersonal psychology, decentralist theory, etc. The irreducible core of this synthesis is the spiritual-political philosophy of P. R. Sarkar, East Indian philosopher and founder of "Ananda Marga.") Teaching classes in Prout theory; teaching classes in meditation adapted for social activists; organizing "movements to provide the minimum necessities of life"; organizing cooperatives; supporting movements for human rights. Publishes a monthly newspaper, *Prout Bulletin*, and a theoretical quarterly, *Prout Journal*.

Psychosynthesis Institute (3352 Sacramento St., San Francisco, Calif. 94118).

Nonprofit educational organization whose purpose is "providing in-depth experience with the principles and practice of psychosynthesis to the lay and professional public." ("Psychosynthesis emphasizes the importance of not only analyzing the individual, but also of reintegrating the released energies around a unifying center of awareness and will—first the 'I' or personal self, and eventually the Transpersonal Self.") Introductory "evening presentations"; day- or weekend-long "thematic" programs (e.g., "Acting and Willing"); a training program in psychosynthesis for professionals; and a counseling service (individual and group psychosynthesis available). Traveling workshops, publications, and a journal (*Synthesis*). Now operating within the Synthesis Graduate School.

Rainbow Family Tribal Council (P.O. Box 5577, Eugene, Ore. 97405).

"We are a loosely organized group of people who sponsor a 'Rainbow Gathering' each July 1–7 in a remote wilderness area . . . a Healing Event to which all people are invited. . . . During this Gathering, which is absolutely free, we share all that we can and provide cooperatively for all our needs in the spirit of love and human kindness. There are classes, workshops, and teach-ins, councils, healing sessions, and spiritual communions. . . . We are also preparing, in harmony and co-effort with as many other groups as possible, to establish a P.E.A.C.E. Village—a permanent ongoing Positive Energy Alternative Community Environment."

The Renascence Project (3611 Walnut St., Kansas City, Mo. 64111).

An "association of community-based entrepreneurs" who are engaged in developing "practical" New Age alternatives through a network of "self-supporting, nonhierarchical, nonprofit, and for-profit corporations. . . . Project activities include: design and development of an $8 million renovated shopping complex, smaller restoration projects, outside consulting and services, seminars and workshops, design of alternative urban habitats from small domes to megacities. . . . The project is funded by voluntary investment from community members and income from goods and services. . . . The project's goal is to demonstrate that alternatives can be cost-effective and profitable, as well as aesthetically, socially, and environmentally desirable."

Rural America (1346 Connecticut Ave., N.W., Washington, D.C. 20036).

National nonprofit membership organization "made up of people who share a common sense of the richness, vitality, and diversity of rural America. . . . Our main goal is to assure rural people equity in the formulation and implementation of public policies and programs. We also serve as a national clearinghouse for information and services to individuals and groups. To meet these objectives, [our] activities include a national program of action-oriented research, the provision of technical assistance and training, . . . public education and advocacy on behalf of small town and rural people." Publications include a monthly newspaper, *ruralamerica*.

SAGE Project, (Claremont Office Park, 41 Tunnel Rd., Berkeley, Calif. 94705).

"A program to generate positive images of aging by demonstrating that people over 60 can grow and transcend the negative expectations of our culture. Through the creation of a humanistically focused self-development program [we] have been exploring the many ways in which the later years of life can be a time of health, vitality, expanded awareness, and the realization of self that comes from having lived a long and full life. . . . [Our] approach is eclectic in technique, drawing from a wide range of Western therapeutic and self-awareness methods as well as a variety of Eastern self-development disciplines and processes." Also training workshops, consultation services.

School of Living (P.O. Box 3233, York, Pa. 17402).

Offers "workshops, seminars, apprenticeships, and long term living opportunities" at various centers relating to such topics as "new age consciousness," decentralism, political action, "intimate relationships," "economics of quality," and nonviolence. Has full time "openings for persons seeking to homestead or to live communally in pursuit of the simple life." Members (resident and non-) are "united in seeking: a philosophy centered in the organic and creative aspects of life; life-styles consistent with this philosophy; social, economic, and political changes to permit such life-styles, particularly ready access to land; insight into and understanding of one's self." Publishes *Green Revolution* (sect. III).

Self Determination: A Personal/Political Network (P.O. Box 126, Santa Clara, Calif. 95052).

A statewide network of persons in California who are "simultaneously committed to our evolving as persons and to humanizing politics and institutions." As distinct from Governor Brown (who speaks of "original sin"), members "share a positive way of looking at ourselves as persons. We have a faithful vision of human potential and what we can be-come. . . . [And] we wish to create institutions which can operate on that same premise." The Network functions as an "empowering structure, affording us an opportunity to help and be helped . . . and to develop tools to improve our personal effectiveness and our political environment." Meetings, journal, and a Network Exchange Program for sharing resources.

Shanti Nilaya (P.O. Box 2396, Escondido, Calif. 92025).

Shanti Nilaya—founded by Dr. Elisabeth Kubler-Ross in 1977—is "dedicated to the promotion of physical, emotional, intellectual, and spiritual health. It is an isolated, yet accessible retreat environment where all people who seek help for whatever reason can look at themselves and find release from fear, guilt, pain, and lack of self-worth with the help of dedicated professional and paraprofessional staff. Shanti Nilaya's purpose is to encourage people to view life not as a threatening and painful ordeal, but as a series of challenging experiences from birth through death." Especially, Shanti Nilaya "provides an environment where all people can come to grips with the 'little deaths' of life's transitions."

Sierra Club (530 Bush St., San Francisco, Calif. 94108).

National nonprofit membership organization whose members work in hundreds of Club committees on urgent campaigns to save threatened areas, wildlife, and resources and to make the environment of the cities "more fit" for people. "A local and worldwide outing program helps you see what needs to be conserved and lets you explore, enjoy, and learn how to properly use what has been conserved. . . ." Founded in the nineteenth century by one of the spiritual forefathers of New Age politics, John Muir (see Chapter 25). Lobbies hard in Washington; publishes books and calendars; publishes a bi-monthly magazine, *Sierra*.

Small Towns Institute (P.O. Box 517, Ellensburg, Wash. 98926).

National nonprofit organization whose members are concerned with "economic prosperity as well as the quality of life in small towns and rural communities," and "finding new solutions to the problems facing small towns and countryside communities." Through the pages of *Small Town*, a monthly newsjournal, and other, occasional publications, the Institute provides information resources to local citizens, planners, public officials, and others "who are interested in maintaining small communities as modern alternatives to urban life." It focuses on "practical . . . new or innovative ways of solving" everyday problems in housing, community health, small business, historic preservation, local government finance, cultural development, etc.

Social Change Network of the Association for Humanistic Psychology (c/o Monica Armour, 60 Albany Ave., Toronto, Ont., Canada M5R-3C3).

Founded in 1978. Some goals: "to raise the consciousness of AHP members *re* the workings of government and other powerful organizations"; "to be a forum . . . for participation in social change projects at all levels of community from local to international"; to involve AHP members in the creation of "social change programs, workshops, and other sessions at regional and annual meetings of AHP"; "to generate an 'issue of the year' of social and political concern around which AHPers can take action"; "to identify and connect with other networks and resources in the area of social change"; "to hold workshops and issue publications."

Synergy Power Institute (P.O. Box 9096, Berkeley, Calif. 94709).

Dedicated to "empowering" individuals and groups by teaching and training them in the uses of Synergic Power—"power to generate creative cooperation," as distinct from the power to use and abuse other people (see Chapter 15). A recent spinoff from SPI is ProAction, Inc., whose stated objective is to develop a series of training programs for "the elimination or reduction of the [mental, interpersonal, and ideological] barriers to social transformation." Publications include sect. I, under Craig; Marguerite Craig et al., *Power from Within: A Work-*

book for Women ($3); and a broadsheet, "18 Synergistic Principles for Support/Task Groups" (free).

Turning Point (7 St. Ann's Villas, London, U.K. W11-4RU).

"International network of people whose individual concerns range widely—environment, sex equality, third world, disarmament, community politics, appropriate technology, and alternatives in economics, health, education, agriculture, religion, etc.—but who share a common feeling that [humankind] is at a turning point. We see that old values, old life-styles, and an old system of society are breaking down, and that new ones must be helped to break through. Turning Point does not demand adherence to doctrines, manifestos, and resolutions. It enables us, as volunteers, to help and seek help from one another." Meetings; newsletter. Coordinating committee includes James Robertson (sect. I).

Twin Oaks Community (eighty-five members; Rt. 4, P.O. Box 169, Louisa, Va. 23093; visitors "write first to set up exact dates").

An intentional community "originally formed as an experiment in communal living. . . . Together we are [still] engaged in an experiment, an attempt to build a social system based on cooperation, egalitarianism (economic as well as political), nonviolence, and interpersonal openness. . . . We are a diverse group, with individual philosophies ranging from the utopian to the spiritual. [And] our approaches to designing our culture reflect this diversity. Ours is a continual struggle to restructure our lives along lines that feel right to all of us." Sponsors an annual "Communities Conference"; publishes a newsletter; co-edits *Communities* (sect. III).

Union of Concerned Scientists (1208 Massachusetts Ave., Cambridge, Mass. 02138).

Takes New Age-oriented stands on issues like air pollution, chemical and biological warfare, the misuse of pesticides, and—first and foremost—nuclear power. "While UCS's income last year was only $139,000, money used primarily to pay its ten staff members, the group has waged a relentless campaign to educate the public and other scientists about the hazards of nuclear power, to pry damaging secrets from the government and the nuclear industry, and, ultimately, to make nuclear power . . . 'an energy source of last resort'." The director of the Federation of American Scientists calls UCS "the spearhead of the scientific opposition" to nuclear power.

Values Party (P.O. Box 137, Wellington, New Zealand).

The English-speaking world's most successful New Age-oriented political party to date (105 branches, 5 percent of the vote). From a campaign flyer: "Values is entirely New Zealand-made. . . . Values is an EXCITING, NECESSARY alternative to the incompetent actions of the Labour [socialist] and National [capitalist] Parties. . . . Values is for everyone, not just those belonging to certain [social or economic] groups. . . . Values is concerned with every aspect of the New Zealand way of life. . . . Values not only fights elections. It is continually involved in community affairs. . . . Values organizes itself in the [same decentralist] way it would like to see society organized." Publishes a newspaper, *Vibes*.

World Future Society (4916 St. Elmo Ave., Washington, D.C. 20014).

An "association of people interested in future social and technological developments." Hopes to "contribute to a reasoned awareness of the future and the importance of its study," "serve as an unbiased forum and clearinghouse for scientific and scholarly forecasts and intellectual explorations of the future," etc. Likes to describe itself as "independent, nonpolitical, and nonideological," though many of its members are clearly in sympathy with the New Age ethics and political values. Local chapters with speakers, seminars, discussion groups, etc.; book service with over 200 titles; conferences and general assemblies; publications (including sect. I, Cornish et al.); tapes; journal, *The Futurist* (sect. III).

World Goodwill (866 United Nations Plaza, Ste. 566–7, New York, N.Y. 10017).

A "world service organization" whose purposes are: (1) "to help mobilize the energy of goodwill"; (2) "to cooperate in the work of preparation for the reappearance of the Christ"; and (3) "to educate public opinion on the causes of the major world problems and to help create the thoughtform of solution." Says, "The major need today is to educate world public opinion in the significance of goodwill as a powerful creative energy and way of life; and to . . . establish goodwill as a keynote of the coming new age civilization." Publishes *World Goodwill Newsletter* and *World Goodwill Commentary* along with numerous pamphlets. Based on the ideas of Alice Bailey (sect. I, under Rudhyar).

Worldwatch Institute (1776 Massachusetts Ave., N.W., Washington, D.C. 20036).

"Independent, nonprofit research organization created to analyze and focus attention on global problems." Research is written up in occasional "Worldwatch Papers" (pamphlets) and in occasional Worldwatch books; for example, *The Twenty-Ninth Day* (sect. I, under Brown), by the president of Worldwatch. Papers and books are "written for a worldwide audience of decision makers [and scholars]" as well as for the general public. Some topics discussed: new sources of inflation; women in politics; redefining "national security" (some new factors: growing dependence on the North American breadbasket, possible climate modification); and how could most of the world's energy come from the sun by the year 2025?

Zen Center (300 Page St., San Francisco, Calif. 94102).

Buddhist awareness "includes knowing our mind, feelings, emotions, and conditions of our physical existence," and Zen Center practice is designed to foster that awareness in us. There are many regular activities (in which "everyone is invited to participate"); there is basic instruction in zazen every Saturday at 8:30 A.M. at no charge; there is living space for about fifty full-time students. "At Zen Mountain Center a more intensive practice is offered that includes all daily activities. . . . The schedule at Green Gulch Farm also includes farm and garden work and maintenance." The City Center tries to serve some of the needs of the people in its rather depressed neighborhood. Publishes an excellent occasional journal, *Wind Bell*.

Zero Population Growth (1346 Connecticut Ave., N.W., Washington, D.C., 20036).

"National nonprofit organization which promotes public and personal planning to end population growth in the U.S. and to stabilize the revolution in balance with environmental and economic resources —by voluntary means. For example, by promoting expanded role opportunities for women; making family planning programs and services more easily available; reducing legal and illegal immigration into the U.S. through improved immigration policy and better economic development in developing countries; and educating youth about future population changes." Has more than forty chapters of local volunteer activists; lobbies effectively in Washington; sponsors educational programs. Publications include a newspaper, the *ZPG National Reporter*.

Mark Satin travels around North America giving talks and workshops on New Age politics. His talks have been called "stirring" (*Seriatim*) and praised for their "tone of positivity" (*Cascade*). He has been asked to speak to groups as diverse as a cultural center in Harlem, a decentralist gathering in Oregon, a world order symposium in New York, the Association for Humanistic Psychology, the American Political Science Association, and many colleges and universities including Harvard and Hawaii. He can be reached most promptly by sending him letters at *both* these addresses: c/o Institute of Noetic Sciences, 600 Stockton St., 6th flr., San Francisco, Calif. 94108; c/o Planetary Citizens, 777 United Nations Plaza, 10th flr., New York, N.Y. 10017.

Mark is also helping to start a new political organization that can bring together many of the insights and understandings that he writes about in this book.